THE

ROSICRUCIANS

Their Rites and Mysteries

FOURTH EDITION, REVISED

BY HARGRAVE JENNINGS

AUTHOR OF 'THE INDIAN RELIGION; OR, RESULTS OF THE
MYSTERIOUS BUDDHISM'; 'PHALLICISM'; 'ONE OF THE
THIRTY', ETC. ETC

Illustrated by Upwards of Three Hundred Engravings and Twelve Full-Page Plates

Vnto the very points and prickes, here are to be found great misteries.

--Nickolas Flammel, 1399.

Quod sit Castellum in quo Fratres degunt? Quinam et quales ipsi sint? Cur, inter alia nomina, appelletur Fratres? cur CRUCIS? cur ROSÆ CRUCIS?

-- Gassendus, 1630.

Quod tanto impendio absconditur, etiam solummodo demonstrare, destruere est.

-- Tertullian.

Preface to the Third Edition

THE words 'Third Edition' to a work of this character, which, it will readily be confessed, prefers claims to being quite sui generis, excite mixed feelings on the part of its Authors.

The present edition has been carefully revised, at the same time that it has been largely extended. It comprises, now, Two VOLUMES. The addition of new engravings--singularly suggestive, prepared with great care, presenting very antique and authentic claims--speaks for value.

The Authors can refer with pride to the numerous letters which reach them, if pride, or even particular gratification (according to ordinary ideas), could actuate in the statement of the fact. This is a serious treatise upon the '*Rosicrucians*'. Letters expressing great interest, some anonymous, some with names, addressed from all parts--from Germany, France, Spain,' the West Indies; from India, Italy, and Denmark, and from remote corners in our own country--these have multiplied since the work was first published. America has displayed unbounded curiosity. To all these communications, with a few exceptions, no answers have been (nor could be) returned. The volumes themselves must be read with attention, or nothing is effected. The book must be its own interpreter, if interpretation is sought. But interpretation does not apply in, this instance.

With one word we shall conclude. The Authors of *The Rosicrucians* would quietly warn (for to do more would imply a greater attention than is due) against all attempts in books, or in print or otherwise, to subscribe with 'letters' or any addition (or affectation), signifying a supposed *personal* connexion with the real 'Rosicrucians'. These haughty Philosophers forbade disclosure--this, of either their real doctrines of intentions, or of their personality.

We may most truly say, that in this work--as it now stands, care being taken to keep all reserves--will be found the best account of this illustrious and mysterious Fraternity.

LONDON:
January the Twenty-First,
1887

Preface to the Second Edition

THE Authors of this important Book--such must obviously be the fact of any work speaking with authority in regard of that extraordinary Brotherhood the 'Rosicrucians'--feel assured that it will only be necessary to penetrate but to the extent of two or three pages therein, to secure vivid curiosity and attention. The Producers--particularly in the instance of this much enlarged Second Edition--are particularly desirous that no one shall identify them with, or consider them as maintaining personally, the strangely abstruse, and, in some instances, the startlingly singular ideas of these Princes among the Mystics. We are--and desire etc) be viewed as--the Historians only of this renowned Body; of whom it may most truly be asserted that no one can boast of having ever--really and in fact--seen or known in any age any supposed (or suspected) 'Member' in the flesh. It is sufficient honour to offer as the medium only, or the Intermediaries to the reading-world--of this Illustrious Membership; whose renown has filled, and whose mystical doctrines (assumed or supposed) have puzzled the ages:--in the intenser degree, still, in the present time; as the inquisitive reception of the Authors' First Edition of *The Rosicrucians* abundantly proved.

Dr. Ginsburg says of the *Cabala*, or *Kabbalah* (regarding the mysteries of which the Rosicrucians claimed to be the only true exponents), that it is a system of religious philosophy, or more properly of theosophy, which has not only exercised, for hundreds of years, an extraordinary influence on the mental development of so shrewd a people as the Jews, but has captivated the minds of some of the greatest thinkers of Christendom in the sixteenth and seventeenth centuries. 'It--and all that refers to it'--therefore claims the greatest attention of both the philosopher and the theologian. 'The thinkers of the past days, after restlessly searching for a scientific system which should disclose to them the "deepest depths" of the Divine Nature, and approve to the understanding the *real tie* which binds all things together, found the craving of their mind SATISFIED by this Theosophy.'

We say enough in reference to the august possessors of this knowledge when we remind the reader that among those who knew how to wield (and to adapt) the stupendous acquisition to which they were supposed to have at last penetrated, were Raymond Lully, the celebrated scholastic, metaphysician, and chemist (died 1315); John Reuchlin, the renowned scholar and reviver of oriental literature in Europe (born 14J5, died 1522); John Picus di Mirandola, the famous philosopher and classical scholar (1463-1494); Cornelius Henry Agrippa, the distinguished philosopher, divine, and physician (1486-1535); John Baptist von Helmont, a remarkable chemist and physician (1577-1644); Dr. Henry More (1614-1687), and lastly and chiefly (in regard of whom this whole Book is but the translation and exposition of his highly-prized and very scarce works), our own countryman[1], Robert Flood or Fludd (Robertus de Fluctibus) the famous physician and philosopher (1574-1637).

HARGRAVE-JENNINGS.
LONDON, *April* 6*th*, 1879.

---

[1] In regard to the value and rarity of Robert Fludd's books it may be mentioned that Isaac D'Israeli says that 'forty' and 'seventy' 'pounds' were given for a 'single volume' abroad in his time--such was the curiosity concerning them. At the present time the value of these books has greatly increased. Fludd's volumes, and any of the early editions of Jacob Bœhmen's books, are worth much money. Indeed they are so scarce as to be caught up everywhere when offered--especially when encountered by foreigners and Americans.

Preface to the First Edition

THIS book, which now leaves our hands, concentrates in a small compass -the results of very considerable labour, and the diligent study of very many books in languages living and dead. it purports to be a history (for the first time treated seriously in English) of the famous Order of the 'Rose-Cross', or of the 'Rosicrucians'. No student of the occult philosophy need, however, fear that we shall not most carefully keep guard--standing sentry (so to speak) not only over this, which is, by far, the pre-eminent, but also over those other recondite systems which are connected with the illustrious Rosicrucians.

An accomplished author of our own period has remarked that 'He who deals in the secrets of magic, or in the secrets of the human mind, is too often looked upon with jealous eyes by the world, which is no great conjuror.'

How is it that, after centuries of doubt or denial--how happens it, in face of the reason that can make nothing of it, the common sense that rejects, and the science which can demonstrate it as impossible, the supernatural still has such vital hold in the human--not to say in the modern--mind? How happens it that the most terrible fear is the fear of the invisible?--this, too, when we are on all hands assured that the *visible* alone is that which we have to dread! The ordinary reason exhorts us to dismiss our fears. That thing 'magic', that superstition 'miracle', is now banished wholly from the beliefs of this clear-seeing, educated age. 'Miracle', we are told, never had a place in the world--only in men's delusions. It is nothing more than a fancy. It never was anything more than a superstition arising from ignorance.

What is fear? It is a shrinking from possible harm, either to the body, or to that thing which we denominate the mind that is in us. The body shrinks with instinctive nervous alarm, like the sensitive leaf, when its easy, comfortable exercise or sensations are disturbed.

Our book, inasmuch as it deals--or *professes* to deal--seriously with strange things and with deep mysteries, needs the means of interpretation in the full attention of the reader: otherwise, little will be made, or can come, of it. It is, in brief, a history of the alchemical philosophers, written with a serious explanatory purpose, and for the first time impartially stated since the days of James. the First and Charles the First. This is really what the book pretends to be--and nothing more. It should be mentioned that the peculiar views and deductions to be found herein were hinted at as demonstrable for the first time by the same Author in the year 1858, when a work entitled *Curious Things of the Outside World* was produced.

Let it be understood, however, that the Author distinctly excepts against being in any manner identified with *all* the opinions religious or otherwise, which are to be found in this book. Some of them are, indeed, most extraordinary; but, in order to do full justice to the speculations of the Hermetic Brethren, he has put forward their ideas with as much of their original- force as he was able; and, in some parts of his book, he believes he has urged them with such apparent warmth, that they, will very likely seem to have been his own most urgent convictions. As far as he can. succeed in being so considered, the Author wishes to be regarded simply as the Historian of, the Rosicrucians, or as an Essayist on their strange, mysterious beliefs.

Whether he will succeed in engaging the attention of modern readers to a consideration of this time-honoured philosophy remains to be seen; but this he is assured of, that the admiration of all students and reflective minds will be excited by the unrivalled powers of thinking of the Rosicrucians. The application, proper or otherwise, of these powers is a matter altogether beside the present inquiry.

The Author has chiefly chosen for exposition the Latin writings of the great English Rosicrucian, Robert Flood, or Fludd (Robertus de Fluctibus), who lived in the times of James the First and Charles the First.

Our final remarks shall be those of a very famous Brother of the 'R.C.', writing under the date of 1653: 'I will now cloze up', saith he, 'with the doxology of a most excellent, renowned Philocryphus:

> *Soli Deo Laus et Potentia!*
> *Amen in MERCURIO, qui pedibus licet carens decurrit AQUA, et metallice universaliter operatur.*'

LONDON, *January* 20*th*, 1870

THE ROSICRUCIANS

PART I

CHAPTER THE FIRST
CRITICS OF THE ROSICRUCIANS CRITICIZED

THAT modern science, spite of its assumptions and of its intolerant dogmatism, is much at fault--nay, to a great extent a very vain thing--is a conclusion that often presents itself to the minds of thinking persons. Thus thoughtful people, who choose to separate themselves from the crowd, and who do not altogether give in with such edifying submission to the indoctrination of the scientific classes--notwithstanding that these latter have the support generally of that which, by a wide term, is called the 'press' in this country--quietly decline reliance on modern science. They see that there are numerous shortcomings of teachers in medicine, which fails frequently, though always with its answer-- in theology, which chooses rather that men should sleep, though not the right sleep, than consider waking--nay, in all the branches of human knowledge; the fashion in regard to which is to disparage the ancient schools of thought by exposing what are called their errors by the light of modern assumed infallible discovery. It never once occurs to these eager, conceited professors that they themselves may possibly have learned wrongly, that the old knowledge they decry is underrated because they do not understand it, and that, entirely because the light of the modern world is so brilliant in them, so dark to them, as eclipsed in this novel artificial light, is the older and better and truer sunshine nearer to the ancients: because time itself was newer to the old peoples of the world, and because the circumstances of the first making of time were more understood in the then first divine disclosure, granting that time ever had a beginning, as man's reason insists it must.

Shelley, the poet, who, if he had not been so great as a poet, would have been perhaps equally eminent as a metaphysician, that is, when age and experience had ripened and corrected his original brilliant crudities of thought--used to declare that most men--at least, most thinking men--spend the latter half of their lives in unlearning the mistakes of the preceding half. This he declares to have been the fact in his own experience--which was, even for this test, a very brief one; .for Shelley was only twenty-nine when his lamentable death occurred. The early departure of three brilliant poetic spirits of our fathers' period, at the same time that it is very melancholy, is worthy of deep remark. Shelley was, as we have said, twenty-nine; Byron was only thirty-six; John Keats--in some respects the most poetically intense and abstract of the three--was only twenty-four. And in these short several lifetimes, measuring so few years, these distinguished persons had achieved that which resulted in the enrolment of their names in a nation's catalogue in a grand branch of human attainment. They live in lasting records, they grow in honour, and their names do not fade, as is the case with those reputations which have been unduly magnified, but which give way to time. Perhaps the lot of some contemporaneous accepted important, not to say great, reputations will be diminution and disappearance. Time is not only an avenger, but a very judicious corrector.

We are so convinced of the irresistible dominancy, all the world over, of opinions, and of the *dicta* relative to this or that merit, or this or that truth, propounded, by people with names and of influence in our good, readily believing England, and of the power of supposed authority in matters of taste and literary acceptance, that we desire to warn querists against the statements about the fraternity--for it is not a body--of the Rosicrucians appearing in all the published accounts, whether of this country or abroad. We have examined all these supposed notices and explanations of who the Rosicrucians were in biographical works, in encyclopædias and histories, and we find them all prejudiced and misrepresenting, really telling no truth, and only displaying a deplorable amount of mischievous ignorance. They are, besides, in the main copied from each other--which is notably the case with the early encyclopædias. Old Fuller, who has some notices of Robert Flood, a famous English member of the order of Rosicrucians, fully admits his ignorance of whom the brotherhood comprised, and of their constitution or purpose. All generally received accounts, therefore, are wrong, principally for three reasons: first, through ignorance; secondly, through prejudice; thirdly, as instigated by distrust, dislike, and envy--for in criticism it is a dogma that the subject must be always *under* the critic, never that, by a chance, the subject may be *above* the critic--that is, above the critic's grasp and comprehension. But suppose the criticized choose to except to the ability of the critic in any way to judge of him?

From this obstinacy and conceit arise such underrating and false comment as is implied in the following which is extracted from *The Encyclopædia Britannica*--which account is copied again into several other encyclopædias, and repeated into smaller works with. pertinacious, with even malicious fidelity

'In fine, the Rosicrucians, and all their fanatical descendants, agree in proposing the most crude and incomprehensible notions and ideas in the most obscure, quaint, and unusual expressions.'--*Encyclopædia Britannica:* article 'Rosicrucians'.

During the age of James the First, Charles the First, even during the Protectorate, and again in the time of Charles the Second, the singular doctrines of the Rosicrucians attracted a large amount of attention, and excited much keen controversy. Sundry replies or 'apologies' appeared on the part of the Rosicrucians. Among them was a most able work published in Latin by Dr. Robert Flood, at Leyden, in 1616. It was a small, closely printed, very learned octavo, entitled *Apologia Compendiaria Fraternitatis de Rosea Cruce*, etc., and abounds in knowledge. It is an exceedingly rare work; but there is a copy in the British Museum. All this long period was marked by considerable speculation regarding these Rosicrucians. Pope's

Rape of the Lock is founded upon some of their fanciful cabalistic ideas. *The Spectator* contains notices of the mystic society; and, to prove. the public curiosity concerning the Rosicrucians, and a strange incident, the particulars of which we are going to supply from the best sources now for the first time, we may state that there is included, in one number of Addison's elegant series of papers called *The Spectator,* a resumption of a notice, and some after-comment, upon the supposed discovery of the burial-place in England of one of these mighty men the Rosicrucians. The story is to the following. purport, as nearly as it can be gathered. We have written much more fully of it from other means; for *The Spectator's* account is very full of errors, and was evidently gained afar off, and merely from hearsay, as it were. It is, besides, poor and ineffective, gathered from no authority, and produced with no dramatic force; for the life and the beliefs of the Rosicrucians were very dramatic, at the same time that the latter were very true, although generally disbelieved.

Delphic E
(With the significant point in the centre)

CHAPTER THE SECOND

SINGULAR ADVENTURE IN STAFFORDSHIRE

DR. PLOT, who was a very well-known and reliable man, and a painstaking antiquary and writer of natural history, in his *History of Staffordshire*, published by him in the time of Charles the Second, relates the following strange story:

That a countryman was employed, at the close of a certain dull summer's day, in digging a trench in a field in a valley, round which the country rose into sombre, silent woods, vocal only with the quaint cries of the infrequent magpies. It was some little time after the sun had sunk, and the countryman was just about giving over his labour for the day. Dr. Plot says that, in one or two of the last languid strokes of his pick, the rustic came upon something stony and hard, which struck a spark, clearly visible in the increasing gloom. At this surprise he resumed his labour, and, curiously enough, found a large, flat stone in the centre of the field. This field was far away from any of the farms or 'cotes', as they were called in those days, with which the now almost twilight country was sparingly dotted. In a short time he cleared the stone free of the grass and weeds which had grown over it; and it proved to be a large, oblong slab, with an immense iron ring fixed at one end in a socket. For half-an-hour the countryman essayed to stir this stone in vain. At last he bethought himself of some yards of rope which he had lying near amongst his tools; and these he converted, being an ingenious, inquisitive, inventive man, into a tackle--by means of which, and by passing the sling round a bent tree in a line with the axis of the stone, he contrived, in the last of the light, and with much expenditure of toil, to raise it. And then, greatly to his surprise, he saw a large, deep, hollow place, buried in darkness, which, when his eyes grew accustomed a little to it, he discovered was the top-story to a stone staircase, seemingly of extraordinary depth, for he saw nothing below. The country fellow had not the slightest idea of where this could lead to; but being a man, though a rustic and a clown, of courage, and most probably urged by his idea that the staircase led to some secret repository where treasure lay buried, he descended the first few steps cautiously, and tried to peer in vain down into the darkness. This seemed impenetrable; but there was some object at a vast, cold distance below. Looking up to the fresh air and seeing the star Venus--the evening star--shining suddenly like a planet, in encouraging, unexpected brilliancy, although the sky had still some beautiful placid sunset light in it, the puzzled man left the upper ground, and descended silently a fair, though a somewhat broken staircase. Here, at an angle, as near as he could judge, of a hundred feet underground, he came upon a square landing-place, with a niche in the wall; and then he saw a further long staircase, descending at right angles to the first staircase, and still going down into deep, cold darkness. The man cast a glance upward, as if questioning the small segment of light from the upper world which shot down, whether he should continue his search or desist and return. All was stillest of the still about him; but he saw no reason particularly to fear. So; imagining that he would in some way soon penetrate the mystery, and feeling in the darkness by his hands upon the wall, and by his toes to make sure first on each step, he resolutely descended; and he .deliberately counted two hundred and twenty steps. He felt no difficulty in his breathing, except a certain sort of aromatic smell of distant incense, that he thought Egyptian, coming up now and then from below, as if from another, though a subterranean, world. 'Possibly', thought he--for he had heard of them--'the world of the mining gnomes: and I am breaking in upon their secrets, which is forbidden for man'. The rustic, though courageous, was superstitious.

But, notwithstanding some fits of fear, the countryman went on, and at a much lower angle he met a wall in his face; but, making a turn to the right, with singular credit to his nerves, the explorer went down again. And now he saw at a vast distance below, at the foot of a deeper staircase of stone, a steady though a pale light. This was shining up as if from a star, or coming from the centre of the earth. Cheered by this light, though absolutely astounded, nay, frightened, at thus discovering light, whether natural or artificial, in the deep bowels of the earth, the man again descended, meeting a thin, humid trail of light, as it looked, mounting up the centre line of the shining though mouldering old stairs, which apparently had not been pressed by a foot for very many ages. He thought now, although it was probably only the wind in some hidden recess, or creeping down some gallery, that he heard a murmur overhead, as. if of the uncertain rumble of horses and of heavy waggons or lumbering wains. Next moment, all subsided into total stillness; but the distant light seemed to flicker, as if in recognition or answer to the strange sound. Half-a-dozen times he paused, and turned as if he would remount-- almost flee for his life upward,. as he thought; for this might be the secret haunt of robbers, or the dreadful abode of evil spirits. What if, in a few moments, he should -come upon some scene to affright, or alight in the midst of desperate ruffians; or be caught by murderers! He listened eagerly. He now almost bitterly repented his descent. Still the light streamed at a distance; but still there was no sound to interpret the meaning of the light, or to display the character of this mysterious place, in which the countryman found himself entangled hopelessly like a knight of romance in an enchanted world.

The discoverer by his time stood still with fear. But at last, summoning courage, and recommending himself devoutly to God, he determined to complete his discovery. Above, he had been working in no strange place; the field he well knew, the woods were very familiar to him, and his own hamlet and his wife and family were only a few miles distant. He now hastily, and more in fear than through courage, noisily with his feet descended the remainder of the stairs; and the light grew brighter and brighter as he approached, until at last, at another turn, he came upon a square chamber, built up of large hewn ancient stones. He stopped, silent and awe-struck. Here was a flagged pavement and a somewhat lofty roof, gathering up into a centre, in the groins of which was a rose, carved exquisitely in some dark stone or in marble. But what was this poor man's fright when, making another sudden turn, from between the jambs, and from under the large archivolt of a Gothic, stone portal, light streamed out over him with inexpressible brilliancy, shining over everything, and lighting up the place with brilliant radiance, like an intense golden sunset. He started back. Then his limbs shook and bent under him as he gazed with terror at the figure of a than, whose face: was hidden, as he sat in a studious attitude in a stone chair, reading in a great book, with his elbow testing on a table like a rectangular altar, in the light of a large, ancient iron lamp, suspended by a thick chain to the middle of the roof. A cry of alarm, which he could not suppress, escaped from the scared discoverer, who involuntarily advanced one pace, beside himself with terror. He was now within the illuminated chamber. As his foot fell on the stone, the figure started bolt upright from his seated position, as if in. awful astonishment. He erected his hooded head, and showed himself as if in anger about to question the intruder. Doubtful if what he saw were a reality, or whether he was not in some terrific dream, the countryman advanced, without being aware of what he was doing, another audacious step. The hooded man now thrust out a long arm, as if in warning; and in a moment the discoverer perceived that this hand was armed with an iron baton, and that he pointed it as if tremendously to forbid further approach. Now, however, the poor man, not being in a condition either to reason or to restrain himself, with a cry, and in a passion of fear, took a third fatal step; and as his foot descended on the groaning stone, which seemed to give way for a moment under him, the dreadful man, or image, raised his arm high like a machine, and with his truncheon struck a prodigious blow upon the lamp, shattering it into a thousand pieces, and leaving the place in utter darkness.

This was the end of this terrifying adventure. There was total silence now, far and near. Only a long, low roll of thunder, or a noise similar to thunder, seemed to begin from a distance, and then to move with snatches, as if making turns; and it then rumbled sullenly to sleep, as if through unknown, inaccessible passages. What these were--if any passages—nobody ever found out. It was only suspected that this hidden place referred in some way to the Rosicrucians, and that the mysterious people of that famous order had there concealed some of their scientific secrets. The place in Staffordshire became afterwards famed as the sepulchre of one of the brotherhood, whom, for want of a more distinct recognition or name, the people chose to call 'Rosicrucius', in general reference to his order; and from the circumstance of the lamp, and its sudden extinguishment by the figure that started up, it was supposed that some Rosicrucian had determined to inform posterity that he had penetrated to the secret of the making of the ever-burning lamps of the ancients-- though, at the moment that he displayed his knowledge, he took effectual means that no one should reap any advantage from it.

The Spectator, in No. 379, for Thursday, May 15th, 1712, under the signature of 'X', which is understood to be that of Budgell, has the following account of that which is chosen there to be designated 'Rosicrucius's Sepulchre':

Rosicrucius, say his disciples, made use of this method to show the world that he had re-invented the ever-burning lamps of the ancients, though he was resolved no one should reap any advantage from the discovery'.

We have chosen the above story as the introduction to our curious history.

Christian Rosencreutz died in 1484. To account for Rosicrucianism not having been heard of until 1604, it has been asserted that this supposed first founder of Rosicrucianism bound his disciples not to reveal any of his doctrines until a period of one hundred and twenty years after his death.

The ancient Romans are said to have preserved lights in their sepulchres many ages by the *oiliness of gold* (here steps in the art of the Rosicrucians), resolved by hermetic methods into a liquid substance; and it is reported that at the dissolution of monasteries, in the time of Henry the Eighth, there was a lamp found that had then burned in a tomb from about three hundred years after Christ--nearly twelve hundred years. Two of these subterranean lamps are to be seen in the Museum of Rarities at

Leyden, in Holland. One of these lamps, in the Papacy of Paul the Third, was found in the Tomb of Tullia (so named), Cicero's daughter, which had been shut up fifteen hundred and fifty years (Second edition of N. Bailey's Φιλόλογος, 1731).

CHAPTER THE THIRD

EVER-BURNING LAMPS

IN the Papacy of Paul the Third, in the Appian Way, where abundance of the chief heathens of old were laid, a sepulchre was opened, where was found the entire body of a fair virgin swimming in a wonderful juice, which kept it from putrefaction so well, that the face seemed no way impaired, but lively and very beautiful. Her hair was yellow, tied up artificially, and kept together with a golden circlet or band. Under her feet burnt lamps, the light of which was extinguished at the opening of the sepulchre. By some inscriptions found about the tomb it appeared that she must have lain there fifteen hundred years. Who she was was never known, although many concluded her to be 'Tulliola', the daughter of Cicero. This discovery has been reported from various hands.

Cedrenus makes mention of a lamp, which, together with an image of Christ, was found at Edessa in the reign of Justinian the Emperor. It was set over a certain gate there, and elaborately enclosed and shut out from the air. This lamp, as appeared from the date attached to it, was lighted soon after Christ was crucified. It was found burning--as in fact it had done for five hundred years--by the soldiers of Cosroes, king of Persia; by whom, at this strange discovery and plunder, the oil was taken out and cast into the fire. As it is reported, this wild act occasioned such a plague as brought death upon numbers of the forces of Cosroes, sufficiently punished for their sacrilegious mischief.

At the demolition of our monasteries here in England, there was found in the monument which was supposed to be that of Constantius Chlorus, father to the great Constantine, a burning lamp, which was thought to have continued burning there ever since his burial, which was about three hundred years after Christ. The ancient Romans are said to have been able to maintain lights in their sepulchres for an indefinite time, by an essence or oil obtained from liquid gold; which was an achievement assumed to have been only known to the Rosicrucians, who boasted this among some other of their stupendous arts.

Baptista Porta, in his treatise on Natural Magic, relates that about the year 1550, in the island of Nesis, in the Bay of Naples, a marble sepulchre of a certain Roman was discovered; upon the opening of which a burning lamp, affording a powerful illumination, was discovered. The light of this lamp paled on the admission of the air, and it was speedily extinguished. It appeared from undoubted tokens in the mode of inscription that this wonderful lamp had been placed in its present receptacle before the advent of the Saviour. Those who saw the lamp declared that the effulgence was of the most dazzling character; that the light did not flicker or change, but burnt marvellously steadily.

A most celebrated lamp, called that of Pallas, the son of Evander, who, as Virgil relates, was killed by Turnus (the account will be found in the tenth book of Virgil's Æneid), is that reported as discovered not far from Rome, as far forward in time as the year 1401. It is related that a countryman was digging in the neighbourhood, and that delving deeper than usual, he came upon a stone sepulchre, wherein there was discovered the body of a man of extraordinary size, as perfect and natural as if recently interred. Above the head of the deceased there was found a lamp, burning with the supposed fabulous perpetual fire. Neither wind nor water, nor any other superinduced means, could extinguish it; but the flame was mastered eventually by the lamp being bored at bottom and broken by the astonished investigators of this consummate light. The man enclosed in this monument had a large wound in the breast. That this was the body of Pallas was evident from the inscription on the tomb, which was as follows:

> Pallas, Evander's son, whom Turnus' spear
> In battle slew, of mighty bulk, lies here.

A very remarkable lamp was discovered about the year 1500 near Ateste, a town belonging to Padua, in Italy, by a rustic who in his explorations in a field came upon an urn containing another urn, in which last was deposited one of these much-doubted miraculous lamps. The aliment of this strange lamp appeared to be a very exquisite crystal liquor, by the ever-during powers of which the lamp must have continued to shine for upwards of fifteen hundred years. And unless this lamp had been so suddenly exposed to the action of the air, it is supposed that it might have continued to burn for any time. This lamp, endowed with such unbelievable powers, was discovered to be the workmanship of an unknown contriver named Maximus Olibius, who must have possessed the profoundest skill in chemical art. On the greater urn some lines were inscribed in Latin, recording the perpetuation of this wonderful secret of the preparation and the starting of these (almost) *immortal* flames.

St. Austin mentions a lamp that was found in a temple dedicated to Venus, which,, notwithstanding that it was exposed to the open weather, could never be consumed or extinguished.

Ludovicus Vives, his commentator, in a supplementary mention of ever-burning lamps, cites an instance of another similar lamp which was discovered a little before his time, and which was considered to have been burning for a thousand and fifty years.

It is supposed that the perpetuity of the flame of these wonderful lamps was owing to the consummate tenacity of the unctuous matter with which the light was maintained; and that the balance was so exquisitely perfect between the feeding material and the strength of the flame, and so proportioned -for everlasting provision and expenditure, that, like the radical moisture and natural heat in animals, neither of them could ever unduly prevail. Licetus, who has advanced this opinion, observes that in order to effectually prevent interference with this balance, the ancients hid these lamps in caverns or in enclosed monuments. Hence it happened that on opening these tombs and secret places, the admission of fresh air to the lamps destroyed the fine equilibrium and stopped the life (as it were) of the lamp, similarly as a blow or a shock stops a watch, in jarring the matchless mechanism.

CHAPTER THE FOURTH

INSUFFICIENCY OF WORLDLY OBJECTS

IT is a constant and very plausible charge offered by the general world against the possession of the power of gold-making as claimed by the alchemists, who were the practical branch of the Rosicrucians, that if such supposed power were in their hands, they would infallibly use it, and that quickly enough; for the acquisition of riches and power, say they, is the desire of all men. But this idea proceeds from an ignorance of the character and inclinations of real philosophers, and results from an inveterate prejudice relative to them. Before we judge of these, let us acquire a knowledge of the natural inclinations of very deeply learned men. Philosophers, when they have attained to much knowledge, which wearies them of merely mundane matters, hold that the ordering of men, the following of them about by subservient people, and the continual glitter about them of the fine things of this world, are, after all, but of mean and melancholy account, because life is so brief, and this accidental pre-eminence is very transitory. Splendour, show, and bowing little delight the raised and abstract mind. That circuit of comfort formed by the owning of money and riches is circumscribed by the possessor's own ken. What is outside of this sight may just as well be enjoyed by any other person as by the owner, since all is the thinking of it; only granting that a man has sufficient for his daily wants, letting the 'morrow, indeed, take thought for itself'. One dinner a day, one bed for each night, in the alternations of sun and darkness, one of everything that is agreeable to (or is desirable for) man, is sufficient for any one man. A man's troubles are increased by the multiplication even of his enjoyments, because he is then beset with anxiety as to their repetition or maintenance. Reduction of things to attend to, and not multiplication, is his policy, because thinking of it is all that can affect him about anything in this world.

By the time that the deep, philosophical chemist has penetrated to the control and conversion of the ultimate elements, so as to have in his view the secret operations of Nature, and to have caught Nature, as it were: preparing her presentments and arranging her disguises behind the scenes, he is no more to be amused with vain book-physics. After his spying into the subtle processes of Nature, he cannot be contented with the ordinary toys of men; for are not worldly possessions, honour, rank, money, even wives and numerous or any children, but toys in a certain sense? Where sink they in importance to him when the great unknown sets in which awaits every man? He who can work as Nature works, causing the sunshine, so to speak, to light fire up independently in itself, and to breed and propagate precious things upon the atmosphere in which it burns, causing the growing supernatural soul to work amidst the seeds of gold, and to purge the material, devilish mass until the excrement is expelled, and it springs in health into condensating, solid splendour, a produce again to be sown, to fructify into fresh harvests--the alchemist, or prince of chemists, who can do this, laughs at the hoards of kings. By the time that the artist is thus so much more than man, is he the less desirous of the gratifying things to the ordinary man. Grandeur fades to him before such high intellectual grandeur. He is nearer to the angels, and the world has sunk infinitely below. His is the sky, and the bright shapes of the clouds of the sky: which he is going to convert, perhaps, into prisms, showering solid triumphs. He can well leave to common man his acres of mud, and the turbid pools spotted over them like the shining, showy discs of a snake. Man, under these enlightened philosophical circumstances, will only value the unseen kingdoms--glimpses of the immortal glories of which and of their Rosicrucian inhabitants he has obtained in his magic reveries. What can the longest ordinary man's life give to such a gifted thinker? Man's senses and their gratification, as long as the inlets and avenues of perception remain--world's music, so long as the strings cling tight, for the air of imagination to play upon them--appetites, with downward eyes to find their satisfaction--

man's mortality, with an exit into the shadows or into the grave while the sun is up: the longest life can but give him repetition to satiety of these things--repetitions until he seems almost to tire of the common sun. Of which he grows weary, as well as of his waste or extent of knowledge.

To some minds, this world does not present such extraordinary attractions. The very possession of the heights of knowledge induces rather stay up there, amidst the stars, thane descent. Every man almost has felt the sublime exaltation of a great height, when he has achieved the top of a high hill, and looks out and over the landscape for miles and miles. How very little the world looks under him! He is obliged to descend, because he has his home under there. But he quits the upper regions with reluctance, although it is somewhat frightening (as though he were going to be flown away with) to stay so, high up. You become giddy by looking up at the stars, which then seem to be so much nearer as to be attainable.

Limited as it is, life itself--very brief, very empty, very much disposed to repeat dull things, gathering up from about you in a strange sensation sometimes, in folds like a dream, or flowing on like a sleep-inducing river to the sea, carrying faces seen and snatched away, and obliterating voices which change into echoes--life, at its very best, ought to be the stoicism of the spectator, who feels that he has come here somehow, though for what purpose he knows not; and he is rather amused as at a comedy in life, than engaged in it as in a business. Even perpetual youth, and life prolonged, with pleasures infinite--even the fancied ever-during life--would, to the deeply thinking man who had risen; as it were, over life, and to that strangely gifted being who has in himself the power of self-perpetuation (like the Wandering Jew), seem vain. Man can be conceived as tiring of the sun--tiring of consciousness even. What an expression is that, 'forgotten by Death'! The only being through whom the scythe of the great destroyer passes scatheless! That life, as a phantom, which is the only conceivable terrible doom of the 'Wanderer' (if such a magical being ever existed); whom as a locomotive symbol, to be perpetuated through the ages, the earth, at the command of the Saviour, refused to hide, and of whom a legend--soon hushed in again--now and then rises to the popular whisper and to the popular distrust!

We only adduce these remarks to show that, in, the face of the spectator of the great ultimate, mysterious man, children are no necessity, but an anxiety, estates are a burden, 'business' is the oft-told purposeless tale to the wearying ear: He who can be the spectator of the ages has no particulars in ordinary life. He has nothing which can interest him. He can have no precise and consolidated likings or affections or admirations, or even aversions, because the world is as a toy-shop to him--its small mechanism is an artificial show, of which (given the knowledge of the wheels) he can predicate as to-the movements safely--completely.

To return for a moment to the idea of the 'Wandering Jew', which some have supposed to be derived from the claim of the Rosicrucians to the possession of a secret means of renewing youth, and to the escape of some notion of it from out their writings. Even supposing that this strange tale was true, nothing can be imagined more melancholy than the state of this lone traveller, moving with his awful secret through the world, and seeing the successive generations, like leaves, perishing from about him. He counts the years like the traveller of a long summer day, to whom the evening will never come, though he sees his temporary companions, at the different hours of the day, depart appropriately and disappearing to their several homes by the wayside. To him the childhood of his companions seems to turn to old age in an hour. He remembers the far-off ancestors of his contemporaries. Fashions fleet, but your unsuspected youth is accommodated to all. Yours is, indeed, the persecution of the day-life, which will not let you fall to sleep and cease to see the vanity of everything. Your friends of any period disappear. The assurance of the emptiness of all things is the stone as into which your heart is turned. Grey hairs (and the old face) have nothing with you, though you see them appearing upon all others.

Familiar objects disappear from about you, and you and the sun seem the only things that survive as old friends. Indeed, it may be doubtful whether, to this supposed man of the ages, the generations would not seem to be produced as a purposeless efflux out of the ground by the sun, like flowers or plants; so as mere matter of mould would all flesh appear, with a phenomenon only going with it in the article of the figure's uprightness as man; it having so strangely set its face against the stars, unlike the creatures doomed to move horizontally.

We make these observations to show that, notwithstanding the opinions of the world to the contrary, there may have been men who have possessed these gifts--that is, the power of making gold and of perpetuating their lives--and yet that the exercise of these powers was forborne; and also that their secrets of production have most carefully been kept, lest less wise men should (to speak in figure) have 'rushed in where they feared to tread', and have abused where the philosophers even would not use--despising wealth, which they could not enjoy, and declining a perpetuated life, which would only add to their weariness--life being only a repetition of the same suns, already found too unmeaning and too long. For it is a mistake to suppose that this life is so equally enjoyable by all. There is a sublime sorrow of the ages, as of the lone ocean. There is the languishment for the ever-lost original home in this tearful mortal state.

The philosophers knew that possession blunted desire, and that rich men may be poor men. A remarkable answer was made by a man who, to all appearance, possessed superabundantly the advantages of life--wealth, honour, wife, children, 'troops of friends', even health, by day: but in his night he lived another life, for in it was presented another picture, and that unfailingly uncomfortable, even to this good man--exchanging joy for horror. 'My friend', replied he to an inquirer, 'never congratulate a man upon his happiness until you become aware how he sleeps. Dreams are as that baleful country into which I pass. every night of my life; and what can be said to a man who dreams constantly (and believes it) that he is with the devil'?

There was no answering this, for every person leads two lives, altogether independent of each other--the days and the nights both full of life, though the night, with the dreams, may be of an opposite order. The world's circumstances may afford you solace and gratification--even happiness--in the day; but you may be very miserable, notwithstanding, if it happen that you have persecution in your dreams. Here the world's advantages are of no use to you, for you are delivered over helpless, night after night, in your sleep--and you must have sleep--to the dominion of Other Powers, whom all your guards cannot keep out, for their inlet is quite of another kind than the ordinary life's access. We advise you, then, to beware of this dark door; the other will perhaps take care of itself, letting in no ugly things upon you: but the former may let in unpleasant things upon you in full grasp with your hands bound.

CHAPTER THE FIFTH

THE HERMETIC PHILOSOPHERS

THERE was among the sages a writer, Artephius, whose productions are very famous among the Hermetic Philosophers, insomuch that the noble Olaus Borrichius, an excellent writer and a most candid critic, recommends these books to the attentive perusal of those who would acquire knowledge of this sublime highest philosophy. He is said to have invented a cabalistic magnet which possessed the extraordinary property of secretly attracting the aura, or mysterious spirit of human efflorescence and prosperous bodily growth, out of young men; and these benign and healthful springs of life he gathered up, and applied by his magic art to himself--by inspiration, transudation, or otherwise--so that he concentred in his own body, waning in age, the accumulated rejuvenescence of many young people: the individual owners of which new fresh life suffered and were consumed in proportion to the extent in which he preyed vitally upon them, and some of them were exhausted by this enchanter and died. This was because their fresh young vitality had been unconsciously drawn out of them in his baneful, devouring society, which was unsuspected because it afforded a glamour delightful. Now this seems absurd; but it is not so absurd as we suppose when considered sympathetically.

Sacred history affords considerable authority to this kind of opinion. We all are acquainted with the history of King David, to whom, when he grew old and stricken in years, Abishag, the Shunammite, was brought to recover him--a damsel described as 'very fair'; and we are told that she 'lay in his bosom', and that thereby he 'gat heat'--which means vital heat, but that the king 'knew her not'. This latter clause in *I Kings* i. 4, all the larger critics, including those who speak in the commentaries of Munster, Grotius, Vossius, and others, interpret in the same way. The seraglios of the Mohammedans have more of this less lustful meaning, probably, than is commonly supposed. The ancient physicians appear to have been thoroughly -acquainted with the advantages of the companionship, without irregular indulgence, of the young to the old in the renewal of their vital powers.

The elixir of life was also prepared by other and less criminal means than those singular ones hinted above. It was produced out of the secret chemical laboratories of Nature by some adepts. The famous chemist, Robert Boyle, mentions a preparation in his works, of which Dr. Le Fevre gave him an account in the presence of a famous physician and of another learned man. An intimate friend of the physician, as Boyle relates, had given, out of curiosity, a small quantity of this medicated wine or preparation to an old female domestic; and this, being agreeable to the taste, had been partaken of for ten or twelve days by the woman, who was near seventy years of age, but whom the doctor did not inform what the liquor was, nor what advantage he was expecting that it might effect. A great change did indeed occur with this old woman; for she acquired much greater activity, a sort of youthful bloom came to her countenance, her face was becoming much more smooth and agreeable; and beyond this, as a still more decided step backward to her youthful period, certain *purgationes* came upon her again with sufficiently severe indications to frighten her very much as to their meaning; so that the doctor, greatly surprised at his success, was compelled to forego his further experiments, and to suppress all mention of this miraculous new cordial, for fear of alarming people with incomprehensible novelties--in regard to which they are very tenacious, having prejudices inveterate.

But with respect to centenarians, some persons have been mentioned as having survived for hundreds of years, moving as occasion demanded from country to country; when the time arrived that, in the natural course of things, they should die, or be expected to die, merely changing their names, and reappearing in another place as new persons--they having long survived all who knew them, and thus being safe from the risk of discovery. The. Rosicrucians always most jealously guarded these secrets, speaking in enigmas and parables for the most part; and they adopted as their motto the advice of one of their number, one of the Gnostics of the early Christian period: 'Learn to know all, but keep thyself unknown'. Further, it is not generally known that the true Rosicrucians bound themselves to obligations of comparative poverty but absolute chastity in the world, with certain dispensations and remissions that fully answered their purpose; for .they were not necessarily solitary people: on the contrary, they were frequently gregarious, and mixed freely with all classes, though privately admitting no law but their own.

Their notions of poverty, or comparative poverty, were different from those that usually prevail. They felt that neither monarchs nor the wealth of monarchs could endow or aggrandize those who already esteemed themselves the superiors of all men; and therefore, though declining riches, they were voluntary in the renunciation of them. They held to chastity, because, entertaining some very peculiar notions about the real position in creation of the female sex, the Enlightened or Illuminated Brothers held the monastic or celibate state to be infinitely that more consonant with the intentions of Providence, since in everything possible to man's frail nature they sought to trample on the pollutions and the great degradation of this his state in flesh. They trusted the great lines of Nature, not in the whole, but in part, as they believed Nature was in certain senses not true and a betrayer, and that she was not wholly the benevolent power to endow, as accorded with the prevailing deceived notion. We wish not to discuss more particularly than thus the extremely refined and abstruse protesting views of these fantastic religionists, who ignored Nature. We have drawn to ourselves a certain frontier of reticence, up to which margin we may freely comment; and the limit is quite extended enough for the present popular purpose, though we absolutely refuse to overpass it with too distinct explanation, or to enlarge further on the strange persuasions of the Rosicrucians.

There is related, upon excellent authority, to have happened an extraordinary incident at Venice, that made a very great stir among the talkers in that ancient place, and which we will here supply at length, as due to so mysterious and amusing an episode. Every one who has visited Venice in these days, and still more those of the old-fashioned time who have put their experience of it on record, are aware that freedom and ease among persons who make a good appearance prevail there to an extent that; in this reserved and suspicious country, is difficult to realize. This doubt of respectability until conviction disarms has a certain constrained and unamiable effect on our English manners, though it occasionally secures us from imposition, at the expense perhaps of our accessibility. A stranger who arrived in Venice one summer, towards the end of the seventeenth century, and who took up his residence in one of the best sections of the city, by the considerable figure which, he made, and through his own manners, which were polished, composed, and elegant, was admitted into the best company--this though he came with no introductions, nor did anybody exactly know who or what he was. His figure was exceedingly elegant and well-proportioned, his face oval and long, his forehead ample and pale, and the intellectual faculties were surprisingly brought out, and in distinguished prominence. His hair was long, dark, and flowing; his smile inexpressibly fascinating, yet sad; and the deep light of his eyes seemed laden, to the attention sometimes of those noting him, with the sentiments and experience of all the historic periods. But his conversation, when he chose to converse, and his, attainments and knowledge, were marvellous; though he seemed always striving to keep himself back, and to avoid saying too much, yet not with an ostentatious reticence. He went by the name of Signor Gualdi and was looked upon as a plain private gentleman, of moderate independent estate. He was an interesting character; in short, one to make an observer speculate concerning him.

This gentleman remained at Venice for some. months, and was known by the name of 'The Sober Signior' among the common people, on account of the regularity of his life, the composed simplicity of, his manners, and the quietness of his costume; for he always wore dark clothes, and these of a plain, unpretending style. Three things were remarked of him during his stay at Venice. The first was, that he had a small collection of fine pictures, which he readily showed to everybody that desired it; the next, that he seemed perfectly versed in all arts and sciences, and spoke always with such minute correctness as to particulars as astonished, nay, silenced, all who heard him, because he seemed to have been present at the occurrences which he related, making the most unexpected correction in small facts sometimes. And it was, in the third place, observed that he never wrote or received any letter, never desired any credit, but always paid for everything in ready money, and made no use of bankers, bills of exchange, or letters of credit. However, he always seemed to have enough, and he lived respectably, though with no attempt at splendour or show.

Signor Gualdi met, shortly after his arrival at Venice, one day, at the coffee-house which he was in the habit of frequenting, a Venetian nobleman of sociable manners, who was very fond of art, and this pair used to engage in sundry discussions; and they had many conversations concerning the various objects and pursuits which were interesting to both of them. Acquaintance ripened into friendly esteem; and the nobleman invited Signor Gualdi to his private house, whereat--for he was a widower-- Signor Gualdi first met the nobleman's daughter, a very beautiful young maiden of eighteen, of much grace and intelligence, and of great accomplishments. The nobleman's daughter was just introduced at her father's house from a convent, or *pension*, where she had been educated by the nuns. This young lady, in short, from constantly being in his society, and listening to his interesting narratives, gradually fell in love with the mysterious stranger, much for the reasons of Desdemona; though Signor Gualdi was no swarthy Moor, but only a well-educated gentleman--a thinker rather than the desirer to be a doer. At times, indeed, his countenance seemed to grow splendid and magical in expression; and he boasted certainly wondrous discourse; and a strange and weird fascination would grow up about him, as it were, when he became more than usually pleased, communicative, and animated. Altogether, when you were set thinking about him, he seemed a puzzling person, and of rare gifts; though when mixing only with the crowd you would scarcely distinguish him from the crowd; nor would you observe him, unless there was something romantically .akin to him in you excited by his talk.

And now for a few remarks on the imputed character of these Rosicrucians. And in regard to them, however their existence is disbelieved, the matters of fact we meet with, sprinkled, but very sparingly, in the history of these hermetic people, are so astonishing, and at the same time are preferred with such confidence, that if we disbelieve--which it is impossible to avoid, and that from the preposterous and unearthly nature of their pretensions--we cannot escape the conviction that, if there is not foundation for it, their impudence and egotism is most audacious. They speak of all mankind as infinitely beneath them; their pride is beyond idea, although they are most humble and quiet in exterior. They glory in poverty, and declare that it is the state ordered for them; and this though they boast universal riches. They decline all human affections, or submit to them as advisable escapes only--appearance of loving obligations, which are assumed for convenient acceptance, or for passing in a world which is composed of them, or of their supposal. They mingle most gracefully in the society of women, with hearts wholly incapable of softness in this direction; while they criticize them with pity or contempt in their own minds as altogether another order of beings from men, They are most simple and deferential in their exterior; and yet the self-value which fills their hearts ceases its self-glorying expansion only with the boundless skies. Up to a certain point, they are the sincerest people in the world; but rock is soft to their impenetrability afterwards. In comparison with the hermetic adepts, monarchs are poor, and their greatest accumulations are contemptible. By the side of the sages, the most learned are mere dolts and blockheads. They make no movement towards fame, because they abnegate and disdain it. If they become famous, it is in spite of themselves: they seek no honours, because there can be no gratification in honours to such people.

Their greatest wish is to steal unnoticed and unchallenged through the world, and to amuse themselves with the world because they are in it, and because they find it about them. Thus, towards mankind they are negative; towards everything else, positive; self-contained, self-illuminated, self-everything; but always prepared (nay, enjoined) to do good, wherever possible or safe.

To this immeasurable exaltation of themselves, what standard of measure, or what appreciation, can you apply? Ordinary estimates fail in the idea of it. Either the state of these occult philosophers is the height of sublimity, or it is the height of absurdity. Not being competent to understand them or their claims, the world insists that these are futile. The result entirely depends upon their being fact or fancy in the ideas of the hermetic philosophers. The puzzling part of the investigation is, that the treatises of these profound writers abound in the most acute discourse upon difficult subjects, and contain splendid passages and truths upon all subjects--upon the nature of metals, upon medical science, upon the unsupposed properties of simples, upon theological and ontological speculation, and upon science and objects of thought generally--upon all these matters they enlarge to the reader stupendously--when the proper attention is directed to them.

CHAPTER THE SIXTH

AN HISTORICAL ADVENTURE

BUT to return to Signor Gualdi, from whom we have notwithstanding made no impertinent digression, since he was eventually suspected to be one of the strange people, or Rosicrucians, or Ever-Livers of whom we are treating. This was from mysterious circumstances which occurred afterwards in relation to him, and which are in print.

The Venetian nobleman was now on a footing of sufficient intimacy with Signor Gualdi to say to him one evening, at his own house, that he understood that he had a fine collection of pictures, and that, if agreeable, he would pay him a visit some day for the purpose of viewing them. The nobleman's daughter who was present, and who was pensively looking down upon the table, more than half in love with the stranger as she had become, thinking deeply of something that the Signor had just said, raised her eyes eagerly at this expression of wish by her father and, as accorded with her feelings, she appeared, though she spoke not, to be greatly desirous to make one of the party to see the pictures. It was natural that she should secretly rejoice at this opportunity of becoming more intimately acquainted with the domestic life, of one whom she had grown to regard with feelings of such powerful interest. She felt that the mere fact of being his guest, and under the roof which was his; would seem to bring her nearer to him; and, as common with lovers, it appeared to her that their being thus together would, in feeling at least, appear to identify both. Signor Gualdi was very polite, and readily invited the nobleman to his house, and also extended the invitation to the young lady, should she feel disposed to accompany her father, since he divined from the expression of her face that she was wishful to that effect. The day for the visit was then named, and the Signor took his departure with the expressions of friendship on all sides which usually ended their pleasant meetings.

It followed from this arrangement, that on the day appointed the father and daughter went to Signor Gualdi's house. They were received by the Signor with warm kindness, and were shown over his rooms with every mark of friendliness and distinction. The nobleman viewed Signor Gualdi's pictures with great attention; and when he had completed his tour of the gallery, he expressed his satisfaction by telling the Signor that he had never seen a finer collection, considering the number of pieces. They were now in Signor Gualdi's own chamber--the last of his set of rooms; and they were just on the point of turning to go out and bidding adieu, and Gualdi was courteously removing the tapestry from before the door to widen the egress, when the nobleman, who had paused to allow him thus to clear the way, by chance cast his eyes upwards over the door, where there hung a picture with the curtain accidentally left un-drawn, evidently of the stranger himself. The Venetian looked upon it with doubt, and after a while his face fell; but it soon cleared, as if with relief. The gaze of the daughter was also now riveted upon the picture, which was very like Gualdi; but she regarded it with a look of tenderness and a blush. The Venetian looked from the picture to Gualdi, and back again from Gualdi to the picture. It was some time before he spoke; and when, he did; his voice sounded strangely.

'That picture was intended for you, sir', said he at last, hesitating, to Signor Gualdi. A slight cold change passed over the eyes of the stranger; but he only made reply by a low bow. 'You look a moderately young man--to be candid with you, sir, I should say about forty-five or thereabouts; and yet I know, by certain means of which I will not now further speak, that this picture is by the hand of Titian, who has been dead nearly a couple of hundred years. How is this possible'? he added, with a polite, grave smile. 'It is not easy', said Signor Gualdi quietly, 'to know all things that are possible or not possible, for very frequently mistakes are made concerning such; but there is certainly nothing strange in my being like a portrait painted by Titian.' The nobleman easily perceived by his manner, and by a momentary cloud upon his brow, that the stranger felt offence.

The daughter clung to her father's arm, secretly afraid that this little unexpected demur might pass into coolness, and end with a consummation of estrangement, which she feared excessively; she dreaded nervously the rupture of their intimacy with the stranger; and, contradictory as it may seem, she wanted to withdraw, even without the demur she dreaded being cleared up into renewed pleasant confidence. However, this little temporary misunderstanding was soon put an end to by Signor Gualdi himself, who in a moment or two resumed his ordinary manner; and he saw the father and daughter downstairs, and forth to the entrance of his house, with his usual composed politeness, though the nobleman could not help some feeling of restraint, and his daughter experienced a considerable amount of mortification; and she could not look at Signor Gualdi, or rather, when she did, she dwelt on his face too much.

This little occurrence remained as a puzzle in the mind of the nobleman. His daughter felt lonely and dissatisfied afterwards, eager for the restoration of the same friendly feeling with Signor Gualdi, and revolving in her mind, with the ingenuity of love, numberless schemes to achieve it. The Venetian betook himself in the evening to the usual coffeehouse; and he could not forbear speaking of the incident among the group of people collected there. Their curiosity was roused, and one or two, resolved to satisfy themselves by looking at the picture attentively the next morning. But to obtain an opportunity to see the picture on this next morning, it was necessary to see the Signor Gualdi somewhere, and to have the invitation of so reserved a man to his lodgings for the purpose. The only likely place to meet with him was at the coffee-house; and thither' the gentlemen went at the usual time, hoping, as it was the Signor's habit to present himself, that he would do so. But he did not come; nor had he been heard of from the time of the visit of the nobleman the day before to the Signor's house--which absence, for the first time almost that he had been in Venice, surprised everybody. But as they did not meet with him at the coffee-house, as they thought was sure, one of the persons who had the oftenest conversed with the Signor, and therefore was the freer in his acquaintance, undertook to go to his lodgings and inquire after him, which he did; but he was, answered by the owner of the house, who came to the street-door to respond to the questioner, that the Signor had gone, having quitted Venice that morning, early, and that he had locked up his pictures with certain orders, and had taken the key of his rooms with him. This affair made a great noise at the time in Venice; and an account of it found its way into most of the newspapers of the year in which it occurred. In these newspapers and elsewhere, an outline of the foregoing particulars may be seen. The account of the Signor Gualdi will also be met with in *Les Mémoires Historiques* for the year 1687, tome i. p. 365. The chief particulars of our own narrative are extracted from an old book in our collection treating of well-attested relations of the sages, and of life protracted by their art for several centuries: *Hermippus Redivivus; or, the Sage's Triumph over Old Age and the Grave.* London, Second Edition, much enlarged. Printed for J. Nourse, at The Lamb, against Catherine Street in the Strand, in, the year 1749.

And thus much for the history of Signor Gualdi, who was suspected to be a Rosicrucian.

We shall have further interesting notices of these unaccountable people as we proceed.

CHAPTER THE SEVENTH

THE HERMETIC BRETHREN

THE following passages occur in a letter published by some anonymous members of the R.C., and are adduced in a translation from the Latin by one of the most famous men of the order, who addressed from the University of Oxford about the period of Oliver Cromwell; to which university the great English Rosicrucian, Robertus de Fluctibus (Robert Flood), also belonged, in the time of James the First and Charles the First. We have made repeated visits to the church where Robert Flood lies buried.

'Every man naturally desires superiority. Men wish for treasures and to seem great in the eyes of the world. God, indeed, created all things to the end that man might give Him thanks; But there is no individual thinks of his proper duties; he secretly desires to spend his days idly, and would enjoy riches and pleasures without any previous labour or danger. When we' (professors of abstruse sciences) 'speak, men either revile or contemn, they either envy or laugh. When we discourse of gold, they assume that we would assuredly produce it if we could, because. they judge us by themselves; and when we debate of it, and enlarge upon it, they imagine we shall finish by teaching them how to make gold by art, or furnish them with it already made. And wherefore or why should we teach them the way to these mighty possessions? Shall it be to the end that men may live pompously in the eyes of the world; swagger and make wars; be violent when they are contradicted; turn usurers, gluttons, and drunkards; abandon themselves to lust? Now, all these things deface and defile man, and the holy temple of man's body, and are plainly against the ordinances of God. For this dream of the world, as also the body or vehicle through which it is made manifest, the Lord intended to be pure. And it was not purposed, in the divine arrangement, that men should grow again down to the earth. It is for other purposes that the stars, in their attraction, have raised man on his feet, instead of abandoning him to the "all fours" that were the imperfect tentatives of nature until life, through the supernatural impulse, rose above its original condemned level--base and relegate.

'We of the secret knowledge do wrap ourselves in mystery, to avoid the objurgation and importunity or violence of those who conceive that we cannot be philosophers unless we put our knowledge to some ordinary worldly use. There is scarcely one who thinks about us who does not believe that our society has no existence; because, as he truly declares, he never met any of us. And he concludes that there is no such brotherhood because, in his vanity, we seek not- him to be our fellow. We do not come, as he assuredly expects, to that conspicuous stage upon which, like himself, as he desires the gaze of the vulgar, every fool may enter; winning wonder, if the man's appetite be that empty way; and, when he has obtained it, crying out "Lo, this is also vanity!"'

Dr. Edmund Dickenson, physician to King Charles the Second, a professed seeker of the hermetic knowledge, produced a book entitled, *De Quinta Essentia Philosophorum:* which was printed at Oxford in 1686, and a second time in 1705. There was a third edition of it printed in Germany in 1721. In correspondence with a French adept, the latter explains the reasons why the Brothers of the Rosy Cross concealed themselves. As to the universal medicine, *Elixir Vitæ*, or potable form of the preternatural *menstruum*, he positively asserts that it is in the hands of the 'Illuminated', but that, by the time they discover it, they have ceased to desire its uses, being far above them; and as to life for centuries, being wishful for other things, they decline availing themselves of it. He adds, that the adepts are obliged to conceal themselves for the sake of safety, because they would be abandoned in the consolations of the intercourse of this world (if they were not, indeed, exposed to worse risks), supposing that their gifts were proven to the conviction of the bystanders as more than human; when they would become simply intolerable and abhorrent. Thus, there are excellent reasons for their conduct; they proceed with the utmost caution, and instead of making a display of their powers, as vainglory is the least distinguishing characteristic of these great men, they studiously evade the idea that they possess any extraordinary. or separate knowledge. They live simply as mere spectators in the world, and they desire to make no disciples, converts, nor confidants. They submit to the obligations of life, and to relationships--enjoying the fellowship of none, admiring none, following none, but themselves. They obey all codes, are excellent citizens, and only preserve silence in regard to their own private convictions, giving the world the benefit of their acquirements up to a certain point: seeking only sympathy at some angles of, their multiform character, but shutting out curiosity wholly where they do not wish its imperative eyes.

This is the reason that the Rosicrucians passed through the world mostly unnoticed, and that people generally disbelieve that there ever were such persons; or believe that, if there were, their pretensions are an imposition. It is easy to discredit things which we do not understand--in fact, nature compels us to reject all propositions which do not consist with our reason. The true artist is supposed to avoid all suspicion, even on the part of those nearest to him. And granting the possibility, of the Rosicrucian means of the renewal of life, and supposing also that it was the desire of the hermetic philosopher, it would not be difficult for him so to order his arrangements as that he should seem to die in one place (to keep up the character of the natural manner of his life), by withdrawing himself, to reappear in another place as a new person at the time that seemed most convenient to him for the purpose. For everything, and every difficult thing, is easy to those with money; nor will, the world inquire with too resolute a curiosity, if you have coolness and address, and if you have the art of accounting for things. The man of this order also is *solus*, and without wife or children to embarrass him in the private disposition of his affairs, or to follow him too closely into his by-corners. Thus it will be seen that philosophers may live in the world, and have all these gifts, and yet be never heard of--or, if heard of, only as they themselves wish or suggest.

As an instance of the unexpected risks which a member of this order may run if he turns his attention to the practical side of his studies, spite of all his precautions, we may cite the accident which happened to a famous Englishman, who disguised himself under the name of Eugenius Philalethes, but whose real name is said to be Thomas Vaughan. He tells us of himself, that going to a goldsmith to sell twelve hundred marks' worth of gold, the man told him, at first sight, that it never came out of the mines, but was the production of art, as it was not of the standard of any known kingdom: which proved so sudden a dilemma to the offerer of the gold, that he withdrew immediately, leaving it behind him. It naturally follows from this, that it is not only necessary to have gold, but that the gold shall be marketable or acceptable gold, as otherwise it is utterly useless for the purposes of conversion into money in this world. Thomas Vaughan, who was a scholar of Oxford, and was vehemently attacked in his lifetime, and who certainly was a Rosicrucian adept if there ever was one, led a wandering life, and fell often into great perplexities and dangers from the mere suspicion that he possessed extraordinary secrets. He was born, as we learn from his writings, about the year 1612, which makes him a contemporary of the great English Rosicrucian, Robert Flood; and what is the strangest part of his history, as we find remarked by a writer in 1749, is, that he is 'believed by those of his fraternity' (so the author adds) 'to be living even now; and a person of great credit at Nuremberg, in Germany, affirms that he conversed with him a year or two ago. Nay, it is further asserted' (continues the author) 'that this very individual is the president of the Illuminated in Europe, and that he sits as such in all their annual meetings'. Thomas Vaughan, according to the report of the philosopher Robert Boyle, and of others who knew him, was a man of remarkable piety, and of unstained morals. He has written and edited several invaluable works upon the secrets of the philosophers, some of which are in our possession; among others: *Introitus Apertus ad occlusum Regis Palatium; Lumen de Lumine; Magia Adamica; Anima Magica Abscondita*, and other learned books; advancing very peculiar theories concerning the seen and the unseen. These books were disbelieved at the time, and remain discredited, principally because they treat of eccentric and seemingly impossible things. It is, however, certain that we go but a very little way out of the usual learned track before we encounter puzzling matters, which may well set us investigating our knowledge, and looking with some suspicion upon its grounds, spite of all the pompous claims of modern philosophers, who are continually, on account of their conceitedness, making sad mistakes; and breaking down with their plausible systems.

'Progress and enlightenment are prerogatives to which no generation in particular can lay a special claim', says a modern writer, speaking of railways and their invention. 'Intelligence like that of the Stephensons is born again and again, at lengthened intervals; and it is only these giants in wisdom who know how to carry on to perfection the knowledge which centuries have been piling up before them. But the age in which such men are cast, is often unequal to appreciate the genius which seeks to elevate its aspiration. Thus it was in 1820 that Mr. William Brougham proposed to consign George Stephenson to Bedlam, for being the greatest benefactor of his time. But now that we have adopted somewhat fully his rejected ideas of steam-locomotion and high rates of speed, which were with so much difficulty forced upon us, we complacently call ourselves "enlightened"; and doubtless we are tolerably safe in doing so, considering that the Stephensons, and similar scientific visionaries, no longer live to contradict us.' We might add, that the Rosicrucians hold their critics in light esteem--indeed in very light esteem.

If such is the disbelief of science of everyday use, what chance of credit has the abstruser knowledge, and those assertions of power which contradict, our most ordinary ideas of possibility? Common sense will answer, None at all. And yet all human conclusions and resolutions upon points which have been considered beyond the possibility of contradiction have been sometimes at fault. The most politic course is not too vigorously to take our stand upon any supposed fixed point of truth, but simply to admit that our knowledge is limited, that absolute truth is alone in the knowledge of God, and that no more truth is vouchsafed to man than he knows how to utilize: most of his uses, even of his little quantum of truth, being perverted. He must await other states for greater light, and to become a higher creature--should that be his happy destiny. As to certainty in this world, there is none--nor can there be any. Whether there is anything outside of man is uncertain. Hume has pointed out that there is no sequence between one and two. Other philosophers have ingeniously detected that our senses are all one, or all none. Man is the picture painted upon external matter, and external matter is the individuality that surveys the picture. In the world of physics, colours are tones in other senses, and tones are colours; sevenfold in either case, as the planetary powers and influences are septenary--which, in the ideas of the Rosicrucians, produce both.

CHAPTER THE EIGHTH

MYTHIC HISTORY OF THE FLEUR-DE-LIS

THE maypole is a *phallos*. The ribbons depending from the discus, or ring, through which the maypole pierces, should be of the seven prismatic colours--those of the rainbow (or *Règne-beau*). According to the *Gnostics and their Remains, Ancient and Modern*, a work by the Rev. C. W. King, M.A., published in 1864, Horapollo has preserved a talisman, or Gnostic gem, in yellow jasper, which presents the engraved figure of a 'Cynocephalus, crowned, with *bâton* erect, adoring the first appearance of the new moon'.

The phallic worship prevailed, at one time, all over India. It constitutes, as Mr. Sellon asserts, to this day one of the chief, if not the leading, dogma of the Hindoo religion. Incontestable evidence could be adduced to prove this--however strange and impossible it seems--the key of all worship the world over; and highest in esteem in the most highly civilized nations. Though it has degenerated into gross and sensual superstition, it was originally intended as the worship of the creative principle in Nature. Innumerable curious particulars lie scattered up and down, in all countries of the world, relating to this worship; mad as it seems--bad as, in its grossness, it is. It is only in modern times that sensuality, and not sublimity, has been actively associated with this worship, however. There was a time when the rites connected with it were grand and solemn enough. The general diffusion of these notions regarding the *Phalli* and the *Ioni*, and of the sacred mystic suggestions implied in both, as well as the inflections in design of these unlikely, repulsive figures for serious worship, prove that there was something very extraordinary, and quite beyond belief to the moderns in the origin of them. The religion of the *Phallos* (and of its twin emblem) is to be traced all over the East. It appears to be the earliest worship practised by man. It prevailed not only amongst the Hindoos, Assyrians, Babylonians, Mexicans, Etruscans,

Greeks, and Romans in ancient times, but it still forms an integral part of the worship of India, Thibet, China, Siam, Japan, and Africa. We cannot, therefore, afford, to ignore this grand scheme of ritual, when we discover it to be a religion so widely spread, and reappearing so unexpectedly, not only in the countries with which we are contemporaneously acquainted, but also in those old countries of which we in reality know very little, or nothing at all; for all history reads doubtfully, being written for popular purposes.

In the *Temple-Herren* of Nicolai there is an account of a Gnostic gem, or talisman, which represents a 'Cynocephalus', with a lunar disc on his head, standing in the act of adoration, with *sceptrum* displayed, before a column engraved with letters, and supporting a triangle. This latter architectural figure is, in fact, an obelisk. All the Egyptian obelisks were *Phalli*. The triangle symbolizes one of the Pillars of Hermes (Hercules). The Cynocephalus was sacred to him. The Pillars of Hermes have been Judaised into Solomon's 'Jachin and Boaz'. So says Herz, in regard to 'Masonic Insignia'. We will explain fully, later in our book, of these interesting sexual images, set up for adoration so strangely and from the meaning of which we foolishly but determinedly avert.

We now propose to deduce a very original and a very elaborate genealogy, or descent, of the famous arms of France, the *Fleurs-de-Lis*, '*Lucifera*', *Lisses*, Luces, 'Lucies', Bees, Scarabs, Scara-bees, or Imperial 'Bees' of Charlemagne, and of Napoleon the First and Napoleon the Third, from a very extraordinary and (we will, in the fullest assurance, add) the most unexpected point of view. The real beginning of these inexpressibly sublime arms (or this 'badge'), although in itself, and apart from its purpose, it is the most refined, but mysteriously grand, in the world, contradictory as it may seem, is also the most ignoble. It has been the *crux* of the antiquaries and of the heralds for centuries! We would rather be excused the mentioning of the peculiar item which has thus been held up to the highest honour (heraldically) throughout the world. It will be sufficient to say that mystically, in its theological Gnostic allusion, it is the grandest device and most stupendous hint that armory ever saw; and those who are qualified to apprehend our hidden meaning will perhaps read correctly and perceive our end by the time that they have terminated this strange section of our history of Rosicrucianism-- for to it it refers particularly.

Scarabæi, Lucifera ('Light-bringers'), Luce, Fleur-de-Lis, Lily, Lucia, Lucy, Lux, Lu(+)x.

The Luce is the old-fashioned name for the 'pike' or jack--a fish famous for the profuse generation of a certain insect, as some fishermen know full well. This once (incredible as it may seem) formed an object of worship, for the sake of the inexpressibly sublime things which it symbolized. Although so mean in itself, and although so far off, this implied the beginning of all sublunary things.

The bees of Charlemagne, the bees of the Empire in France, are 'scarabs', or figures of the same affinity as the Bourbon 'lilies'. They deduce from a common ancestor. Now, the colour heraldic on which they are always emblazoned is *azure*, or blue--which is the colour of the sea, which is salt. In an anagram it may be expressed as 'C'. Following on this allusion, we may say that 'Ventre-saint-gris!' is a very ancient French barbarous expletive, or oath. Literally (which, in the occult sense, is always obscurely), it is the 'Sacred blue (or grey) womb'--which is absurd. Now, the reference and the meaning of this we will confidently commit to the penetration of those among our readers who can felicitously privately surmise it; and also the apparently circuitous deductions, which are yet to come, to be made by us.

Blue is the colour of the 'Virgin Maria'. Maria, Mary, *mare, mar, mara*, means the 'bitterness' or the 'saltness' of the sea. Blue is expressive of the Hellenic, Isidian, Ionian, Yonian (Yoni-Indian) Watery, Female, and Moonlike Principle in the universal theogony. It runs through all the mythologies.

The 'Lady-Bird' or 'Lady-Cow' (there is no resemblance between a *bird* and a *cow*, it may be remarked, *en passant*, except in this strangely occult, almost ridiculous, affinity), and the rustic rhyme among the children concerning it, may be here remembered:

> Lady-Bird, Lady-Bird, fly away home!
> Your House is on fire--your children at home!

Such may be heard in all parts of England when a lady-bird is seen by the children. Myths are inextricably embodied--like specks and straws and flies in amber--amidst the sayings and rhymes of the common people in all countries; and they are there preserved for very many generations, reappearing to recognition after the lapse sometimes of centuries. Now, how do we explain and re-render the above rude couplet? The 'Lady-Bird' is the 'Virgin Maria', Isis, the 'Mother and Producer of Nature'; the 'House' is the 'Ecliptic'--it is figuratively 'on fire', or 'of fire', in the path of the sun; and the 'children at home' are the 'months' produced in the house of the sun, or the solar year, or the 'signs of the Zodiac'--which were originally 'ten', and not twelve'[2], each sign answering to one of the letters of the primeval alphabet, which were in number 'ten'. Thus, re-read, the lines run:

> Lady-Bird, Lady-Bird (*Columba*, or Dove), fly away home!
> Your House is of *Fire*--your children are *Ten!*

---

[2] Lady-Cow, Lady-Cow,
  Fly away home!
Thy house is on fire,
  Thy Children are flown.

All but a Little One
  Under a 'Stone':
Fly thee home, Lady-Cow,
  Ere it be gone.

The 'Lady-Bird', or 'Cow', is the Virgin Mary, the 'Little One' under the 'Stone', or the 'Mystic Human Possibility', is the 'Infant Saviour' born in the mysterious 'Month of the Propitiation', or the mystical Astrological and Astronomical 'Escaped Month' of the Zodiac; and the 'Stone' is the 'Philosopher's Stone'.

The name of the flying insect called in England 'Lady-Bird' is *Bête-à-Dieu* in French, which means 'God-creature' or 'God's creature'. The Napoleonic green is the mythic, magic green of Venus. The Emerald is the *Smaragdus*, or Smaragd. The name of the insect Barnabee, Barnbee, 'Burning Fire-Fly', whose house is of fire, whose children are ten, is *Red Chafer, Rother-Kaefer, Sonnen-Kaefer, Unser-Frauen Kohlein*, in German; it is 'Sun-Chafer', 'Our Lady's Little Cow', Isis, or Io, or C--ow, in English. The children *Tenne* (*Tin*, or *Tien*, is fire in some languages) are the earliest 'Ten Signs' in the Zodiacal Heavens --each 'Sign' with its Ten Decans, or Decumens, or 'Leaders of Hosts'. They are also astronomically called 'Stalls', or 'Stables'. We may here refer to Porphyry, Horapollo, and Chifflet's Gnostic Gems. The Speckled Beetle was flung into hot water to avert storms (Pliny, *Nat. Hist.*, lib. xxxvii, ch. x). The antiquary Pignorius has a beetle 'crowned with the sun and encircled with the serpent'. Amongst the Gnostic illustrations published by Abraham Gorlæus is that of a talisman of the more abstruse Gnostics--an onyx carved with a 'beetle which threatens to gnaw at a thunderbolt'. See *Notes and Queries*: 'Bee Mythology'.

The 'Lilies' are said not to have appeared in the French arms until the time of Philip Augustus. See Montfauçon's *Monumens de la Monarchie Française*, Paris, 1729. Also Jean-Jacques Chifflet, *Anastasis de Childeric*, 1655. See also *Notes and Queries*, 1856, London, 2d Series, for some learned papers on the 'Fleur-de-lis'. In the early armorial bearings of the Frankish kings, the 'lilies' are represented as 'insects', *seméed* (seeded), or spotted, on the blue field. These are, in their origin, the *scarabæi* of the Orientals; they were dignified by the Egyptians as the emblems of the 'Enlightened'. If the reader examines carefully the sculpture in the British Museum representing the Mithraic Sacrifice of the Bull, with its mystic accompaniments (No. 14, Grand Central Saloon), he will perceive the *scarabæus*, or crab, playing a peculiar part in the particulars of the grand rite so strangely typified, and also so remotely. The motto placed under the 'lilies', which are the arms of France, runs as follows: 'Lilia non laborant, neque nent'. This is also (as all know) the legend, or motto, accompanying the royal order of knighthood denominated that of the 'Saint-Esprit' in France. We are immediately now recalled to those exceedingly obscure, but very significant, words of our Saviour, which have always seemed very erroneously interpreted, on account of their obvious contradictions: 'Consider the lilies of the field, how they grow; they toil not, neither do they spin' [3]. Now, in regard to this part of the text, what does the judicious speculator think of the following Rosicrucian gloss, or explanation? *Lilia non laborant* (like bees); *neque nent*, 'neither do they spin' (like spiders). Now of the 'lisses', as we shall elect to call, them. They *toil not* like 'bees' (*scarabæi*); neither do they *spin* like 'spiders' (*arachnidæ*).

To be wise is to be enlightened. *Lux* is the *Logos* by whom all things were made; and the *Logos* is *Rasit*--R.s.t.: 'ρ.'σ.'τ = 600; and *Lux* makes *Lucis;* then LX, ξ'ς = 666. Again, L = 50, ו v = 6, ש s = 300, י i = 10, ש s = 300 = 666.

The Fleur-de-lis is the Lotus (water-rose), the flower sacred to the *Lux*, or the *Sul*, or the Sun. The 'Auriflamme' (the flame of fire, or fire of gold) was the earliest standard of France. It was afterwards called *Oriflamme*. It was the sacred flag of France, and its colour was red--the heraldic, or 'Rosicrucian red, signifying gold. The three 'Lotuses', or 'Lisses', were the coat of arms-- emblems of the Trimurti, the three persons of the triple generative power, or of the Sun, or 'Lux'. שלה, *sle*, 'Shilo', is probably שיל, *sil* = 360, or χ = 600, λ = 50 = 10, ו = 6 = 666. This is Silo, or Selo. 'I have no doubt it was the invocation in the Psalms called "Selah", שלה(ס)'. Thus asserts the learned and judicious Godfrey Higgins.

'The Holie Church of Rome herself doth compare the incomprehensible generation of the Sonne of God from His

---

[3] The full quotation is the following: 'Consider the lilies of the field, how they grow; they toil not, neither do they spin: and yet I say unto you, That even Solomon' (here steps in some of the lore of the Masonic order) 'in all his glory was not arrayed' (or *exalted*, or *dignified*, as it is more correctly rendered out of the original) 'like one of these' (*St. Matt.* vi. 28).

Father, together with His birth out of the pure and undefiled Virgine Marie, unto the Bees--which were in verie deede a great blasphemie, if the bees were not of so great valour and virtue' (value and dignity).--'Beehive of the Romish Church': Hone's *Ancient Mysteries Described*, p. 283.

In the second edition of *Nineveh and its Palaces*, by Bonomi (London, Ingram, 1853), p. 138, the headdress of the divinity Ilus is an egg-shaped cap terminating at the top in a *fleur-de-lis*; at p. 149, the Dagon of Scripture has the same; at p. 201, fig. 98, the same ornament appears; at p. 202, fig. 99, a bearded figure has the usual '*fleur-de-lis*'. In the same page, the tiaras of two bearded figures are surmounted with *fleurs-de-lis*. At p. 322, fig. 211, the Assyrian helmet is surmounted with a *fleur-de-lis*; at p. 334, fig. 217, the head-dress of the figure in the Assyrian standard has a *fleur-de-lis*; at p. 340, fig. 245, the bronze resembles a *fleur-de-lis*; at p. 350, fig. 254, an Egyptian example of the god Nilus, as on the thrones of Pharaoh-Necho, exhibits the *fleur-de-lis*.

Vert, or green, and *azure*, or blue (feminine tinctures), are the colours on which respectively the golden 'bees', or the silver 'lisses', are emblazoned. The Egyptian *Scarabæi* are frequently cut in stone, generally in *green-coloured* basalt, or *verdantique*. Some have hieroglyphics on them, which are more rare; others are quite plain. In the tombs of Thebes, Belzoni found *scarabæi with human heads*. There is hardly any symbolical figure which recurs so often in Egyptian sculpture or painting as the *scarabæus*, or beetle, and perhaps scarcely any one which it is so difficult to explain. He is often represented with a ball between his forelegs, which some take for a symbol of the world, or the sun. He may be an emblem of fertility. The 'crab' on the Denderah Zodiac is by some supposed to be a 'beetle' (*Egyptian Antiquities*). It is for some of the preceding reasons that one of the mystic names of Lucifer, or the Devil, is the 'Lord of Flies', for which strange appellation all antiquaries, and other learned decipherers, have found it impossible to account.

Of the figure of the Fleur-de-Luce, Fleur-de-Lis, or Flower-de-*Luce* (*Lus, Luz,* Loose), the following may be remarked. On its sublime, abstract side, it is the symbol of the mighty self-producing, self-begetting Generative Power deified in many myths. We may make a question, in the lower sense, in this regard, of the word 'loose', namely, wanton, and the word 'Lech', or 'leche', and 'lecher', etc. Consider, also, in the solemn and terrible sense, the name Crom-Lech, or 'crown', or 'arched entry', or 'gate', of death. The Druidical stones were generally called *cromlechs* when placed in groups of two[4], with a *coping* or *capstone* over, similarly to the form of the Greek letter *pi* (Π, π), which was imitated from that temple of stones which we call a cromlech:

Cromlechs were the altars of the Druids, and were so called from a Hebrew word signifying 'to bow'. There is a Druidic temple at Toulouse, in France, exhibiting many of these curious Druidical stones. There is a large, flat stone, ten feet long, six feet wide, one foot thick, at St. David's, Pembrokeshire. It is called in Cymric '*Lêch Lagar*, the speaking stone'. We may speculate upon the word 'Lich, Lych, Lech' in this connexion, and the terms 'Lich-gate', or 'Lech-gate', as also the name of 'Lich-field'. There is a porch or gateway, mostly at the entrance of old-fashioned churchyards, which is called the 'Lyke-Porch', or 'Litch-Porch'. *Lüg*, or *Lük*, is a word in the Danish signifying the same as *Lyk* in the Dutch, and *Leiche*, in the German. Thus comes the word 'Lich-gate'. *Lich* in the Anglo-Saxon means a 'dead body'. See *Notes and Queries*, vol. ii. p. 4. The 'Lich-gates' were as a sort of triumphal arches (*Propylæa*) placed before the church, as the outwork called the 'Propylon', or 'Propylæum', was advanced before the Egyptian and the Grecian temples. They are found, in the form of separate arches, before the gates even of *Chinese* cities, and they are there generally called 'triumphal arches'.

---

[4] The whole forming a 'capital', 'chapter', 'chapitre', 'chapel', 'cancel', or 'chancel'--hence our word, and the sublime judicial office of 'Chancellor', and 'Chancery'.

Propylæa is a name of Hecate, Dis, Chronos, or the Π, to which sinister deity the *Propylon* or *Propylæum* (as also, properly, the Lych-gate) is dedicated. Hence its ominous import, *Pro*, or 'before', the *Pylon* or passage. Every Egyptian temple has its Propylon. The Pyramid also in Nubia has one. We refer to the ground plans of the Temples of Denderah, Upper Egypt; the Temple of Luxor, Thebes; the Temple of Edfou, Upper Egypt; the Temple of Carnac (or Karnak), Thebes.

Colonel (afterwards General) Vallancey, in the fourth volume, p. 80, of his *General Works*, cited in the *Celtic Druids*, p. 223 (a valuable book by Godfrey Higgins), says: 'In Cornwall they call it' (i.e. the rocking-stone) 'the Logan-Stone.' Borlase, in his *History of Cornish Antiquities*, declares that he does not understand the meaning of this term Logan, as applied to the Druidical stones. 'Had Dr. Borlase been acquainted with the Irish MSS', significantly, adds Colonel Vallancey, 'he would have found that the Druidical oracular stone called *Loghan*, which yet retains its name in Cornwall, is the Irish *Logh-oun*, or stone into which the Druids pretended that the *Logh*, or divine essence, descended when they consulted it as an oracle.' *Logh* in Celtic is the same as *Logos* in the Greek'; both terms mean the *Logos* ('Word') or the Holy Ghost.

Sanchoniathon, the Phœnician, says that Ouranus contrived, in Bœtulia, 'stones that moved as having life'. Stukeley's *Abury*, p. 97, may be here referred to for further proofs of the mystic origin of these stones, and also the *Celtic Druids* of Godfrey Higgins, in contradiction to those who would infer that these 'poised stones' simply mark *burial-places*, or foolish conclusions of shallow and incompetent antiquaries.

The Basilidans were called by the orthodox *Docetæ*, or Illusionists. The Deity of the Gnostics was called 'Abraxas' in Latin, and 'Abrasax' in Greek. Their last state, or condition for rescued sensitive entities, as they termed souls, was the 'Pleroma', or 'Fullness of Light'. This agrees precisely with the doctrines of the Buddhists or Bhuddists. The regulating, presiding genius was the *Pantheus*. The Pythagorean record quoted by Porphyry (*Vit.*

Pythag.) states that the 'numerals of Pythagoras were hieroglyphical symbols by means whereof he explained ideas concerning the nature of things'. That these symbols were ten in number, the *ten original signs of the zodiac, and the ten letters of the primeval, alphabet,* appears from Aristotle (*Met.* vii. 7). 'Some philosophers hold', he says, 'that ideas and numbers are of the same nature, and amount to *ten* in all.' See *The Gnostics and their Remains,* p. 229.

But to return to the arms of France, which are the 'Fleurs-de-lis', and to the small representative creature (sublime enough, as the farthest-off symbol which they are imagined in their greatness to indicate). A Bible presented to Charles the Second, A.D. 869, has a miniature of this monarch and his court. His throne is terminated with three flowers of the form of 'fleurs-de-lis sans pied'. On his head is a crown 'fermée à fleurons d'or, relevez et recourbez d'une manière singulière'. Another miniature in the Book of Prayers shows him on a throne surmounted by a sort of 'fleurs-de-lis sans pied'. His crown is of 'fleurs comme de lis', *and the robe is fastened with a rose,* 'd'où sortent trois pistils en forme de fleurs-de-lis'. His sceptre terminates in a fleur-de-lis.--*Notes and Queries.*

Sylvanus Morgan, an old-fashioned herald abounding in suggestive disclosures, has the following: 'Sir William Wise having lent to the king, Henry VIII, his signet to seal a letter, who having powdered' (*seméed,* or spotted) 'eremites' (they were emmets--ants) 'engray'd in the seale, the king paused and lookit thereat, considering'. We may here query whether the field of the coat of arms of Sir William Wise was not 'ermine'; for several of the families of Wise bear this fur, and it is not unlikely that he did so also.

'"Why, how now, Wise!" quoth the king. "What! hast thou lice here?" "An', if it like your majestie", quoth Sir William, "a louse is a rich coat;" for by giving the louse I part arms with the French king, in that he giveth the *flour-de-lice.*" Whereat the king heartily laugh'd, to hear how prettily so byting a taunt (namely, proceeding froth a prince) was so suddenly turned to so pleasaunte a conceit.'--Stanihurst's *History of Ireland*, in Holinshed's *Chron*. Nares thinks that Shakespeare, who is known to have been a reader of Holinshed, took his conceit of the 'white lowses which do become an old coat well', in

The Merry Wives of Windsor, from this anecdote. See *Heraldic Anomalies*, vol. i. p. 204; also Lower's *Curiosities of Heraldry*, p. 82 (1845). It may here be mentioned, that the mark signifying the royal property (as it is used in France), similarly to the token, or symbol, or 'brand', denoting the royal domain, the property, or the sign upon royal chattels (the 'broad arrow'), as used in England, is the 'Lis', or the 'Fleur-de-Lis'. The mark by which criminals are 'branded' in France is called the 'Lis--Fleur-de-lis'.

The English 'broad-arrow', the mark or sign of the royal property, is variously depicted, similarly to the following marks:

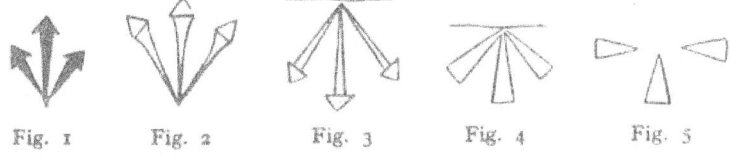

Fig. 1   Fig. 2   Fig. 3   Fig. 4   Fig. 5

These are the Three Nails of the Passion. In figs. 1 and 2 they are unmistakably so, with the points downwards. Figs. 3 and 4 have the significant horizontal mark which, in the first centuries of Christianity, stood for the Second (with feminine meanings) Person of the Trinity; but the points of the spikes (*spicæ*, or thorns) are gathered upwards in the centre. In fig. 5 there are still the three nails; but a suggestive similarity to be 'remarked in this figure is a disposition resembling the *crux-ansata*--an incessant symbol, always reappearing in Egyptian sculptures and hieroglyphics. There is also a likeness to the mysterious letter '*Tau*'. The whole first chapter of Genesis is' said to be contained in this latter-emblem--this magnificent, all-including '*Tau*'.

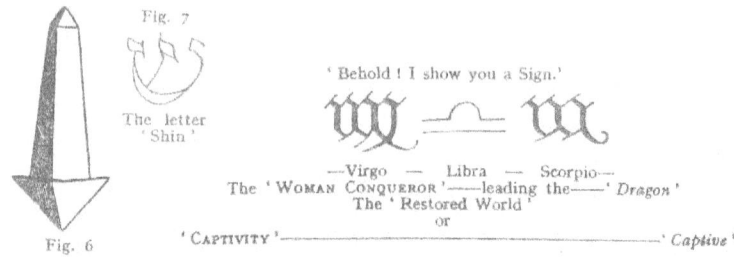

Three bent spikes, or nails, are unmistakably the same symbol that Belus often holds in his extended hand on the Babylonian cylinders, afterwards discovered by the Jewish cabalists in the points of the letter 'Shin', and by the mediæval mystics in the 'Three Nails of the Cross'.-- *The Gnostics and their Remains, Ancient and Mediæval*, p. 208.

This figure, which is clearly a nail, has also characteristics, which will use remarked in its upper portion, which suggest a likeness to the obelisk, pin, spike, upright or phallus.

The Hebrew letter '*Shin*', or '*Sin*', counts for 300 in the Hebraic numeration. Each *spica*, or spike, may be taken to signify 100, or ten tens. We have strong hints here of the origin of the decimal system, which reigns through the universal laws of computation as a natural substratum, basis, or principle. This powerful symbol, also, is full of secret important meanings. It will be remarked as the symbol or figure assigned in the formal zodiacs of all countries, whether original zodiacs, or whether produced in figure-imitations by recognizing tradition. The marks or symbols of the zodiacal signs, 'Virgo-Scorpio', are closely similar to each other, with certain differences, which we recommend to the judicious consideration of close and experienced observers.

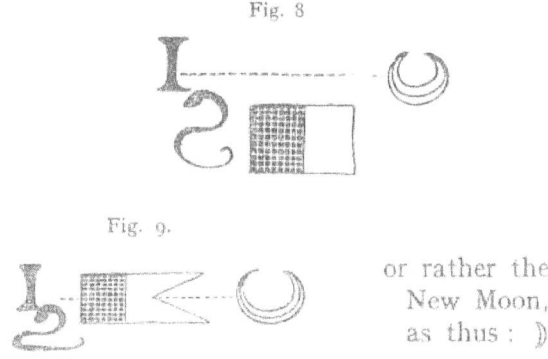

The Templar Banner: the famous 'Beauséant'

Fig. 8 is the symbol, or hook, of Saturn, the colour of whom, in the heraldic configuration, is *sab.*, *sable*, or black, divided, *party per pale*, with the opening light of the first crescent moon of the post-diluvian world[5]. Fig. 9 is the same grandly mystic banner, denominated Beauséant ('Beau-Séant'), revealing a whole occult theosophy to the initiate, which the leaders of the Templars undoubtedly were. The difference between these two figures, fig. 8 and fig. 9, is, that the 'fly' of the ensign marked fig. 9 is bifurcated (or cloven) in the 'lighted' part.

---

[5] The Shining Star as the Harbinger in the Moon's Embrace. Meaning the Divine Post-diluvian Remission and Reconciliation. Thus the sublime Mahometan mythic device or cognisance--the Crescent of the New Moon (lying on her back), and the Shining Star in this display:

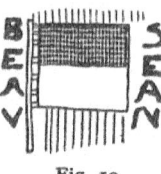 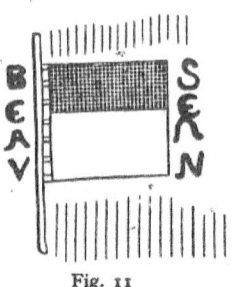

Fig. 10   Fig. 11

We subjoin the representation of the wondrous banner of the 'Poor soldiers of the Temple as depicted abundantly 'on the spandrels of the arches of the Temple Church, London. Von Hammer's *Mystery of Baphomet Revealed* contains much suggestive matter relative to these mysterious supposed dreadful Templars. The Parisian '*Templiers*' assert that there is a connexion between the recent Niskhi letter and the 'Cufic' characters, and that the origin of the secrets of the order of the Temple is contemporary with the prevalence of the latter alphabet. We here refer to the work entitled *Mysterium Baphometis Revelatum; seu, Fratres Militiæ Templi, qua Gnostici et quidem Ophiani, apostasiæ, idololatriæ, et quidem impuritatis convicti per ipsa eorum monumenta*, published in the *Mines' de l'Orient*, vol. vi. This treatise is illustrated with numerous admirably executed copper-plates of magical statuettes, architectural ornaments, mystical inscriptions, vases, and coins. Amidst these there is a bearded, yet female, figure, '*Mete*' (*magna*, or *maxima*), whom Von Hammer, following Theodosius and others, makes the same as the 'Sophia' of the Ophites. Some particulars to these subjects are contained in *The Gnostics and their Remains, Ancient and Mediæval;* although there is an evident betraying of total ignorance on the part of the author, throughout his book, as to the purpose, meaning, and reality of the, whole of these remote and mysterious subjects to which he is, however, blindly constantly referring, without the merit of even feeling his way. It is well known that the preservation of Gnostic symbols by Freemasons was, and remains so to this day, exceedingly sedulous.

We will terminate this part of our long dissertation, which commenced with the explanation of the descent, or the genealogy, or the generation of the famous 'fleurs-de-lis' of France--the noblest and sublimest symbol, in its occult or mysterious meaning, which the 'monarch sun' ever saw displayed to it, inexpressibly mean and repellant as the 'Lis' seems: we will finish, we say, thus far, by commenting in a very original and unexpected, but strictly corroborative, manner upon some words of Shakespeare which have hitherto been passed wholly without remark or explanation.

We may premise by recalling that the *luce* is a pike (*pic*), or Jack: Jac, Iacc (*B* and *I* are complementary in this mythic sense), Bacc, Bacche, Bacchus. Shakespeare's well-known lampoon, or satirical ballad, upon the name of 'Lucy' may be cited as illustrative proof on this side of the subject:

Lucy is lowsie, *as some volke miscalle it.*

The Zodiacal sign for February is the 'fishes'. Now, the observances of St. Valentine's Day, which point to courtship and to sexual love, or to loving invitation, bear direct reference to the 'fishes', in a certain sense. The arms of the Lucys--as they are at present to be seen, and where we not long since saw them, beautifully restored upon the great entrance-gates of Charlecote Hall, or Place, near Stratford-upon-Avon--are 'three luces or pikes, *hauriant, argent*'.

'The dozen white luces' are observed upon with intense family pride by Shallow (Lucy), in *The Merry Wives of Windsor*.

'*Shallow.* It is an old coat.

'*Evans.* The dozen white *louses* do become an old coat well'. The significant part of the passage follows to this effect, though deeply hidden in the sly art of our knowing, but reticent, Shakespeare: 'I agrees well *passant*' (we would here read *passim*, 'everywhere', which makes clear sense). 'It is a familiar beast to Man, and signifies--love' (the generative act).--*Merry Wives of Windsor*, act i. sc. I.

We commend the above history of the 'Fleur-de-Lis' to the thoughtful attention of our reader, because he will find under it the whole explanation of the arms of France. And yet, although the above is all-essentially 'feminine', this is the country that imported amidst its Frankish or Saxon progenitors (Clodio, the 'long-haired', to the example, who first passed the Rhine and brought his female 'ultramarine' to supersede and replace, in blazon, the martial, manly 'carmine' or 'gules' of the Gauls)--this is the country that adopted and maintains '*la Loi Salique*'.

CHAPTER THE NINTH

SACRED FIRE

THE appearance of God to mortals seems always to have been in brightness and great glory, whether He was angry and in displeasure, or benign and kind. These appearances are often mentioned in Scripture. When God appeared on Mount Sinai, it is said 'The Lord descended upon it in Fire' (*Exod.* xix. 18). And when Moses repeats the history of this to the children of Israel, he says 'The Lord spake unto you out of the midst of the Fire' (*Deut.* iv. 12). So it was when the Angel of the Lord appeared to Moses in a flame of fire out of the midst of the bush: 'The bush burned with Fire, and the bush was not consumed' (*Exod.* iii. 3). The appearances of the Angel of God's presence, or that Divine Person who represented God; were always in brightness; or, in other words, the Shechinah was always surrounded with glory. This seems to have given occasion to those of old to imagine fire to be what God dwelt in.

'Ipse' (Darius) 'solem Mithren, sacrumque et æternum invocans IGNEM, ut illis dignam vetere gloria majoremque monumentis fortitudinem inspirarent.'--Q. Curtius, l. iv. c. 13.

Whether it was that any fire preceded from God, and burnt up the oblation in the first sacrifices, as some ingenious men have conjectured, we know not. It is certain that in after ages this was the case. We are sure that a fire from the Lord consumed upon the altar the burnt-offering of Aaron (*Lev.* ix. 24); and so it did the sacrifice of Gideon, 'both the flesh and the unleavened cakes' (*Judg.* vi. 21). When David 'built an altar unto the Lord, and offered burnt-offerings and peace-offerings, and called upon the Lord, He answered him from heaven by Fire, upon the altar of burnt-offerings' (*1 Chron.* xxi. 26). The same thing happened at the dedication of Solomon's temple: 'The fire came down from heaven, and consumed the burnt-offering and the sacrifices, and the glory of the Lord filled the house' (*2 Chron.* vii. 1). And much about a hundred years afterwards, when Elijah made that extraordinary sacrifice in proof that Baal was no god, 'The Fire of the Lord fell and consumed the burnt sacrifice, and the wood, and the stones, and the dust, and licked up the water that was in the trench' (*I Kings* xviii. 38). And if we go back long before the times of Moses, as early as Abraham's days, we meet with an instance of the same sort: 'It came to pass that when the sun went down, and it was dark, behold a smoking furnace and a burning lamp, that passed between these pieces' (*Gen.* xv. 17).

The first appearance of God, then, being in glory--or, which is the same thing, in light or fire--and He showing His acceptance of sacrifices in so many instances, by consuming them with fire, hence it was that the Eastern people, and particularly the Persians, fell into the worship of fire itself, or rather they conceived fire to be the symbol of God's presence-, and they worshipped God in, or by, fire. From the Assyrians, or Chaldæans, or Persians, this worship was propagated southwards among the Egyptians, and westward among the Greeks; and by them it was brought into Italy. The Greeks were wont to meet together to worship in their *Prytaneia*, and there they consulted for the public good; and there was a. constant fire kept upon the altar, which was dignified by the name of Vesta, by some. The fire itself was properly Vesta; and so Ovid:

> Nec te aliud Vestam, quam vivam intelligere flammam.

The *Prytaneia* were the *atria* of the temples, wherein a fire was kept that was never suffered to go. out. On the change in architectural forms from the pyramidal (or the horizontal) to the obeliscar (or the upright, or vertical), the flames were transferred from the altars, or cubes, to the summits of the typical uprights, or towers; or to the tops of the candles, such as we see them used now in Catholic worship, and which are called 'tapers', from their tapering or pyramidal form, and which, wherever they are seen or raised, are supposed always to indicate the divine presence or influence. This, through the symbolism that there is in the living light, which is the last exalted show of fluent or of inflamed brilliant matter, passing off beyond into the unknown and unseen world of celestial light (or occult fire), to which all the forms of things tend, and in which even idea itself passes from recognition as meaning, and evolves--spiring, as all flame does, to escape and to wing away.

Vesta, or the fire, was worshipped in circular temples, which were the images or the miniatures, of the 'temple' of the world, with its dome, or cope, of stars. It was in the atria of the temples, and in the presence of, and before the above-mentioned lights, that the forms of ceremonial worship .were always observed. It is certain that Vesta was worshipped at Troy; and Æneas brought her into Italy

> manibus vittas, Vestamque potentem,
> Æternumque adytis effert penetralibas Ignem.
> --*Æneid* ii. 296.

Numa settled an order of Virgin Priestesses, whose business and care it was constantly to maintain the holy fire. And long before Numa's days, we find it not only customary, but honourable, among the Albans to appoint the best-born virgins to be priestesses of Vesta, and to keep up the constant, unextinguished fire.

When Virgil speaks (*Æneid* iv. 200) of Iarbas, in Africa, as building a hundred temples and a hundred altars, he says:

> vigilemque sacraverat Ignem,
> Excubias Divum æternas,

that he had 'consecrated a fire that never went out'. And he calls these temples and these lights, or this fire, the 'perpetual watches', or 'watch-lights', or proof of the presence, of the gods. By which expressions he means, that places and things were constantly protected, and solemnized where such lights burned, and that the celestials, or angel-defenders, 'camped', as it were, and were sure to be met with thickly, where these flames upon the altars, and these torches or lights about the temples, invited them and were studiously and incessantly maintained.

Thus the custom seems to have been general from the earliest antiquity to maintain a constant fire, as conceiving the gods present there. And this was not only the opinion of the inhabitants in Judæa, but it extended all over Persia, Greece, Italy, Egypt, and most other nations of the world.

Porphyry imagined that the 'reason why the most ancient mortals kept up a constant, ever-burning fire in honour of the immortal Gods, was because Fire was most like the Gods. He says that the ancients kept an unextinguished fire in their temples to the Gods, because it was most like them. Fire was not like the Gods, but it was what they appeared in to mortals. And so the true God always appeared in brightness and glory, yet no one would say that brightness was most like the true God, but was most like the Shechinah, in which God appeared. And hence the custom arose of keeping up an unextinguished fire in the ancient temples.

Vesta is properly an Oriental word, derived from the Hebrew אש, *As*--'Fire'. Thence the word Astarte, in the Phœnician dialect. The signification of the term is the same as the πῦρ ἄσβεστον, the *ignis æternus*, the perpetual fire itself. They that worshipped either Vesta or Vulcan, or the master-power of nature which is known under those names, were properly Fire-worshippers.

God, then, being wont to appear in Fire, and being conceived to dwell in Fire, the notion spread universally, and was universally admitted. First, then, it was not at all out of the way to think of engaging in friendship with God by the same means as they contracted friendship with one another. And since they to whom God appeared saw Him appear in Fire, and they acquainted others with such His appearances, He was conceived to dwell in Fire. By degrees, therefore, the world came to be over-curious in the fire that was constantly to be kept up, and in things to be sacrificed; and they proceeded from one step to another, till at length they filled up the measure of their aberration, which was in reality instigated by their zeal, and by their intense desire to mitigate the displeasure of their divinities--for religion was much more intense as a feeling in early days--by passing into dreadful ceremonies in regard to this fire, which they reverenced as the last possible physical form of divinity, not only in its grandeur and power, but also in its purity. It arose from this view that human sacrifices came to be offered to the deities in many parts of the world, particularly in Phœnicia, and in the colonies derived from thence into Africa and other places. In the intensity of their minds, children were sacrificed by their parents, as being the, best and dearest oblation that could be made, and the strongest arguments that nothing ought to. be withheld from God. This was expiation for that sad result, the consequence of the original curse, issuing from the fatal curiosity concerning the bitter fruit of that forbidden 'Tree',

> whose mortal taste
> Brought death into the world, and all our woe,
> With loss of Eden,

according to Milton. That peculiar natural sense of shame in all its forms lesser and larger, and with all the references inseparably allied to propagation in all its multitudinous cunning (so to speak), wherever the condemned material tissues reach, puzzled the thoughtful ancients as to its meaning. This they considered the convicted 'Adversary', or Lucifer, 'Lord of light'-- that is, material Light', 'Eldest Son of the Morning'. Morning, indeed! dawning with its light from behind that forbidden Tree of the Knowledge of Good and Evil. What is this shame, urged the philosophers, this reddening, however good and beautiful, and especially the ornament of the young and inexperienced and of children, who are newest from the real, glowing countenance of Deity, with the bloom of the first angelic word scarcely yet fading from off their cherub faces, gradually darkening and hardening in the degradation and iniquity of being here as presences in this world, although the most glorious amidst the forms of flesh? What is this shame, which is the characteristic singly of human creatures? All other creatures are sinless in this respect, and know not the feeling of that--correctly looked at--strange thing which men call 'shame', something which is not right that the sun even should see, and therefore stirring the blood, and, reddening the face, and confusing the speech, and causing man to hang down his head, and to hide himself, as if guilty of something: even as our guilty first parents, having lost the unconsciousness of their child-like, innocent first state--that of sinless virginity--hid themselves and shunned their own light in the umbrage of Paradise, all at once convicted to the certainty that they must hide, because they were exposed, and that they had themselves broken that original intention regarding them.

'Suffer the little children to come unto Me, and forbid them not, for of such is the kingdom of heaven'.

That is, the innocent children should come up for salvation, who, though suffering under the mortal liability incurred by all flesh in that first sin (and incident in the first fall, which has empoisoned and cursed all nature), are yet free by the nature of their ungrown possibility, and from their unconsciousness of it. They know not the shame of the condition adult, and therefore they bear not the badge of men, and are not of this world really, but of another world.

To recur for a moment to the theory of human sacrifices which once largely prevailed. Interwoven inseparably with the forms of architecture from the earliest times, proof of which we see constantly in classical buildings particularly, and in the Italian modifications displayed in the cities of Europe, was the habit of exposing as talismans the members (and particularly the heads) of human sacrifices. This is observable in the innumerable masks (or heads full-faced) placed on the keystones of arches or portals. They are either deified mortals or demigods. Sometimes, but very rarely (because it is, a sinister *palladium*), the head of Medusa is seen. Exposure of the heads of criminals on town-gates, over bridges, or over arches, follows the same idea, as ranging in the list of protecting, protesting, or appealing *Palladia*, which are supposed to possess the same objurgating or propitiating power as the wild, winged creatures--children of the air--affixed in penitential, magic brand or exposure on the doors of barns, or on the outside of rustic buildings. All this is ceremonial sacrifice, addressed to the harmful gods, and meant occultly and entreatingly for the eyes of the observant, but invisible, wandering angels, who move through the world--threading unseen the ways of men, and unwitted of by them, and most abundant and most active there where the mother of all of them is in the ascendant with her influences; or when Night is abroad, throned in her cope of stars--letters, from their first judiciary arrangement in the heavens, spelling out continually new astrological combinations. For Astrology. was the mother, as she was the precursor, of Astronomy, and was once a power; into whatever mean roads the exercise of the art of her servants has strayed now, in unworthy and indign divination, and in the base proffer of supposed Gipsy arts--ministration become ridiculous (or made so), which was once mighty and sublime.

The pyramidal or triangular form which Fire assumes in its ascent to heaven is in the monolithic typology used to signify the great generative power. We have only to look at Stonehenge, Ellora, the Babel-towers of Central America, the gigantic ruins scattered all over Tartary and India, to see how gloriously they symbolized the majesty of the Supreme. To these uprights, disks, or *lithoi*, of the old world, including the *Bethel*, or Jacob's Pillar, or Pillow, raised in the Plain of 'Luz', we will add, as the commemorative or reminding shape of the fire, the Pyramids of Egypt, the Millenarius, Gnomon, Mete-Stone, or Mark, called 'London Stone', all Crosses raised at the junction of four roads, all Market-Crosses, the *Round Towers of Ireland*, and, in all the changeful aspects of their genealogy, all spires and towers, in their grand hieroglyphic proclamation, all over the world. All these are *Phalli*, and express a sublime meaning.

(♈) Aries, (♉) Taurus, (♊) Gemini, (♋) Cancer, (♌) Leo, (♍) Virgo, are the first six 'Signs'; and they collectively (in their annual succession) form 'the Macrocosmos' of the Cabalists. Then succeeds the 'turning-point', 'balances', or 'nave' (*navel*), of the astronomical wheel, represented by the sign 'Libra' (♎), which, be it remembered, was added by the imaginative (and therefore practically inventive) Greeks. The foregoing, up to 'Libra', represent the 'ascending signs', or six of the spokes, so to speak, of the annual zodiacal wheel, circling to the zenith or vertex. The last six 'Signs' of the zodiac are called 'descending signs', and they are the sinister, autumnal, or changing, in reverse, monthly spaces, each of thirty degrees, and again comprising six *radii* of this celestial wheel, or this 'Ezekiel's Wheel'. The turning-point is 'Virgo-Scorpio', which, until separated in the mythical interruption from without at the 'junction-point' between ascent and descent, were the same 'single sign'. The latter half (or left wing of this grand zodiacal 'army', or 'host of heaven', drawn up in battle array, and headed--as, by a figure, we shall choose to say--by the 'Archangel Michael', or the Sun, at the centre, or in the 'champion' or 'conquering point') is called by the Cabalists--and therefore by the Rosicrucians--the abstract 'Microcosmos'--in which 'Microcosm', or 'Little World', in opposition to the 'Macrocosm', or 'Great World', is to be found 'Man', as produced in it from the operations from above, and to be saved in the 'Great Sacrifice' (Crucifixion-Act), the phenomena of the being (Man) taking place 'in the mythic return. of the world'. All this is incomprehensible, except in the strange mysticism of the Gnostics and the Cabalists; and the whole theory requires a key of explanation to render it intelligible; which key is only darkly referred to as possible, but refused absolutely, by these extraordinary men, as not permissible to be disclosed. As they, however, were very fond of diagrams and mystic figures, of which they left many in those rarities (mostly ill-executed, but each wonderfully suggestive) called Gnostic gems ',we will supply a seeming elucidation of this their astrological assumption of 'what was earliest'; for which see the succeeding figure.

(♎) Libra (the Balances) leads again off as the 'hinge-point,' introducing the six winter signs, which are: (♎) Libra again, (♏) Scorpio, (♐) Sagittarius, (♑) Capricornus, (♒) Aquarius, and (♓) Pisces.

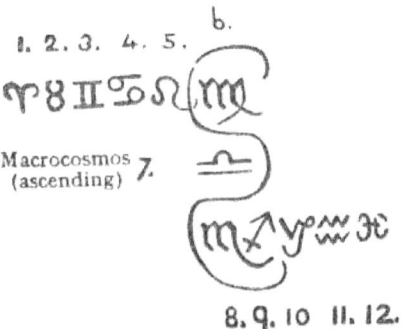

Fig. 12 (A) 'Ezekiel's Wheel'

Turning-point--Libra. (The sign 'Libra' was added by the Greeks.)

The first six signs, or ascending signs, are represented by the celestial perpendicular, or descending ray, as thus: (Fig. 13).

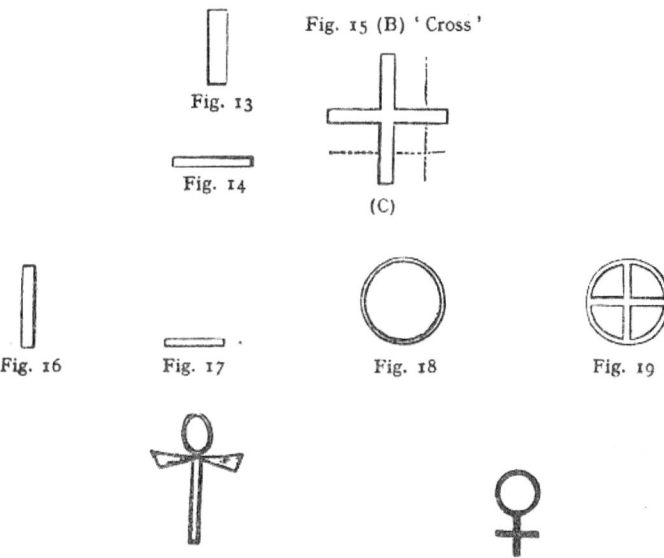

Figs. 13-21

The last six signs, or descending signs, are 'represented by the terrestrial ground-line, or horizontal, or 'equatorial' (symbol or *sigma*), as thus: (Fig. 14).

The union of these (at the intersection of these rays) at the junction-point, or middle point, forms the 'Cross', as thus: (Fig 15-19).

In figure C, the union of fig. 16 and fig. 17 forms the cross. Fig. 18 is the mundane circle. Fig. 19 is the astronomical cross *upon* the mundane circle. The union of fig. 18, fig. 17, and fig. 16, in this respective order, gives the *crux-ansata*, so continual in all the Egyptian sculptures, which mark or sign is also the symbol of the Planet Venus, as below (Fig. 20, 21).

Their origin is thus traced clearly to the same original meanings, which reappear .under all sorts of disguises, and are varied in innumerable ingenious ways, in all the mythologies--incessantly disclosing, and inviting, and as continually evading and escaping discovery. This abstruse mark particularly abounds in the Egyptian temples, where every object and every figure presents it. Its real meaning is, however, intended to be buried in profound darkness.

In regard to the mysteries implied in the Christian Cross, the schismatics contended (1st) 'that Christ, alive upon the cross, humbled Himself, *usque ad inferni tremenda tormenta*, even unto the dreadful torments of hell'. (Paget's *Catech. Latin.*) (2nd) 'Endured for a time those torments, *qualis reprobi in æternum sensuri sunt*, which the reprobates shall everlastingly suffer in hell'. (Pisc. in *Luc.* xii. 10.) 'Even despaired of God's mercy, finding God, at this time, *Non patrem sed tyrannum*, not a Father, but a Tyrant: and overcame despair by despair; death by death; hell by hell; and Satan by Satan' (Ferus *in Matth.* 27): 'suffered actually all the torments of hell for our redemption, and descended into the heaviest that hell could yield; endured the torments of hell, the second death, abjection from God, and' was made a curse; that is, had the bitter anguish of God's wrath in his soul and body, which is the fire that shall never be quenched'.--*Faith and Doctrine* (Thomas Rogers), London, 1629. Jacob

Böhmen produces some of these most stringent and dark shades in his profound mysticism--although essentially Christian.

It may be here distinctly mentioned that it is a mistake to suppose any of the Egyptian hieroglyphics tell the story of that most profound and most ancient religion. There are various series of hieroglyphics, more or less reserved, but the real beliefs of the Egyptian Priest were never (indeed, they *dared not* so have been hazarded in sigma, or writing, or hieroglyphic of any kind--being forbidden to be spoken, still more written. Consequently all supposed readings of hieroglyphics are guesswork only--implying earnest and plausible but mistaken effort alone.

CHAPTER THE TENTH

FIRE-THEOSOPHY OF THE PERSIANS

THE Fire-Philosophers, or *Philosophi per ignem*, were a fanatical sect of philosophers, who appeared towards the close of the sixteenth century. They made a figure in almost all the countries of Europe. They declared that the intimate essences of natural things were only to be known by the trying efforts of fire, directed in a chemical process. The Theosophists also insisted that human reason was a dangerous and deceitful guide; that no real progress could be made in knowledge or in religion by it; and that to all vital--that is, supernatural--purpose it was a vain thing. They taught that divine and supernatural illumination was the only means of arriving at truth. Their name of Paracelsists was derived from Paracelsus, the eminent physician and chemist, who was the chief ornament of this extraordinary sect. In England, Robert Flood, or Fludd, was their great advocate and exponent. Rivier, who wrote in France; Severinus, an author of Denmark; Kunrath, an eminent physician .of Dresden; and Daniel Hoffmann, Professor of Divinity in the University of Helmstadt--have also treated largely on Paracelsus and on his system.

Philippus Aureolus Theophrastus Paracelsus was born in 1493, at Einsiedeln, a small town of the Canton of Schwitz, distant some leagues from Zurich. Having passed a troubled, migratory, and changeful life, this' great chemist, and very original thinker, died on the 24th of September 1541, in the Hospital of St. Stephen, in the forty-eighth year of his age. His works may be enumerated as follows: I. The German editions: Basil, 1575, in 8vo; lb. I, 1589-90, in 10 vols. 4to; and Strasbourg, 1603-18, in 4 vols. folio. 2. The Latin editions: *Opera Omnia Medico-chymico-chirurgica*, Francfort, 1603, in 10 vols. 4to; and Geneva, 1658,. in 3 vols. folio. 3. The French editions: *La Grand Chirurgerie de Paracelse*, Lyons, 1593 and 1603, in 4to; and Montbéliard, 1608, in 8vo. See Adelung, *Histoire de la Folie*

Humaine, tom. vii; Biographie Universelle, article 'Paracelse'; and Sprengel, *Histoire Pragmatique de la Médecine*, tom. iii.

'Akin to the school of the ancient Fire-Believers, and of the magnetists of a later period', says the learned Dr. Ennemoser, in his *History of Magic* (most ably rendered into English by William Howitt), 'of the same cast as these speculators and searchers into the mysteries of nature, drawing from the same well, are the Theosophists of the sixteenth and seventeenth, centuries. These practised chemistry, by which they asserted that they could explore the profoundest secrets of nature. As they strove, above all earthly knowledge, after the divine, and sought the divine light and fire, through which all men can acquire the true wisdom, they were called the Fire-Philosophers (*philosophi per ignem*). The most distinguished of these are Theophrastus Paracelsus, Adam von Boden, Oswald Croll; and, later, Valentine Weigel, Robert Flood, or Fludd, Jacob Böhmen, Peter Poiret, etc.' Under this head we may also refer to the Medico-surgical Essays of Hemmann, published at Berlin in 1778; and Pfaff's *Astrology*.

As a great general principle, the Theosophists called the soul a fire, .taken from the eternal ocean of light.

In regard to the supernatural--using the word in its widest sense--it may be said that 'all the difficulty in admitting the strange things told us lies in the non-admission of an internal causal world as absolutely real: it is said, in intellectually admitting, because the influence of the arts proves that men's feelings always have admitted, and do still admit, this reality'.

The Platonic philosophy of vision is, that it is the view of objects really existing in interior light, which assume form, not according to arbitrary laws, but according to the state of mind. This interior light, if we understand Plato, unites with exterior light in the eye, and is thus drawn into a sensual or imaginative activity; but when the outward light is separated, it reposes in its own serene atmosphere. It is, then, in this state of interior repose, that the usual class of religions, or what are called inspired visions occur. It is the same light of eternity so frequently alluded to in books that treat of mysterious subjects; the light revealed to

Pimander, Zoroaster, and all the sages of the East, as the emanation of the spiritual sun. Böhmen writes of it in his *Divine Vision or Contemplation*, and Molinos in his *Spiritual Guide*--whose work is the ground of Quietism: Quietism being the foundation of the religion of the people called Friends or Quakers, as also of the other mystic or meditative sects. We enlarge from a very learned, candid, and instructive book upon the Occult Sciences.

Regard Fire, then, with other eyes than with those soulless, incurious ones, with which thou hast looked upon it as the most ordinary thing. Thou hast forgotten what it is--or rather thou hast never known. Chemists are silent about it; or may we not say that it is too loud for them? Therefore shall they speak fearfully of it in whispers. Philosophers talk of it as anatomists discourse of the constituents (or the parts) of the human body--as a piece of mechanism, wondrous though it be. Such the wheels of the clock; say they in their ingenious expounding of the 'whys' and the 'wherefores' (and the mechanics and the mathematics) of this mysterious thing, with a supernatural soul in it, called world. Such is the chain, such are the balances, such the larger and the smaller mechanical forces; such the 'Time-blood', as it were, that is sent circulating through it; such is the striking, with an infinity of bells. It is made for man, this world and it is greatly like him--that is *mean*, they would add. And they do think it, if they dare add their thinkings. But is this all? Is this the sum of that casketed lamp of the human body--thine own body, thou unthinking world's machine--thou Man! Or, in the fabric of this clay lamp (lacquered in thy man's Imperial splendours), burneth there not a Light? Describe that, ye Doctors of Physics! Unwind the starry limbs of *that* phenomenon, ye heavy-browed doctorial wielders of the scalpel--useful, however, as ye be, in that 'upholstery warehouse' of nature to which bodies and their make be referred by the materialists as the godless origin of everything. Touch at its heart, ye dissectors of fibres and of valves; of sinews and of leaves (hands, perchance); of the vein-work, of the muscles, as bark-integument; of the trunk! Split and pare, as with steel tools and wedge, this portent, this 'Tree' (human though it be), round which ye cluster to examine, about which ye gather, with your 'persuasions' to wind into the innermost secret of Cyclops--one-eyed and savage--break into meaning this portent, Man, on your science-wheels.

Note the goings of the Fire, as he creepeth, serpentineth, riseth, slinketh, broadeneth. Note him reddening, glowing, whitening. Tremble at his face, dilating; at the meaning that is growing into it, to you. See that spark from the blacksmith's anvil--struck, as an insect, out of a sky containing a whole cloud of such. Rare locusts, of which Pharaoh and the Cities of the Plain read of old the secret! One, two, three sparks; dozens come: faster and faster the fiery squadrons follow, until, in a short while, a whole possible army of that hungry thing for battle, for food for it--Fire--glances up; but is soon warned in again--lest acres should glow in the growing advance. Think that this thing is bound as in matter-chains. Think that he is outside of all things, and deep in the inside of all things; and that thou and thy world are only *the thing between*; and that outside and inside are both identical, couldst thou understand the supernatural truths! Reverence Fire (for 'its meaning), and tremble at it; though in the Earth it be chained, and the foot of the Archangel Michael--like upon the Dragon--be upon it! Avert the face from it, as the Magi turned, dreading, and (as the Symbol) before it bowed askance. So much for this great thing--Fire!

Observe the multiform shapes of fire; the flame-wreaths, the spires, the stars, the spots, the cascades, and the mighty falls of it; where the roar, when it grows high in Imperial masterdom, is as that of Niagara. Think what it can do, what it is. Watch the trail of sparks, struck, as in that spouting arch, from the metal shoes of the trampling horse. It is as a letter of the great alphabet. The familiar London streets, even, can give thee the Persian's God: though in thy pleasures, and in thy commerce-operations, thou so oft forgettest thine own God. Whence liberated are those sparks? as stars, afar off, of a whole sky of flame; sparks deep down in possibility, though close to us; great in their meaning, though small in their show; as distant single ships of whole fiery fleets; animate children of, in thy human conception, a dreadful, but, in reality, a great world, of which thou knowest nothing. They fall, foodless, on the rejecting, barren, and (on the outside) the coldest stone. But in each stone, flinty and chilly as the outside is, is a heart of fire, to strike at which is to bid gush forth the *waters*, as it were, *of very Fire*, like waters of the rock! Truly, out of sparks can be displayed a whole acreage of fireworks. Forests can be conceived of flame--palaces of the fire; grandest things--soul-things--last things--all things!

Wonder no longer, then, if, rejected so long as an idolatry, the ancient Persians and their masters the Magi--concluding that they saw 'All' in this supernaturally magnificent element--fell down and worshipped it; making of it the visible representation of the very truest; but yet, in man's speculation, and in his philosophies--nay, in his commonest reason--impossible God: God being everywhere, and in us, and, indeed, us, in the God-lighted man; and impossible to be contemplated or known outside--being All!

Lights and flames, and the *torches*, as it were, of fire (all fire in this world, the last background on which all things are painted), may be considered as 'lancets' of another world--the last world: circles, enclosed by the thick walls (which, however, *by the fire* are kept from closing) of this world. As fire waves and brandishes, will the walls of this world wave, and, as it were, undulate from about it. In smoke and disruption, or combustion of matter, we witness a phenomenon of the *burning* as of the edges of the matter-rings of this world, in which world is fire, like a spot; that dense and hard thing, matter, holding it in. Oxygen, which is the finest of air, and is the means of the quickest burning out, or the supernatural (in this world) exhilaration of animal life, or extenuation of the Solid; and above all, the heightening of the capacity of the Human, as being the quintessence of matter: this oxygen is the thing which feeds fire the most overwhelming. Nor would the specks and spots and stars of fire stop in this dense world-medium, in this tissue or sea of things--could it farther and farther fasten upon and devour the solids: eating, as it were, through them. But as this thick world is a thing the thickest, it presses out, thrusts, or gravitates upon, and stifles, in its too great weight; and conquers not only that liveliest, subtlest, thinnest element of the solids, the finest air, by whatever chemical name--*oxygen; azote, azon*e, or what not--it may be called; which, in fact, is merely the nomenclature of its *composition*, the naming of the ingredients which make the thing (but not the thing). The denseness of the world not only conquers this, we repeat; but, so to figure it, matter stamps upon, effaces, and treads out fire: which, else, would burn on, back, as in the beginning of things, or into itself--consuming, as in its great revenge of any thing being created *other than it*, all the. mighty worlds which, in Creation, were permitted out of it. - This is the teaching of the ancient Fire-Philosophers (re-established and restored, to the days of comprehension of them, in the conclusions of the Rosicrucians, or *Illuminati*, of later times), who claimed to have discovered the Eternal Fire, or to have found out 'God' in the 'Immortal Light'.

There are all grades or gradations of the density of matter; but it all coheres by the one law of gravitation. Now, this gravitation is mistaken for a force of itself, when it is nothing but the sympathy, or the taking away of the supposed thing between two other things. It is sympathy (or appetite) seeking its food, or as the closing-together of two like things. It is not because one mass of matter is more ponderable or attracting than another (out of our- senses, and in reality), but. that, they are the same, with different amounts of affection, and that like seeks like, not recognizing or knowing that between. Now, this thing which is, as it were; slipped between, and which we strike into show of itself, or into fire--surprised and driven out of its ambush--is Fire. It is as the letter by which. matter spells itself out--so to speak.

Now, matter is only to be finally forced asunder by heat; flame being the bright, subtle something which comes last, and is the expansion, fruit, crown, or glory of heat: it is the vivid and visible soul, essence, and spirit of heat--the last evolvement before rending and before the forcible closing again of all the centre-speeding weights, or desires, of matter. Flame is as the expanding-out (or even *exploding*) flower to this growing thing, heat: it is as the bubble of it--the fruit (to which before we have likened it), or seed, in the outside Hand upon it. Given the supernatural Flora, heat is as the gorgeous plant, and flame the glorying flower; and as growth is greater out of the greater *matrix*, or matter of growing, so the thicker the material of fire (as we may roughly figure it, though we hope we shall be understood), so the stronger shall the fire be, and of necessity the fiercer will it be perceived to be--result being according to power.

Thus we get more of fire--that is, heat--out of the hard things: there being more of the thing Fire in them.

Trituration, mechanical division, multiplication, cutting up, precipitating, or compounding, are states into which the forces outside can place matter, without searching into and securing its bond, and gathering up (into hand off it) its chains, and mastering it. These changes can be wrought in matter, and; as it, were, it can be taken in pieces; and all this dissolution of it may be effected without our getting as at the fire-blood of our subject.

But Fire disjoints, as it were, all the hinges of the house--laps out the coherence of it--sets ablaze the dense thing, matter--makes the dark metals run like waters of light--conjures the black devils out of the minerals, and, to our astonishment, shows them much libelled, blinding, angel-white! By Fire we can lay our hand upon the solids, part them, powder them, melt them, fine them, drive them out to more and more delicate and impalpable texture--firing their invisible molecules, or imponderables, into cloud, into mist, into gas: out of touch, into hearing; out of hearing, into seeing; out of seeing into smelling; out of smelling, into nothing--into real NOTHING--not even into the last blue sky. These are the potent operations of Fire--the crucible into which we can cast all the worlds, and find them, in their last evolution, not even smoke. These are physical and scientific facts which there can be no gainsaying--which were seen and found out long ago, ages ago, in the reveries first, and then in the practice of the great

Magnetists, and those who were called the Fire-Philosophers, of whom we have spoken before.

What is that mysterious and inscrutable operation, the striking fire from flint? Familiar as it is, who remarks it? Where, in that hardest, closest pressing together of matter--where the granulation compresses, shining even in its hardness, into the solidest *laminæ* of cold, darkest blue, and streaky, core-like, agate-resembling white--lie the seeds of fire, spiritual flame-seeds, to the so stony fruit? In what folds of the flint, in. the block of it--in what invisible recess--speckled and spotted in what tissue--crouch the fire-sparks?-- to issue, in showers, on the stroke of iron--on the so sudden clattering (as of the crowbars of man) on its stony doors: Stone caving the thing Fire, unseen as its sepulchre; Stroke warning the magical thing forth. Whence comes that trail of the fire from the cold bosom of the hard, secret, unexploding flint?-- children as from what hard, rocky breast; yet hiding its so sacred, sudden fire-birth! Who--and what science-philosopher--can explain this wondrous darting forth of the hidden something, which he shall try in vain to arrest, but which like a spirit, escapes. him? If we ask what fire is, of the men of science, they are at fault. They will tell us that it is a *phenomenon*, that their vocabularies can give no further account of it. They will explain to us that all that can be said of it is, that it is a last affection of matter, to the results of which (in the world of man) they can only testify, but of whose coming and of whose going--of the place from which it comes, and the whereabout to which it goeth--they are entirely ignorant--and would give a world to know!

The foregoing, however feebly expressed, are the views of the famous Rosicrucians respecting the nature of this supposed familiar, but yet puzzling, thing--Fire.

We will proceed to some of their further mystic reveries. They are very singular.

But the consideration of these is exceedingly abstract, and difficult. The whole subject is abstruse in the highest degree.

In regard to the singular name of the Rosicrucians, it may be here stated that the Chemists, according to their *arcana*, derive the

Dew from the Latin *Ros*, and in the figure of a cross (+) they trace the three letters which compose the word *Lux*, Light. Mosheim is positive as to the accuracy of his information.

CHAPTER THE ELEVENTH

IDEAS OF THE ROSICRUCIANS AS TO THE CHARACTER OF FIRE

SPARK surrenders out of the world, when it disappears to us, in the universal ocean of Invisible Fire. That is its disappearance. It quits us in the supposed light, but *to it* really darkness--as fire-born, the last level of all--to reappear in the true light, which is *to us* darkness. This is hard to understand. But, as the real is the direct contrary of the apparent, so that which shows as light to us is darkness in the supernatural; and that which is light to the supernatural is darkness to us: matter being darkness, and soul light. For we know that light is material; and being material, it must be dark. For the Spirit of God is not material, and therefore, not being material, it cannot be light to us, and therefore darkness to God. Just as (until discovered otherwise) the world it is that is at rest, and the sun and the heavenly bodies in daily motion--instead of the very reverse being the fact. This is the belief of the oldest Theosophists, the founders of magical knowledge in the East, and the discoverers of the Gods; also the doctrine of the Fire-Philosophers, and of the Rosicrucians, or *Illuminati*, who taught that all knowable things (both of the soul and of the body) were evolved out of Fire, and finally resolvable into it: and that Fire was the last and only-to-be-known God: as that all things were capable of being searched down into it, and all things were capable of being thought up into it. Fire, they found-- when, as it were, they took this world, solid, to pieces (and also, as metaphysicians, distributed and divided the mind of man, seeking for that invisible God-thing, coherence of ideas)--fire, these thinkers found, in their supernatural light of mind, to be the latent, nameless matter started out of the tissues--certainly out of the body, presumably out of the mind--with groan, disturbance, hard motion, and flash (when forced to sight of it), instantly disappearing, and relapsing, and hiding its Godhead in the closing-violently-again solid matter--as into the forcefully resuming mind. Matter, the agent whose remonstrance at disturbance out of its Rest was, in the winds, murmur, noises, cries, as it were, of air; in the waters, rolling and roaring; in the piled floors of the sky, and their furniture, clouds, circumvolvence, contest, and war, and thunders (defiant to nature, but groans to God), and intolerable lightning-rendings; matter tearing as a garment, to close supernaturally together again as the Solid, fettered and chained--devil-bound--in the Hand upon it, 'To Be!' In this sense, all noise (as the rousing or conjuration of matter by the outside forces) is the agony of its penance. All motion is pain, all activity punishment; and fire is the secret, lowest--that is, foundation-spread--thing, the ultimate of all things, which is disclosed when the clouds of things roll, for an instant, off it--as the blue sky shows, in its fragments, like turquoises, when the canopy of clouds is wind-torn, speck-like, from off it. Fire is that floor over which the coats or layers, or the spun kingdoms of matter, or of the subsidences of the past periods of time (which is built up of objects), are laid: tissues woven over a gulf of it: in one of which last, We Are. To which Fire we only become sensible when we start it by blows or force, in the rending up of atoms, and in the blasting out of them that which holds them, which then, as Secret Spirit, springs compelled to sight, and as instantly flies, except to the immortal eyes, which receive it (in the supernatural) on the other side.

The Fire-Philosophers maintained that we transcend everything into Fire, and that we lose it there in the flash; the escape of fire being as the door through which everything disappears to the other side. In their very peculiar speculations, and in this stupendous and supernatural view of the universe, where we think that fire is the exception, and is, as it were, *spotted over the world* (in reality, to go out *when it goes out*), they held that the direct contrary was the truth, and that we, and all things, were *spotted upon fire*: and that we conquer patches only of fire when we put it out, or win torches (as it were) out of the *great flame*, when we enkindle fire--which is our master in the truth, making itself, in our beliefs (in our human needs), the slave.

Thus fire, when it is put out, only goes into the under world, and the matter-flags close over it, like a grave-stone.

When we witness Fire, we are as if peeping only through a door into another world. Into this, all the (consumed into microscopical smallness) things of this world, the compressed and concentrate matter-heaps of defunct tides of Being and of Time, are in combustion rushing: kingdoms of the floors of the things passed through--up to this moment held in suspense in the invisible inner worlds. All roars through the hollow. All that is mastered in the operations of this Fire, and that is rushing through the hollow made by it in the partition-world of the Knowable--across, and out on the other side, into the Unknowable--seeks, in the Fire, its last and most perfect evolution into ABSOLUTE NOTHING-- as a bound prisoner urges to his feet, in his chains, and shrieks for freedom when he is smitten. In Fire, we witness a grand phenomenon of the subsidiary (or further, and under, and inner, and multiplied) birth and death, and the supernatural transit of microscopic worlds, passing from the human sense-worlds to other levels and into newer fields. Then it is that the Last Spirit, of which they are composed, is playing before us; and playing, into last extinction, out of its rings of this-side matter; all which matter, in its various stages of thickening, is as the flux of the Supernatural Fire, or inside God.

It will appear no wonder now, if the above abstractions be caught by the Thinker, how it was that the early people (and the founders of Fire-Worship) considered that they saw God, standing face to face with Him--that is, with all that, in their innermost possibility of thought, they could find as God--in Fire. Which Fire is not our vulgar, gross fire; neither is it the purest material fire, which has something of the base, bright lights of the world still about it--brightest though they be in the matter which makes them the *Lightest* to the material sight; but it is an occult, mysterious, or inner--not even magnetic, but a supernatural--Fire: a real, sensible, and the only possible Mind, or God, as containing all things, and as the soul of all things; into whose inexpressibly intense, and all-devouring and divine, though fiery, gulf, all the worlds in succession, like ripe fruit to the ground, and all things, fall--back into whose arms of Immortal Light: on the other side, as again receiving them, all things, thrown off as the smoke off light, again fall!

At the shortest, then, the theory of the Magi may be summed up thus. When, as we think, fire is spotted over all the world, as we have said, it is we who make the mistake, necessitated in our man's nature and we are that which is spotted over it--just as, while we think we move, we are moved; and we conclude the senses are in us, while we are in the senses; everything--out of this world--being the very opposite of that which we take it. The views of these mighty thinkers amounted to the suppression of human reason, and the institution of magic, or god head, as all. It will be seen at once that this knowledge was possible but for -the very few. It is only fit for men when they seek to pass out of the world, and to approach--the nearer according to their natures--God.

The hollow world in which that essence of things, called Fire, plays, in its escape, in violent agitation--to us, combustion--is deep down inside of us; that is, deep-sunk inside of the time-stages; of which rings of being (subsidences of spirit) we are, in the flesh--that is, in the human show of things, in the OUTER. It is exceedingly difficult, through language, to make this idea intelligible; but it is the real mystic dogma of the ancient Guebres, or the Fire-Believers, the successors of the Buddhists, or, more properly, Bhuddists.

What is explosion? It is the lancing into the layers of worlds, whereinto we force, through turning the edges out and driving through; in surprisal of the reluctant, lazy, and secret nature, exposing the hidden, magically microscopical stores of things, passed inwards out of the accumulated rings of worlds, out of the (within) supernaturally buried wealth, rolled in, of the past, in the procession of Being. What is smoke but the disrupted vapour-world to the started soul-fire? The truth is, say the Fire-Philosophers, in the rousing of fire we suddenly come upon

Nature, and start her violently out of her ambush of things, evoking her secretest and immortal face to us. Therefore is this knowledge not to be known generally of man; and it is to be assumed at the safest in the disbelief of it: that disbelief being as the magic casket in which it is locked. The keys are only for the Gods, or for god-like spirits.

This is the true view of the religion of the leaders of the ancient Fire-Believers, and of the modern *Illuminati*.

We shall proceed to demonstrate, in the chapters following, other strange things, hitherto wholly unsuspected in the philosophical short-sight of the modern metaphysicians.

We imagine that it will be said that it is impossible that any religionists could have seriously entertained such extraordinary doctrines; but, incredible as it may seem, because it requires much preparation to understand them, it is certainly true, that it is only in this manner the ideas of the divinity of fire, which we know once prevailed largely, can be made intelligible--we mean, to the philosopher, who knows how properly to value the ancient thinkers, who were as giants in the earth. We shall shortly show that the monuments raised to this strange faith still remain, and that, surviving from the heathen times, the forms still linger and lurk largely amidst the Christian European institutions--the traces of the idolatry, if not the idolatry itself.

Obelisks, spires, minarets, tall towers, upright stones (Menhirs), monumental crosses, and architectural perpendiculars of every description, and, generally speaking, all erections conspicuous for height and slimness, were representatives of the sworded, or of the pyramidal, Fire. They bespoke, wherever found, and in whatever age, the idea of the First Principle, Or the male generative emblem.

Having given, as we hope, some new views of the doctrine of Universal Fire, and shown that there has been error in imagining that the Persians and the ancient Fire-Worshippers were idolaters simply of fire, inasmuch as, in bowing down before it, they only regarded Fire as a symbol, or visible sign, or thing placed as standing for the Deity--having, in our preceding chapters, disposed the mind of the reader to consider as a matter of solemnity, and of much greater general significance, this strange fact of Fire-Worship, and endeavoured to show it as a portentous, first, all-embracing as all-genuine principle--we will proceed to exemplify the widespread roots of the Fire-Faith. In fact, we seem to recognize it everywhere.

Instead of--in their superstitions--making of fire their God, they obtained Him, that is, all that we can realize of Him; by which we mean, all that the human reason can find of the Last Principle--out of it. Already, in their thoughts, had the Magi exhausted all possible theologies; already had they, in their great wisdom, searched through physics--their power to this end (as not being distracted by world's objects) being much greater than that of the modern faith-teachers and doctors; already in their reveries, in their. observations (deep within their deep souls) upon the nature of themselves, and of the microcosm of a world in which they found themselves, had the Magi transcended. They had arrived at a new world in their speculations and deductions upon facts, upon all the things behind which (to men) make these facts. Already, in their determined climbing into the heights of thought, had these Titans of mind achieved, past the cosmical, through the shadowy borders of Real and Unreal, into Magic. For, is Magic wholly false?

Passing through these mind-worlds, and coming out, as we may figure it, *at the other side*, penetrating into the secrets of things, they evaporated all Powers, and resolved them finally into the Last Fire. Beyond this, they found nothing; as into this they resolved all things. And then, on the Throne of the Visible, they placed this--in the world, Invisible--Fire: the sense-thing to be worshipped *in the senses*, as the last thing of them, and the king of them--that is, that which we know as the phenomenon, Burning Fire--the Spiritual Fire being impalpable, as having the visible only for its shadow; the Ghostly Fire not being even to be thought upon; thought being its medium of apprehension when it itself had slipped; the waves of apprehension of it only flowing back when it--being intuition--had vanished. We only know that a thought is in us when the thought is off the object and in us: another thought being, at that simultaneous instant, in the object, to be taken up by us only when the first has gone out of us, and so on; but not *before* to be taken up by us--that thought being *all of us*, and a deceptive and unreal thing to pass at all to us through the reason, and there being no resemblance between it and its original: the true thing being 'Inspiration', or 'God in us', excluding all matter or *reason*, which is only built up of matter. It is most difficult to frame language in regard to these things. Reason can only unmake God; He is only possible in His own development, or in His. seizing of us, and 'in possession'. Thus Paracelsus and his disciples declare that Human Reason become our master, that is, in its perfection--but not used as our servant-- transforms, as it were, into the Devil, and exercises *his* office in leading us away *from* the throne of Spiritual Light--other, and, in the world, seeming *better*; in his false and deluding World-Light, or Matter-Light, really showing himself God. This view of the Human Reason, intellectually trusted, transforming into the Angel of Darkness, and effacing God out of the world, is borne out by a thousand *texts of Scripture*. It is equally in the belief and in the traditions of all nations and of all time, as we shall by and by show. Real Light is God's shadow, or the soul of matter; the one is the very brighter, as the other is the very blacker. Thus, the worshippers of the Sun, or Light, or Fire, whether in the Old or the New Worlds, worshipped not Sun, or Light, or Fire-- otherwise they would have worshipped the Devil, he being all conceivable Light; but rather they adored the Unknown Great God, in the last image that was possible to man of anything--the Fire. And they chose that as His shadow, as the very opposite of that which He really. was; honouring the Master through His Servant; bowing before the manifestation, Eldest of Time, for the Timeless; paying homage to the spirit of the Devil-World, or rather to the Beginning and End, on which was the foot of the ALL, that the ALL, or the LAST, might be worshipped; propitiating the Evil Principle in its finite shows, because (as by that alone a world could be made, whose making is alone

Comparison) it was permitted as a means of God, and therefore the operation of God Downwards, as part of Him, though Upwards dissipating as before Him--before Him in whose presence Evil, or Comparison, or Difference, or Time, or Space, or anything, should be Impossible: real God being not to be thought upon.

But it was not only in the quickening Spirit of Divinity that these things could be seen. Otherwise than in faith, we can hope that they shall now--in our weak attempts to explain them--be gathered as not contradictory, and merely intellectual, and seen as vital and absolute. They need the elevation of the mind in the sense of 'inspiration', and not the quickening and the *sharpening* of the Intellect, as seeking wings--devil-pinions--wherewith to sail into the region only of its own laws, where, of course it will not find God. Then step in the mathematics, then the senses, then the reason--then the very perfection of matter-work, or this world's work, sets in--engines of which the Satanic Powers shall realize the work. The Evil Spirit conjures, as even by holy command, the translucent sky. The Archangelic, clear, child-like rendering-up in intuitive belief--intense in its own sun--is FAITH. Lucifer fills the scope of belief with imitative, dazzling clouds, and built splendours. With these temptations it is sought to dissuade, sought to rival, sought to put out Saints' sight--sought even to surpass in seeming a further and truer, because a more solid and a more sensible, glory. The apostate, real-born Lucifer is so named as the intensest Spirit of Light, because he is of the things that perish, and of the things that to Mind--because they are all of Matter--have the most of glory! Thus is one of the names of the Devil, the very eldest-born and brightest Star of Light, that of the very morning and beginning of all things--the clearest, brightest, purest, as being soul-like, of Nature; but only of Nature. Real law, or Nature, is the Devil; real Reason is the Devil.

Now we shall find, with a little patience, that this transcendental, beyond-limit-or-knowledge ancient belief of the Fire-God is to be laid hand upon--as, in a manner, we shall say-- in all the stories and theologies of the ancient world--in all the countries (and they, indeed, *are* all) where belief has grown--yea, as a thing with the trees and plants, as out of the very ground, in all the continents, and in both worlds. And out of this great fact of its universal diffusion, as a matter of history the most innate and coexistent, shall we not assume this fire-doctrine as being of truth--as a thing really, fundamentally, and vitally true? As in the East, so in the West; as in the old time, so in the new; as in the preadamite and postdiluvian worlds, so in the modern and latter-day world; surviving through the ages, buried in the foundations of empires, locked in the rocks, hoarded in legends, maintained in monuments, preserved in beliefs, suggested in tradition, borne amidst the roads of the multitude in emblems, gathered up--as the recurring, unremarked, supernaturally coruscant, and yet secret, evading, encrusted, and dishonoured jewel--in rites, spoken (to those capable of the comprehension) in the field of hieroglyphics, dimly glowing up to a fitful suspicion of it in the sacred rites of all peoples, figured forth in the religions, symbolized in a hundred ways; attested, prenoted, bodied forth in occult body, as far as body can--in fine, in multitudinous fashions and forms forcibly soliciting the sharpness of sight directed to its discovery, and spelt over a floor as under-placing all things, we recognize, we espy, we descry, and we may, lastly, ADMIT the mysterious sacredness of Fire. For why should we not admit it?

Of course, it will not for a moment be supposed that we mean anything like--or in its nature similar to--ordinary fire. We hope that no one will be so absurd as to suppose that this in any manner could be the mysterious and sacred element for which we are contesting. Where we are seeking to transcend, this would be simply sinking back into vulgar reason. While we are seeking to convict and dethrone this world's reason as the real devil, this would be distinctly deifying common sense. Of common sense, except for common-sense objects, we make no account. We have rather in awed contemplation the divine, ineffable, transcendental SPIRIT--the Immortal fervour-- into which the whole World evolves. We have the mystery of the Holy Spirit in view, called by its many names.

It is because theologies will contest concerning divers names of the same thing, that we therefore seek, in transcending, but to identify. It is because men will dispute about forms, that we seek philosophically to show that all forms are impossible--that, when we take the human reason into account, all forms of belief are alike. Reason has been the great enemy of religion. Let us see if this world's reason cannot be mastered:

We are now about--in a new light--to treat of facts, and of various historical monuments. They all bear reference to this universal story of the mystic Fire.

We claim to be the first to point out how strikingly--and yet how, at the same time, without any suspicion of it--these emblems and remains, in so many curious and unintelligible forms, of the magic religion are found in the Christian churches.

CHAPTER THE TWELFTH

MONUMENTS RAISED TO FIRE-WORSHIP IN ALL COUNTRIES

WE think that we shall be able fully in our succeeding chapters to place beyond contradiction an extraordinary discovery. It is, that the whole round of disputed emblems which so puzzle antiquaries, and which are found in all countries, point to the belief in Fire as the First Principle. We seek to show that the Fire-Worship was the very earliest, from the immemorial times--that it was the foundation religion--that the attestation to it is preserved in monuments scattered all over the globe--that the rites and usages of all creeds, down even to our own day, and in everyday use about us, bear reference to it--that problems and puzzles in religion, which cannot be otherwise explained, stand clear and evident when regarded in this new light--that in all the Christian varieties of belief--as truly as in Bhuddism, in Mohammedanism, in Heathenism of all kinds, whether Eastern, or Western, or Northern, or Southern--this 'Mystery of Fire' stands ever general, recurring, and conspicuous--and that in being so, beyond all measure, old, and so, beyond all modern or any idea of it, general--as universal, in fact, as man himself, and the thoughts of man; and, as being that beyond which, in science and in natural philosophy, we cannot further go, it must carry truth with it, however difficult to comprehend, and however unsuspected: that is, as really being the manifestation and Spirit of God, and--to the confounding and annihilation of Atheism--Revelation.

Affirmatively we shall now, therefore, offer to the attention of the reader the universal scattering of the Fire-Monuments, taking up at the outset certain positions about them.

Narrowly considered, it will be found that all religions transcend up into this spiritual Fire-Floor, on which, to speak metaphysically, the phases of Time were laid. Material Fire, which is the brighter as the matter which constitutes it is the blacker, is the shadow (so to express, or to speak, necessarily with 'words', which have no meaning in the spirit) of the 'Spirit-Light', which invests itself in it as the mask in which alone it can be possible. Thus, material light being the very opposite of God, the Egyptians--who were undoubtedly acquainted with the Fire-Revelation--could not represent God as light. They therefore expressed their Idea of Deity by darkness. Their chief adoration was paid to *Darkness*. They bodied the Eternal forth under Darkness.

In the early times before the Deluge--of which 'phenomenon', as there remains a brighter or fainter tradition of it among all the peoples of the globe, it must be true--Man walked with the Knowledge of Spirit in him. He has derogated, through time, from this primeval, God-informed Type. Knowledge of Good and Evil, or the *power of perceiving difference*, became his faculty, with his power of propagation, only in his fallen state-- that is, his gods only came to him in his fallen state. As one of two things must of necessity be under the other, and as 'one' and 'two' are double in succession--one being, as a matter of course, before the other--and 'positive' or 'particled', existence being in itself denial of 'abstract', or 'imparticled', existence--existence needing something other than itself to find itself--logicians must see at once in this that Comparison is constituted; from out of which *difference* is built Light and Shadow, or a world, whether the moral world or the real world.

The immemorial landmark, in the architectural form, is the upright. We find the earliest record of this in the setting-up of monumental stones. Seth is said to have engraved the wisdom of the Antediluvians upon two pillars--one of brick, the other of stone--which he erected in the 'Siriadic land'--a *Terra Incognita* to modern antiquaries. This raising of the 'reminding-stone' prevails in all places, and was the act of all time. It is the only independent thing which stands distinct out of the clouds of the past. It would seem universally to refer to the single Supernatural Tradition--all that is heired out of Time. A mysterious Cabalistic volume of high repute, and of the greatest antiquity, is *The Book of Light*, whose doctrine divides. The first dogma is that of 'Light-Enlightened', or 'Self-Existent', which signifies God, or the Light Spiritual, which is darkness in the world, or Manifestation or Creation. This Light-Enlightened is Inspiration, or blackness to men (God), opposed to knowledge, or brightness to men (the Devil). The second Light is the Enlightening Light, or the Material Light, which is the producer, foundation, and God of *this World*--proceeding, nevertheless, from God; for He is All. It is in reverence to this second light, and to the Mysterious Identity of both (the third power Three in One)--but only in the necessity of 'being'--all dark-being constituting all bright-being in the Spirit, and Both, and their identity, being One--that these monumental pillars are raised--being really the mark and the signal (warning on, in Time) of supernatural, or magic, knowledge.

Stones were set up by the Patriarchs: the Bible records them. In India, the first objects of worship were monoliths. In the two peninsulas of India, in Ceylon, in Persia, in the Holy Land, in Phœnicia, in Sarmathia, in Scythia, everywhere where worship was attempted (and in what place where man exists is it not?), everywhere where worship was practised (and where, out of fears, did not, first, come the gods, and then their propitiation?)--in all the countries, we repeat, as the earliest of man's work, we recognize this sublime, mysteriously speaking, ever-recurring monolith, marking up the tradition of the supernaturally real, and only real, Fire-dogma. Buried so far down in time, the suspicion assents that there must somehow be truth in the foundation; not fanciful, legendary, philosophical creed-truth, unexplainable (and only to be admitted without question) truth; but truth, however mysterious and awing, yet cogent, and not to be of philosophy (that is, illumination) denied.

The death and descent of Balder into the Hell of the Scandinavians may be supposed to be the purgatory of the Human Unit (or the God-illuminate), from the Light (through the God-dark phases of being), back into its native Light. Balder was the Scandinavian Sun-God, and the same as the Egyptian

Osiris, the Greek Hercules, Bacchus, and Phœbus, or Apollo, the Indian Crishna, the Persian Mithras, the Aten of the empires of insular Asia; or, even of the Sidonians, the Athyr or Ashtaroth. The presences of all these divinities--indeed, of all Gods--were of the semblance of Fire; and we recognize, as it were, the mark of the foot of them, or of the Impersonated Fire, in the countless uprights, left, as memorials, in the great ebb of the ages (as waves) to nations in the latter divisions of that great roll of periods called Time; yet so totally unguessing of the preternatural mystery--seeming the key of all belief, and the reading of all wonders--which they speak.

It is to be noted that all the above religions--all the Creeds of Fire--were exceedingly similar in their nature; that they were all fortified by rites, and fenced around with ceremonies; and that, associated as they were with mysteries and initiations, the disciple was led through the knowledge of them in stages, as his powers augmented and his eyes saw, until, towards the last grades (as he himself grew capable and illuminate), the door was closed upon all after-pressing and unrecognized inquirers, and the Admitted One was himself lost sight of.

There was a great wave to the westward of all knowledge, all cultivation of the arts, all tradition, all intellect, all civilization, all religious belief. The world was peopled westwards. There seems some secret, divine impress upon the world's destinies--and, indeed, ingrain in cosmical matter--in. these matters. All faiths seem to have diverged out, the narrower or the wider, as rays from the great central sun of this tradition of the Fire-Original. It would seem that Noah, who is suspected to be the Fo, Foh, or Fohi, of the Chinese, carried it into the farthest Cathay of the Middle Ages. What is the Chinese Tien, or Earliest Fire? The pagodas of the Chinese (which name, *pagoda*, was borrowed from the Indian; from which country of India, indeed, probably came into China its worship, and its Bhuddist doctrine of the exhaustion back into the divine light, or unparticled nothingness, of all the stages of Being or of Evil)--the Chinese pagodas, we repeat, are nothing but innumerable gilt and belled fanciful repetitions of the primeval monolith. The fire, or light, is still worshipped in the Chinese temples; it has not been perceived that, in the very form of the Chinese pagodas, the fundamental article of the Chinese religion--transmigration, through stages of being; out into nothingness of this world--has been architecturally emblemed in the diminishing stories, carried upwards, and fining away into the series of unaccountable discs struck through a vertical rod, until all culminates, and--as it were, to speak heraldically of it--the last *achievement* is blazoned in the gilded ball, which means the final, or Bhuddist, glorifying absorption. Buildings have always telegraphed the *insignia* of the mythologies; and, in China, the fantastic speaks the sublime. We recognize the same embodied *Mythos* in all architectural spiring or artistic diminution, whether tapering to the globe or exaltation of the Egyptian *Uræus*, or the disc, or the Sidonian crescent, or the lunar horns, or the *acroterium* of the Greek temple, or the pediment of the classic *pronaos* itself (crowning, how grandly and suggestively, at solemn dawn, or in the 'spirit-lustres' of the dimming, and, still more than dawn, solemn twilight, the top of some mountain, an ancient of the days). Here, besetting us at every turn, meet we the same mythic emblem: again, in the crescent of the Mohammedan fanes, surmounting even the Latin, and therefore the once Christian, St. Sophia. Last, and not least, the countless 'churches' rise, in the Latter-day Dispensation, sublimely to the universal signal, in the glorifying, or top, or crowning Cross: last of the Revelations!

In the fire-towers of the Sikhs, in the dome-covered and many-storied spires of the Hindoos, in the vertically turreted and longitudinally massed temples of the Bhudds, of all the classes and of all the sects, in the religious buildings of the Cingalese, in the upright flame-fanes of the Parsees, in the original of the *campaniles* of the Italians, in the tower of St. Mark at Venice, in the flame-shaped or pyramidal (*pyr* is the Greek for fire) architecture of the Egyptians (which is the parent of all that is called architecture), we see the recurring symbol. All the minarets that, in the Eastern sunshine, glisten through the Land of the

Moslem; indeed, his two-horned crescent, equally with the moon, or disc, or two-pointed globe of the Sidonian Ashtaroth (after whose forbidden worship Solomon, the wisest of mankind, in his defection from the God of his fathers, evilly thirsted); also, the mystic *discus*, or 'round' of the Egyptians, so continually repeated, and set, as it were, as the forehead-mark upon all the temples of the land. of soothsayers and sorcerers--this Egypt so profound in its philosophies, in its wisdom, in its magic-seeing, and in its religion, raising out of the black Abyss a God to shadow it--all the minarets of the Mohammedan, we say, together with all the other symbols of moon, of disc, of wings, or of horns (equally with the shadowy and preternatural beings in all mythologies and in all theologies, to which these adjuncts or *insignia* are referred, and which are symbolized by them)--all these monuments, or bodied meanings, testify to the Deification of Fire.

What may mean that 'Tower of Babel' and its impious raising, when it sought, even past and over the clouds, to imply a daring sign? What portent was that betrayal of a knowledge not for man--that surmise forbidden save in infinite humility, and in the whispered impartment of the further and seemingly more impossible, and still more greatly mystical, meanings? In utter abnegation of self alone shall the mystery of fire be conceived. Of what was this Tower of Belus, or the Fire, to be the monument? When it soared, as a *pharos*, on the rock of the traditional ages, to defy time in its commitment to 'form' of the unpronounceable secret--stage on -stage and story on story, though it climbed the clouds, and on its top should shine the ever-burning fire--first idol of the world, 'dark, save with neglected stars'--what was the Tower of Babel but a gigantic monolith? Perhaps to record and to perpetuate this ground-fire of all; to be worshipped, an idol, in its visible form, when it should be alone taken as the invisible *thought:* fire to be waited for (spirit-possession), not waited on (idolatry). Therefore was the speech confounded, that the thing should not be; therefore, under the myth of climbing into heaven by the means of it, was the first colossal monolithic temple (in which the early dwellers upon the earth sought to enshrine the Fire) laid prostrate in the thunder of the Great God! And the languages were confounded from that day--speech was made babble--thence its name--that the secret should remain a secret. It was to be only darkly hinted, and to be fitfully disclosed, like a false-showing light, in the theosophic glimmer, amidst the world's knowledge-lights. It was to reappear, like a spirit, to the 'initiate', in the glimpse of reverie, in the snatches of sight, in the profoundest wisdom, through the studies of the ages.

We find, in the religious administration of the ancient world, the most abundant proofs of the secret fire-tradition. Schweigger shows, in his *Introduction into Mythology* (pp. 132, 228), that the Phœnician Cabiri and the Greek Dioscuri, the Curetes, Corybantes, Telchini, were originally of the same nature, and are only different in trifling particulars. All these symbols represent electric and magnetic phenomena, and that under the 'ancient name of twin-fires, hermaphrodite fire. The Dioscuri is a phrase equivalent to the Sons of Heaven: if, as Herodotus asserts, 'Zeus originally represented the whole circle of heaven'.

According to the ancient opinion of Heraclitus, the contest of opposing forces is the origin of new bodies, and the reconcilement of these contending principles is called combustion. This is, according to Montfauçon, sketched in the minutest detail in the engravings of the ancient Phœnician Cabiri.

From India into Egypt was imported this spiritual fire-belief. We recognize, again, its never-failing structure-signal. Rightly regarded, the great Pyramids are nothing but the world-enduring architectural attestation, following (in the pyramidal) the well-known leading law of Egypt's templar-piling--moundlike, spiry-- of the universal Flame-Faith. Place a light upon the summit, star-like upon the sky, and a prodigious altar the mighty Pyramid then becomes. In this tribute to the world-filling faith, burneth expressed devotion to (radiateth acknowledgment of) the immemorial magic religion. There is little doubt that as token and emblem of fire-worship, as indicative of the adoration of the real, accepted deity, these Pyramids were raised. The idea that they were burial-places of the Egyptian monarchs is untenable, when submitted to the weighing of meanings, and when it comes side by side with this better fire-explanation. Cannot we accept these Pyramids as the vast altars on whose top should burn the flame--flame commemorative, as it were, to all the world? Cannot we see in these piles, literally and really transcendental in origin, the Egyptian reproduction, and a hieroglyphical signalling-on, of special truth, eldest of time? Do we not recognize in the Pyramid the repetition of the first monolith--all the uprights constituting the grand attesting pillar to the supernatural tradition of a Fire-Born World?

The ever-recurring globe with wings, so frequent in the sculptures of the Egyptians, witnesses to the Electric Principle. It embodies the transmigration of the Indians, reproduced by Pythagoras. Pythagoras resided for a long period in Egypt, and acquired from the priests the philosophic 'transition'-knowledge, which was afterwards doctrine. The globe, disc, or circle of the Phœnician Astarte, the crescent of Minerva, the horns of the Egyptian Ammon, the deifying of the ox--all have the same meaning. We trace among the Hebrews, the token of the identical mystery in the horns of Moses, distinct in the sublime statue by Michael Angelo in the Vatican; as also in the horns of the Levitical altar: indeed, the use of the 'double hieroglyph' in continual ways. The *volutes* of the Ionic column, the twin-stars of Castor and Pollux, nay, generally, the employment of the double emblem all the world over, in ancient or in modern times, whether displayed as points, or *radii,* or wings on the helmets of those barbarian chiefs who made war upon Rome, Attila or Genseric, or broadly shown upon the head-piece of the Frankish Clovis; whether emblemed in the rude and, as it were, savagely mystic horns of the Asiatic idols, or reproduced in the horns of the Runic Hammerer (or Destroyer), or those of the Gothic Mars, or of the modern devil; all this double-spreading from a common point (or this figure of HORNS) speaks the same story.

The Colossus of Rhodes was a monolith, in the human form, dedicated to the Sun, or to fire. The Pharos of Alexandria was a fire-monument. Heliopolis, or the City of the Sun, in Lower Egypt (as the name signifies), contained a temple, wherein, combined with all the dark superstitions of the Egyptians, the flame-secret was preserved. In most jealous secrecy was the tradition guarded, and the symbol alone was presented to the world. Of the Pyramids, as prodigious Fire-Monuments, we have before spoken. Magnificent as the principal Pyramid still is, it is stated by an ancient historian that it originally formed, at the base, 'a square of eight hundred feet, and that it was eight hundred feet high'. Another informs us that 'three hundred and sixty-six thousand men were employed twenty years in its erection'. Its height is now supposed to be six hundred feet. Have historians and antiquaries carefully weighed the fact (even in the *name* of the Pyramids), that *Pyr*, or *Pur*, in the Greek, means Fire? We would argue that that object, in the Great Pyramid, which Ms been mistaken for a tomb (and which is, moreover, rather fashioned like an altar, smooth and plain, without any carved work), is, in reality, the vase, urn, or depository, of the sacred, ever-burning *fire*: of the existence of which ever-living, inextinguishable fire, to be found at some period of the world's history, there is abundant tradition. This view is fortified by the statements of Diodorus, who writes that 'Cheops, or Chemis, who founded the principal Pyramid, and Cephren, or Cephrenus, who built the next to it, were neither buried here, but that they were deposited elsewhere'.

Cheops, Cephrenus, and Mycerinus, the mighty builders of these super-gigantic monuments, of which it is said that they look as if intended to resist the, waste of the ages, and, as in a front of supernatural and sublime submission, to await, in the undulation of Time (as in the waves of centuries), the expected revolution of nature, and the new and recommencing series of existence, surely had in view something grander, something still more universally portentous, than sepulture--or even death! Is it at all reasonable to conclude, at a period when knowledge was at the highest, and when the human powers were, in comparison with ours at the present time, prodigious, that all these indomitable, scarcely believable, physical efforts--that such achievements as those of the Egyptians--were devoted to a mistake? that the Myriads of the Nile were fools labouring in the dark, and that all the magic of their great men was forgery? and that we, in despising that which we call their superstition and wasted power, are alone the wise? No! there is much more in these old religions than, probably, in the audacity of modern denial, in the confidence of these superficial-science times, and in the derision of these days without faith, is in the least degree supposed. We do not understand the old time.

It is evident from their hieroglyphics that the Egyptians were acquainted with the wonders of magnetism. By means of it (and by the secret powers which lie in the hyper-sensual, 'heaped floors' of it), out of the every-day senses, the Egyptians struck together, as it were, a bridge, across which they paraded into the supernatural; the magic portals receiving them as on the other and *armed* side of a drawbridge, shaking in its thunders in its raising (or in its lowering), as out of flesh. Athwart this, in trances, swept the adepts, leaving their mortality behind them: all, and their earth-surroundings, to be resumed at their reissue upon the plains of life, when down in their humanity again.

In the cities of the ancient world, the Palladium, or Protesting Talisman (invariably set up in the chief square or place), was--there is but little doubt--the reiteration of the very earliest monolith. All the obelisks--each often a single stone, of prodigious weight--all the singular, solitary, wonderful pillars and monuments of Egypt, as of other lands, are, as it were, only tombstones of the Fire! All testify to the great, so darkly hinted secret. In Troy was the image of Pallas, the myth of knowledge, of the world, of manifestation, of the fire-soul. In Athens was Pallas-Athene, or Minerva. In the Greek cities, the form of the deity changed variously to Bacchus, to Hercules, to Phœbus-Apollo; to the tri-formed Minerva, Dian, and Hecate; to the dusky Ceres, or the darker Cybele. In the wilds of Sarmathia, in the wastes of Northern Asia, the luminous rays descended from heaven, and, animating the Lama, or 'Light-Born', spoke the same story. The flames of the Greeks, the towers of the Phœnicians, the emblems of the Pelasgi; the story of Prometheus, and the myth of his stealing the fire from heaven, wherewith to animate the man (or ensoul the visible world); the forges of the Cyclops, and the monuments of Sicily; the mysteries of the Etrurians; the rites of the Carthaginians; the torches borne, in all priestly demonstrative processions, at all times, in all countries; the vestal fires of the Romans; the very word *flamen*, as indicative of the office of the officiating sacerdote; the hidden fires of the ancient Persians, and of the grimmer (at least in name) Guebres; the whole mystic meaning of flames on altars, of the ever-burning tombs-lights of the earlier peoples, whether in the classic or in the barbarian lands--everything of this kind was intended to signify the deified Fire. Fires are lighted in the funeral ceremonies of the Hindoos and of the Mohammedans, even to this day, though the body be committed whole to earth. Wherefore fire, then? Cremation and urn-burial, or the burning of the dead--practised in all ages--imply a profounder meaning than is generally supposed. They point to the transmigration of Pythagoras, or to the purgatorial reproductions of the Indians, among whom we the earliest find the dogma. The real signification of fire-burial is the commitment of human mortality into the last of all matter, overleaping the intermediate states; or the delivering over of the man-unit into the Flame-Soul, past all intervening spheres or stages of the purgatorial: the absolute doctrine of the Bhudds, taught, even at this day, among the *initiate* all over the East. Thus we see how classic practice and heathen teaching may be made to reconcile--how even the Gentile and Hebrew, the mythological and the (so-called) Christian, doctrine harmonize in the general faith--founded in magic. That magic is indeed possible is the moral of our book.

    We have seen that Hercules was the myth of the Electric Principle. His pillars (Calpe and Abyla) are the Dual upon which may be supposed to rest a world. They stood in the days when giants might really be imagined--indeed, they almost look as impressive of it *now*--the twin prodigious monoliths, similar in purpose to the artificial pyramids. They must have struck the astonished and awed discoverer's gaze, navigating that silent Mediterranean (when men seemed as almost to find themselves alone in the world), as the veritable, colossal, natural pillars on which should burn the double Lights of the forbidden Baal: witness of the ever-perpetuated, ever-perpetuating legend of the fire-making! So to the Phœnician sailors, who, we are told, first descried, and then stemmed royally through, these peaked and jagged and majestic Straits--doorway to the mighty floor of the new blue ocean, still of the more Tyrian crystal depth--rolling, in walls of waves, under the enticing blaze of the cloud-empurpled, all-imperial, western sun, whose court was fire indeed--God's, not Baal's! --so to these men of Sidon, emblemed with the fire-white horns of the globed Astarte, or Ashtaroth, showed the monster rocks: pillar-portals--fire-topped as the last world-beacon--to close in (as gate) that classic sea, and to warn, as of the terrors of the unknown, new, and second world of farthest waters, which stretched to the limits of possibility. Forsaking, indeed, daringly, were these Iberi their altars, to tempt perils, when they left behind them that mouth of their Mediterranean: that sea upon whose embayed and devious margin were nations the most diverse, yet the mightiest of the earth. The very name of the Iberia which they discovered, and to which they themselves gave title, hints the *Cabiri*, who carried, doubtless, in their explorations, as equally with their commerce and their arts, their religious usages and their faith, as pyramidically intensifying, until it flashed truth upon the worlds in the grand Fire-Dogma--that faith to which sprung monuments from all the sea-borders at which glittered the beak-- itself an imitation flame--of every many-oared, single ship of their adventurous, ocean-dotting fleets--the precursors of the exploring ships of the Vikings.

We claim the cauldron of the witches as, in the original, the vase or urn of the fiery transmigration, in which all the things of the world change. We accept the sign of the double-extended fingers (pointed in a fork) or of *horns*, which throughout Italy, the Greek Islands, Greece, and Turkey, is esteemed as the counter-charm to the Evil Eye, as the occult Magian telegraphic. The horns, or *radii* of the Merry-Andrew, or Jester, or Motley, and the horns of Satan; indeed, the figure of horns generally[6], even have a strange affinity in the consecrate and religious. The horseshoe, so universally employed as a defensive charm, and used as a sign to warn-off and to consecrate, when--as it so frequently is--displayed at the entrance of stables, outhouses, and farm-buildings in country places, speaks the acknowledgment of the Devil, or Sinister Principle. The rearing aloft, and 'throwing out' as it were, of protesting, and--in a certain fashion--badge-like, magic signs, in the bodies of bats, and wild nocturnal creatures, fixed upon barn doors, we hold to be the perpetuation of the old heathen sacrifice to .the harmful gods, or a sort of devil-propitiation. Again, in this horse-shoe we meet the *horse*, as indicative of, and connected with, spirit power: of which strange association we shall by and by have more to say. The horse-shoe is the, mystic symbol of the Wizard's Foot, or the *sigma*, or sign, of the abstract 'Four-footed', the strangely secret, constantly presented, but as constantly evading, magic meaning conveyed in which (a tremendous cabalistic sign) we encounter everywhere. May the original, in the East, of the horse-shoe arch of the Saracens, which is a foundation-form of our Gothic architecture-- may the horse-shoe form of all arches and cupolas (which figure is to be met everywhere in Asia)--may these strange, rhomboidal curves carry reference to the ancient mysterious blending of the ideas of the horse and the supernatural and religious? It is an awing thought but Spirits and supernatural embodiments-- unperceived by our limited, vulgar senses--may make their daily walk amidst us, invisible, in the ways of the world. It may indeed be that they are sometimes suddenly *happened upon*, and, as it were, surprised. The world--although so silent--may be noisy with

---

[6] Horns generally--whether the horns of the *cocu*, which need not be those of the 'wittol', or contented, betrayed husband, but generally implying the mysterious ultra-natural scorn, ranging in meaning with the 'attiring' and stigmatizing of Acton turned into the stag, and hunted by his own hounds, for surprising Diana naked.

ghostly feet. The Unseen Ministers may every day pass in and out among our ways, and we all the time think that we have the world to ourselves. It is, as it were, to this *inside*, unsuspected world that these recognitive, deprecatory signs of horseshoes and of charms are addressed; that the harming presences, unprovoked, may pass harmless; that the jealous watch of the Unseen over us may be assuaged in the acknowledgment; that the unrecognized presences amidst us, if met with an unconsciousness for which man cannot be accountable, may not be offended with carelessness in regard of them for which he may be punishable.

CHAPTER THE THIRTEENTH

DRUIDICAL STONES AND THEIR WORSHIP

THE monolith, talisman, mysterious pillar, or stone memorial, raised in attestation of the fire-tradition, and occupying the principal square or place, Forum, or middle-most or navel-point of the city in ancient times, is the original of our British market-crosses. The *cromlech*, or *bilithon*, or *trilithon*; the single, double, or grouped stones found in remote places--in Cornwall, in Wales, in various counties of England, in by-spots in Scotland, in the Scottish Isles, in the Isle of Man, and in Ireland--all these stones of memorial--older than history--speak the secret faith of the ancient peoples. These stones are also to be found in Brittany, in various parts of France and Spain; nay, throughout Europe, and occurring to recognition, in fact, in all parts of the world--old and new.

Stonehenge, with its inner and outer circles of stones, enclosing the central mythic object, or altar; all the Druidic or Celtic remains; stones on the tops of mountains, altar-tables in the valley; the centre measuring, or obelisk, stones, in market-places or centre-spaces in great towns, from which the highways radiated, spaced--in mileage--to distance; that time-honoured relic, 'London Stone', still extant in Cannon Street, London; the Scottish 'sacred stone', with its famous oracular gifts, vulgarly called Jacob's Pillow, transported to England by the dominant Edward the First, and preserved in the seat of the Coronation Chair in Westminster Abbey; even the placing of upright stones as tombstones, which is generally accepted as a mere means of personal record--for, be it remembered, the ancients placed *tablets* against their walls by way of funeral register; all follow the same rule. We consider all these as variations of the upright commemorative pillar.

The province of Brittany, in France, is thickly studded with stone pillars, and the history and manners of its people teem with interesting, and very curious, traces of the worship of them. In these parts, and elsewhere, they are distinguished by the name of *Menhirs and Peulvans*. The superstitious veneration of the Irish people for such stones is well known. M. de Fréminville says in his *Antiquités du Finisterre*, p. 106: 'The Celts worshipped a divinity which united the attributes of Cybele and Venus'. This worship prevailed also in Spain--as, doubtless, throughout Europe--inasmuch as we find the Eleventh and Twelfth Councils of Toledo warning those who offered worship to stones that they were sacrificing to devils.

We are taught that the Druidical institution of Britain was Pythagorean, or patriarchal, or Brahminical. The presumed universal knowledge which this order possessed, and the singular customs which they practised, have afforded sufficient analogies and affinities to maintain the occult and remote origin of Druidism. A Welsh antiquary insists that the Druidical system of the Metempsychosis was conveyed to the Brahmins of India by a former emigration from Wales. But, the reverse may have occurred, if we trust the elaborate researches which would demonstrate that the Druids were a scion of the Oriental family. The reader is referred to Toland's *History of the Druids*, in his *Miscellaneous Works*, vol. ii, p. 163; also to a book published in London in 1829, with the title *The Celtic Druids; or, An Attempt to show that the Druids were the Priests of Oriental Colonies, who emigrated from India*, by Godfrey Higgins. A recent writer confidently intimated that the knowledge of Druidism must be searched for in the Talmudical writings; but another, in return, asserts that the Druids were older than the Jews.

Whence and when the British Druids transplanted themselves to this lone world amid the ocean, no historian can write. We can judge of the Druids simply by the sublime monuments which are left of them, surviving, in their majestic loneliness, through the ages of civilization. Unhewn masses or heaps of stones tell alone their story; such are their *cairns*, and *cromlechs*, and *corneddes*, and that wild architecture, whose stones hang on one another, still frowning on the plains of Salisbury.

Among the most remarkable ancient remains in Wales (both North and South) are the Druidical stones: poised in the most extraordinary manner--a real engineering problem--the slightest touch will sometimes suffice to set in motion the *Logan*, or rocking, stones, whether these balanced masses are found in Wales or elsewhere. We think that there is very considerable ground for concluding that all these mounted stones were oracular, or, so to express it, speaking; and that, when sought for divine responses, they were caused first to tremble, then to heave, and finally, like the tables of the modern (so-called) Spiritualists, to tip intelligibly. To no other reason than this could we satisfactorily refer the name under which they are known in Wales: namely, 'bowing-stones'. For the idea that they were denominated 'bowing-stones' because to the people they formed objects of adoration is a supposition infinitely less satisfactory. The reader will perceive that we admit the phenomenon, when the mysterious *rapport* is effected, of the spontaneous sensitiveness and ultimate sympathetic motion of solid objects. No one who has witnessed the strange, unexplained power which tables, after proper preparation, acquire of supplying intelligent signals--impossible as it may seem to those who have not witnessed and tested these phenomena--but will see that there is great likelihood of these magic stones having been reared and haunted by the people for this special sensitive capacity. This idea would greatly increase the majesty and the wonder of them; in other respects, except for some extraordinary and superstitious use, these mysterious, solitary stones appear objectless.

The famous 'Round Table' of King Arthur--in regard to which that mystic hero is understood to have instituted an order of knighthood[7]--may have been a magical consulting-disc, round which he and his peers sat for oracular directions. As it is of large dimensions, it presents a similarity not only to some of the

---

[7] It was also something else--to which we make reference in other parts of our book.

prophesying-stones, but also, in a greater degree, to the movable enchanted drums of the Lapps and Finns, and to the divining-tables of the Shamans of Siberia. There lies an unsuspected purpose, doubtless of a mysterious (very probably of a superstitious and supernatural) character, in this exceedingly ancient memorial of the mythic British and heroic time at Winchester.

When spires or steeples were placed on churches, and succeeded the pyramidal tower, or square or round towers, these pointed erections were only the perpetuations of the original monolith. The universal signal was reproduced through the phases of architecture. The supposition that the object of the steeple was to point out the church to the surrounding country explains but half its meaning. At one period of our history, the signal-lights abounded all over the country as numerously as church-spires do in the present days. Exalted on eminences, dotting hills, spiring on cliffs, perched on promontories--from sea inland, and from the interior of the country to broad river-side and to the sea-shore--rising from woods, a universal telegraph, and a picturesque landmark--the tower, in its meaning, spoke the identical, unconscious tradition with the blazing Baal, Bael, or Beltane Fires: those universal votive torches, which are lost sight of in the mists of antiquity, and which were so continual in the Pagan countries, so reiterated through the early ages, and which still remain so frequent in the feudal and monastic periods--these were all connected closely with religion. The stone tower was only, as it were, a 'stationary flame'. The origin of beacons may be traced to the highest antiquity. According to the original Hebrew (which language as the Samaritan, is considered by competent judges as the very oldest), the word 'beacon' may be rendered a mark, monolith, pillar, or upright. At one time the ancient Bale, Bel, or religious fires of Ireland were general all over the country. They have been clearly traced to a devotional origin, and are strictly of the same character as the magic, or Magian, fires of the East. During the political discontents of 1831 and 1832, the custom of lighting these signal-fires was very generally revived amidst the party-distractions in Ireland. In the ancient language of this country, the month of May is yet called '*nic Beal tienne*', or the month of Beal (Bel or Baal's) fire. The Beltane festival in the Highlands has been ascribed to a similar origin. Druidical altars are still to be traced on many of the hills in Ireland, where Baal (Bel or Beal) fires were lighted. Through the countries, in the present day, which formed the ancient Scandinavia, and in Germany, particularly in the North, on the first of May, as in celebration of some universal feast or festival, fires are even now lighted on the tops of the hills. How closely this practice accords with the superstitious usages of the Bohemians, or 'Fire-kings,' of Prague, is discoverable at a glance. All these western flames are representative of the early fire, which was as equally the object of worship of the Gubhs, Guebres, or Gaurs of Persia, as it is the admitted natural principle of the Parsees. Parsees, Bohemians, the Gipsies or Zingari, and the Guebres, all unite in a common legendary fire-worship.

Beside the ancient market-crosses and wayside Gothic uprights, of which so many picturesque specimens are yet to be found in England, Wales, and Scotland, we may enumerate the splendid funeral-crosses raised by the brave and pious King Edward to the memory of his wife. Holinshed writes: 'In the nineteénth yeare of King Edward, quéene Elianor, King Edward's wife, died, upon saint Andrew's euen, at Hirdebie, or Herdelie (as some haue), neere to Lincolne. In euerie towne and place where the corpse rested by the waie, the King caused a crosse of cunning workmanship to be erected in remembrance of hir'. Two of the like crosses were set up at London--one at 'Westcheape' (the last but one), 'and the other at Charing', which is now Charing Cross, and where the last cross was placed.

The final obsequies were solemnized in the Abbey Church at Westminster, on the Sunday before the day of St. Thomas the Apostle, by the Bishop of Lincoln; and the King gave twelve manors and hamlets to the Monks, to defray the charges of yearly *obits*, and of gifts to the poor, in lasting commemoration of his beloved consort. Some writers have stated. the number of crosses raised as above at thirteen. These were, Lincoln, Newark, Grantham,, Leicester, Stamford, Geddington, Northampton, Stoney-Stratford, Woburn, Dunstable, St. Alban's, Waltham, Westcheape (Cheapside), not far from where a fountain for a long time took the place of another erection, and where the statue of Sir Robert Peel now stands. The last place where the body rested, whence the memorial-cross sprung, and which the famous equestrian statue of King Charles the First now occupies, is the present noisy highway of Charing Cross; and, as then, it opens to the royal old Abbey of Westminster. What a changed street is this capital opening at Charing Cross, Whitehall, and Parliament Street from the days--it almost then seeming a river-bordered country road--when the cross spired at one end, and, the old Abbey closed the views southwards.

In regard to the royal and sumptuous obsequies of Queen Eleanor, Fabian, who compiled his *Chronicles* towards the latter part .of the reign of Henry VII, speaking of her burial-place, has the following remark: '*She hathe II wexe tapers brennynge upon her tombe both daye and nyght. Which so hath contynned syne the day of her buryinge to this present daye*'.

The beacon-warning, the Fiery Cross of Scotland, the universal use of fires on the tops of mountains, on the seashore, and on the highest turrets of castles, to give the signal of alarm, and to telegraph some information of importance, originated in the first religious flames. Elder to these summoning or notifying lights was the mysterious worship to which fire rose as the, answer. From religion the beacon passed into military use. On certain set occasions, and on special Saints' Days, and at other times of observance, as the traveller in Ireland well knows, the multitude of fires on the tops of the hills, and in any conspicuous situation, would gladden the eyes of the most devout Parsee. The special subject of illumination, however We may have become accustomed to regard it as the most ordinary expression of triumph, and of mere joyous celebration, has its origin in a much more abstruse and sacred source. In Scotland, particularly, the reverential ideas associated with these mythic fires are strong.

Perhaps in no country have the impressions of superstition deeper hold than in enlightened, thoughtful, educated, and (in so many respects) prosaic Scotland; and in regard to these occult and ancient fires, the tradition of them, and the ideas concerning their origin, are preserved as a matter of more than cold speculation. Country legendary accounts and local usages--obtained from we know not whence--all referring to the same myth, all pointing to the same Protean superstition, are traceable, to the present, in all the English counties. Cairns in Scotland; heaps of stones in by-spots in England, especially--solitary or in group--to be found on the tops of hills; the Druidical mounds; the raising of crosses on the Continent, in Germany, amongst the windings of the Alps, in Russia (by the roadside, or at the entrance of villages), in Spain, in Poland, in lonely and secluded spots; probably even the first use of the 'sign-post' at the junction of roads; all these point, in strange, widely radiant suggestion, to the fire-religion.

Whence obtained is that word 'sign' as designating the guide, or. direction, post, placed at the intersection of cross-roads? Nay, whence gained we that peculiar idea of the sacredness, or of the 'forbidden', attaching to the spot where four roads meet? It is *sacer*, as sacred, in the Latin; 'extra-church', or 'heathen', supposedly 'unhallowed', in the modernacception. The appellative *ob* in the word 'obelisk' means occult, secret; or magic. *Ob* is the biblical name for sorcery. It is also found as a word signifying converse with forbidden spirits; among the negroes on the coast of Africa, from whence--and indicating the practices marked out by it--it was transplanted to the West Indies, where it still exists.

It is well known that a character resembling the Runic alphabet was once widely diffused throughout Europe. 'A character, for example, not unlike the hammer of Thor, is to be found in. various Spanish inscriptions, and lurks in many magical books. Sir William Jones', proceeds our author--we quote from the *Times* of the 2nd of February 1859, in reviewing a work upon Italy by the late Lord Broughton--'has drawn a parallel between the deities of Meru and Olympus; and an enthusiast might perhaps maintain that the vases of Alba Longa were a relic of the times when one religion prevailed in Latium and Hindustan. It is most singular that the Hindoo cross is precisely the hammer of Thor.' All our speculations tend to the same conclusion. One day, it is a discovery of cinerary vases; the next, it is etymological research; yet again, it is ethnological investigation; and, the day after, it is the publication of unsuspected tales from the Norse; but all go to heap up the proofs of our consanguinity with the peoples of History--and of an original general belief, we might add.

What meaneth the altar, with its mysterious lights? What mean the candles of the Catholic worship, burning even by day, borne in the sunshine, blazing at noon? What meaneth this visible fire, as an element at Mass, or at service at all? Wherefore is this thing, Light, employed as a primal witness and attestation in all worship? To what end, and expressive of what mysterious meaning--surviving through the changes of the faiths and the renewal of the Churches, and as yet undreamt--burn the solemn lamps in multitude, in their richly worked, their highly wrought, cases of solid gold or of glowing silver, bright-glancing in the mists of incense, and in the swell or fall of sacredly melting or of holily entrancing music? Before spiry shrine and elaborate drop-work tabernacle; in twilight hollow, diapered as into a 'glory of stone', and in sculptured niche; in the serried and starry ranks of the columned wax, or in rows of bossy cressets--intertwine and congregate the perfumed *flames* as implying the tradition eldest of time! What meaneth, in the Papal architectural piles, wherein the Ghostly Fire is enshrined, symbolic *real fire*, thus before the High Altar? What speak those constellations of lights? what those 'silvery stars of Annunciation'? What signifieth fire *upon* the altar? What gather we at all from altars and from sacrifice--the delivering, as through the *gate of fire*, of the first and the best of this world, whether of the fruits, whether of the flocks, whether of the primal and perfectest of victims, or the rich spoil of the 'world-states'? What mean the human sacrifices of the Heathen; the passing of the children through the fire to Moloch; the devotion of the consummate, the most physically perfect, and most beautiful, to the glowing Nemesis, in that keenest, strangest, yet divinest fire-appetite; the offered plunder, the surrendered lives, of the predatory races? What signifies the sacrifice of Iphigenia, the burning of living people among the Gauls, the Indian fiery immolations? What is intended even by the patriarchal sacrifices? What is the meaning of the burnt offerings, so frequent in the Bible? In short, what read we, and what seem we conclusively to gather, we repeat, in this mystic thing, and hitherto almost meaningless, if not contradictory and silencing institution of sacrifice by fire? What gather we, otherwise than in the explanation of the thing signified, by it? We speak of sacrifice as practised in all ages, enjoined in all holy books, elevated into veneration, as a necessity of the highest and most sacred kind. We, find it in all countries--east, west, north, and south; in the Old equally as in the New World. From whence should this strange and unexplainable rite come, and what should it mean? as, indeed, what should mean the display of bright fire *at all* in the mysteries, Egyptian, Cabiric, Scandinavian, Eleusinian, Etrurian, Indian, Persian, Primal American, Tartarian, Phœnician, or Celtic, from the earliest of time until this very modern, instant, English day of candles on altars, and of the other kindred religious High-Church lightings?--respecting which there rankleth such scandal, and intensifieth such purposeless babble, such daily dispute! What should all this inveterate ritualistic (as it is absurdly called) controversy, and this ill-understood bandying, be about? Is it that, even at this day, men do not understand anything about the symbols of their religion, and that the things for which they struggle are mere words? really that the principles of their wonderful and supernatural faith are perfectly unknown, and that they reason with the inconclusiveness, but with nothing of the simplicity of children--nothing of the divine light of children?

But, we would boldly ask, what should all this wealth of fire-subjects mean, of which men guess so little, and know less? What should this whole principle of fire and of sacrifice be? What should it signify but the rendering over, and the surrender-up, in all abnegation, of the state of man, of the best and most valued 'entities' of this world, past and through the fire, which is the boundary and border and wall between this world and the next?--that last element of all, on which is all--Fire--having most of the light of matter in it, as it hath most of the blackness of matter in it, to make it the fiercer; and both being copy, or shadow, of the Immortal and Ineffable Spirit-Light, of which, strange as it may sound, the sun is the very darkness! because that, and the whole Creation--as being Degree, or even, in its wonders, as Greater or Less--beautiful and godlike as it is to man, is as the shadow of God, and hath nothing of Him; but is instituted as the place of purification, 'being', or punishment: the opposite of God, the enemy of God, and, in its results, apart from the Spirit of God--which rescues supernaturally from it--the denier of God! This world and its shows--nay, Life--stands mystically as the Devil, Serpent, Dragon, or 'Adversary', typified through all time; the world terrestrial being the ashes of the fire celestial.

The torches borne at funerals are not alone for light; they have their mystic meaning. They mingle largely, as do candles on altars, in all solemn celebrations. The employment of light in all religious rites, and in celebration in the general sense, has an overpoweringly great meaning. Festival, also, claims flame as its secret signal and its password to the propitious Invisible. Lights and *flambeaux* and torches carried in the hand were ever the joyous accompaniment of weddings. The torch of Hymen is a proverbial expression. The ever-burning lamps of the ancients; the steady, silent tomb-lights (burning on for ages), from time to time discovered among the mouldering monuments of the past in the *hypogea*, or sepulchral caves, and buildings broken in upon by men in later day; the bonfires of the moderns; the fires on the tops of hills; the mass of lamps disposed about sanctuaries, whether encircling the most sacred point of the mosque of the Prophet, the graded and cumulative Grand Altar in St Peter's, of the saint-thrones in the churches of the Eternal City, or elsewhere, wherever magnificence riseth into expansion, and intensifieth and overpowereth in the sublimity which shall be *felt*; the multitudinous grouped lamps in the Sacred Stable--the Place of the Holy Nativity, meanest and yet highest--at Bethlehem; the steady, constant lights ever burning in mystic, blazing attestation in Jerusalem, before the tomb of the Redeemer; the *chapelle ardente* in the funeral observances of the ubiquitous Catholic Church; the congregated tapers about the bed of the dead--the flames in mysterious grandeur (and in royal awe), placed as in waiting, so brilliant and striking, and yet so terrible, a court, and surrounding the stately *catafalque;* the very word *falcated,* as bladed, sworded, or scimitared (as with the guard of waved or sickle-like flames); the lowly, single candle at the bedside of the poverty-attenuated dead--thus by the single votive light only allied (yet in unutterably mystic and godlike bond) as with the greatest of the earth; the watch-lights everywhere, and in whatever country; the crosses (spiry memorials, or monoliths) which rose as from out the earth, in imitation of the watching candle, at whatever point rested at night, in her solemn journey to her last home, the body of Queen Eleanor, as told in the English annals (which flame-memorials, so raised by the pious King Edward in the spiry, flame-imitating stone, are all, we believe, obliterate or put out of things, but the well-known, magnificent, restored cross at Waltham); all these, to the keen, philosophic eye, stand as the best proofs of the diffusion of this strange Fire-Dogma: mythed as equally, also, in that 'dark veiled Cotytto':

> She to whom the flame
> Of midnight torches burns.

'She', this blackest of concealment in the mysteries, Isis, Io, Ashtaroth, or Astarte; or Cybele- or Proserpine; 'he', this Baal, Bel, 'Baalim', Foh, Brahm, or Bhudd; 'it'--for the Myth is no personality, but sexless--Snake, Serpent, Dragon, or Earliest at all of Locomotion, under whatever 'Letter of the Alphabet'--all these symbols, shapes, or names, stand confessed in that first; absolutely primal, deified element, Fire, which the world, in all religions, has worshipped, is worshipping, and will worship to the end of time, unconsciously; we even in the Christian religion, and in our modern day, still doing it--unwitting the meaning of the mysterious symbols which pass daily before our eyes: all which.

point, as we before have said, to Spirit-Light as the soul of the World--otherwise, to the inexpressible mystery of the Holy Ghost.

Little is it suspected what is the myth conveyed in the Fackeltanz and Fackelzug of Berlin, of which so much was heard, as a curious observance, at the time of the marriage of the Princess Royal of England with the Prince Frederick William of Prussia. This is the Teutonic perpetuation of the 'Bacchic gloryings', of the Saturnian rout and flame-brandishing of the earliest and last rite.

The ring of light, glory, *nimbus, aureole,* or circle of rays, about the heads of sacred persons; the hand (magnetic and mesmeric) upon sceptres; the open hand borne in the standards of the Romans; the dragon crest of Maximin, of Honorius, and of the Barbarian Leaders; the Dragon of China and of Japan; the Dragon of Wales; the mythic Dragon trampled by St. George; the 'crowned serpent' of the Royal House of Milan; the cairns, as we have already affirmed, and the Runic Monuments; the *Round Towers of Ireland* (regarding which there hath been so much, and so diverse and vain speculation); the memorial piles, and the slender (on seashore and upland) towers left by the Vikinghs, or Sea-Kings, in their adventurous and predatory voyages; the legends of the Norsemen or the Normans; the vestiges so recently, in the discovery of the forward-of-the-old-time ages, exposed to the light of criticism, in the time-out-of-mind antique and quaint cities of the extinct peoples and of the forgotten religions in Central America: the sun or fire-worship of the Peruvians, and their vestal or virgin-guardians of the fire; the priestly fire-rites of the Mexicans, quenched by Cortez in the native blood, and, the context of their strange, apparently incoherently wild, belief; the inscriptions of amulets, on rings and on talismans; the singular, dark, and in many respects, uncouth *arcana* of the Bohemians, Zingari, Gitanos, or Gipsies; the teaching of the Talmud; the hints of the Cabala: also that little-supposed thing, even, meant in the British golden collar of 'S.S.', which is worn as a relic of the oldest day (in perpetuation of a *mythos* long ago buried--spark-like--and forgotten in the dust of ages) by some of our officials, courtly and otherwise, and which belongs to no known order of knighthood, but only to the very highest order of knighthood, the Magian, or to Magic; all these point, as in the diverging radii of the greatest of historical light-suns, to the central, intolerable ring of brilliancy, or the phenomenon--the original God's revelation, eldest of all creeds, survivor, almost, of Time--of the Sacred Spirit, or Ghostly Flame- the baptism of Fire of the Apostles!

In this apparently strange--nay, to some minds, alarming-- classification, and throwing under one head, of symbols diametrically opposed, as holy and unholy, benign and sinister, care must be taken to notice that the types of the 'Snake' or the 'Dragon' stand for the occult 'World-Fire', by which we mean the 'light of the human reason', or 'manifestation' in the general sense, as opposed to the spiritual light, or unbodied light; into which, as the reverse--although the same--the former transcends. Thus, *shadow* is the only possible means of demonstrating light. It is not reflected upon that we must have means whereby to be lifted. After all, we deal only with *glyphs*, to express inexpressible things. Horns mean spirit-manifestation; Radius signifies the glorying absorption (into the incomprehensible) of that manifestation. Both signify the same: from any given point, the One Spirit working downwards, and also transcending upwards. From any given point, in height, that the intellect is able to achieve, the same spirit downwards intensifies into Manifestation; upwards, dissipates into God. In other words, before any knowledge of God can be formed at all, it must have a shape. God is an abstraction; Man is an entity.

CHAPTER THE FOURTEENTH

INQUIRY AS TO THE POSSIBILITY OF MIRACLE

THE definition of a miracle has been exposed to numerous erroneous views. Inquirers know not what a miracle is. It is wrong to assume that nature and human nature are alike invariably, and that you can, interpret the one by the other. There may be in reality great divergence between the two, though both start from the common point--individuality. A miracle is not a violation of the laws of nature (because nature is not everything), but a something independent of all laws--that is, *as we know laws*. The mistake that is so commonly made is the interpreting--or rather the perceiving, or the becoming aware of--that thing we denominate a miracle through the operation of the human senses, which in reality have nothing whatever to do with a miracle, because they cannot know it. If nature, as we understand it, or law, as we understand it, be universal, then, as nothing can be possible to us which contradicts either the one or the other (both being the same)--nature being law, and law being nature--miracle must be impossible, and there never was, nor could there ever be, such a thing as a miracle. But a miracle works outwardly from us at once, and not by a human path--moves away from the world (that is, man's world) as a thing impossible to it, though it may be true none the less, since our nature is not all nature; nor perhaps any nature, but even a philosophical delusion. In the conception of a miracle; however, the thing apprehended revolves to us, and can come to us in no other way, and we seize the idea of it through a machinery--our own judgment--which is a clear, sight compounded of our senses--a synthesis of senses that, in the very act of presenting an impossible idea, destroys it as *humanly* possible. Miracle can be of no date or time, whether earlier, whether later, if God has not withdrawn from nature; and if He has withdrawn from nature, then nature must have before this fallen to pieces of itself; for God is intelligence--not life only; and matter is not intelligent, though it may be living. It is not seen that during that space--which is a space taken out of time, though independent of it--in which miracle is possible to us, we cease to be men, because time, or rather sensation, is man's measure; and that when we are men again, and back in ourselves, the miracle is gone, because the conviction of the possibility of a thing and its non-possibility has expelled it. The persuasion of a miracle is intuition, or the operation of God's Spirit active in us, that drives out nature for the time, which is the opposite of the miracle.

No miracle can be justified to men's minds, because no amount of evidence can sustain it; no number of attestations can affirm that which we cannot in our nature believe. In reality, we believe nothing of which our senses do not convince us--even these not always. In other matters, we only believe *because we think we believe;* and since the conviction of a miracle has nothing of God except the certain sort of motive of possessed, excluding exaltation, which, *with the miracle,* fills us, and to which exaltation we can give no name, and which we can only feel as a certain something in us, a certain power and a certain light, conquering and outshining another light, become fainter--it will follow that the conviction of the possibility of a miracle is the same sort of unquestioning assurance that we have of a dream *in the dream itself;* and that, when the miracle is apprehended in the mind, it just as much ceases to be a miracle when we are in our senses, as a dream ceases to be that which it was, a reality, and becomes that which it is, nonentity, when we awake. But to the questions, what is a dream?--nay, what is waking?--who shall answer? or who can declare whether in that broad outside, where our minds and their powers evaporate or cease, where nature melts away into nothing that we can know as nature, or know as anything else, in regard to dreams and realities, the one may not be the other? The dream may be man's life to him--as another life other than his own life--and the reality may be the dream (in its various forms), which he rejects as false and confusion simply because it is as an unknown language, of which, out of his dream, he can never have the alphabet, but of which, in the dream, he has the alphabet, and can spell well because *that* life is natural to him.

'A pretence that every strong and peculiar expression is merely an Eastern hyperbole is a mighty easy way of getting rid of the trouble of deep thought and right apprehension, and has helped to keep the world in ignorance.'--*Morsels of Criticism*, London, 1800.

It is very striking that, in all ages, people have clothed the ideas of their dreams in the same imagery. It may therefore be asked whether that language, which now occupies so low a place in the estimation of men; be not the actual waking language of the higher regions, while we, awake as we fancy ourselves, may be sunk in a 'sleep of many thousand years, or at least, in the echo of their dreams, and only intelligibly catch a few dim words of that language of God, as sleepers do scattered expressions from the loud conversation of those around them'. So says Schubert, in his *Symbolism of Dreams*. There is every form of the dream-state, from the faintest to the most intense, in which the gravitation of the outside world overwhelms the man-senses, and absorbs the inner unit. *In fact, the lightest and faintest form of dream is the very thoughts that we think.*

A very profound English writer, Thomas de Quincey, has the following: 'In the English rite of Confirmation, by personal choice, and by sacramental oath, each man says, in effect: "Lo! I rebaptize myself; and that which once was sworn on my behalf, now I swear for myself." Even so in dreams, perhaps, under some secret conflict of the midnight sleeper, lighted up to consciousness at the time, but darkened to the memory as soon as all is finished, each several child of our mysterious race may complete for himself the aboriginal fall.'

As to what is possible or impossible, no man, out of his presumption and of his self-conceit, has any right to speak, nor can he speak; for the nature of his terms with all things outside of him is unknown to him. We know that miracle (if once generally believed in) would terminate the present order of things, which are perfectly right and consistent in their own way. Things that contradict nature are not evoked by reason, but by man in his miracle-worked imagining, in all time; and such exceptions are independent of reason, which elaborates to a centre downwards, but exhales to apparent impossibilty (but to real truth) upwards, that is, truth out of this world.

Upwards has nothing of man; for it knows him not. He ceases there; but he is made as downwards, and finds his man's nature there, lowest of all--his mere bodily nature there perhaps, even to be found originally among the four-footed; for by the raising of him by God alone has Man got upon his feet, and set his face upward to regard the stars--those stars which originally, according to the great 'Hermes Trismegistus' (Thrice-Master), in the astrological sense, raised him from the primeval level; for we refer heaven always to a place over our heads, since there only we can be free of the confinements of matter; but above us or below us is equally the. altitude.

May not the sacrificial, sacramental rites--may not those minute acts of priestly offering, as they succeed each other, and deepen in intensity and in meaning--may not those aids of music to enlarge and change and conjure the sense of hearing, and to react on sight (it being notorious that object's change their character really as we look at them when operated upon by beautiful music)--may not those dream-producing, somnolent, enchanting vapours of incense, which seem to loosen from around each of us the walls of the visible, and to charm open the body, and to let out (or to let in) new and unsuspected senses, alight with a new light not of this world, the light of a new spiritual world, in which we can yet see things, and see them as things to be recognized--may not all this be true, and involve impossibilities as only seeming so, but true enough; inasmuch as miracle possibly is true enough?

May not all these effects, and may not the place and the persons in the body, and may not the suggestions, labouring to that end, of unseen, unsuspected, holy ministries, such as thronging angels, casting off from about us our swathes and bands of thick mortality in the new, overmastering influence--may not all this be as the bridge across which we pass out from this world gladly into the next, until we meet, as on the other side,

Jesus, the Ruler in very deed, but now felt as the Offered, the Crucified, the complete and accepted 'Living Great Sacrifice'? May we not in *this* 'Eucharist' partake, not once, but again and again, of that--even of that solid--which was our atonement, and of that blood which was poured out as the libation to the 'Great Earth', profaned by 'Sin', partaking of that reddest (but that most transcendently lucent) sacrament, which is to be the new light of a new world? Is not the very name of the intercommunicating High-Priest that of the factor. of this mystic, glorious, spirit-trodden, invisible 'bridge'? Whence do we derive the word *Pontifex*, or *Pontifex Maximus* (the Great, or the Highest, Bridge-Maker, or Builder), elicited in direct translation from the two Latin words *pons* and *facio* in the earliest pre-Christian theologies, and become 'Pontiff' in the Roman and the Christian sense--'Pontiff' from 'Pontifex'?

It is surely this meaning--that of fabricator or maker of the bridge between things sensible and things spiritual, between body and spirit, between this. world and the next world, between the spiritualizing 'thither' and the substantiating 'hither', *trans* being the transit. The whole word, if not the whole meaning, may be accepted in this Roman Catholic sense of 'transubstantiation', or the making of miracle. Never 'Idolatry'--but 'Idea' recognizing and acknowledging.

CHAPTER THE FIFTEENTH

CAN EVIDENCE BE DEPENDED UPON?
EXAMINATION OF HUME'S REASONING

'OUR evidence for the truth of the Christian religion is less than the evidence for the truth of our senses; because, even in the first authors of our religion, it was no greater. It is evident it must diminish in passing from them to their disciples; nor can any one rest such confidence in their testimony as in the immediate object of his senses.'

This is wrong, The testimony of some men is more valid than is the evidence of the senses of some others. All depends upon the power of the mind judging.

'It is a general maxim, that no objects have any discoverable connexion together. All the inferences which we can draw from one to another are founded merely on our experience of their constant and regular conjunction; It is evident that we ought not to make an exception to this maxim in favour of human testimony, whose connexion with any event seems in itself as little necessary as any other.'

It may be put to any person who carefully considers Hume's previous position as to the fixedness of the proofs of the senses, whether this last citation does not upset what he previously affirms.

'The memory is tenacious to a certain degree. Men commonly have an inclination to truth and a principle of probity. They are sensible to shame when detected in a falsehood. These are qualities in human nature.'

This is a mistake; for they are *not* qualities in human nature. They are the qualities of grown men, because they are reflective of the state of the man when he is living in community--not as man.

'Contrariety of evidence, in certain cases, may be derived from several different causes: from the opposition of contrary testimony--from the character or number of the witnesses--from the manner of their delivering their testimony--or from the union of all these circumstances. We entertain a suspicion concerning any matter of fact when the witnesses contradict each other--when they are but few, or of a doubtful character--when they have an interest in what they affirm--when they deliver their testimony with hesitation, or, on the contrary, with too violent asseverations. There are many other particulars of the same kind, which may diminish or destroy the force of any argument derived from human testimony.'

Now, we contest these conclusions; and we will endeavour to meet them with a direct overthrowing answer. The recognition of likelihood--not to say of truth--is intuitive, and does not depend on testimony. In fact, sometimes our belief goes in another direction than the testimony, though it be even to matters of fact.

Hume resumes with his cool, logical statements: 'The reason why we place any credit in witnesses and historians is not derived from any connexion which we perceive *a priori* between testimony and reality, but *because we are accustomed to find a conformity between them*.'

Just so! we would add to this 'because we are accustomed to find a conformity between them.'

We are now arrived at the grand dictum of cool-headed, self-possessed Hume, who thought that by dint of his logical clearness, and by his definitions, he had exposed the impossibility of that unaccountable thing which men call a miracle, and upon the possibility or the non-possibility of which religion will, be ultimately found to wholly depend, because religion is, entirely opposed to laws of 'must be' and 'must not be'.

'A miracle is a violation of the *laws of nature*' he declares.

Not so, we will rejoin. It is only a violation of the laws of *our* nature. A very different thing. We have no right to set *our* nature up as the measure of *all* nature. This is merely the mind's assumption; and it is important to expose its real emptiness, because all Hume's philosophy turns upon this, which he imagines to be a rigid axiom, to which all argument must recur.

'A firm and unalterable experience has established the laws of nature. The proof against a miracle, from the very nature of the fact, is as entire as any argument from experience can possibly be imagined.' So says Hume.

But experience has nothing to do with a miracle, because it is a sense not comprised in the senses, but an unexperienced sensation or perception, exposing the senses as dreams, and overriding their supposed certainty and totality by a *new dream*, or apparent certainty, contradicting the preceding. If this were not possible, then the senses, or the instantaneous judgment which comes out of their sum--or the thing 'conviction' as we call it-- would be the measure of everything past, present, and to come-- which we know it is not.

Hume, or any. philosopher, is wrong in dogmatizing at all; because he only speaks from his own experience; and individual experience will in no wise assist towards the discovery of real truth. In philosophy, no one has a right to lay down any basis, and to assume it as true. The philosopher must always argue negatively, not affirmatively. The moment he adopts the latter course, he is lost. Hume presupposes all his *Treatise on Miracles* in this single assumption that nature itself has laws, and not laws *only to our faculties.* The mighty difference between these two great facts will be at once felt by a thinker; but we will not permit Hume to assume anything where he has no right, and so to turn the flank of his adversary by artfully putting forward unawares and carrying an assumption. Nature is only nature in man's mina, but not true otherwise, any more than that the universe exists out of the mind--or out of the man, who has in thinking to make it. Take away, therefore, the man in whom the idea of it is, and the universe disappears. We will question Hume, the disbelieving philosopher, as to his right to open his lips, because it is very doubtful if language, which is the power of expression, any more than that which we call consistent thought, is inseparably consistent to man, who is all inconsistence in his beginning, middle, and end--in his coming here and in his going hence from here, out of this strange world; to which he does not seem really to belong, and in which world he seems to have been somehow obtruded, as something not of it--strange as this seems.

As to the philosophy of Hume, granting the ground, you have, of course, all the basis for, the constructions raised upon that ground. But suppose we, who argue in opposition to Hume, dispute his ground?

Hume, in his *Treatise on Miracles*, only begs the question; and there is therefore no wonder that, having first secured his position by consent or negligence of the opponent, he may deal from it the shot of what artillery he pleases; and his opponent, having. once allowed the first ground--or the capacity to argue--has unwittingly let in all the ruinous results which follow; these philosophically are indisputable. We would urge that Hume has no capacity to argue in this way, inasmuch as he has taken the 'human 'mind' as the capacity of arguing. Either .reason or miracle must be first removed, because you can admit either; for they are opposites, and cannot camp in the same mind one is idea, the other is no idea--in this world; and as we are in this world, we can only judge as in this world. In another world, Hume the philosopher may himself be an impossibility, and therefore be a miracle, through his own philosophy, and the application of it.

Hume is the man of ideas, and is therefore very correct, as a philosopher, if philosophy were possible; but we deny that it is possible in regard to any speculation out of this world. Ideas--that is, philosophical ideas--may be described as the steps of the ladder by which we philosophically descend *from* God. Emotions are also the steps by which alone we can ascend *to* Him. Human reason is a possibility, from the line drawn by which either ascent or descent may be made. The things Necessity, or Fate, and Free Will, passing into the mind of man (*both* may be identical in their nature, though opposite in their operation), *dictate* from the invisible, but *persuade* from the visible.

Hume asserts that 'a uniform experience amounts to a proof'. It does not do so, any more than 'ninety-nine' are a 'hundred'.

He also says that 'there is not to be found in all history any miracle attested by a sufficient number of men to be believed.' Now, we will rejoin to this, that a public miracle is a public impossibility; for the moment it has become public, it has ceased to be a miracle. 'In the case of any particular assumed miracle', he further says, 'there are not a sufficient number of men of such unquestioned good sense, education, and learning as to secure us against all delusion in themselves--of such undoubted integrity as to place them beyond all suspicion of any design to *deceive others.*' Now, to this our answer is, that our own senses deceive us; and why, then, should not the asseverations of others?

Hume adduces a number of circumstances which, he insists, 'are requisite to give us a full assurance in the testimony of men'; but nothing can give us this assurance in other men's testimony that he supposes. We judge of circumstances ourselves, upon our own ideas of the testimony of men--not upon the testimony itself; for we sometimes believe that which the witnesses, with the fullest reliance upon themselves, deny. We judge upon our own silent convictions--that is, upon all abstract points. It is for this reason that assurances even by angels, in Scripture, have not been believed by the persons to whom the message was directly sent. Of course, if the miracle was displayed through the ordinary channels of human comprehension, it was no miracle; for comprehension never has miracle in it.

'The maxim by which we commonly conduct ourselves in our reasonings is, that the objects of which we have no experience resemble those of which we have' says Hume.

Now, this remark is most true; but we cannot help this persuasion. We conclude inevitably that things unknown should resemble things known, because, whatever may be outside of our nature, we have no means of knowing it, or of discovering anything else that is other than ourselves. We can know nothing, except through our own machinery of sense. As God made outside and inside, God alone works, though we think that *we--*that is, Nature--work. God (who is Himself miracle) can effect impossibilities, and make two one by annihilating the distinction between them.

Hume says that 'where there is an opposition of arguments, we ought to give the preference to such as are founded on the *greatest number of past observations.*'

So we ought, if the world were real; but, as it is not, we ought not. Things unreal cannot make things real.

Hume declares that 'if the spirit of religion join itself to the love of wonder, there is an end of common sense. Human testimony, in these circumstances, loses all pretensions to authority. A religionist may be an enthusiast, and imagine he sees what has no reality. He may know his narrative to be false, and yet persevere in it with the best intentions in the world, for the sake of promoting so holy a cause. Even where this delusion has not taken place, vanity, excited by so strong a temptation, operates on him more powerfully than on the rest, of mankind in any other circumstances, and self-interest with equal force. His auditors may not have, and commonly have not, sufficient judgment to canvass his evidence. What judgment they have, they renounce by principle in these sublime and mysterious subjects. If they were ever so willing to employ it, passion and a heated imagination disturb the regularity of its operations. Their credulity increases his impudence, and his impudence overpowers their credulity.'

Now, the reverse of all this is more nearly the fact. Ordinary minds have more incredulity than credulity. It is quite a mistake to imagine that credulity is the quality of an ignorant mind; it is rather *incredulity* that is.

'Eloquence, when at its highest pitch', says Hume, 'leaves little room for reason or reflection.'

Now, on the contrary, true eloquence is the embodiment or *synthesis* of reason and reflection.

'Eloquence', resumes Hume, 'addresses itself entirely to the fancy or the affections, captivates the willing hearers, and subdues their understanding. Happily, this pitch it seldom attains; but what a Tully or a Demosthenes could scarcely effect over a Roman or Athenian audience, every capuchin, every itinerant or stationary teacher, can perform over the generality of mankind, and in a higher degree, by touching such gross and vulgar passions.'

All the above is simply superficial assumption.

Hume then of 'forged miracles and prophecies'; but there is no proof of any *forged* miracle or prophecy. He says that 'there is a strong propensity in mankind to the extraordinary and the marvellous. There is no kind of report which rises so easily and spreads so quickly, especially in country places and provincial towns, as those concerning marriages, insomuch that two young persons of equal condition never see each other, twice, but the whole neighbourhood immediately join them together.'

This is all nonsense. There is always a reason for these suppositions.

Hume then goes on to adduce this same love of inspiring curiosity and delight in wonders as the cause of the belief in miracles.

'Do not', he asks, 'the same passions, and others still stronger, incline the generality of mankind to believe and report, with the greatest vehemence and assurance, all religious miracles?'

Now, this is only very poor.; and, besides, it is all assumption of truths where they are not.

Hume speaks of supernatural and miraculous relations as having been received from 'ignorant and barbarous ancestors'. But what is ignorance and barbarism?--and what is civilization? He says that they have been 'transmitted with that inviolable sanction and authority which always attend received opinions'. But supernatural and miraculous relations have never been received opinions. They have always been contested, and have made their way *against* the common sense of mankind, because the common sense of mankind is common sense, and nothing more; and, in reality, common sense goes but a very little way, even in the common transactions of life; for *feeling* guides us in most matters.

'All belief in the extraordinary', Hume declares, 'proceeds from the usual propensity of mankind towards the marvellous, which only receives a check at intervals from sense and learning'. But what are sense and learning both but mere *conceits?*

'"It is strange", a judicious reader is apt to say', remarks Hume, 'upon the perusal of these wonderful histories, "that such prodigious events never happen in our days".' But such events *do* occur, we would rejoin; though they are never believed, and are always treated as fable, when occurring in their own time.

'It is experience only', says Hume, 'which gives authority to human testimony'. Now, it is not experience only which induces belief, but recognition. It is not ideas, but light. We do not go to the thing in ideas, but the thing comes into us, as it were: for instance, a man never finds that he is awake by experience, but by influx of the thing 'waking'--whatever the act of waking is, or means.

'When two kinds of experience are contrary, we have nothing to do but to *subtract the one from the other*, and embrace an opinion either on one side or the other, with that assurance which arises from the remainder.'

This which follows may be a conclusion in regard to the above. If beliefs were sums, we should, and could, subtract the difference between two amounts of evidence, and accept the product; but we cannot help our beliefs, because they are intuitions, and not statements.

Hume towards the close of his strictly hard and logical *Treatise on Miracles*, brings forward an argument, which to all appearance is very rigid and conclusive, out of this his realistic philosophy--if that were true:

'Suppose that all the historians who treat of England should agree that on the 1st of January 1600 Queen Elizabeth died, that both before and after her death she was seen by her physicians and the whole court, as is usual with persons of her rank, that her successor was acknowledged and proclaimed by the parliament, and that, after being interred a month, she again appeared, resumed the throne, and governed England for three years. I must confess that I should be surprised at the concurrence of so many odd circumstances, but should not have the least inclination to believe so miraculous an event. *I should not doubt of her pretended death, and of those other public circumstances that followed it.*'

Now, in their own sequence, as they occur to us as real facts in the world, so unreal even are true, positive circumstances, that we only believe them by the same means that we believe dreams--that is, by intuition. There is no fact, so to say. Startling as it may appear, I appeal to the consciousness of those who have witnessed death whether the death itself did not seem unreal, and whether it did not remain without belief as' a fact until the negative--that, is 'The dead man is not here'--affirmed it, not through present persuasions, but through unreal incidents, post-dating reappearance.

As to the belief in miracles, Hume asserts that the Christian religion cannot be believed by any reasonable person without a miracle. 'Mere reason', he assures us, 'is insufficient to convince us of its veracity; and whoever is moved by faith to assent to it, is conscious of a continued miracle in his own person, which subverts all the principles of his understanding.'

The theosophic foundation of the Bhuddistic *Maya*, or Universal Illusion, has been finely alluded to by Sir William Jones, who was deeply imbued with the Oriental mysticism and transcendental religious views.

'The inextricable difficulties', says he, 'attending the *vulgar notion of material substances*, concerning which we know this only, that we know nothing, induced many of the wisest among the ancients, and some of the most enlightened among the moderns, to believe that the whole creation was rather an *energy* than a work, by which the Infinite Being, who is present at all times and in all places, exhibits to the minds of His creatures a set of perceptions, like a wonderful picture or piece of music, always varied, yet always uniform; so that all bodies and their qualities exist, indeed, to every wise and useful purpose, but exist only as far as they are *perceived*--a theory no less pious than sublime, and as different from any principle of atheism as the brightest sunshine differs from the blackest midnight.'

CHAPTER THE SIXTEENTH.

FOOTSTEPS OF THE ROSICRUCIANS AMIDST ARCHITECTURAL OBJECTS

THOMAS VAUGHAN, of Oxford, a famous Rosicrucian, whom we have before mentioned, and who in the year 1650 published a book upon some of the mysteries of the Rosicrucians, has the following passage. His work is entitled *Anthroposophia Theomagica*; it has a supplemental treatise, called *Anima Magica Abscondita*; we quote from pages 26 and 27 of the united volume:

'In regard of the *Ashes of Vegetables*', says Vaughan, 'although their *weaker exterior Elements* expire by violence of the *fire*, yet their *Earth* cannot be *destroyed*, but is *Vitrified*. The *Fusion* and *Transparency* of this substance is occasioned by the *Radicall moysture* or *Seminal water* of the *Compound*. This water resists the fury of the Fire, and cannot possibly be vanquished. "*In hac Aqua* (saith the learned Severine), *Rosa latet in Hieme*." These two principles are never separated; for *Nature* proceeds not so *far* in her Dissolutions. When Death hath done her worst, there is an *Vnion* between *these two*, and out of them shall God *raise* us at the last day, and restore us to a *spiritual constitution*. I do not conceive there shall be a Resurrection of every *Species*, but rather their *Terrestrial* parts, together with the element of Water *(for there shall be "no more sea*"; *Revelation*), shall be united in one mixture with the Earth, and fixed to a pure *Diaphanous substance*. This is St. John's Crystall gold, a *fundamentall* of the New Jerusalem--so called, not in respect of Colour, but constitution. Their *Spirits*, I suppose, shall be reduced to their first *Limbus*, a *sphere* of pure, ethereall *fire*, like rich Eternal Tapestry spread under the Throne of God.'

Coleridge has the following, which bespeaks (and precedes), be it remarked, Professor Huxley's late supposed original speculations. The assertion is that the matrix or formative substance is, at the base, in all productions, 'from mineral to man', the same.

'The germinal powers of the plant transmute the fixed air and the elementary base of water into grass or leaves; and on these the organific principle in the ox or the elephant exercises an alchemy still more stupendous. As the unseen agency weaves its magic eddies, the foliage becomes indifferently the bone and its marrow, the pulpy brain or the solid ivory; and so on through all the departments of nature.'--Coleridge's *Aids to Reflection*, 6th edn., vol. i. p. 328. See also Herder's *Ideen*, book v. cap. iii.

We think that we have here shown the origin of all Professor Huxley's speculations on this head appearing in his *Lectures*, and embodied in articles by him and others in scientific journals and elsewhere.

In a lecture delivered at the Royal Institution, Mr. W. S., Savory made the following remarks: 'There is close relationship between the animal and the vegetable kingdoms. The organic kingdom is connected with both by the process of crystallization, which closely resembles some of the processes of vegetation and of the growth of the lower orders of animal creation.'

The 'Philosopher's Stone', in one of its many senses, may be taken to mean the magic mirror, or translucent 'spirit-seeing crystal', in which things impossible to ordinary ideas are disclosed. 'Know', says Synesius, 'that the *Quintessence*' (five-essence) 'and hidden thing of our "stone" is nothing less than our celestial and glorious soul, drawn by our magistery out of its mine, which engenders itself and brings itself forth.' The term for 'Chrystal', or 'Crystal' in Greek, is the following; which may be divided into twin or half-words in the way subjoined:

$$\text{ΧΡΥΣΤ} \mid \text{---} \mid \text{ΑΛΛΟΣ}$$

Crystal is a hard, transparent, colourless 'stone' composed of simple plates, giving fire with steel, not fermenting with acid *menstrua*, calcining in a strong fire, of a regular angular figure, supposed by some to be '*formed of dew* coagulated with nitre'.

Amber is a solidified resinous gum, and is commonly full of electricity. It was supposed, in the hands of those gifted correspondingly, to abound with the means of magic. In this respect it resembles the *thyrsus* or pinecone, which was always carried in processions--Bacchanalian or otherwise--in connexion with the mysteries. We can consider the name of the palace, or fortress or 'royal' house in Grenada, in Spain, in this respect following. The word 'Alhambra' or 'Al-Hambra', means the 'Red'. In Arabia this means the place of eminence, the 'place of places', or the 'Red', in the same acceptation that the sea between Arabia and. Egypt is called the 'Red Sea'. All spirits generally (in connexion with those things supposed to be evil or indifferent especially) are 'laid' in the 'Red Sea', when disposed of by exorcism, or in forceful conjuration. We think that this 'Hambra', 'ambra', or 'ambre', is connected with the substance amber, which is sometimes very red, and which amber has always been associated with magical influence, magical formularies, and with spirits. We have seen an ancient crucifix, carved in amber, which was almost of the *redness* of coral. Amber has always been a substance (or gem, or gum) closely mingling with superstitions, from the most ancient times. For further connected ideas of the word 'amber,' and the substance 'amber' in relation to magic and sorcery, and for the recurrence of the word 'amber' and its varieties in matters referring to the mysteries and the mythology generally of ancient times, the reader will please to refer to other parts of this volume.

While excavations were in progress at a mound in Orkney, described by Mr. John Stuart, Secretary of the Society of Antiquaries of Scotland, on July 18th, 1861, numerous lines of 'runes' of various sizes were found on the walls and on the roof of a large vaulted chamber in the earth. When the discoveries were completed, the series of runes exceeded 700 in number; figures of '*dragons and a cross*' were also cut on some of the slabs. There are many mounds of various forms and sizes in this part of Orkney, and there is a celebrated circle of Druidical Stones on the narrow peninsula which divides the two lochs of Stennis.

Pliny says that the word 'boa', for a snake, comes from 'bovine', because '*young snakes are fed with cow's milk*'. Here we have the unexpected and unexplained connexion of the ideas of 'snake' and 'cow'. The whole subject is replete with mystery, as well as the interchange of the references to the 'Cross' and the 'Dragon' found in the *insignia* of all faiths, and lurking amongst all religious buildings.

On a Phœnician coin, found at Citium or Cyprus, and engraved in Higgins's *Celtic Druids*, p. 117, may be seen a cross and an animal resembling a *hippocampus*, both of which, or objects closely similar, appear on ancient sculptured stones in Scotland. The same two things, a cross and a strange-looking animal, half mammal, half fish or reptile, but called by Mr. Hodgson, of Newcastle-upon-Tyne, a Basilisk; appear together on a Mithraic sculptured slab of the Roman period, found in the North of England. What is more remarkable still, the 'star' and 'crescent', or 'sun' and 'moon', also appear, the whole being enclosed in what has been called the 'Fire-Triangle', or 'Triangle with its Face Upwards'.

The Builder, of June 6th, 1863, has some valuable observations on 'Geometrical and other Symbols'.

In regard to the word 'Alhambra', we may associate another word appropriated to Druidical Stones in England, *Men-Amber*. A famous Logan-Stone, commonly called 'Men-Amber', is in the parish of Sethney, near Pendennis, Cornwall. It is 11 feet long, 4 feet deep, and 6 feet wide. From this the following derivatives may be safely made: Men-Amber, Mon-Amber, Mon-Ambra, Mon-Amrha, Mon-Amra (M'Om-Ra, Om-Ra), 'Red Stone', or Magic, or Angelic, or Sacred Stone. This red colour is male--it signifies the Salvator.

The following is the recognitory mark or talisman of the Ophidiæ: Φ. The Scarabæus, Bee, Ass, Typhon, Basilisk, Saint-Basil, the town of Basle (Basil, or Bâle), in Switzerland (of this place it may be remarked, that the appropriate cognisance is a 'basilisk' or a 'snake'), the mythic horse, or *hippocampus*, of Neptune, the lion, winged (or natural), the Pegasus or winged horse, the Python, the Hydra, the Bull (Osiris), the Cow (or Io), are mythological ideas which have each a family connexion. All the above signify an identical myth. This we shall presently show conclusively, and connect them all with the worship of fire.

Our readers have no doubt often wondered to see on the table-monuments in Christian cathedrals a creature resembling a dog, or generally like some four-footed animal, trampled by the feet of the recumbent effigy. It is generally a male which is represented as performing this significant efforcement, trampling or piercing with the point of his sword, or the butt of the crosier (in his *left hand*, be it remembered). This crosier is the ancient *pedum*, or *lituus*. At Brent-Pelham, in Hertfordshire, there is a tomb, bearing the name of a knight, Pierce Shonke, *built in the wall*. He is said to have died A.D. 1086. Under the feet of the figure there is a *cross-flourie*, and under the cross a serpent (Weever, p. 549). There is an inscription which, translated, means:

Nothing of Cadmus nor Saint George, those names of great renown, survives them but their names;
But Shonke *one serpent kills*, *t'other defies*, And in this wall, *as in a fortress*, lies.

See Weever's *Ancient Funeral Monuments*. He calls the place '*Burnt* Pelham', and he says: 'In the wall of this Church lieth a most ancient Monument: A Stone wherein is figured a man, and about him an Eagle, a Lion, and a Bull, having all wings, and a fourth of the shape of an Angell, as if they should represent the four Evangelists: under the feet of the man is a crosse Flourie.'

'The being represented cross-legged is not always a proof of the deceased having had the merit either of having been a *crusader*, or having made a pilgrimage to the Holy Sepulchre. I have seen at Milton, in Yorkshire, two figures of the *Sherbornes* thus represented, who, I verily believe, could never have had more than a wish to enter the Holy Land.' Pennant writes thus of the Temple, London. Weever points out, in relation to the monument of Sir Pierce or Piers Shonke described above: 'Under the Cross is a Serpent. Sir Piers Shonke is thought to havve been sometime the Lord of an ancient decaied House, well moated, not farre from this place, called "O Piers Shonkes". He flourished *Ann. a conquestu, vicesimo primo*.'--Weever, p. 549.

'The personation of a *dog*--their invariable accompaniment, as it is also found amongst the sculptures of Persepolis, and in other places in the East--*would*

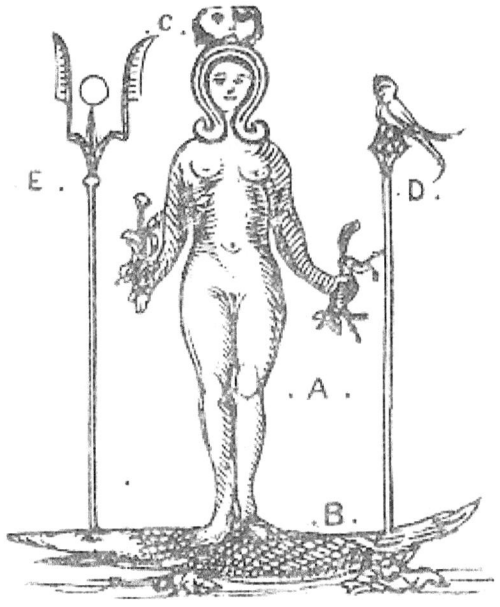

Fig. 23

in itself be sufficient to fix the heathen appropriation of these crosses' (the ancient Irish crosses), 'as that animal can have no possible relation to Christianity; whereas, by the Tuath-de-danaans, it was accounted *sacred*, and its maintenance enjoined by the ordinances of the state, as it is still in the Zend books, which remain after Zoroaster.'--O'Brien's *Round Towers of Ireland*, 1834, p. 359.

'I apprehend the word "Sin" came to mean Lion when the Lion was the emblem of the Sun at his summer solstice, when he was in his glory, and the Bull and the "Man" were the signs of the Sun at the Equinoxes, and the Eagle at the winter solstice.'--*Anacalypsis*, vol. ii. p. 292.

Figure 23 is an Egyptian bas-relief, of which the explanation is the following: A is the Egyptian Eve trampling the Dragon (the goddess Neith, or Minerva); B, a Crocodile; C, Gorgon's head; D, Hawk (wisdom); E, feathers (soul).

'The first and strongest conviction which will flash on the mind of every ripe antiquary, whilst surveying the long series of Mexican and Toltecan monuments preserved in these various works, is the similarity which the ancient monuments of New Spain bear to the monumental records of Ancient Egypt. Whilst surveying them, the glance falls with familiar recognition on similar graduated pyramids, on similar marks of the same primeval *Ophite worship*, on vestiges of the same Triune and Solar Deity, on planispheres and temples, on idols and sculptures, some of rude and some of finished workmanship, often presenting the most striking affinities with the Egyptian.'--Stephens and Catherwood's *Incidents of Travel, in Central America*.

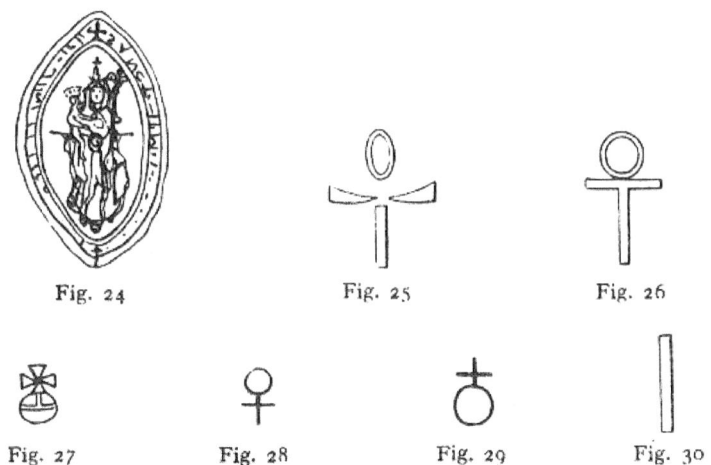

Fig. 24 Fig. 25 Fig. 26
Fig. 27 Fig. 28 Fig. 29 Fig. 30

CHAPTER THE SEVENTEENTH

THE ROUND TOWERS OF IRELAND

IT is astonishing how much of the Egyptian and the Indian symbolism of very early ages passed into the usages of Christian times. Thus: the *high cup* and the *hooked staff* of the god became the bishop's mitre and crosier; the term *nun* is purely Egyptian, and bore its present meaning; the *erect oval*, symbol of the Female Principle of Nature, became the Vesica Piscis, and a frame for Divine Things; the *Crux Ansata*, testifying the union of the Male and Female Principle in the most obvious manner, and denoting fecundity and abundance as borne in the god's hand, is transformed, by a simple inversion, into the Orb surmounted by the Cross, and the ensign of royalty. Refer to *The Gnostics and their Remains*, p. 72.

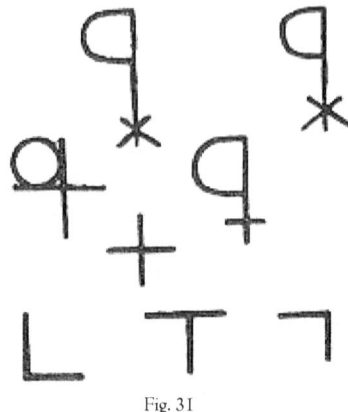

Fig. 31

The famous 'Stone of Cabar', Kaaba, Cabir, or Kebir, at Mecca, which is so devoutly kissed by the faithful, is a talisman. It is called the 'Tabernacle' (*Taberna*, or Shrine) of the Star Venus. 'It is said that the figure of Venus is seen to this day engraved upon it, with a crescent.' The very Caaba itself was at first an idolatrous temple, where the Arabians worshipped 'Al-Uza'--that is, Venus. See Bobovius, Dr. Hyde Parker, and others, for particulars regarding the Arabian and Syrian Venus. She is the 'Uraniæ-corniculatæ sacrum' (Selden, *De Venere Syriaca*). The 'Ihrâm is a sacred habit, which consists only of two woollen wrappers; one closed about the middle of devotees, to cover', etc., 'and the other thrown over the shoulders.' Refer to observations about Noah, later in our book; Sale's *Discourse*, p. 121; Pococke's *India in Greece*, vol. ii. part i. p. 218. The Temple of Venus at Cyprus was the Temple of Venus-Urania. 'No woman entered this temple' (Sale's *Koran*, chap. vii. p. 119; note, p. 149). Accordingly, Anna Commena and Glycas (in Renald. *De Mah.*) say that 'the Mahometans do worship Venus'. Several of the Arabian idols were no more than large, rude stones (Sale's *Discourse*, p. 20; *Koran*, chap. v. p. 82). The stone at Mecca is *black*. The crypts, the subterranean churches and chambers, the choirs, and the labyrinths, were all intended to enshrine (as it were) and to conceal the central object of worship, or this sacred 'stone'. The pillar of Sueno, near Forres, in Scotland, is an obelisk. These obelisks were all astrological *gnomons*, or 'pins', to the imitative stellar mazes, or to the 'fateful charts', in the 'letter-written' skies. The astronomical 'stalls', or 'stables' were the many 'sections' into which the 'hosts' of the starry sky were distributed by the Chaldæans. The *Decumens* (or tenths), into which the ecliptic was divided, had also another name, which was *Ashre*, from the Hebrew particle *as*, or *ash*, which means 'fiery', or 'FIRE'. The Romans displayed reverence for the ideas connected with these sacred stones. Cambyses, in Egypt, left the obelisks or single magic stones. The *Linghams* in India were left untouched by the Mohammedan conquerors. The modern Romans have a *phallus* or *lingha* in front of almost all their churches. There is an obelisk, altered to suit Christian ideas (and surmounted in most instances in modern times by a cross), in front of every church in Rome. There are few churchyards in England without a *phallus* or obelisk. On the top is usually now fixed a dial. In, former times, when the obeliscar form was adopted for ornaments of all sorts, it was one of the various kinds of Christian acceptable cross which was placed on the summit. We have the single stone of memorial surviving yet in the Fire-Towers (*Round Towers of Ireland*). This *phallus*, upright, or 'pin of stone', is found in every Gilgal or Druidical Circle. It is the boundary-stone or *terminus*, the parish mark-stone; it stands on every motehill lastly (and chiefly), this stone survives in the stone in the coronation chair at Westminster (of which more hereafter), and also in the famous 'London Stone', or the *palladium*, in Cannon Street, City of London: which stone is said to be 'London's fate'--which we hope it is not to be in the unprosperous sense.

The letter 'S', among the Gnostics, with its. grimmer or harsher brother (or sister) 'Z', was called the 'reprobate' or 'malignant' letter. Of this portentous *sigma* (or sign) 'S' (the angular *and not serpentine* 'S' is the grinding or bass 'S'--the letter 'Z'), Dionysius the Halicarnassian says as follows: that the '*letter S makes a noise more brutal than human.* Therefore the ancients used it very sparingly' ('Περὶ συνθες': see, also, sect. 14 p of *Origin and Progress of Language*, vol. ii. p. 233).

Notwithstanding the contentions of opposing antiquaries, and the usually received ideas that the 'Irish Round Towers' were of Christian, and not heathen, origin, the following book, turning up very unexpectedly, seems to settle the question in favour of O'Brien, and of those who urge the incredibly ancient devotion of the Round Towers to a heathen myth--fire-worship, in fact.

'John O'Daly, 9 Anglesea Street, Dublin. Catalogue of Rare and Curious Books, No. 10, October 1855, Item 105: *De Antiquitate Turrum Belanorum Pagana Kerriensi, et de Architectura non Campanilis Ecclesiasticæ*, T. D. Corcagiensi, Hiberno. Small 4to, old calf, with numerous woodcut engravings of Round Towers interspersed through the text, £10. Lovanii, 1610.' The bookseller adds 'I never saw another copy of this curious old book.' This book--which there is no doubt is genuine--would seem finally to settle the question as to the character of these Irish Round Towers, which are not Christian belfries, as Dr. George Petrie, and others sharing his erroneous beliefs, persistently assure us, but heathen *Lithoi*, or obelisks, in the sense of all those referred to in other parts of this work. They were raised in the early religions, as the objects of a universal worship. All antiquaries know of what object the *phallus* stands as the symbolical representation. It needs not to be more particular here.

The '*Fleur-de-Lis*' is a sacred symbol descending from the Chaldæans, adopted by the Egyptians, who converted it into the deified '*scarab*', the emblem of the Moon-god; and it is perpetuated in that mystically magnificent badge of France, the female 'Lily', or 'Lis'. All the proofs of this lie concealed in our Genealogy of the Fleur-de-Lis, and the 'Flowers-de-Luce', or the 'Fleurs-de-Lis', *passim*. It means 'generation', or the vaunt realized of the Turkish Soldan, '*Donec totum impleat orbem*'. The 'Prince of Wales's Feathers', we believe to be, and to mean, the same thing as this sublime 'Fleur-de-Lis'. It resembles the object closely, with certain effectual, ingenious disguises. The origin of the

Prince of Wales's plume is supposed to be the adoption of the king's crest (by Edward the Black Prince, at the battle of Cressy), on the discovery of the slain body of the blind King of Bohemia. Bohemia again!--the land of the 'Fire-worshipping Kings' whose palace, the Radschin, still exists on the heights near Prague. We believe the crest and the motto of the Prince of Wales to have been in use, for our Princes of Wales, at a much earlier period, and that history, in this respect, is perpetuating an error--perhaps an originally intended mistake. We think the following, which appears now for the first time; will prove this fact. Edward the Second, afterwards King of England, was the first Prince of Wales. There is reason to suppose that our valiant Edward the First, a monarch of extraordinary acquirements, was initiated into the knowledge of the abstruse Orientals. An old historian has the following: 'On their giving' (i.e. the assembled Welsh) 'a joyful and surprised assent to the King's demand, whether they would accept a king born really among them, and therefore a true Welshman, he presented to them his new-born son, exclaiming in broken Welsh "Eich dyn!", that. is "This is your man"--which has been corrupted into the present motto to the Prince of Wales's crest, "Ich dien", or "I serve". The meaning of 'I serve' in this view, is, that 'I' suffice, or 'the Lis', or '*the act*', suffices (refer to pages and figures *post*), for all the phenomena of the world.

CHAPTER THE EIGHTEENTH

PRISMATIC INVESTITURE OF THE MICROCOSM

THE chemical dark rays are more bent than the luminous. The chemical rays increase in power as you ascend the *spectrum*, from the red ray to the violet. The chemical rays typified by the Egyptians under the name of their divinity, Taut or Thoth, are most powerful in the morning; the luminous rays are most active at noon (Isis, or abstractedly 'manifestation'); the heating rays (Osiris) are most operative in the afternoon. The chemical rays are the most powerful in spring (germination, 'producing', or 'making'), the most luminous in the summer (ripening, or 'knowing'), the most heating in the autumn (perpetuating). The chemical rays have more power in the Temperate Zone; the luminous and heating, in the Tropical. There are more chemical rays given off from the centre of the sun than from the parts near its circumference.

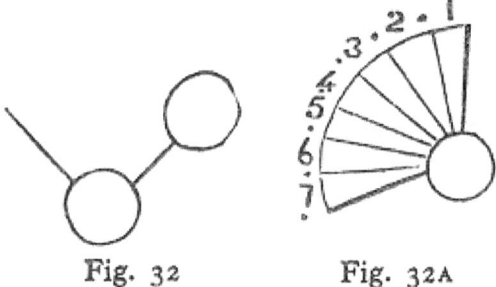

Fig. 32   Fig. 32A

Each prismatic atom, when a ray of light strikes upon it, opens out on a vertical axis, as a *radius* or fan of seven different 'widths' of the seven colours, from the *least* refrangible red up to the *most* refrangible violet. (Refer to diagram above.)

'The Egyptian Priests chanted the seven vowels as a hymn addressed to Serapis' (*Eusebe-Salverte*, Dionysius of Halicarnassus). 'The vowels were retained to a comparatively late period in the mystic allegories relative to the Solar System.' 'The seven vowels are consecrated to the seven principal planets' (Belot, *Chiromancie*, 16th cent.).

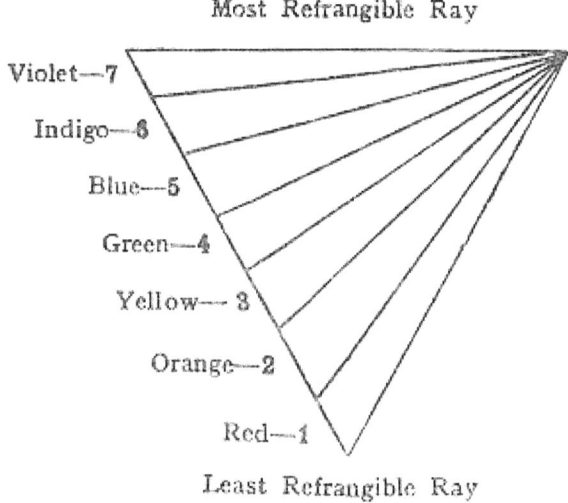

Fig. 33 : PRISMATIC SPECTRUM

The cause of the splendour and variety of colours lies deep in the affinities of nature. There is a singular and mysterious alliance between colour and sound. There are seven pure tones in the diatonic scale, because the harmonic octave is on the margin, or border, or rhythmic point, or the First and Seventh, like the chemical dark rays on the margin of the solar *spectrum*. (See explanatory chart of the Prismatic Colours above.)

Red is the *deep bass* vibration of ether. To produce the sensation of red to the eye, the luminous line must vibrate 477 millions of millions of times in a second. Blue, or rather purple, is the *high treble* vibration, like the upper C in music. There must be a vibration of 699 millions of millions in a second to produce it; while the cord that produces the high C must vibrate 516 times per second.

Heat, in its effect upon nature, produces colours and sounds. The world's temperature declines one degree at the height of 100 feet from the earth. There is a difference of one degree in the temperature, corresponding to each 1,000 feet, at the elevation of 30,000 feet. Colouration is effected, at the surface of the earth, to the same amount in one minute that takes half an hour over three miles high, in the full rays of the sun. The dissemination of light in the atmosphere is wholly due to the aqueous vapour in it. The *spectrum* is gained from the sun. In the air opposite to it, there is no *spectrum*. These conclusions result from balloon observations made in April 1863, and the philosophical deductions are a victory for 'aqueous vapour'.

It has been demonstrated that flames are both sensitive and sounding; they have, therefore, special affinities.

'The author of *The Nature and Origin of Evil* is of opinion that there is some inconceivable *benefit* in Pain, abstractly considered; that Pain, however inflicted or wherever felt, communicates some good to the General System of Being; and that every animal is some way or other the better for the pain of every other animal. This opinion he carries so far as to suppose that there passes some principle of union through all animal life, as attraction is communicated to all corporeal nature; and that the evils suffered on this globe may by some inconceivable means contribute to the felicity of the inhabitants of the remotest planet.'--Contemporary review of the *Nature and Origin of Evil*.

'Without subordination, no created System can exist: all subordination implying Imperfection; all Imperfection, Evil; and all Evil, some kind of Inconveniency or Suffering.'--Soame Jenyns, *Free Enquiry into the Nature and Origin of Evil.*

'Whether Subordination implies Imperfection may be disputed. The means respecting themselves may be as perfect as the end. The Weed as a Weed is no less perfect than the Oak as an Oak. Imperfection may imply primitive Evil, or the Absence of some Good; but this Privation produces no Suffering, but by the Help of Knowledge.' 'Here the point of view is erroneously taken for granted. The end of the oak, in another comprehension, may be the weed, as well as the end of the weed the oak. The contraries may be converse, *out of our* appreciation.'--Review of the above work in *Miscellaneous and Fugitive Pieces*. London: T. Davies, 1774.

'There is no evil but must inhere in a conscious being, or be referred to it; that is, Evil must be *felt* before it is Evil.'--Review of *A Free Enquiry into the Nature and Origin of Evil*, p. 5 of the same *Miscellaneous and Fugitive Pieces*. London: T. Davies, Russell Street, Covent Garden, Bookseller to the Royal Academy. 1774. Query, whether the Review of this Book, though attributed to Dr. Johnson, be not by Soame Jenyns himself, the author of the book?

'Thoughts, or ideas, or notions--call them what you will--differ from each other, not in *kind*, but in *force*. The basis of all things cannot be, as the popular philosophy alleges, mind. It is infinitely improbable that the *cause* of *mind*--that is, of *existence*--is similar to mind.'--Shelley's *Essays*. The foregoing is contained in that on Life. He means Reason, in this objection to MIND. Shelley further remarks: 'The words I, and YOU, and THEY, are grammatical devices, invented simply for arrangement, and totally devoid of the intense and exclusive sense usually attached to them.'

In the *Memoirs of the Life and Writings of Mr. William Whiston*, part ii. (1749), there occur the following observations: 'N.B.--I desire the reader to take notice that the very learned *Gerard John Vossius*, in his three accurate dissertations, *De Tribus Symbolis*, or *Of The Three Creeds*--that called *The Apostles' Creed*, that called *The Athanasian Creed*, and that called the *Nicene* or *Constantinopolitan Creed*, with the *Filioque*, has proved them to be all falsely so called: that the first was only the Creed of the *Roman* Church about A.D. 400; that the second was a forgery about 400 years after Athanasius had been dead, or about A.D. 767, and this in the West and in the Latin Church only, and did not obtain in the *Greek* Church till about 400 years afterwards, or about A.D. 1200; and that the third had the term *Filioque* first inserted into it about the time when the *Athanasian Creed* was produced, and not sooner, or about A.D. 767.'

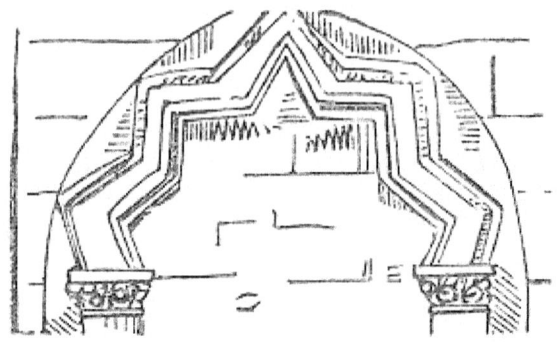

CHAPTER THE NINETEENTH

CABALISTIC INTERPRETATIONS BY THE GNOSTICS

To indicate God's existence, the ancient sages of Asia, and many Greeks, adopted the emblem of pure fire, or ether.

'Aerem amplectatur immensus æther, qui constat exaltissimis ignibus' (Cicero, *De Natura Deorum*, lib. ii. c. 36.) 'Cœlum ipsum stellasque colligens, omnisque siderum compago, æther vocatur, non ut quidem putant quod ignitus sit et insensus, sed quod cursibus rapidis semper rotatur' (Apuleius, *De Mundo*). Pythagoras and Empedocles entertained similar theories (Brucker, I, c. i. p. 113). Parmenides also represented God as a universal fire which surrounded the heavens with its circle of light and fire (Cicero, *De Natura Deorum*, lib. iii. c. 2). Hippasus, Heraclitus, and Hippocrates imagined God as a reasoning and immortal fire which permeates all things (Cudworth, *Systema Intellectuale*, p. 104; and Gesnerus, *De Animis Hippocratis*). Plato and Aristotle departed but little from this in their teachings; and Democritus called God 'the reason or soul in a sphere of fire' (Stobæus, *Eclogæ Physicæ*, lib. vii. c. 10.) Cleonethes considered the sin as the highest god (Busching, *Grundriss einer Geschichte dir Philosophie*, I Th. p. 344) We find, therefore, in the earliest ages, an æther (spiritual fire) theory, by which many modern theorists endeavour to explain the phenomena of magnetism. This is the 'Ætheræum' of Robert Flood, the Rosicrucian.

Fire, indeed, would appear to have been the chosen-element of God. In the form of a flaming 'bush' He appeared to Moses on Mount Sinai. His presence was denoted by torrents of flame, and in the form of fire He preceded the band of Israelites by night through the dreary wilderness; which is perhaps the origin of the present custom of the Arabians, 'who always carry fire in front of their caravans' (Reade's *Veil of Isis*). All the early fathers held God the Creator to consist of a 'subtile fire'. When the Holy Spirit descended upon the Apostles on the Day of Pentecost, it was in the form of a tongue of fire, accompanied by a rushing wind. See *Anacalypsis*, vol. i. p. 627 (Parkhurst, *in voce* ברנ).

The personality of Jehovah is, in Scripture, represented by the Material Trinity of Nature; which also, like the divine antitype, is of one substance. The primal, scriptural type of the *Father* is *Fire*; of the *Word*, *Light*; and of the *Holy Ghost*, *Spirit*, or *Air in motion*. This material Trinity, as a type, is similar to the material trinity of Plato as, a type, it is used to conceal the 'Secret Trinity'. See *Anacalypsis*, vol. i. p. 627. Holy fires, which were never suffered to die, were maintained in all the temples: of these were the fires in the Temple of the Gaditanean Hercules at Tyre, in the Temple of Vesta at Rome, among the Brachmans of India, among the Jews, and principally among the Persians. Now to prove that all 'appearances' are 'born of Fire', so to speak, according to the ideas of the Rosicrucians.

Light is not radiated from any intensely heated *gas* or *fluid*. If nitre is melted, it will not be visible but throw into it any *solid* body, and as soon as that becomes heated it will radiate light; hence the phenomenon, 'Nasmyth's willow-leaves', in the sun, must be solid, not gaseous; and through their medium the whole of our light from the sun is doubtless derived. See the records of the British Association for the Advancement of Science (Cambridge Meeting), October 1862. These physical facts were known to the ancient Persians.

The ancient ideas upon these subjects have not come down to us at all definitely. The destruction of ancient manuscripts was effected upon a large. scale. Diocletian has the credit of having burned the books of the Egyptians on the chemistry of gold and silver (alchemy). Cæsar is said to have burned as many as 700,000 rolls at Alexandria; and Leo Isaurus 300,000 at Constantinople in the eighth century, about the time that the Arabians burned the famous Alexandrian Library. Thus our knowledge of the real philosophy of the ancient world is exceedingly limited; almost all the old records, or germinating means of knowledge, being rooted out.

In regard to 'Boudhisme, ou système mystique' as he denominates it, a learned author describes it as 'Métaphysique visionnaire, qui, prenant à tâche de contrarier l'ordre naturel, voulut que le monde *palpable* et *matériel* fût *une illusion* fantastique; que l'existence de l'homme fût *un réve dont la mort la était le vrai réveil:* que son corps fût une *prison impure* dont il devait se hâter de sortir, ou une *enveloppe grossière* que, pour la rendre perméable à la lumière interne, il devait atténuer, diaphaniser par le jeûne les macérations, les contemplations, et par une foule de pratiques anachorétiques si étranges que le vulgaire étonné ne put s'expliquer le caractère de leurs auteurs qu'en les considérant comme des êtres surnaturels, avec cette difficulté de savoir s'ils furent *Dieu devenu homme*, ou *l'homme devenu Dieu.*'--Volney. (C. F.), *Les Ruines*, p. 210.

'Mind cannot *create*, it can only *perceive*.' This hazardous statement, in its utmost extent, is used simply as an argument against there being the *philosophical* possibility of religion as derivable from *reason* only--which will be found to be the mere operation of the forces of the 'world'. No religion is philosophically capable of being defended on the grounds of *reason*; though one religion may seem (but, in the inner light, it will *seem* only) to be more reasonable (or probable) than another. Divine light, or faith, or intuition--in other words, the enlightenment of the Holy Spirit (to be recognized under its many names)--is that means alone which can carry truth, through the exposure of the futility of all *knowable* (that is, of all intellectual) truth. Such are the abstract notions of the Gnostics, or 'Illuminati', concerning religion.

'The curtains of Yesterday drop down, the curtains of To-morrow roll up; but Yesterday and To-morrow both *are*' (*Sartor Resartus*, edit. 1838, Natural-Supernaturalism', p. 271). To the divine knowledge, the future must be as much present as the present itself.

The explorations of the Rosicrucians may be said to be 'as keys to masked doors in the ramparts of nature, which no mortal can pass through without rousing dread sentries never seen upon this side' (*A Strange Story*, Lord Lytton, vol. i. p. 265). 'Omnia ex Uno, Omnia in Uno, Omnia ad Unum, Omnia per Medium, et Omnia in Omnibus' (*Hermetic axiom*).

In the speculations of the Gnostics, the astronomical points Cancer and Capricorn are called the 'Gates of the Sun'. Cancer, moreover, is termed the 'Gate of Man'; Capricorn, is the 'Gate of the Gods'. These are Platonic views, as Macrobius declares. With the influences of the planets, Saturn brings reason and intelligence; Jupiter, power of action; Mars governs the irascible principle, the Sun produces sensation and speculation, Venus inspires the appetites, Mercury bestows the power of declaring and expressing, and the Moon confers the faculty of generating and augmenting the body. The Egyptian 'winged disc' is a symbol of 'Tat', Taut', or 'Thoth' (Plutarch, *De Iside et Osiride*). The lions' heads, so frequently observable, in the sculptures decorating fountains, bespeak the astral influences under Leo, which produce the rains in the ardent month of July; and in this view they are regarded as the discharges of the 'sacred fountains'. Lions' heads, with fountains, are observable in architecture all the world over. All architecture is primarily derivable from two mathematical lines (| and --), which, united (and intersecting), form the 'cross'. The first 'mark' is the origin of the 'upright' tower, pyramid, or imitation ascending 'flame of fire', which aspires *against the force of gravity*; also of the steeple, or *phallus*, all over the world. The second, or horizontal, 'mark' is the symbol of the tabernacle, chest, or ark, or fluent or base-line, which is the expression of all Egyptian, Grecian, and Jewish templar architecture. The union of the two lines gives the Christian, universal cross-form, in the blending of the 'two dispensations'--Old and New, or 'Law' and 'Gospel'. Now, both of these lines, in the Rosicrucian sense, have special magic 'powers', or gifts, according to their several places, and according to the 'supernatural extra forces brought' specially to bear on them through the operations of those who know *how* (and *when*) to direct the occult power.

Those powers bestowed upon the original deserving 'Man', and not extinguished in the existing 'Man', are his still--if he retain any glimpse of his original spark of light.

Justinus Kerner, in his *Scherin von Prevorst*, most ingeniously anatomizes the inner man, and makes him consist of 'Seele', 'Nerven-geist', and' 'Geist'. The 'Nerven-geist', or nervous energy, being of a grosser nature, continues united with the 'Seele' on its separation from the body, rendering it visible *in the form of an apparition*, and enabling it to effect material objects, make noises, move articles, and suchlike things perceptible to the living sense--in short, to 'spucken'. According to its nature, this composite being takes a longer or shorter time to be dissolved; the 'Geist' alone being immortal (*The Gnostics and their Remains*, note to p. 46).

An *Ancient Homily on Trinity Sunday* has the following: 'At the deth of a manne, three bells should be ronge as his knyll in worship of the Trinitie. And for a woman[8], *who was the Second Person of the Trinitie*, two bells should be ronge.' Here we have the source of the emblematic difficulty among the master-masons, who constructed the earlier cathedrals, as to the addition and as to the precise value of the second (or feminine) tower at the western end (or Galilee) of a church.

Valentinus is called the 'profoundest doctor of the Gnosis'. According to him, the 'Eons' (angels, or effusions) number fifteen pairs, which represent the thirty degrees of each sign of the zodiac. The name of the great Gnostic deity, Abraxas, is derived as follows: 'Ab' or 'Af' ('Let it be'); 'Rax' or 'Rak' ('Adore'); 'Sas' or 'Sax' for 'Sadshi' ('Name'). 'The entire Gnostic system was not derived either from the Kabala, or from the Grecian philosophy; but from the East, as Mosheim long ago maintained': so declares the author of *The Gnostics and their Remains*; but it is a thorough mistake, both in his authority (Mosheim), and also in himself. We shall successfully show this before we have done.

As soon as Jesus was born, according to the Gnostic speculative view of Christianity, Christos, uniting himself with

---

[8] This is a curious direct assertion that the Saviour of the World was feminine.

Sophia (Holy Wisdom), descended through the seven planetary regions, assuming in each an analogous form to the region, and concealing his true nature from its genii, whilst he attracted into himself the sparks of Divine Light they severally retained in their angelic essence. Thus Christos, having passed through the seven *Angelic Regions* before the 'THRONE', entered into the man Jesus, at the moment of his baptism in the Jordan. 'At the moment of his baptism in the Jordan'--mark. Up to that point he was natural--but not the 'Christ'. This will recall his exclamation of world's disclaimer to the Virgin:--'Woman, what have I to do with thee?' From that time forth, being supernaturally gifted, Jesus began to work miracles. Before that, he had been completely ignorant of his mission. When on the cross, Christos and Sophia left his body, and returned to their own sphere. Upon his death, the two took the man 'Jesus', and abandoned his material body to the earth; for the Gnostics held that the true Jesus did not (and could not) physically suffer on the cross and die, but that Simon of Cyrene, who bore his cross, did in reality suffer in his room: 'And they compel one Simon a Cyrenian, who passed by, coming out of the country, the father of Alexander and Rufus, to bear his cross' (*St. Mark* xv. 21). The Gnostics contended that a portion of the real history of the Crucifixion was never written.

Asserting that a miraculous substitution of persons took place in the great final act of the 'Crucifixion', the Gnostics maintained that the 'Son of God' could not suffer physically upon the cross, the apparent sufferer being .human only--real body having no part with him.

At the point of the miraculous transference of persons, Christos and Sophia (the Divine) left his body, and returned to their own heaven. Upon his death on earth, the two withdrew the 'Being' Jesus (spiritually), and gave him another body, made up of ether (Rosicrucian *Æthereum*). Thenceforward he consisted of the two first Rosicrucian principles only, soul and spirit; which was the cause that the disciples did not recognize him after the resurrection. During his sojourn upon earth of eighteen months after he had risen, he received from Sophia (*Soph, Suph*), or Holy

Wisdom, that perfect knowledge or illumination, that true 'Gnosis', which he communicated to the small number of the Apostles who were capable of receiving the same:

The Gnostic authorities are St. Irenæus in the first place, Tertullian, Clemens Alexandrinus, Origen, St. Epiphanius. The Gnostics are divided into sects, bearing the names of Valentinians, Carpocratians, Basilideans, and Manichæans. Γνωσις, Gnosis, Gnossos: thence 'Gnostics'.

As the Son of God remained unknown to the world, so must the disciple of Basilides also remain unknown to the rest of mankind. As they know all this, and yet must live amongst strangers, therefore must they conduct themselves towards the rest of the world as invisible and unknown. Hence their motto, 'Learn to know all, but keep thyself unknown' (Irenæus).

The speech of an angel or of a spirit with man is heard as sonorously as the speech of one man with another, yet *it is not heard by others who stand near*, but by the man himself alone. The reason is, that the speech of an angel or of a spirit flows first into the man's thought, and, by an internal way, into his organ of hearing, and thus actuates it *from within*; whereas the speech of man flows first into the air, and, by an external way, into his organ of hearing, which it actuates *from without*. Hence it is evident that the speech of an angel and of a spirit with man is *heard in man*, and, since it equally affects the organs of hearing, that it is equally sonorous (Swedenborg; also *Occult Sciences*, p. 93; London, 1855).

The Greek Bacchanals were well acquainted with the *mythos* of Eve, since they constantly, invoked her, or a person under her name, in their ceremonies.

Black is the Saturnian colour--also that of the Egyptian Isis. Under the strange head of the embodiment of Deity under darkness, the following remarkable facts may be considered: the Virgin and Child are depicted *black* at the Cathedral at Moulins, at the famous Chapel of the Virgin at Loretto, in the Church of the Annunciation at Rome, at the Church of St. Lazaro and the Church of St. Stephen at Genoa, at that of St. Francisco at Pisa, at the Church of Brixen in the Tyrol, at a church in (and at the Cathedral of) Augsburgh, where the black figures are as large as life, at the Borghese Chapel in Rome, at the Church of Santa Maria Maggiore in the Pantheon, and in a small chapel at St. Peter's, on the right-hand side, on entering, near the door. The reader can make references in his memory to these places, if he be a traveller.

The writer, who goes by the name of Dionysius Areopagita, teaches that the highest spiritual truth is revealed only to those who have transcended every ascent of every holy height, and have left behind all divine lights and sounds and heavenly discoursing, and have passed into that *Darkness* where HE really is (as saith the Scripture) who is ALL, above all things (*De Mystica Theologia*, cap. i. sec. 3; *Hours with the Mystics*, by R. A. Vaughan, note to book i. chap. 2).

The words graven upon the zone and the feet of the Ephesian Diana, which Hesychius has preserved, are the following:

Aski-Kataski		'Darkness--Light'
Haix-Tetrax	interpreted as	'Himself'
Damnameneus		'The Sun'
Aision		'Truth'

'These Ephesian words', says Plutarch (*Sympos*), 'the Magi used to recite over those possessed with devils.' 'Damnameneus' is seen on a Gnostic amulet in the De la Turba Collection (*The Gnostics*, p. 94).

The Argha had the form of a crescent. The *Argo, arc,* or *arche,* is the *navis biprora.* It is clear that, as neither the full moon nor the half-moon was ever the object of worship, it is the *crescent horns* of the moon which imply the significance. These mean the woman-deity in every religion.

The snake associated with the mysteries among the Hindoos is the cobra-di-capella. It is said that the snake on the heads of all the Idols in Egypt was a Cobra. The name of the monarch or Chief Priest in Thibet is the Lama, or the Grand Lama. Prester-

John is the great Priest, or Prestre (*Prêtre*), Ian, Ion, Jehan, or John (the Sun). Lamia is the '*snake*' among the Ophidians; Lama is the hand: *lamh*, hand, is a divine name in the Scythian tongue. It also means the number 10, and the Roman numeral X, which is a cross. Now, the double pyramid, or

and, (*a*) ∆, of the Egyptians comprises the mystic mark signifying the two original principles water and fire, as above--(*b*)--the union of which, as intersecting triangles, forms the famous Hexalpha, or 'Solomon's Seal', or 'Wizard's Foot', which, according to the Eastern allegory, is placed (as that of St. Michael) upon the Rebellious Spirits in their 'abyss', or 'prison'.

Pyr is the Greek name of fire (thence Pyramid), and mythologically of the *sun*, who was the same as Hercules. And the great analyser of mythology assures us that *Pur* was the ancient name of Latian *Jupiter*, the father of Hercules; that he was the deity of fire; that his name was particularly retained amongst the people of Præneste, who had been addicted to the *rites* of *fire*. Fire, in short, in these mythologies, as also in all the Christian churches, meets us at every turn. But we must not mix up heathen ideas and Christian ideas in these matters.

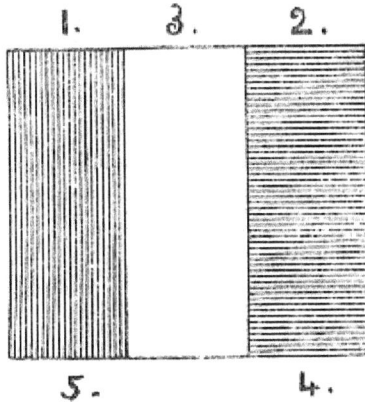

Moorish Arch.   Cathedral of Cordova

CHAPTER THE TWENTIETH

MYSTIC CHRISTIAN FIGURES AND TALISMANS

OUR engraving borrows from the West Front of Laon Cathedral, France, a Catherine-Wheel (or 'Rose') Window. The twelve pillars, or *radii*, are the signs of the Zodiac, and are *issuant* out of the glorified centre, or opening 'rose'--the sun, or 'beginning of all things'. 'King Arthur's Round Table' displays the 'crucified' Rose in its centre.

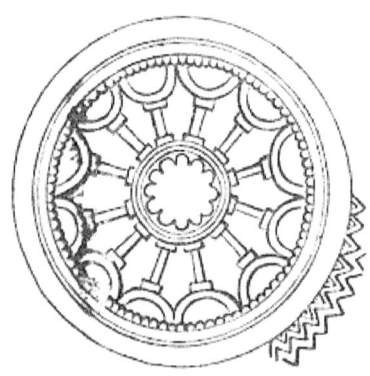

Fig. 34

In the 'tables' (*Tablier*, Fr. = Apron), alternating with tying-knots, of the Order of the Garter--which 'Most Noble Order' was originally dedicated, be it remembered, to the Blessed Lady, or to the Virgin Mary--the microcosmical, miniature 'King Arthur's

Round Table' becomes the individual female *discus*, or organ, waxing and waning, negative or in flower, positive or natural, alternately red and white, as the Rose of the World: *Rosamond, Rosa mundi.* And here we will adduce, as our justification for this new reading of the origin of the Order of the Garter, the very *motto* of the princely order itself:

Honi soit qui mal y pense!

or,

'YONI' *soit qui mal y pense!*

What this 'Yoni' is, and the changes meant and apotheosized through it, the discreet reader will see on a little reflection.

All the world knows the chivalric origin of this Most Noble Order of the Garter[9]. It arose in a princely act--rightly considered princely, when the real, delicate, inexpressibly high-bred motive and its circumstances are understood, which motive is systematically and properly concealed. Our great King Edward the Third picked up, with the famous words of the motto of the Order of the Garter, the 'garter'--or, as we interpret it, by adding a new construction with hidden meanings, the 'Garder' (or special *cestus*, shall we call it?)--of the beautiful and celebrated Countess of Salisbury, with whom, it is supposed, King Edward was in love.

The following is from Elias Ashmole: 'The Order of the Garter by its motto seems to challenge inquiry and defy reproach. Everybody must know the story that refers the origin of the name to a piece of gallantry: either the Queen or the Countess of Salisbury having been supposed to have dropped one of those very useful pieces of female attire at a dance; upon which old Camden says, with a great deal of propriety, and a most just compliment to the ladies, "*Hæc vulgus perhibet, nec vilis sane hæc videatur origo, cum* NOBILITAS *sub* AMORE *jacet.*" The ensign of the order, in jewellery or enamel, was worn originally on the *left arm*. Being in the form of a *bracelet* to the arm, it might possibly divert the attention of the men from the reputed original; it might be dropped and resumed without confusion; and the only

---

[9] See post, and through a subsequent Chapter, for particular facts--very important in the authentic history of the 'Garter'.

objection I can see to the use of such an ornament is the hazard of mistake from the double meaning of the term *periscelis*, which signifies not only a *garter*, but breeches, which our English ladies never wear: "Quæ Græcī ερισχελῆ vocant, nostri Braccas" (braces or breeches) "dicunt", says an ancient Father of the Church.' The Garter, to judge thus from Camden, was not a garter at all for the leg, but an occasional very important item of feminine under-attire; and King Edward's knightly feeling, and the religious devotion of the object, will be perceived upon close and delicately respectful consideration.

There is great obscurity as to the character of Abraxas, the divinity of the Gnostics. The Eons, or Degrees of Advance in the Zodiacal Circle, are thirty in number to each of the Twelve Signs, and consequently there are 360 to the entire Astronomical Circle, or 365, counting for each day of the solar year. The inscription upon the Gnostic gems, CEOY, is probably intended for ΘEOY; 'for the Arabs yet substitute the *s* for the *th* in their pronunciation' (*Gnostics*, p. 233; Matter, *Histoire Critique du Gnosticisme*). In this '*s*', and the '*th*' standing for it, lie all the mysteries of Masonry.

+, Christos, was designed for the guide of all that proceeds from God. Sophia-Achamoth is the guide, according to the Gnostics, for all proceeding out of 'matter'. St. Irenæus, whose period is the end of the second century, draws all these startling inferences from the Book of Enoch, and names 'Sophia' as signifying the Divine Wisdom. The Ophite scheme seems evidently the Bhuddistic Bythos, answering to the first Buddha. Sige, Sophia, Christos, Achamoth, Ildabaoth, answer to the successive five others (*Gnostics*, p. 27; Bellermann's *Drei Programmen über die Abraxasgemmen*, Berlin, 1820; Basilides; Tertullian; *De Præscript.*: 'Serpentem magnificant in tantum, ut ilium etiam Christo præferant.' See Tertullian, Epiphanius, and Theodoret.: *St. John* iii. 14, also). We now refer the reader to some significant figures towards the end of our volume, which will be found according to their numbers.

Figure 289: The Abraxas-god, invested with all the attributes of Phœbus. Green jasper; a unique type. The Egyptians call the moon the mother of the world, and say it is of both sexes (Plutarch; Spartian, *Life of Caracalla*). The moon, in a mystic sense, is called by the Egyptians male and female. The above is a gem in the Bosanquet Collection. In the *exerque* is the address, CABAΩ, 'Glory unto Thee!' On the reverse, in a *cartouche* formed by a coiled asp--precisely as the Hindoos write the ineffable name 'Aum'--are the titles ΙΑΩ.ΑΒΡΑCΑΞ (*The Gnostics*, p. 86).

Figure 311 represents Venus standing under a canopy supported on twisted columns, arranging her hair before a mirror held up by a Cupid; two others hover above her head, bearing up a wreath. In the field, ΦΑΣΙΣ ΑΡΙΩΡΙΦ--'The Manifestation of Arioriph'. Venus here stands for the personification of the Gnostic *Sophia*, or Achamoth, and as such is the undoubted source of our conventional representation of Truth (Montfauçon, pl. clxi). *Reverse*, figure 312, which represents Harpocrates seated upon the lotus, springing from a double lamp, formed of two phalli united at the base. Above his head is his title 'Abraxas', and over that is the name 'Iao'. In the field are the seven planets. The sacred animals--the scarab, ibis, asp, goat, crocodile, vulture, emblems of so many deities (viz. Phre, Thoth, Isis, Merides, Bebys, Neith)--the principal in the Egyptian mythology, arranged by *threes*, form a frame to the design. Neatly engraved on a large, bright loadstone (*The Gnostics*, p. 211).

ORIGIN OF THE TRICOLOR

'THEORY OF SACRAMENTAL MYSTICISM', ADAPTED FROM
THE SPECULATIONS OF THE SOPHISTS OR GNOSTICS

Blue	*White*	*Red*
(B.V.M.)	(S.S.)	(Φ, Fire)
Baptism by water	Air or Light	
Natural	Intermediate	Supernatural
	Nexus	
Bread ('Host')	and	Wine (cup denied to the Laity)
Body		Spirit: symbolical 'Blood

Sacramenta; 'Baptism and the Supper of the Lord'

From the above cabalistic estimate of the virtues of colours, it happens that the colour blue (sky-blue) is chosen as the colour for the investiture of infants at baptism, and as the colour for children's coffins. Blue or white (not white as meaning the 'S.S.' in the sacred sense, but white as the *synthesis* of material elements, or of light, or of 'sinlessness in irresponsibility') are children's colours at other times. There were two great ordeals--by water, and by fire. The one is the occult trial-baptism by water in the sinister or left-handed sense, applied to those suspected of witchcraft. The other (more perfect and more perfecting) baptism is by symbolical fire. Both rites were in use among the Egyptians. (Refer to mystic heraldic *formulæ* elsewhere in our book.) The three ordeals (or sacraments) of the Ancient Mysteries were by 'Water, Air, and Fire'. Thus, also, the Egyptian Initiations: 'Cave, Cloud, Fire'. So, too, the Masonic Initiations. With these meanings, royal coffins and investitures are always red (Mars), as meaning 'royalty active'; or imperial purple (Jupiter, or perhaps Mercurius--Thoth, Taut, Tat), as 'royalty passive', or implying the 'lord of regions'.

According to the cabalistic view, 'Jacob's 'Ladder', which was disclosed to him in a vision, is a metaphorical representation of the powers of alchemy, operating through visible nature. The 'Ladder' was a 'Rainbow', or prismatic staircase, set up between earth and heaven. Jacob's Dream implied a history of the whole hermetic creation. There are only two original colours, red and blue, representing 'spirit' and 'matter'; for orange is red mixing with the yellow light of the sun, yellow is the radiance of the sun itself, green is blue and yellow; indigo is blue tinctured with red, and violet is produced by the mingling of red and blue. The sun is alchemic gold, and the moon is alchemic silver. In the operation of these two potent spirits, or mystic rulers of the world, it is supposed astrologically that all mundane things were produced.

The next following pages explain the mystic analogy between colours, language; music, and the seven angelic adverse intelligences, supposed by the Gnostics to be operative in the 'dissonance of creation'. These represent the descending half of the 'Machataloth', as the cabalistic Jews called the Zodiac united. The whole is made up from abstruse sigmas, or the application of Rosicrucianism on its hieroglyphic and representative side.

CHARTS 1-3.

HERALDIC AND FIGURATIVE CHART, ACCORDING TO THE OLDEST HERALDIC SYSTEMS

(No. 1)

(Musical Notes also)		REGION ELEMENTARY	
Y.	1--Violet (Red and Blue)--*Most Refrangible Ray* Sanguine. Sardonyx Dragon's Tail	(Red Matter qualified by 3-- Light	3-- Cherubim
W.	2--Indigo (Opaque Blue) Purpure. Amethyst (?). Mercury(☿).	Matter 'coagulate' (as the sea)	
U.	3--Blue (Azure) Sapphire. Jupiter (♃).	Pure elemental matter (as the 'sky')	
O.	4--Green (Yellow and Blue) Vert. Emerald. Venus (♀).	Living forms in matter (disclosed in light). Fixed and stationary natural forms, and their spirits SECOND ÆTHERÆUM	
I.	5--Yellow Or. Topaz. Gold. Sol	Red inflamed, or Light 2-- Fire in its flower, or *Seraphim*	

	(☉).	glory	
E.	6--Orange (Red and Yellow) Tawny. Tenne. Jacynth Dragon's head	Fire inflaming, or 'flowering' (in stage of flowering) Blooming fire (as a being)	
A.	7--Red--*Least Refrangible Ray* Gules. Ruby. Mars (♂).	*Elementum Ignis* First affection, or results (πῦρ) 'Phrodite	Pyr-Fri-ga.

Vowels

FIRST.-- EMPYRÆUM

I-- *Teraphim*

'JACOB'S LADDER', 'And he dreamed, and behold a ladder set up on the earth, and the top of it reached to heaven: and behold the ANGELS of GOD ascending and descending on it' (*Genesis* xxviii. 12)
Also the Chromatic Scale of seven Musical Notes

'*Linea viridis seu Benedicta* whereon he saw 'Angels', *Viriditas*': the celebrated 'Seal of Solomon' (or 'Sword of Solomon') or 'Gladius of Saint Michael the Archangel.' (With the celebrated 'Seal of Solomon', he--Solomon-- *mastered* the Genii). It is 'the most potent Cabalistic, or Talismanic, sign.

HERALDIC AND FIGURATIVE CHART, ACCORDING TO THE OLDEST HERALDIC SYSTEMS

(No. 2)

Prismatic Colours

1.--Blue Ark. Arc (Patient)

Sigma

Blue.--Material World, or 'Great Deep', or 'Ark', or world made manifest, or sea, or 'C', or 'Patient', or Isis, or Venus, or 'Regina Cœli', or 'Heva or Eve'

חָדָה

or Th(ת)oth, etc., etc., etc.

VALOIS
Therefore the 'Lis', or creature-forms in the 'deep', or 'blue'

2.--White Produced (Neuter)

White. Synthesis of the colours, or Light. (Green, when living, inorganic forms--such as the 'herb of the field', or trees, etc. Colour of the 'fairy races'. Smaragdine). Or White in perfect light. 'Saint John'. Mystic Illumination. 'Saint-Esprit.'

BOURBON
Therefore 'White' with the 'Lilies' or creature-forms, in 'white' or the 'light'. Or Green (Charlemagne, Emperor, or Cæsar, or Kaisar of the West), with the golden '*scarabs*' or bees, in lieu of the 'Lisses' or 'Lilies'. Napoleon the First and Third. Scarabæus of Egypt. 'Lucifera'. 'Morning Star.'

3.	Red	*Red*. Baal. Bel. Osiris. Phœbus-Apollo (in manifestation). Aphrodite (sexless in this sense). The Producing Power (Agent)	GAULOIS
	Producer. (Agent.)		Red. Therefore the 'Oriflamme' (or 'Fire of Gold') is red. And from this original, the red of the Gauls and the red of England is derived. Red is the national colour of the Welsh--as witness the 'Red Dragon' (Rouge Dragon) of Wales, etc.

Obeliscus: Mystic Figure

Also Triad of the Diatonic Scale
Musical Harmony
'Music of the Spheres'
(Jacob's metaphorical 'LADDER')

HERALDIC AND FIGURATIVE CHART, ACCORDING TO THE OLDEST HERALDIC SYSTEMS

(No. 3)

Rationale of the 'Tricolor', or the three united, national, successive Colours of France.

1--*Red.* Fire. Gaulois. Represented by vertical lines, as indicative of the aspiring rays of this noblest and most active element. Salique, or Salic, from the Salii, or Priests of Mars. *Teraphim*

In Heraldry, there are only two chief colours: Red (Gules), or the 'Princedom' of this world; and Blue (Azure), or the 'Queendom' of this world.'

2--*White.* Illumination. Light: synthesis of colours. It is magic, or sacred, because it stands for the 'Third Person' of the 'Triune'. It is the colour of the Bourbons. It also supplies the field, or ground-colour, to the emblazonment of the order of the 'Saint-Esprit', or of the H. G. It also refers mystically to 'Revelation' and to Saint John. *Seraphim*

Also, in regard to the heraldic metals, Sol is the sun, the procreative or producing power (Gold); and Luna, the moon, Astarte ('receptive, or female power'), is the metal argent (or silver). [10]

3--*Blue.* It stands for the 'great deep' or for 'matter' in the *Cherubim*

The colour azure, or blue,

---

[10] These are the two chief metals of the Alchemists, and the two chief mystic symbols of the Rosicrucians. Red is blazoned by the old priestly heralds, or augurs, by the name of the Planet Mars. Vert (or Verd), and Argent, or silver (Hermes, or Thoth, or Taut, or Luna, or Astarte, indifferently), are represented by the Planet Venus and by the Moon.

abstract': It is represented heraldically by horizontal lines which stand for fluid-levels, whether of the sea or of the air. This colour is assigned to the 'Blessed Lady', or 'Notre Dame de Paris'. In heathen representations of the Ruling Feminine Principle, it stands for the 'Virgin of the Sea'.

mystically signifies the 'deep' or the world usurped, or won, out of chaos (Chronos, Saturn, or Time); and it is represented by the Planet Jupiter (Zeus), as 'Lord of the Worlds'.

CHAPTER THE TWENTY-FIRST

THE ROSY CROSS IN INDIAN, EGYPTIAN, GREEK, ROMAN, AND MEDIÆVAL MONUMENTS

THOUGH fire is an element in which everything inheres, and of which it is the life, still, according to the abstruse and unexplained ideas of the Rosicrucians, it is itself another element, in a second non-terrestrial element, or inner, non-physical; ethereal fire, in which the first coarse fire, so to speak, flickers, waves, brandishes, and spreads, floating (like a liquid) now here, now there. The first is the natural, material, gross fire, with which we are familiar, contained in a celestial, unparticled, and surrounding medium (or celestial fire), which is its *matrix*, and of which, in this human body, we can know nothing.

In 1867, in Paris, a suggestive philosophical book was published, under the title of *Hébreu Primitif; Formation des Lettres, ou Chiffres, Signes du Zodiaque et Racines Hébraiques, avec leurs Dérivés dans les Langues de l'Orient et de l'Europe*, par Ad. Lethierry-Barrois.

Ptha is the emblem of the Eternal Spirit from which everything is created. The Egyptians represented it as a pure ethereal fire which burns for ever, whose radiance is raised far above the planets and stars. In early ages the Egyptians worshipped this highest being under the name of Athor. He was the lord of the universe. The Greeks transformed Athor into Venus, who was looked upon by them in the same light as Athor (Apuleius, Cicero, Ovid; Ptolemæus, *in tetrabibla*; Proclus; Ennemoser, vol. i. p. 268, trans. by Howitt). Among the Egyptians, Athor also signified the night (Hesiod; Orpheus). 'According to the Egyptians', says Jablonski, 'matter has always been connected with the mind. The Egyptian priests also maintained that the gods appeared to man, and that spirits communicated with the human race.' 'The souls of men are, according to the oldest Egyptian doctrine, formed of ether, and at death return again to it.'

The alchemists were a physical branch of the Rosicrucians. The more celebrated authors (and authorities) upon the art and mystery of alchemy are Hermes (whose seven chapters and 'smaragdine table', as it is called, contain the whole alchemical system); Geber, the '*Turba*', 'Rosary', *Theatrum Chemicum, Bibliothèque Hermétique, Chymical Cabinet*; Artephius, Arnoldus de Villa Nova, Raimondus Lullius, Trevisan, Nicholas Flamel, Zachareus, Basilius Valentinus, Cosmopolita, and Philalethes (Thomas Vaughan). Refer also to *The Hermetical Triumph, or the Victorious Philosopher's Stone*. London, 1723; Lucas's *Travels*, p. 79; Count Bernard of Treviso. Two leading works, however, on the hermetic subject are *La Chiave del Gabinetto*[11], Col. 1681, 12mo, by Joseph Francis Borri, an Italian; and *Le Compte de Gabalis, ou Entretiens sur les Sciences Secrètes*; imprimée à Paris, par Claude Barbin, 1671, 12mo, pp. 150. This book is the work of the Abbé de Villars, or is supposed to be so. J. V. Andrea, a writer upon hermetic subjects, was Almoner to the Duke of Wurtemberg, and wrote early in the seventeenth century. The Emperor Rudolphus the Second greatly encouraged learned men who had made acquaintance with alchemical lore. At the supposed revival of Rosicrucianism -in Paris, in March 1623, the Brethren were said to number thirty-six; of whom there were six in Paris, six in Italy, six in Spain, twelve in Germany, four in Sweden, and two in Switzerland. In 1616, the famous English Rosicrucian, Robertus de Fluctibus (Robert Fludd), published his defence of the society, under the title *Apologia Compendiaria, Fraternitatem de Rosea-Cruce, Suspicionis et Infamiæ maculis aspersam abluens*, published in 1616 at Frankfort. Since this time, there has been no authentic account of the Rosicrucians. We are now the first translators of Robert Fludd.

'Amongst an innumerable multitude of images and symbolical figures, with which the walls'--i.e. those of the caverns of initiation at Salsette--'are covered, the Linga or Phallus was

---

[11] Mark--the letters G and C are convertible: Thus Gab or Cab ('Gab' ala or 'Cab' ala). The 'Compte' de 'Gabalis' is, properly the 'Compte' de 'Cabalis', or the Count of the 'Cabala'.

everywhere conspicuous, often alone, sometimes united with the petal and calyx of the lotus, the point within the circle, and the intersection of two equilateral triangles' (Dr. Oliver, *History of Initiation*. See also Maurice on the *Indian Initiations*).

The Linga, or pillar, or stone of memorial, in its material form, is the perpetuation of the idea of the male generative principle, as the physical means, in conjunction with the Yoni (Ioni), or *discus*, of the production of all visible things. In this connexion, the addition to the name of Simon Peter (Petra, or Pietra, Cephas, Jonas, Bar-Jonas, Ionas) will be recalled as suggestive. There is a sacred stone in every Temple in India. The Stone, or Pillar, or 'Pillow', of Jacob was sacred among the Jews. It was anointed with oil. There was a sacred stone among the Greeks at Delphi, which was also anointed with oil in the mystic ceremonies. The stone of Caaba, or black stone at Mecca, is stated to have been there long before the time of Mohammed. It was preserved by him when he destroyed the dove and images. The obelisks at Rome were, and are, Lingas (or Linghas). In the Temple of Jerusalem, and in the Cathedral of Chartres, they are in vaults. They are the idea of the abstract *membrum*, or 'affluence', or MEANS. To the initiated mind they imply glory, not grossness.

Figs. 25-26 are the *Crux Ansata* of the Egyptians. This emblem is also found in India. According to Ruffinus and Sozomen, it imports the '*time that is to come*'. It is a magical symbol. Fig. 27 is the imperial mound, and cross-sigma surmounting it.

Figs. 28-29 are symbols of Venus (Aphrodite), the deity of the Syrians and Phœnicians. They are phallic emblems.

Fig. 30 is the Phallus proper. It is the *sigma* of Zeus, Mithras, 'Baalim', Bacchus.

Figures numbered 31, 'Osiris': these various figures signify also Jupiter-Ammon. The rectangular marks denote the Scandinavian Tuisco, Thoth (Mercurius, or Hermes). Fig. 35 is the Indian form of the same idea.

The figure marked 36 is to be found on the breast of one of the mummies in the museum Fig. 35 of the London University.

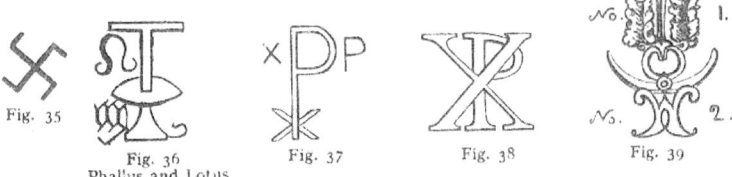

Fig. 35 Fig. 36 Phallus and Lotus Fig. 37 Fig. 38 Fig. 39

Upon a monument discovered in Thebes, Anubis is represented as St. Michael and St. George are in Christian paintings, armed in a cuirass, and having in his hand a lance, with which he pierces a monster that has the head and tail of a serpent (A. Lenoir, *Du Dragon du Metz, etc.: Mémoires de l'Académie Celtique*, tome ii. pp. 11, 12).

Figure 37 is the 'Labarum'. The celebrated sign which is said to have appeared in the sky at noonday to the Emperor Constantine was in this form.

Figure 38 is the monogram of the Saviour. To show the parallel in symbolical forms, we will add some further authorities from the Temple of Solomon at Jerusalem.

Figure 39, No. 1, is an evidently Corinthian foliation. It is from a pillar in the vaults of the Temple of Solomon at Jerusalem. (Probably a Lotus-Acanthus.) No. 2 is evidently the 'Crux Ansata', combining the indications of 'Lotus' and 'Lily'. Here is a union of the classic, the Judaic, and Gothic forms, all presenting the same idea at once. Buddha was the sun in 'Taurus'; Cristna (Crishna, Krishna) was the sun in 'Aries'.

In regard to the origin of speech, of writing, and of letters, it may be remarked that the Egyptians referred the employment of a written symbol (to record and communicate the spoken word) to a Thoth; the Jews, to Seth or his children (Josephus, *Ant.* I, 2, 3); the Greeks, to Hermes. But 'Thout' in Coptic (Pezron, *Lexicon Lingua Copticæ*, s.v. *Gen.* xix. 26 in the Coptic version), also שׁת in Hebrew, and Ερμῆς (Hermes) in Greek are all names for *a pillar or post*. This is the Homeric use of ἕρμα and ἕρμις (*Il. á,*

486; *Od.* ή, 278; Kenrick's *Essay on Primeval History*, p. 119). Αρχα is the ship, *navis* (from thence come 'nave' and 'navel'), in which the germ of animated nature was saved. Thebes, or Theba, means the 'ark'. Carnac, or Karnak, in Egypt, is reckoned to be older than the days of Moses--at least dating from 1600 A.C.

The opinion of M. Dupuis was (see his learned memoir concerning the origin of the constellations), that 'Libra' was formerly the sign of the vernal equinox, and 'Aries' of the nocturnal, autumnal equinox; that is, that since the origin of the actual astronomical system, the procession (precession?) of the equinoxes had carried forward by seven signs the primitive order of the Zodiac. Now, estimating the procession (precession?) at about 70½ years to a degree, that is, 2115 years to each sign, and observing that 'Aries' was in its fifteenth degree 1447 before Christ, it follows that the first degree of 'Libra' could not have coincided with the vernal equinox more lately than 15,194 years before Christ, to which, if you add 1790 years since Christ, it appears, that 16,984 years have elapsed since the origin of the 'Zodiac' (Volney, *Ruins of Empires*, 1st English edition, 1792, p. 360). All white things express the celestial and luminous gods; all circular ones, the world, the moon, the sun, the destinies; all semicircular ones, as arches and crescents, are descriptive of the moon, and of lunar deities and meanings.

HERALDIC GENEALOGY OF THE 'FLEUR-DE-LIS', OR 'FLOWER-DE-LUCE'

APOTHEOSIS OF THE SYMBOL
Fig. 40

4. Bee   6. Bee   7. Imperial Bee   8. Fleuron   9. Charlemagne
10. A Babylonian Gem

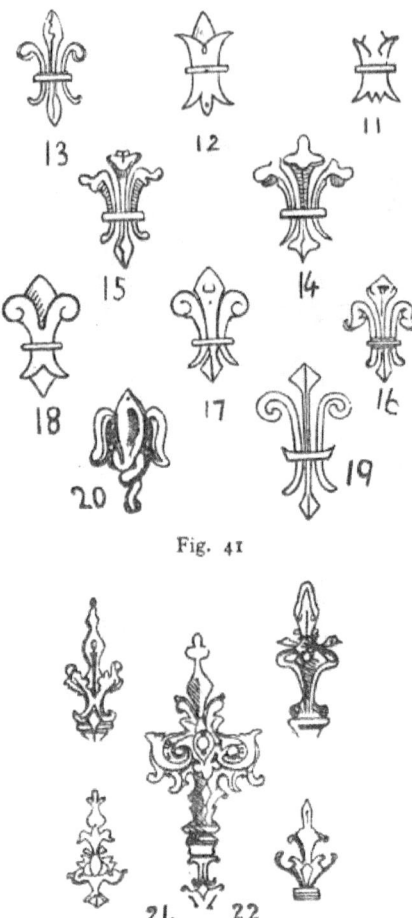

Fig. 41

11-12. Early French (also Babylonian) 13. Middle French 14. Later French 16. Valois 17. Henry of Navarre 18. In England, thus. 19. Bourbon 20. Egyptian Sculptures: Fleur-de-Lis; Asp: Speed calls them the 'Flower de Lize.'

21. Finial: meaning the 'Fleur-de-Lis' 22. Finial[1]

---

[12] See figs, 190, 191, 192, 195, *post.* See, also, pages preceding.

'The Egyptians', says Porphyry, 'employ every year a talisman in remembrance of the world. At the summer solstice, they mark their houses, flocks, and trees with red, supposing that on that day the whole world had been set on fire. It was also at the same period that they celebrated the Pyrrhic or "Fire Dance".' (And this illustrates the origin of the purifications by fire and water.)

There are seven planets in the solar system. These seven planets are signified in the seven-branched candlestick of the Jewish ritual. The number is a sacred number. These seven 'prophets', or angels, have each twelve apostles, places, *stella*, 'stalls', or regions or dominions (stalls as 'stables'), for the exercise of their powers. These are the twelve divisions of the great Circle, or the twelve signs of the Zodiac. All this is Cabalistic, Magical, Sabaistical, and Astrological. The name Ashtaroth or Astarte has been derived from *Ashre, aster, ast*, star, or 'starred'; in the same way as the word Sephi-roth comes from the Hebrew root, 'roth'.

On the black sacred stone ('Kebla', or 'Cabar') at Mecca, 'there appears the figure of a human head cut', 'which some take to be the head of a Venus' (Enthumius Zyabenus, *Mod. Un. Hist.* i. 213; Sale's *Discourse*, p. 16; *Bibliotheca Biblia*, i. 613, 614).

Man's ideas, outwards from himself, must always become more dreamlike as they recede from him, more real as they approach him.

CHAPTER THE TWENTY-SECOND

MYTH OF THE SCORPION, OR THE SNAKE, IN ITS MANY DISGUISES

ONE of the Targums says that חיא, a serpent, tempted Adam, or the first man, and not היה, Eve, his wife. Here we have the object of adoration of the Ophites--the female generative power--the Destroying, Regenerating Power among the Ophites, and, indeed, the Gnostics generally. The Serpent was called the Megalistor, or Great Builder of the Universe (*Maia*, or Bhuddist illusion). Here again we recognize, under another name (Ophites), the Cyclopes, or the builders of the circular Temples at Stonehenge and everywhere else. Mr. Payne Knight has repeated an observation of Stukeley, that the original name of the temple at Abury was the "Snake's Head".' And he adds, 'It is remarkable that the remains of a similar circle of stones (circular temple) in Bœotia had the same name in the time of Pausanias' (Pausanias, *Bœot.* cap. xix. s. 2).

The famous oracular stone, enclosed in the seat of St. Edward's chair (the Coronation Chair) in Westminster Abbey, was at one time a, stone to which adoration was paid. It was possessed of imagined miraculous gifts. This stone is asserted to be the same which the Patriarch rested his head upon in the *Plain of 'Luza*', and is said to have been carried first to Brigantia, a city of Gallicia, in Spain. From thence it was brought into, Ireland by Simon Brech, the first King of the Scots, about 700 years before Christ; and from there, about 370 years, after, into Scotland, by King Fergaze (Fergus). In the year of Christ 850 it was placed at the Abbey of Scone (in the county of Perth) by King Kenneth; this being the place where the Scottish Kings were generally crowned in those days. In the year 1297 this Scottish wooden throne or chair, together with their crown and sceptre, was brought into England by the English King Edward the First, and placed in Westminster Abbey.

> Si quid habent veri vel chronica, cana fidesve,
> Clauditur hac Cathedra nobilius ecce lapis,
> Ad caput eximius Jacob quondam Patriarcha
> Quem posuit, cernens numina mirapoli.
> Quem tulit ex Scotis, spolians quasi victor honoris,
> Edwardus Primus, Mars velut armipotens;
> Scotorum Domitor, noster Validissimus Hector,
> Anglorum Decus & gloria militiæ.
> *Antiquities of Westminster Abbey*, 1711.

It is still supposed, in accordance with the ancient prophecies, that the stone in the Coronation Chair has miraculous gifts, and that the sovereignty of England depends upon it. This magical stone carries with it the tradition (how or whence derived no one knows), that it murmurs approval at the coronation when the rightful heir assumes his or her seat on it; but that, on the contrary, it would clap with terrific noise, and fire flash from it, implying protest and denunciation, should an usurper attempt to counter-work or control its mysteries. It still has hooks for the chain which in former unknown times suspended it, when it was borne as a talisman of victory at the head of the army--when doubtless it was regarded as a Palladium of Prosperity, and a Divinity. It is also said that the pre-eminence of London is connected with the preservation of London Stone.

Both the ancient relic, London Stone, and the Coronation Stone in Westminster Abbey, seem of the same character. They appear to have been either worn down to their present smallness in the lapse of the ages, or to have been mutilated at some unknown, remote period--possibly thrown down and broken as objects of superstitious reverence, if not of direct and positive idolatry, thus very probably exciting indignation, which, as it found opportunity and scope for its exercise, was successful in their demolition. In both these stones we certainly .have only fragments--perhaps of Obelisks, or of Jewish 'Bethel' Pillars or 'Stones'--for all these supposed magical stones are of the same sacred family.

The supposed magical stone, enclosed in the wooden block at the base of the Coronation Chair, has been reputed, from time immemorial, to murmur its approval or disapproval of the royal occupant, only at the moment when the Sovereign was placed in the chair for investiture with the sacred *pallium* or with the state robes, on the occasion of the King's or the Queen's coronation.

In this respect the stone is very similar in its ascribed supernatural gifts, and in this special oracular speaking-power, to all sacred or magical stones; and more particularly to the famous statue of Memnon in Egypt, which is said to give forth a long, melodious tone with the first ray of sunrise, like that produced by the wind through the Æolian harp. It is not quite clear whether this sound is expected to issue from the stone in the royal chair at Westminster when approval is intended, and the meaning of the stone is benign, or whether sounds at all are to be heard only when displeasure is to be expressed. This strange asserted power of the sacred stone at Westminster to become vocal directly allies it with ether oracular stones all over the world. The prevalence everywhere, and in all time, of the existence of special stones having this miraculous gift is a striking and curious proof of the continual, invincible yearning of man for supernatural direct help and direction from powers exterior and invisible to him. He earnestly desires the possibility of personal communication with that intelligent, unseen world, which he cannot avoid thinking is close about him, surveying his doings. Man tries to overcome the assurance that this invisible, recognitive, responsive world, to betake himself to in his time of trouble, is, so far as his senses insist, so hopelessly out of reach. He languishes to think it attainable.

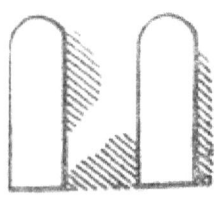

The oracular stone at Westminster seems only a piece of some pillar or *lithos*: but no one will attempt to dispute that it is an object of prodigious antiquity, and that its history is very remarkable and interesting. Its place of deposit, too, the shrine of Edward the Confessor, is worthy of it; and both inspire deep reverence--nay, an awful feeling.

CHAPTER THE TWENTY-THIRD

OMINOUS CHARACTER OF THE COLOUR 'WHITE' TO ENGLISH ROYALTY

WE beg to premise that the following fears are not our belief, but that they are educed from old traditions--old as England.

It is a very ancient idea, derived from the highest antiquity, that the colour 'white'--which, considered in the mystic and occult sense, is feminine in its origin--is fateful in its effects sometimes; and that, as a particular instance of its unfortunate character, it is an unlucky colour for the royal house of England-- at all events, for the king or queen of England personally-- singular as the notion would appear to be. We are not aware whether this sinister effect of the ominous colour white is supposed to extend to the nation generally. It is limited, we believe, to the prince or sovereign of England, and to his immediate belongings. The name John, which comes from *Iona*, a remote feminine root, has also been reckoned unfortunate for the king's name both in England and in France. The reason of this does not appear to be anywhere stated. The origin of the prophecy, also, as to the formidable character of the colour white to England, is unknown; but it is imagined to be at least as old as the time of Merlin. Thomas de Quincey, who takes notice of the prophecy of the 'White King', says of King Charles the First, that the foreboding of the misfortunes of this 'White King' were supposed to have been fulfilled in his instance, because he was by accident clothed in white at his coronation; it being remembered afterwards that white was the ancient colour for a victim. This, in itself, was sufficiently formidable as an omen.' De Quincey's particular expressions are; 'That when King Charles the First came to be crowned, it was found that, by some oversight, all the store in London was insufficient to furnish the purple velvet necessary for the robes of the king and for the furniture of the throne. It was too late to send to Genoa for a supply; and through

186

this accidental deficiency it happened that the king was attired in *white* velvet at the solemnity of his coronation, and not in red or purple robes, as consisted with the proper usage.'

As an earlier instance of this singular superstition, the story of that ill-fated royal *White Ship* occurs to memory, as the vessel was called wherein Prince William, the son of King Henry the First, the heir-apparent, with his natural sister, the Countess of Perche, and a large company of the young nobility, embarked on their return to England from Normandy. It might be supposed that the misfortunes of King Charles the First, which were accepted, at that time of monarchical dismay, as the reading (and the exhaustion) of this evil-boding prophecy, were enough; but there are some reasons for imagining that the effects are not--even in our day--altogether expended. The fatalities of the colour 'white' to English royalty certainly found their consummation, or seemed so to do, in the execution of King Charles the First, who was brought out to suffer before his own palace of 'Whitehall'-- where, again, we find 'white' introduced in connexion with royalty and tragical events. Whitehall is the Royal 'White' Palace of England. The 'White Rose' was the unfortunate rose (and the conquered one) of the contending two Roses in this country. This is again a singular fact, little as it has been remarked. We will pursue this strange inquiry just a little further, and see if the lights of Rosicrucianism will not afford us a measure of help; for it is one of the doctrines of the Rosicrucians that the signatures, as they call them, of objects have a magical marking-up and a preternatural effect, through hidden spiritual reasons, of which we have no idea in this mortal state-in other words, that magic and charming, through talismans, is possible; common sense being not all sense.

The colour white is esteemed both of good and of bad augury, according to the circumstances and the periods of its presentation. In relation to the name of our present King, the supposedly unfortunate prefix 'Albert' has been practically discarded in favour of 'Edward' only. This name of Edward is an historical, triumphant, and auspicious name; for all our Edwards, except the weak King Edward the Second, have been powerful or noteworthy men. Now, very few people have had occasion to remark, or have recalled the fact as significant and ominous in the way we mean, that the word 'Albert' itself means 'White'. The root of 'Albert' is, in most languages, to be found in 'white'; *albus*, white; *alp*, white; *Albania*, the 'white' country. We here recall the '*snowy* camëse', to which Byron makes reference as worn in *Alb*ania. 'Albion' (of the 'white' cliffs), Alb, Al, El, Æl, all mean 'white'. Examples might be multiplied. Αλφος, αλπε, *albus*, 'white', are derived from the Celtic *alp*; and from thence came the word 'Alps', which are mountains always white, as being covered with snow. '*Albus*, "white", certainly comes from the Celtic *alp*, or *alb*' says the historian Pezron; 'for in that language, as well as in many others, the *b* and the *p* frequently interchange; from whence the ancient Latins, and the Sabines themselves, said *Alpus* for white. I consider it therefore as certain', continues Pezron, 'that from *Alpus* the word Alps came, because the mountains are always white, as being covered with snow; the words "Alp" or "Alb", and their compounds, meaning white everywhere. I conclude, also, that from the *Pen* of the Celtæ, Umbrians, and Sabines, which signifies a "head", "top", or "high place", they made *Penninus Mons*, the Apennines, vast mountains in Italy. Thus these celebrated words proceed certainly from the Gaulish tongue, and are older by several ages than the city of Rome.' The following are all Teutonic or German words: *alb*, *alf* (Qy. Alfred?), and *alp*, which' all signify 'white' as their original root. Thus much for white.

White is also a colour not auspicious to the Prussian royal family, although, again, in a contradictory way, the ensigns of Prussia (Borussia, or 'of the Borussi') are, as armorists well know, the original 'white and black' of the Egyptians, which were adopted by the Teutons and the Templars. These white and black tinctures are heraldically *argent and sable*: Luna, or *pearl*, for 'tears'; Saturn, or *diamond*, for 'sadness, penance, and ashes'. In these strange senses, the Rosicrucians accepted colours as in themselves talismanic, powerfully operative through their planetary 'efficients', or 'signatures', as the astrologers call them. These ideas, more or less pronounced, have prevailed in all ages and in all countries, and they lurk largely in suspicion through our own land. We are all aware, in England, of the objection to the colour 'green' in certain cases. It is the spirit-colour, a magic colour, the colour of the 'fairies', as the cabalistic, tutelary, miniature spirits are called, who are supposed to be very jealous of its use. In Ireland, green, is universally regarded with distrust; but with veneration, in the spiritual sense. It is the national colour; for the Patroness of Ireland is the female deity, the. Mother of Nature, known in the classic mythology as Venus--equally Venus the graceful and Venus the terrible, as the Goddess of Life and of Death. The various *verts*, or greens, are the 'colour-rulers' in the emblazonry of the Emerald Isle. The presiding deity of the Land of Ierna, or of Ireland, is the mythic 'Woman', born out of the fecundity of nature, or out of the 'Great Deep'. This is the genius (with certain sinister, terrible aspects, marked out grandly in the old forms) 'who is 'impaled' or 'crucified'--in its real, hidden meaning--upon the stock, of 'Tree of Life', indicated by the Irish Harp. Her hair, in the moment of agony, streams Daphne-like, as 'when about to be transformed into the tree', behind her in the wind, and twines, in the mortal, mythical stress, into the seven strings of the magic Irish Harp, whose music is the music of the spheres, or of the Rosicrucian, assumed penitential, visible World. These seven strings stand for the seven vowels, by means of which came speech to man, when the 'new being', man (this is cabalistic again, and therefore difficult of comprehension), 'opened his mouth and spake'. The seven strings of the Irish Harp, it will be remembered, are blazoned 'Luna', or the 'Moon'--the feminine moon--according to the practice of the old heralds, in regard to all royal or, ruling achievements, which are blazoned by the names of the planets. The seven strings of the Irish Harp mean also the seven pure tones in music; these, again, stand for the seven prismatic colours; which, again, describe the seven vowels; and these, again, represent their seven rulers, or the seven planets, which have their seven spirits, or 'Celestial Flames', which are the seven Angels or Spirits of God, who keep the way round about 'the Throne of the Ancient of Days'.

There is in most countries an objection to Friday, although it is the Mohammedan sacred day or Sabbath. Friday is the day of the 'Green'. Emeralds, or *smaragds*, are proper to be worn on Friday, and bring good fortune, as exercising occult influences on this particular day.

The breastplate of the Jewish High-Priest had its oracular gems, which were the Urim and Thummim. The reputed enchanter, Apollonius Tyaneus, is said, for the purposes of his magic, to have worn special rings, with their appropriate gems, for each day of the sevenfold week, to command the particular spirits belonging to the different days. The Hermetic Brethren had certain rules that they observed in relation to this view of the power of precious stones to bring good or bad fortune through the planetary affinities of certain days, because they imagined that the various gems, equally as gold and silver, were produced through the chemic operation of the planets, working secretly in the telluric body. They thought that gold and silver, and all the gems, had but one foundation in nature, and were simply augmented, purified, and perfected through the operation of the hermetic or magnetic light--invisible and unattainable under ordinary circumstances, and unknown, except to the alchemists. All yellow gems, and gold, are appropriate to be worn on Sunday, to draw down the propitious influences, or to avert the antagonistic effects, of the spirits on this day, through its ruler and name-giver, the Sun. On Monday, pearls and white stones (but not diamonds) are to be worn, because this is the day of the Moon, or of the second power in nature. Tuesday, which is the day of Mars, claims rubies, and all stones of a fiery lustre. Wednesday is the day for turquoises, sapphires, and all precious stones which seem to reflect the blue of the vault of heaven, and that imply the lucent azure of the supposed spiritual atmosphere, wherein, or under which, the Rosicrucian sylphs dwell--those elementary children who, according to the cabalistic theogony, are always striving for intercourse with the race of Adam, seeking a share of his particular privilege of immortality, which has been denied to them. Thursday demands amethysts and deep-coloured stones of sanguine tint, because Thursday is the day of Thor--the Runic impersonated Male Divine Sacrifice. Friday, which is the day of Venus, has its appropriate emeralds, and reigns over all the varieties of the imperial, and yet strangely the sinister, colour green. Saturday, which is Saturn's day, the oldest of the gods, claims for its distinctive talisman the most splendid of all gems, or the queen of precious stones, the lustre-darting diamond, which is produced from, the black of Sab, Seb, or Saturn, the origin of all visible things, or the 'Great Deep', or 'Great Mother', in one sense.

This is the day on which all green gems, and the colour green, should be universally used. Friday is the 'woman's day' of the sevenfold weekly period; and therefore, as some ill-natured people might say, it is the unlucky day. Certain it is, however, that although it presents the exact contradiction of being especially the woman's day, few or no marriages would be celebrated on this day, as popularly bearing the mark of ill luck, which suppositions few would like Openly to defy, or, according to the familiar expression, 'fly in the face of'. May is also forbidden for marriages, although it is the 'woman's month', or month in which 'May-day' occurs, and in which 'May-poles' used to be set up everywhere. (See figures of May-poles later in our book.)

But to return to the ill-omened colour to England, white, and to the important shape in which we find it to appear in the name borne by our present--'King Albert Edward;' inheriting his name 'Albert' from perhaps the most lovable prince whom this country has ever known as casting in his destinies, by marriage, with it, but whose end--in the prime of life, and in the fullness of his influence--was surely unfortunate enough, when the eyes of hope of all Europe, in various respects, were fixed upon him! The name 'Albert' has happily, however, been passed over in the person of the King as a name laid aside; and he is known by the name--the propitious name--of Edward only, 'Edward the Seventh'.

The 'White Lady of Berlin' and her mysterious appearances from time to time are well known to the writers of modern romantic biographical story. Whom she is supposed to represent seems to be unknown to all. Those who have recorded her fitful revelations of herself venture no surmise; but she is considered in some way the evil genius of the Hohenzollern family, much in the same manner as the unaccounted-for figure might have been regarded who revealed himself to Brutus on the Plains of Philippi, and who announced the crowning misfortunes of the next day. The Irish have a name for this supernatural appearance in the 'banshee', or the speaker, or exponent, of fate. The 'White Lady of Berlin' is supposed to be seen by some person in the palace before any pre-eminent disaster supervenes, occurring to a member of the royal house. The glimpses of this White Lady are only momentary and delusive--so vague, indeed, as to be readily contradicted or explained away (perhaps willingly) even by the supposed seers themselves. It is also a fact not a little curious, when we come to consider it by the side-glance, as it were, that the colour white (the English unfortunate colour), besides being that of the 'White Rose' and of 'Whitehall', is that white of the unlucky Stuarts, whose history through centuries, both in Scotland and in England, was but one long catalogue of mishaps, woes, and disasters. Prince Charles Edward and his famous 'white cockade', and the evil fortunes of all his followers and of the Jacobite cause in general in' 1715 and 1745, emblemed in the virgin, holy colour white, supply a touching, nay tragical, page in public and in private history. Lastly, we may adduce as a supposed exemplification of the terrible general effects of this evil-boding name albus, and colour white, in France, the history of all the Bourbons, whose colour is white in particular, from the first of that name who displayed his snowy banner, and who fell by the dagger of an assassin, to the last Bourbon in modern history, whose fate we will not attempt to forecast, nor in any manner to seem to bespeak. Merlin, whose prophecy of the dangers, at some time, of 'white' to the kingdom of England was supposed to refer to the invasion of this country by the pale

Saxons, whose device or token was the 'white horse', until further associations of white and misfortune in England came to dispel the idea, may even still have his original prophetic forecast unfulfilled. The colour white, or some strange, at present unimagined, association of 'white', may yet lie, like a dream, *perdu* in the future (of the chances of which no man can speak), to justify Merlin at once, and to astonish and bewilder, by the long-delayed evolvement of the centuries in which at last the realization and the misfortune become simultaneously apparent: for which, and for the possibilities of which, we will terminate in the adjuration of the sublime Romans, those masters in the art of augury and of divination, 'Absit omen! But thus much we have chosen to explain about the colour white, in justification of the ideas of the Rosicrucians as to the supernatural power of colours; and as to the magical qualities of those occult influences which they determined, in their philosophical vocabularies, strangely and mysteriously to call the 'signatures of things'.

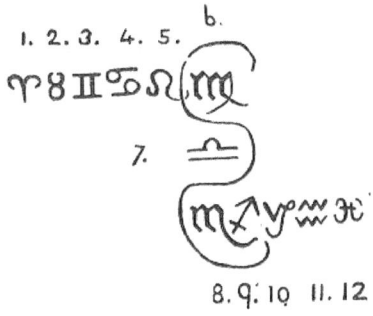

CHAPTER THE TWENTY-FOURTH

THE BELIEFS OF THE ROSICRUCIANS--MEANING OF LIGHTS AND OF COMMEMORATIVE FLAMBEAUX IN ALL WORSHIP

FROM the name of the Temple, now Stonehenge, comes the name of Ambresbury, which stands a few miles from it. This is called the 'Ambres of the Abiri'. It is two words, and means the 'Ambres of the *Dii Potentes*', or of the אבירי, or 'Cabiri'--for they are the same.

The star of the *Légion d'Honneur* bears the inscription '*Napoléon, Empereur des Français*'. This order was instituted by the Emperor Napoleon the First, after the discovery and dissolution of the Secret Society, or Brotherhood, of which General Pichegru, Georges Cadoudal; the famous Moreau, and other noted revolutionary men were members. This order possessed, it is stated, a talisman or mystic head, which served as a recognitive mark, and was supposed to be a sort of bond to the brotherhood. After their death, their secret insignia were discovered; and it has been stated that the Emperor Napoleon, whose attention was instantaneously arrested by great and unusual ideas or supernatural suggestions, in suppressing this mystic symbol or head, adopted it in another form, and substituted his own head in profile, as the *palladium*, or talisman, for his new order of the 'Legion of Honour'.

The saffron robe of Hymen is of the colour of the Flame of Fire. The Bride, in ancient days, was covered with a veil called the '*Flammeum*'; unless made under this, no vow was considered sacred. The ancients swore, not by the altar, but by the flame of fire *which was upon the altar.* Yellow, or flame-colour, was the colour of the Ghebers, or Guebres, or Fire-Worshippers. *The Persian lilies are yellow;* and here will be remarked a connexion between this fact of the yellow of the Persian lilies and the mystic symbols in various parts of our book. Mystic rites, and the symbolical lights, which mean the Divinity of Fire, abound at

Candlemas-day (February 2nd), or the Feast of the Purification; in the torches borne at weddings, and in the typical flame-brandishing at marriage over almost all the world; in the illuminations at feasts; in the lights on, and set about, the Christian altar; at the festival of the Holy Nativity; in the ceremonies at preliminary espousals; in the Bale, or Baal, fires on the summits of the mountains; in the watch-lights, or votive sanctuary-lights, in the hermitage in the lowest valley; in the *chapelle ardente*, in the Romish funereal observances, with its abundance of silent, touching lights around the splendid *catafalque*, or twinkling, pale and ineffectual, singly at the side of the death-bed in the cottage of the peasant. Starry lights and innumerable torches at the stately funeral, or at any pompous celebration, mean the same. In short, light all over the world, when applied to religious rites, and to ceremonial, whether in the ancient or in the modern times, bespeaks the same origin, and struggles to express the same meaning, which is Parseeism, Perseism, or the worship of the deified FIRE, disguised in many theological or theosophic forms. It will, we trust, never be supposed that we mean, in this, *real fire*, but only the inexpressible something of which real fire, or rather its flower or glory (bright light), is the farthest off--because, in being visible at all, it is the grossest and most inadequate image.

All this strange, dreamy, ethereal view of a vital, accessible something, entirely separate from the suggestions of mere sensation, is Gnosticism, or Bhuddism, in its own profoundest depth. It follows on similarly to the 'intoxication,' or suffusion with the very certainty of the presence of God, which, in the poetic sense, was said to fill the mind of even the supposed arch-atheist Spinoza.

The Rosicrucians, through the revelations concerning them of their celebrated English representative, Robertus de Fluctibus, or Robert Fludd, declare, in accordance with the Mosaic account of creation--which, they maintain, is in no instance to be taken literally, but metaphorically--that two original principles, in the beginning, proceeded from the Divine Father. These are Light and Darkness, or form or idea, and matter or plasticity. Matter, downwards, becomes fivefold, as it works in its forms, according to the various operations of the first informing light; it extends four-square, according to the points of the celestial compass, with the divine creative effluence in the centre. The worlds spiritual and temporal, being rendered subject to the operation of the original Type, or Idea, became, in their imitation of this Invisible Ideal, first intelligible, and then endowed with reciprocal meaning outwards from themselves. This produced the being (or thought) to whom, or to which, creation was disclosed. This is properly the 'Son', or Second Ineffable Person of the Divine Trinity. Thus that which we understand as a 'human mind' became a possibility. This second great, only intelligible world, the Rosicrucians call 'Macrocosmos'. They distribute it as into three regions or spheres; which, as they lie near to, or dilate the farthest from, the earliest opening divine 'Brightness', they denominate the Empyræum, the Ætheræum, and the Elementary Region, each filled and determinate and forceful with less and less of the First Celestial Fire. These regions contain innumerable invisible nations, or angels, of a nature appropriate to each. Through these immortal regions, Light, diffusing in the emanations of the cabalistic Sephiroth, becomes the blackness, sediment, or ashes, which is the second fiery, real world. This power, or vigour, uniting with the Ethereal Spirit, constitutes strictly the 'Soul of the World'. It becomes the only means of the earthly intelligence, or man, knowing it. It is the Angel-Conqueror, Guide, Saviour born of 'Woman', or 'Great Deep', the Gnostic Sophia, the 'Word made flesh' of St. John. The Empyræum is properly the flower, or glory (effluent in its abundance), of the divine Latent Fire. It is penetrated with miracle and holy magic. The Rosicrucian system teaches that there are three ascending hierarchies of beneficent Angels (the purer portion of the First Fire, or Light), divided into nine orders. These threefold angelic hierarchies are the Teraphim, the Seraphim, and the Cherubim. This religion, which is the religion of the Parsees, teaches that, on the Dark Side, there are also three counter-balancing resultant divisions of operative intelligences, divided again into nine spheres, or inimical regions, populated with splendidly endowed adverse angels, who boast still, the relics of their lost, or eclipsed, or changed, light. The elementary world, or lowest world, in which man and his belongings, and the lower creatures, are produced, is the flux, subsidence, residuum, ashes, or deposit, of the Ethereal Fire. Man is the microcosm, or 'indescribably small copy', of the whole great world. Dilatation and compression, expansion and contraction, magnetic sympathy, gravitation to, or flight from, is the bond which holds all imaginable things together. The connexion is intimate between the higher and the lower, because all is a perpetual aspiration, or continuous descent: one long, immortal chain, whose sequence is never-ending, reaches by impact with that immediately above, and by contact with that immediately below, from the very lowest to the very highest. 'So true is it that God loves to retire into His clouded Throne; and, thickening the Darkness that encompasses His most awful Majesty, He inhabits an Inaccessible Light, and lets none into His Truths but the poor in spirit.' The Rosicrucians contended that these so 'poor in spirit' meant themselves, and implied their submission and abasement before God.

The Rosicrucians held that, all things visible and invisible having been produced by the contention of light with darkness, the earth has denseness in its innumerable heavy concomitants downwards, and they contain less and less of the original divine light as they thicken and solidify the grosser and heavier in matter. They taught, nevertheless, that every object, however stifled or delayed, in its operation, and darkened and thickened in the solid blackness at the base, yet contains a certain possible deposit, or jewel, of light--which light; although by natural process it may take ages to evolve, as light will tend at last by its own native, irresistible force upward (when it has opportunity), can be liberated; that dead matter will yield this spirit in a space more or less expeditious by the art of the alchemist. There are worlds within worlds--we, human organisms, only living in a deceiving, or Bhuddistic, 'dreamlike phase' of the grand panorama.

Unseen and unsuspected (because in it lies magic), there is an inner magnetism, or divine aura, or ethereal spirit, or possible eager fire; shut and confined, as in a prison, in the body, or, in. all sensible solid objects, which have more or less of spiritually sensitive life as they can more successfully free themselves from this ponderable, material obstruction. Thus all minerals, in this spark of light, have the rudimentary possibility of plants and growing organisms; thus all plants have rudimentary sensitives, which might (in the ages) enable them to perfect and transmute into locomotive new creatures, lesser or higher in their grade, or nobler or meaner in their functions; thus all plants and all vegetation might pass off (by side-roads) into more distinguished highways, as it were, of independent, completer advance, allowing their original spark of light to expand and thrill with higher and more vivid force, and to urge forward with more abounding, informed purpose--all wrought by planetary influence, directed by the unseen spirits (or workers) of the Great Original Architect, building His *microcosmos* of a world from the plans and powers evoked in the *macrocosm*, or heaven of first forms, which, in their multitude and magnicence, are as changeable shadows cast off from the Central Immortal First Light, whose rays dart from the centre to the extremest point of the universal circumference. It is with terrestrial fire that the alchemist breaks or sunders the material darkness or atomic thickness, all visible nature yielding to *his* furnaces, whose scattering heat (without its sparks) breaks all doors of this world's kind. It is with immaterial fire (or ghostly fire) that the Rosicrucian loosen contraction and error, and conquers the false knowledge and the deceiving senses which bind the human soul an in its prison. On this side of his powers, on this dark side (to the world) of his character, the alchemist (rather now become the Rosicrucian) works in invisible light, and is a magician. He lays the bridge (as the Pontifex or Bridge-Maker) between the world possible and the world impossible: and across this bridge, in his Immortal Heroism and Newness, he leads the votary out of his dream of life into his dream of temporary death, or info extinction of the senses and of the powers of the senses;

which world's blindness is the only true and veritable life, the envelope of flesh falling metaphorically off the now liberated glorious *entity*--taken up, in charms, by the invisible fire into rhapsody, which is as the gate of heaven.

Now, a few words as to the theory of alchemy. The alchemists boasted of the power, after the elimination and dispersion of the ultimate elements of bodies by fire (represented by the absent difference of their weights before and after their dissolution), to recover them back out of that exterior, unknown world surrounding this world: which world men reason against as if it had no existence, when if has real existence; and in which they were in ignorance in their 'Pre-State', as they will be (perhaps also in ignorance) in their 'After-State'. In respect of which state ('before' and 'after' this life), all people, in all time, have had an idea. It is 'Purgatory', if is '*Limbus*', it is 'Suspension in Repose', it is as the 'Twilight' of the Soul before and after the 'Day' of Full Life, or complete consciousness. These ideas are as equally Christian as Pagan. How little is all this supposed in the ignorance of the moderns!

It is this other world (just off this real world) into which the Rosicrucians say they can enter, and bring back, as proofs that they have been there, the old things (thought escaped), metamorphosed into new things. This act is *transmutation*. This product is magic gold, or 'fairy gold', condensed as real gold, This growing gold, or self-generating and multiplying, gold, is obtained by invisible transmutation (and in other light) in another world out of this world; immaterial to us creatures of limited faculties, but material enough, farther on, on the heavenly side, or on the side *opposite* to our human side. In other words, the Rosicrucians claim not to be bound by the limits of the present world, but to be able to pass into this next world (inaccessible only in appearance), and to be able to work in it, and to come back safe (and selfsame) out of it, bringing their trophies with them, which were gold, obtained out of this master-circle, or outside elementary circle, different from ordinary life, though enclosing it; and the *elixir vitæ*, or the means of the renewal or the perpetuation of human life through this universal, immortal medicine, or *magisterium*, which, being a portion of the light outside, or magic, or breath of the spirits, fleeing from man, and only to be won in the audacity of God-aided alchemic exploration, was independent of those mastered natural elements, or nutritions, necessary to ordinary common life. The daily necessary food which is taken for the sustenance of the body was, as the Rosicrucians contended, the means of dissolution, or death daily passing through and the real cause of the destruction of the body, by the slowest of all processes, but yet, in instalments, the effectual one. They asserted that man *dies daily* in his own native bodily corruptions. These singular philosophers ventured the assertion that God did not, in the beginning, intend that man's life should be terminated by diseases, nor that he should be made subject to accidental, violent means of end. In the abstract sense, and apart from our knowledge of man as man, the Rosicrucians contended that diseases are not necessarily incidental to the body, and that death may be said to have become an imported accident into the scheme of things; our ideas being erroneous as to the original design in regard of us.

Man was to have lived as the angels, of an impregnable, impassable vitality, taking his respiration, not by short snatches, as it were, but as out of the great cup of the centuries. *He* was to be the spectator of nature--not nature *his* spectator. The real objects of the adepts were, in truth, to remain no longer slaves to those things supposed to be *necessities*, but, by the assistance of Heaven, to remove back to Heaven's original intention; to rise superior to the consequences of the original Curse, and to tread under foot, in vindicating the purpose of God, that mortal (however seductive), sexual, distinctive, degradation entailing dissolution, heired from Adam, or from the First Transgressor. That poverty and celibacy (under certain limitations) must be the obligations of the true Brothers of the 'R. C.' will at once be seen from the above reasons, however wild and mistaken--barely even comprehensible. This is the real original reason for the monastic state--defying and denying nature.

The original curse was entailed upon mankind by eating of
> The fruit
> Of that forbidden 'Tree', whose mortal taste
> Brought death into the world, and all our woe.

What that 'Tree' was, and what are its votive, idolatrous (in the bad sense) symbols in the old world and in the new, we think we have abundantly shown--at least, in the occult, shadowy idea. Why, supposing that the alchemists ever possessed the power of universal gold-making, they fail of producing any, or of offering one of their rich gifts to the world, is at once answered in these two conclusive, obvious facts: Firstly, that if this power of gold-making, or of transmutation, were a recognized possibility, like any other art allowed or authorized, it would inevitably become penal or impossible, in order to preserve the existing value of gold, the richest metal; and the professor of the art would be at once put out of sight. Secondly, if supposed to be true, and not fable, like any ordinary art or science, the man who had arrived at such a stupendous secret would be sacrificed or martyred in the insatiate haste of the people to compel him to produce gold, in order to satisfy *them*--that gold, moreover, which will destroy, but can never satisfy. 'Ye cannot serve God and Mammon.' These things the alchemists too well know, and therefore they (if any exist now) hide, as they have always hidden, and deny, as they have always denied; being desirous of stealing through the world unknown and of serving God alone, whose inaccessible great glory, as we see, has been imitated in the golden lights of the inexpressibly grand (in the worldly and mortal sense), apostate constructions of the magnificent Mammon, Lord of the Treasures of this World, for which men offer themselves willing victims even to Him, King of the Visible, whose semblance is that of the most brilliant yellow element--Fire--*Or*, 'Golden Flame', the 'Flower' of the Fire.

The alchemists maintain that the metals are produced in the secret operations of the planets, that grow them daily in the bowels of the earth; that the sun and moon, red and white, fire and water, light and darkness, male and female, night and day, are active in the generation of the precious metals, of which gold is due wholly to the invisible operation of the sun and moon, and silver is referable to the whitening or bleaching lucidity of the moon; that gold is produced quicker or slower according to the faster or slower operations of nature; that it vivifies and vegetates, bears bright seed and multiplies, germinating as fructifying in the matrix, or the laboratories of the earth; that gold is produced with infinite pains, as it were, by these chemic operations of nature, very slowly under certain circumstances, but very rapidly under other more favourable, more powerful conditions; that it is possible for the adept to act as the midwife of nature, and to assist in her deliverance, and in the birth of gold, in these occult senses; that the work of nature being thus expedited by this alchemical art, the hitherto thwarted intention of Providence is effected in the predetermined liberation of the divine gold, 'Lux', or light, which is again united to its radix or producing-point, in. heaven. A spark of the original light is supposed by the Rosicrucians to remain deep down in the interior of every atom.

The Rosicrucian Cabala teaches that the three great worlds above--Empyræum, Ætheræum, and the Elementary Region--have their copies in the three points of the body of man: that his head answers to the first; his breast, or heart, to the second; and his ventral region to the third. In the head rests the intellect, or the magnetism of the assenting judgment, which is a phenomenon; in his heart is the conscience, or the *emotional* faculty, or the Saviour; and in the umbilical centre reside the animal faculties, or all the sensitives. Nutrition is destruction in the occult sense, and dissolution is rescue in the occult sense; because the entity, or visible man, is constructed in the elements, and is as equally ashes, or condemned matter, as they are; and because the fire that feeds the body (which is its natural respiration or maintenance) is in itself that which (however slowly) destroys it. Man lives upon the lees of nature, or (in the Bhuddistic view) upon the 'gross purgations of the celestial fire', which is urging itself clear through the operation of the divine rescuing spirit in it. It follows that metaphysically all the wonderful shows of life are *phantasmata* only, and their splendours false and a show only. But as these shows are the medium and the instruments of life, without which intelligence (in the human sense) would be impossible, this celestial 'Second Fire' has been deified in the acknowledgments of the first inhabitants of the world, who raised pillars and stones in its honour as the first idol. Thus man bears in his own body the picture of the 'Triune'. Reason is the head, feeling is the breast, and the mechanical means of both feeling and reasoning, or the means of his being Man, is the epigastric centre, from which the two first spring as emanations, and with which the two first form ultimately but 'one'. The invisible magnetic, geometrical bases, or latitudes, of these three vital points, whose consent, or coincidence, or identity, forms the 'microcosm', which is a copy of the same form in heaven, answer magically to their stellar originals. This is astrological 'ruling' by pyramidal culmination; and by trilinear descent or efflux, to an intersecting point in the latitudes of the heavens and in the man's body, at which upper and lower, or heaven and earth; interchange; and Man is therefore said to be made 'in the image' of the Archetype, who has 'descended' to man, who has 'ascended' to Him. This is the 'hinge-point' of the natural and the supernatural, upon which the two wings of the worlds real and unreal revolve. The starry heavens, through whose astrological cross-work complications (as in a snap) all these infinite effects are produced, and on whose (for, taking gravitation away, they are the same) floor of lights, or cope or dome of signs or letters, all the 'past, present, and future' has been written by the finger of God (although to man they are ever rearranging), can be read by the competent as Fate Natural and supernatural, though one is only the reversed side of the other, as 'darkness is only the reversed side of light, and light is only the reversed side of darkness',[13] are mistaken by man for opposites, although they are the same: man living in this state in darkness, although his world is light; and heaven in this state being darkness, although this state is light.

---

[13] '*Comte de Gabalis*': Rosicrucian.

Music (although it is unheard by man) is necessarily produced in the ceaseless operations of material nature, because nature itself is penitential and but the painful (and musical) expression between two dissonant points. The Bhuddist contends that all forms are but the penance of nature. Music is life, and life is music. Both are pain, although made delightful. Phenomena are not real.

Thus colours to the human are negative as music addressed to the ear, the musical notes negative as colours addressed to the eye, and so on of the other senses, although they are all the same in the imagination, without the *sensorium*--as dreams show. And life and the world, in this view, are all imagination: man being made in idea, and only in his own belief. This, again, is only pure Parseeism; and the whole will be rightly regarded as the most extraordinary dream of philosophy--as depth of depths beyond idea.

Schubert, in his *Symbolism of Dreams*, has the following passages, which we have before adduced and made use of for illustration: 'It may be asked whether. that language, which now occupies so low a place in the estimation of men, be not the actual waking language of the higher regions, while we', adds the philosopher, coming out with something very strange, 'awake as we fancy ourselves, may be sunk *in a sleep of many thousand years*, or, at least, in the echo of their dreams, and only intelligibly catch a few dim words of that language of God, as sleepers do scattered expressions from the loud conversation of those around them.'

The following is a fair view of the Rosicrucian theory concerning music.

The whole world is taken as a musical instrument; that is, a chromatic, sensible instrument. The common axis or role of the world celestial is intersected--where this superior diapason, or heavenly concord or chord, is divided--by the spiritual sun, or centre of sentience. Every man has a little spark (sun) in his own bosom. Time is only protracted consciousness, because there is no world out of the mind conceiving it. Earthly music is the faintest tradition of the angelic state; it remains in the mind of man as the dream of, and the sorrow for, the lost paradise. Music is yet master of the man's emotions, and therefore of the man.

Heavenly music is produced from impact upon the paths of the planets, which stand as chords or strings, by the cross-travel of the sun from note to note, as from planet to planet; and earthly music is microscopically an imitation of the same, and a 'relic of heaven'; the faculty of recognition arising from the same supernatural musical efflux which produced the planetary bodies, in motived projection from the sun in the centre, in their evolved, proportional, .harmonious order. The Rosicrucians taught that the 'harmony of the spheres' is a true thing, and not simply a poetic dream: all nature, like a piece of music, being produced by melodious combinations of the cross-movement of the holy light playing over the lines of the planets: light flaming as the spiritual ecliptic, or the *gladius* of the Archangel Michael, to the extremities of the solar system. Thus are music, colours, and language allied.

Of the Chaldæan astrology it may figuratively be said that, although their knowledge, in its shape of the 'Portentous Stone'-- in this instance, their grave-stone--shut up the devils in the depths of the 'Abyss', and made the sages their masters (Solomon being the Priest or King, and his seal the 'Talisman' that secures the 'Deep'): Man, on account of his having fallen into the shadow and the corruptions of EXISTENCE, needs that mighty exterior HAND (before which all tremble) to rescue him back into his native original Light or Rest. All the foregoing is pure Bhuddism.

Thinkers who have weighed well the character of those supposed infractions of natural laws which have admitted, as it were philosophically, the existence of other independent, absent, thinking spirits, communicating intelligibly in this world of ours, insist 'that it is impossible to suppose that the partitions between this world and the other world are so thin as that you can hear the movers in the other through.'

Nevertheless thoughtful people are equally able to convict modern philosophical realists of absurdity, when the former adduce the following insurmountable objection against them: 'When we tell you of a supernatural thing', say the supernaturalists to the realists; 'you directly *have recourse to a natural thing in which to find it.*' This is contrary to common dense; and therefore the realistic arguer has no right to dispose in this manner of that which is supernatural; for his objections are futile and vain, and his arguments contradict themselves. Spirit and matter, when sought to be explained, are totally opposed; and hence, arises the reason why there can never be any belief of impossible things, and only the conviction that such things have been in the mind, notwithstanding the insurmountable contradiction of the senses.

CHAPTER THE TWENTY-FIFTH

THE GREAT PYRAMID

IN a very elaborate and interesting book, published in the year 1867, the title of which, at length, is the following: *Life and Work at the Great Pyramid*, by C. Piazzi Smyth, Professor of Practical Astronomy in the University of Edinburgh, and Astronomer Royal for Scotland. Edinburgh, 1867: the conclusions (though a mistake) which we now supply from the author are offered as definitions, after infinite care, of this important name or word, 'PYRAMID'. 'Pyramid' is derived in this book from two Greek terms. υρός, 'wheat'; μετρον, 'measure'; or from Coptic roots, signifying *pyr*, 'division'; *met*, 'ten'. However, we offer to deduce this term 'Pyramid' from quite another source. The present writer originally sought to do. this in the year 1860, in a dissertation on the origin and purpose of the 'Pyramids of Egypt'. It is well known that the letters *P* and *F* are radically the same letter (as is evidenced by their peculiar pronunciation in certain countries), and that they are interchangeable. In Professor Smyth's book, Πυρός is wrongly translated 'wheat'. It signifies 'product', or 'growth', or 'elimination'; in other words, and in the symbolical sense, it means 'sun-begotten', or 'fire-begotten'. The Coptic derivation (re-read by a new light) is the true one. Thus we obtain another reason upon which we rely as the real interpretation of the name of the pyramid, or obelisk, or great original altar or upright, raised in the divinity working secondarily in nature. Πυρ is fire (or Division produced by fire); Μετρον is Ten (or measures or spaces numbered as ten). The whole word means, and the entire object bearing this name means, the original Ten Measures or Parts of the Fiery Ecliptic or Solar Wheel, or the Ten Original Signs of the Zodiac. Therefore the Pyramids are commemorative altars raised to the divinity Fire.

The *Ophites* are said to have maintained that the serpent of Genesis was the Λογος, and the 'Saviour'. The *Logos* was Divine

Wisdom, and was the Bhudda, or Buddha, of India. The Brazen Serpent was called Λογος, or the 'Word', by the Chaldee Paraphrast (Basnage, lib. iv. ch. xxv). It is very certain that, in ancient times, the serpent was an object of adoration in almost all nations. The serpent-worshippers seem to have placed at the head, or nearly at the head, of all things (Maia), and most intimately connected with the serpent, a certain principle which they called 'Sophia'. This is clearly a translation of the word 'Bhudda' into Greek. It also reminds us that the old Bhuddas are always under the care of the Cobra-Capella. This is evidenced in all the Memnonian or Egyptian heads; and in the asp (or fleur-de-lis), more or less veiled or altered, displayed as the chief symbol upon the universal Sphynxes. The serpent, in one view, was the emblem of the evil principle, or destroyer. But, as we have seen before, the 'destroyer' was the 'creator'. Hence he had the name, among his numerous appellations, of ΟΦΙΣ; in Hebrew, אוב, *Ob*; and as he was the 'logus', or 'linga', he was also ΟΨ, and in Hebrew מ·מרא. Query, hence, Συφαρ, a seraph or serpent?--see Jones's *Lexicon* (*in voce*), and Σοφος, wise. The Συφ and Σοφ are both the same root. The famous 'Brazen Serpent', called Nehustan, set up by Moses in the Wilderness, is termed in the Targum a 'Saviour'. It was probably a 'serpentine crucifix', as it is called a cross by Justin Martyr. All the foregoing is allegorical, and hides deep Gnostic myths, which explain serpent-worship, united with the adoration paid to a perpendicular.

The three most celebrated emblems carried in the Greek mysteries were the Phallus, I; the Egg, O and the Serpent, Φ; or otherwise the Phallus, the Ioni or Umbilicus, and the Serpent. The first, in each case. is the emblem of the sun, or of fire, as the male, or active, generative power. The second denotes the passive nature, or feminine principle, or the element of water. The third symbol indicates the destroyer, the reformer, or the renewer (the uniter of the two), add thus the preserver or perpetuator-- eternally renewing itself. The universality of the serpentine worship (or phallic adoration) is attested by emblematic sculpture and architecture all over the world. This does not admit of denial.

Its character and purpose are, however, wholly misunderstood. Not only is the worship of the serpent found everywhere, but it everywhere occupies an important station; and the farther back we go, the more universally it is found, and the more important it appears to have been considered. The Destroyer or Serpent of Genesis is correctly the Renovator or Preserver. In Genesis there is a 'Tree of Knowledge' and a 'Tree of Life'. Here we have the origin of the *Ophites, Ophiones,* or Oriental emblematical serpent-worshippers, to account for whom, and for whose apparently absurd object of adoration, our antiquaries have been so much perplexed. They worshipped the Saviour-Regenerator under the strangest (but the sublimest) aspect in the world; but not the devil, or malific principle, in our perverse, mistaken ideas, and with the vulgar, downward, literal meanings which we apply. The mythic and mimetic art of the Gnostics is nowhere more admirably or more successfully displayed than in their hieroglyphs and pictured *formulæ*. Even in the blazonry and in the collars and badges of chivalry (which seems so remote from them), we find these Ophite hints. The heathen temples and the modern ritualistic churches alike abound in unconscious Gnostic emblems. State ceremony harbours them; they mix with the insignia of all the orders of knighthood; and they show in all the heraldic and masonic marks, figures, and patterns, both of ancient and of modern times. The religion of the Rosicrucians is also concealed, and unconsciously carried forward, perpetuated, and ignorantly fostered, by the very persons and classes who form, contrive, and wear decorations with special mysterious marks, all the world over. Every person, in unconsciously repeating certain figures, which form an unknown language, heired from the ancient times; carries into futurity, and into all parts of the world, the same carefully guarded traditions, for the knowing to recognize, to whose origin the sun, in his first revolution, may be figuratively said to be the only witness. Thus the great inexpressible 'Talisman' is said to be borne to the 'initiate' through the ages.

Proposals were published some years ago for a book entitled, 'The Enigma of Alchemy and of Œdipus resolved; designed to elucidate the fables, symbols, and other mythological disguises, in which the Hermetic Art has been enveloped and signalized in various ages, in ecclesiastical ceremonies, masonic *formulæ*, astronomical signs, and constellations--even in the emblazonments of chivalry, heraldic badges, and other emblems; which, without explanation, have been handed down, and which are shown to have originated in the same universal mystic school, through each particular tracing their allusion to the means and mechanism.' This intended work was left in MS. by its anonymous author, now deceased, but was never published. The unknown author of it produced also in the year 1850, in one vol. 8vo, a book displaying extraordinary knowledge of the science of alchemy; which bore the name *A Suggestive Enquiry into the Hermetic Mystery; with a Dissertation on the more celebrated of the Alchemical Philosophers*. This book was published in London; but it is now extinct, having been bought up--for suppression, as we believe--by the author's friends after his decease, who probably did not wish him to be supposed to be mixed up in such out-of-the-way inquiries.

The Vedas describe the Persian religion (Fire-Worship) as having come from Upper Egypt. 'The mysteries celebrated within the recesses of the "hypogea"' (caverns or labyrinths) 'were precisely of that character which is called Freemasonic, or Cabiric. The signification of this latter epithet is, as to written letters, a desideratum. Selden has missed it; so have Origen and Sophocles. Strabo, too, and Montfauçon, have been equally astray. Hyde was the only one who had any idea of its composition when he declared that "It was a *Persian word*, somewhat altered from *Gabri* of *Guebri*, and signifying FIRE-WORSHIPPERS".' See O'Brien's *Round Towers of Ireland*, 1834, p. 354). Pococke, in his India in Greece, is very sagacious and true in his arguments; but he tells only half the story of the myths in his supposed successful divestment of them of all unexplainable character, and of exterior supernatural origin. He supposes that all the mystery must necessarily disappear when he has traced, and carefully pointed out, the identity and transference of these myths from India into Egypt and into Greece, and their gradual spread westward. But he is wholly mistaken; and most other modern explainers are equally mistaken. Pococke contemplates all from the ethnic and realistic point of view. He is very learned in an accumulation of particulars, but his learning is 'of the earth, earthy'; by which we mean that, like the majority of modern practical philosophers, he argues from below to above, and not, in the higher way, from above to below, or (contrary to the inductive, or Aristotelian, or Baconian method) from generals to particulars, or from the light of inspiration into the *sagacities* of darkness, as we may call unassisted world's knowledge--always vain.

The Feast of Lanterns, or Dragon-Feast, occurs in China at their New Year, which assimilates with that of the Jews, and occurs in October at the high tides. They salute the festival with drums and music, and with explosions of crackers. During the Feast, nothing is permitted to be thrown into water (for fear of profaning it). Here we have the rites of Aphrodite or Venus, or the Watery Deity, observed even in China, which worship, in Protean forms, being also the worship of the Dragon or Snake, prevails, in its innumerable contradictory and effective disguises, over the whole world. How like are the noises and explosions of crackers, etc., to the tumult of the festivals of Dionusus or Dionysius, to the riot or rout of the Corybantes amongst the Greeks, to the outcry and wild music of the priests of the Salii, and, in modern times, to the noises said to be made at initiation by the Freemasons, whose myths are claimed to be those (or imitative of those) of the whole world, whose Mysteries are said to come from that First Time, deep-buried in the blind, unconscious succession of the centuries! In the Royal-Arch order of the Masons, as some have said, at an initiation, the 'companions' fire pistols, clash swords, overturn chairs, and roll cannon-balls about. The long-descended forms trace from the oldest tradition; the origin, indeed, of most things is only doubt or conjecture, hinted in symbols.

The Egyptian Deities may always be recognized by the following distinctive marks:

Phthas, Ptah, by the close-fitting Robe, Four Steps, Baboon, Cynocephalus.

Ammon, Amn, by a Ram's Head, Double Plume, Vase, Canopus.

The Sun-God (Phre or Ra) has a Hawk's Head, Disc, Serpent, Uræus.

Thoth, or Thoyt, is Ibis-headed (means a scribe or priest).

Sochos, or Suches, has a Hawk. Hermes Trismegistus (Tat) displays a Winged Disc.

The Egyptians, however, *never* committed their greater knowledge to marks or figures, or to writing of any kind.

Figure 313: the Gnostics have a peculiar talisman of Fate (Homer's Αισα). This is one of the rarest types to be met with in ancient art. In Stosch's vast collection, Winckelmann was unable to find a single indubitable example. It is of brown agate, with transverse shades, and is an Etruscan intaglio or Gnostic gem. *The Gnostics*, p. 238, makes a reference to this figure.

Later in our book (figs. 191, 300, 301) we give a figure of the 'Chnuphis Serpent' raising himself aloft. Over, and corresponding to the rays of his crown, are the *seven vowels*, the elements of his name. The usual triple 'S.S.S.' and bard, and the name '**XNOYBIC**', are the reverse of, this Gnostic gem. It is a beautiful intaglio on a pale plasma of the finest quality, extremely convex, as it has been found on examination.

In the Ophic planetary group (*Origen in Celsum*, vi. 25) Michael is figured as a lion, Suriel as a bull, Raphael as a serpent, Gabriel as an eagle, Thautabaoth as a bear, Eratsaoth as a dog, Ouriel as an ass. Emanations are supposed to pass through the seven planetary regions, signified by these Chaldæan names, on their way to this world. It was through these seven planetary spiritual regions, or spheres, filled with their various orders of angels, that the Gnostics mythed the Saviour Jesus Christ to have passed secretly; disguising Himself and His Mission in order to win securely to His object. In evading recognition, in His acceptable disguises, through these already-created 'Princedoms of Angels', He veiled His purpose of His Voluntary Sacrifice for the Human Race till He was safe, in His investment in 'Humanity' for the accepted 'Propitiation'--through the 'Virgin' for production only; not for 'office'.

There was deep mystery in the Gnostic method of teaching that, although the 'Sacrifice' (the source of sacrifice in all faiths) was complete and real and perfect, the Saviour did not--nor could--suffer *bodily* or be nailed *really*, and *die* upon the Cross, but that He suffered in appearance only, and vicariously--the Scripture being misread. The Gnostics maintained that Simon the Cyrenean--who, the Evangelist states, bore His Cross--did really bear it as the culprit, and suffered upon it. As human and divine are totally different, this could not impair the efficacy of the 'Crucifixion', for the substitution of persons was miraculous and remote (of course) from human sense.

THE ROSICRUCIANS

PART II

CHAPTER THE FIRST

HISTORY OF THE TOWER OR STEEPLE

WE have asserted, in an earlier part of our book, that the pyramidal or triangular form which fire assumes in its ascent to heaven was, in the monolithic typology, used to signify the Great Generative Power. The coarse sensuality which seems inseparable from modern ideas about the worship of the pillar or upright had no place really in the solemn ancient mind, in which ideas of religion largely and constantly mingled. We must not judge the ancients by too rigid an adherence to our own prepossessions-- foolish and inveterately hardened as they continually are.

The adoration paid to this image of the *phallus*, which has persisted as an object of worship through all the ages, in all countries, was only the acknowledgment, in the ancient mind, of wonder at the seemingly accidental and unlikely, but certainly most complete and effectual, means by which the continuation of the human race is secured. The cabalistic arguers contended that 'Man' was a phenomenon; that he did not, otherwise than in his presentment, seem intended; that there appeared nothing even in the stupendous chain of organisms that seemed specially to hint his approach, or to explain his appearance (strange as this seems), according to likelihood and sequence; that between the highest of the animals and the being 'Man' there was a great gulf, and seemingly an impassable gulf; that some 'after-reason', to speak according to the means of the comprehension of man, induced his introduction into the Great Design; that, in short, 'Man' originally was not intended. There is a deep mystery underlying all these ideas, which we find differently accounted for in the various theologies.

We are here only speaking some of the abstruse speculations of the old philosophers, whose, idea of creation, and of the nature of man and his destiny, differed most materially--if not wholly--from the acceptable ideas which they chose to inculcate, and which they wished to impress upon ordinary minds. Thus their deeper speculations were never committed to writing, because they did not admit of, interpretation in this way; and if so handed down or promulgated, they would have been sure to have been rejected and disbelieved, on account of the impossibility of their being believed. In indicating some of the strange notions propounded by the Sophists, and, if possible, still more remarkably by the early Christian Fathers, we desire to disclaim

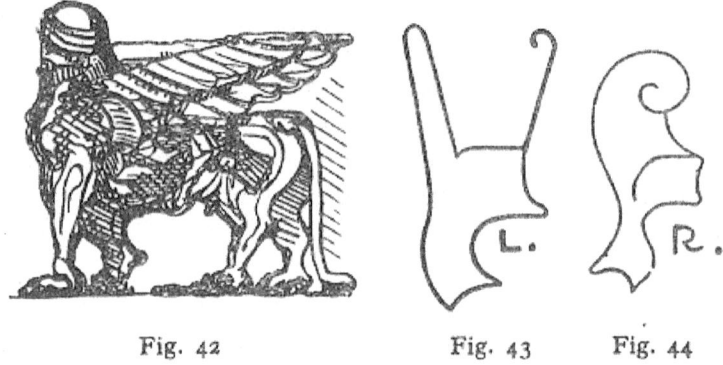

Fig. 42   Fig. 43   Fig. 44

any participation with them. Our personal belief of these theories must not be necessarily supposed from our seeming to advocate them. There is no doubt that they were very acute and profound persons who undertook the examination and reconcilement of the philosophical systems at the introduction of Christianity.

Fig 46: Pyramid; Fig. 47: Tower or 'Tor'; Fig 48: Tower; Fig. 49: Tower of Babel; Fig. 50: Pyramid; Fig 51: Scarabæus.

The succeeding array of phallic figures will be found interesting, as tracing out to its progenitor or prototype that symbol which we call the 'upright'. This architectural descent we shall call the 'Genealogy of the Tower or Steeple'.

The Architectural Genealogy of the 'Tower' or 'Steeple' (so to speak) is full of suggestion, and is closely connected with the story of the phallus.

The insignia on the heads of the cobras in the friezes of the Egyptian Court in the Crystal Palace are coloured on the Right,

White, on the Left, *Red*. These imply masculine and feminine ideas.

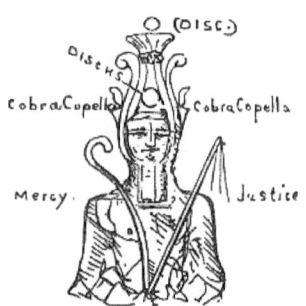

Fig. 52 : Egyptian Colossus

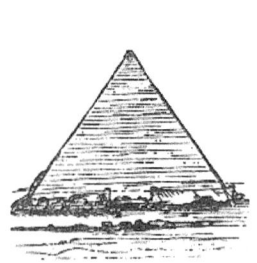

Fig. 53 : Pyramid

Fig. 54
Egyptian Seated Figure (British Museum)

Fig. 42 is the Winged Human-headed Lion. It comes from the Nineveh Gallery. It may be recognized as the Winged Bull, and also as the Winged 'Lion of St Mark'.

The 'Lion', 'Bull', 'Eagle', 'Man', are the symbols of the Evangelists; the 'Man', or 'Angel' standing for St. Matthew, the 'Lion' for St. Mark, the 'Bull' for St. Luke, and the 'Eagle' for St. John. In these strange aspects the Evangelists figured in many ancient churches, and on most fonts. These representative forms are also said to have been the 'Four Cherubim' of the Ark of the Hebrews. Hermetically they signify the 'four elements', or the four corners or angle-points of the 'Lesser' or 'Manifested World', or the 'Microcosm' of the Cabalists.

Fig. 55 : Colossal Head (British Museum)

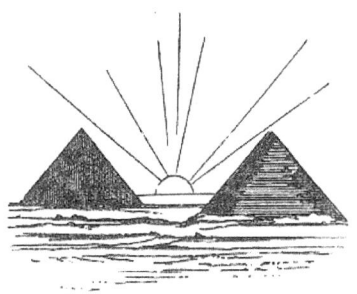

Fig. 56

Fig. 55: Colossal Head (British Museum)

Fig. 45 represents an Obelisk at Nineveh, now in the British Museum. Jacob's Pillar, the Sacred Stone in Westminster Abbey, 'Bethel', etc., 'Gilgal', have a mythic alliance with the obelisk.

Regarding the pyramids the following may be advanced: Murphy, the delineator of the Alhambra, considered the Pointed Arch to be a system founded on the principle of the Pyramid. The pointed or vertical Saracenic or Gothic arch presents the form of the upper portion of the human φαλλος. The Saracenic arch denotes the union of the Linga and Yoni.

In fig. 56 we have the sun rising from between the horns of Eblis (here taken for the pyramids). This is a poetical superstition of the Arabians, who therefore turn to the *North* to pray it

Fig. 58: Figures on the Egyptian Sarcophagus in the British Museum

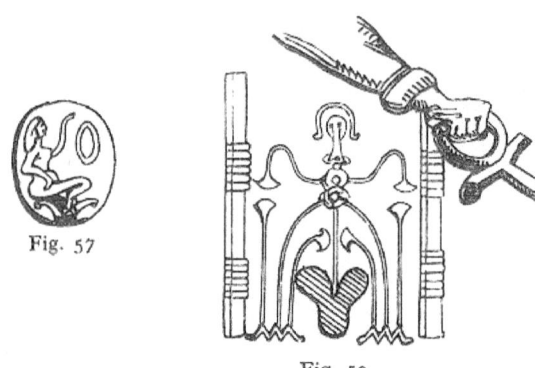

Fig. 57

Fig. 59

contradiction to the practice of the Persians, who adore the rising sun. The Arabians avert in prayer from this malific sign of the 'horns', because the sun is seen rising from between them; and when disclosing from between these mythic pillars, the sun becomes a portent.

Fig. 57 is an Egyptian seal, copied by Layard (*Nineveh and Babylon*, p. 156). Subject: the Egyptian god Harpocrates, seated on the mythic lotus, in adoration of the Yoni, or הוה, or *havah*.

The Druidical Circles, and single stones standing in solitary places, are all connected with the mystic speculations of the Rosicrucians.

The eminences, St. Michael's Mount and Mont St.-Michel, were dedicated by the Phœnicians to the Sun-God (Hercules), as the 'Hydra' or 'Dragon-slayer'.

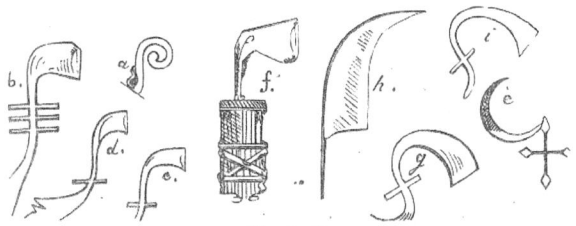

Figs. 60, 61

Heads of Ships ; *a.* Fiddle-head ; *b, c, d.* Gondola ; *e.* Ceres' Reaping-hook, also Saturn ; *f.* Blade and Fasces ; *g.* Beak of Galley ; *h.* Glaive ; *i.* Prow of Grecian Galley.

Fig. 62: Stonehenge

These mounts in the Channel are secondary 'Hercules' Pillars', similar to Calpe and Abyla.

The Architectural Genealogy of the 'Tower' or 'Steeple' displays other phases of the alterations of the 'upright'. All towers are descendants of the biblical votive stones, and in multiplying have changed in aspect according to the ideas of the people of the country in which they were raised. This Architectural Genealogy of the 'Tower' or 'Steeple' gives many varieties.

The groups on Figs. 86-91 supply new changes in the Tower or Upright, and furnish evidence how it passed into the Christian times, and became the steeple. When thus changed and reproduced, according, to the architectural ideas of the builders of the different countries. where the same memorial pillar was raised, it assumed in time the peculiarities of the Gothic or pointed style. The steeples of the churches, the figures of which we give (fig. 86 – 98), indicate the gradual growth and expansion of the romantic or pointed architecture, which is generally called Gothic; and they prove how the upright, or original phallic form, was adopted and gradually mingled in Christian architecture--in reality at last becoming its dominant feature.

Fig. 63
Druidical Stone in Persia

Fig. 64
Druidical Circle at Darab, in Arabia

Fig. 65
'Kit's Cotty-house', Kent

Figs. 66. 67
Ancient British Coin, mentioned by Camden

Fig. 68
England: St. Michael's Mount, Mount's Bay, Cornwall. 'Dragon', Horns, or Fires. (Moloch or Baal)

British Channel, 'Dragonmouth' (Galilee from the West)

Fig. 69
France, Normandy: Mont St.-Michel. ('Montjoie !.' 'Montjoy !'—old "Battlecry of the Gauls.) 'Dragon'. Horns, or Fires. (Moloch or Baal).

St. Michael or the Sun (Hercules).

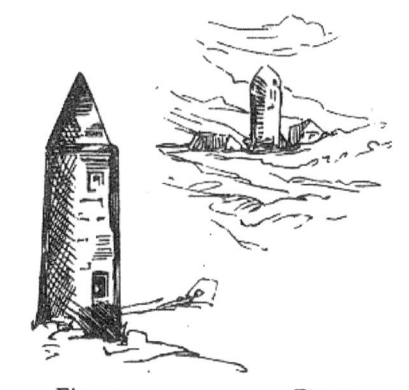

Fig. 71
Round Tower
Devenish, Ireland

Fig. 70
Round Tower, Ireland

73 75 72

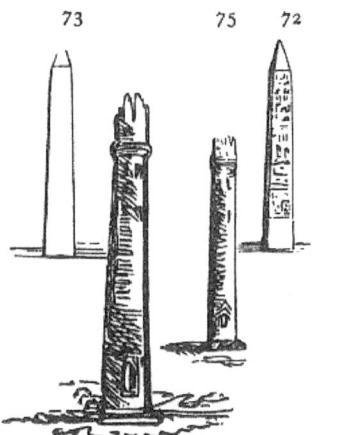

Fig. 72 : Obeliscus Fig. 73 : Obelisk Fig. 75 : Two Round Towers

Fig. 74 : Propylon, Thebes

77   78   76

Fig. 77
The 'Cootub Minar', near Delhi, supposed to have been built *circa* 1220

Fig. 78
Antrim Round Tower

Fig. 76
Round Tower at Bhaugulpore, India

Fig. 96 represents one of the Western Towers of St. Paul's Cathedral, London, which is one of the double *lithoi* (or obelisks), placed always in front of every temple, Christian as well as heathen. It is surmounted by the 'fir-cone' (*thyrsus*) of Bacchus, and the sculptured urns below it are represented as flaming with the mystic fire.

The Architectural Genealogy of the 'Tower' or 'Steeple' in fig. 97, exemplifies a parallel of growth between all the uprights, and exhibits their changes of form, and proves their reproduction through the centuries, both in the East, and more particularly in the western countries of Europe. In the lower portion of this fig. 97 we have a further outline-configuration of various towers and steeples, displaying the new character given, and the gradual variations of the 'Tower', in the first instance, and afterwards of the 'Steeple'; both being reproductions of the first idea of the *lithos*, upright, or *phallus:* the 'Idol' imitative of the 'Flame of Fire'.

The two pillars in fig. 102 are monuments in Penrith Churchyard. These are the familiar double, 'Runic' uprights, pillars, or spires.

All the minarets and towers in the East display in the peculiar curves of their summits the influence of the same phallic idea, as an attentive examination will prove.

There seems to be little or no reason to doubt that the much-disputed origin of the pointed Gothic arch, or lancet-shaped arch, and the Saracenic or Moorish horseshoe arch, is the union and blending of the two generative figures, namely, the 'discus' or round, and the upright and vertical, or 'phallic', shape, as indicated in the diagrams on Fig. 104-115. These forms, in their infinite variety, are the parents of all architecture.

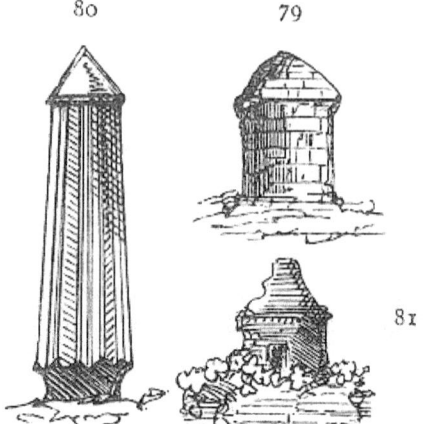

Fig. 79 : Round Tower, Peru
Fig. 80 : Persian Round Tower (From Hanway)
Fig. 81 : Round Tower, Central America

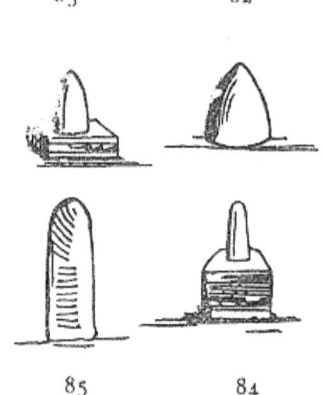

Fig. 82 : Mudros of Phœnicia (Dr Hyde)
Fig. 83 : Mahody of Elephanta (Capt. Pyke)
Fig. 84 : Muidhr of Inismurry
Fig. 85 : Pillar-stone, Hill of Tara

Fig. 86
Brixworth Church, Northamptonsh., supposed *circa* 670

Fig. 87
Tower in Dover Castle, *circa* 400

Fig. 88
Turret at the east end of St. Peter's Church, Oxford, *circa* 1180

Fig. 89 : Little Saxam Church, Suffolk, *circa* 1120
Fig. 90 : Rochester Cathedral (Turret), 1180
Fig. 91 : Bishop's Cleeve Church, Gloucestershire, *circa* 1180

Fig. 92 : Almondsbury Church, Gloucestershire, *circa* 1150
Fig. 93 : (Decorated Period) Salisbury Cathedral, Central Spire, 1350
Fig. 94 : St. Mary's Church, Cheltenham, *circa* 1250

Fig. 95 : Bayeux Cathedral, Normandy, *circa* 1220
Fig. 96 : St Paul's Cathedral

The Zodiac itself is, in certain senses, a Genesis, or 'History of Creation'. The 'Twelve Signs' may be interpreted as the 'Twelve Acts' of the Divine Drama. Some of the Mosques in the East are surmounted with twelve minarets, and the number twelve occurs frequently in connexion with the theology of the Moslems.

Fig: 115A is a scale Fig. 117 is a Masonic, Mosaic, or Tesselated Pavement. (Query, whether this pavement of black and white squares is not the origin of the ancient Chess Table, or Chess-Board?) The game of Chess, with enrichment, introduced into architecture, to symbolize the Female Deity, or 'Virgin born of the Waters'.

The spectator looks to the faces of the figure marked 116. the board upon which it is played, is probably 'Masonic' in its invention.

In old representations of the cathedral church of Notre Dame at Paris, the symbols of the masculine divinity--such as the sun and some others--are placed over the right hand, or masculine western tower, flanking the Galilee, or Great Western Porch; thus unmistakably hinting, its meaning. Over the corresponding left hand, or female tower, are placed the crescent horns of the moon, and some other indications, announcing its dedication to the female deified principle.

In all Christian churches--particularly in Protestant churches, where they figure most conspicuously--the two tables of stone of the Mosaic Dispensation are placed over the altar, side by side, as a united stone, the tops of which are rounded.

Fig. 118, on p. 250, represents the separated original 'Lithoi', when united. They then form the 'Double Tables' (or 'Table') of Stone. In the 'Latter'; or 'Christian (+) 'Dispensation', the 'Ten Commandments are over the Altar', composed of the 'Law' (Five

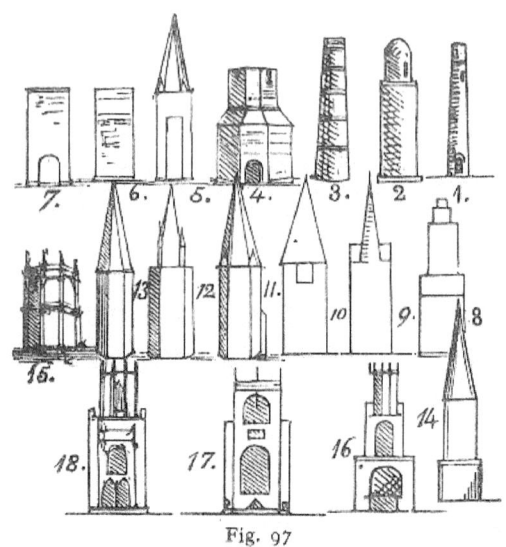

Fig. 97

98

99

102

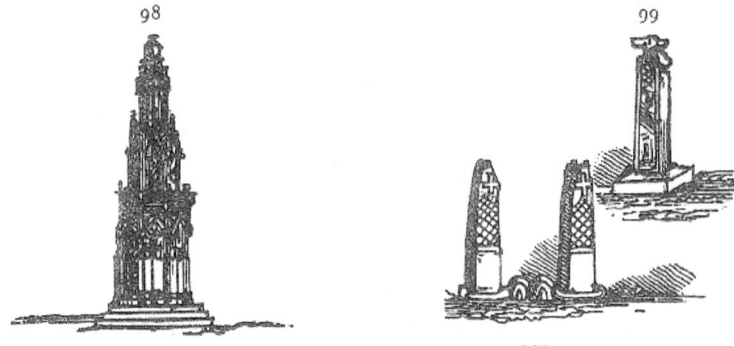

Fig. 98 : Waltham, Essex (one of the Eleanor Crosses)
Fig. 99 : Ancient Cross, Langherne, Cornwall
Fig. 102 : Memorial Stones

Fig. 100: Ancient Cross, Margam, South Wales
Fig. 101: Ancient Cross, St. Patrick, County of Louth

Fig. 103
Group of Minarets or Towers, selected from Examples in Oriental Towns

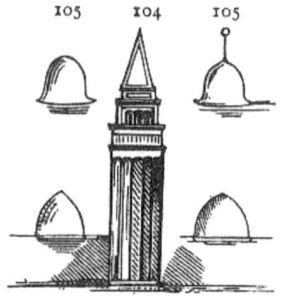
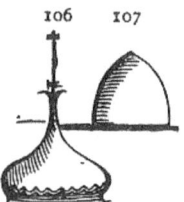

Fig. 104 : Column (Campanile of San Marco, at Venice)
Fig. 105 : Domes at Jerusalem
Fig. 106 : Top of the 'Phallus', Mosque of Ibu Tooloon, Cairo
Fig. 107 : Small Mohammedan Mosque

Fig. 108 : Mosque of Omar
Fig. 110A : Curves of a Moorish or Saracenic Horseshoe Arch
Fig. 112 : Cathedral of Cordova : form of the Arches
Fig. 113 : Patterns of Moorish Doors
Fig. 114 : Moresque Arch
Fig. 110 : Moorish Tower
Fig. 115 : Alhambra

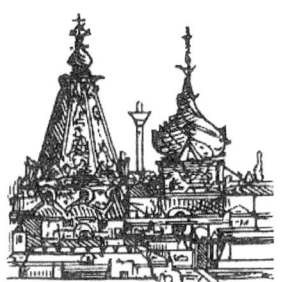

Fig. 109 : Russian Cathedral, Moscow

Russian architecture is strongly infused with the eastern picturesque spirit. The curves of its domes and the forms of its steeples are all oriental.

111

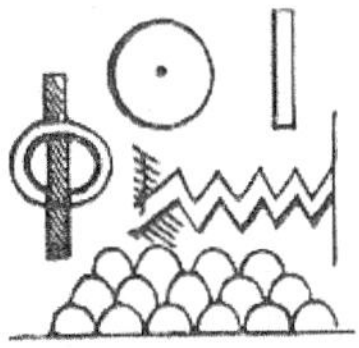

114A

115A

Fig. 111 : The Phallus and Discus, as seen in fig. 110A, united
Fig. 114A : Query, Aquarius ? Fig. 115A, Scale Enrichment

Fig. 116   Fig. 117
1 : Rosicrucian 'Macrocosmos'
2 : Rosicrucian 'Microcosmos'
A : Jachin (יָכִין)
B : Boaz (בֹּעַז)—Isis

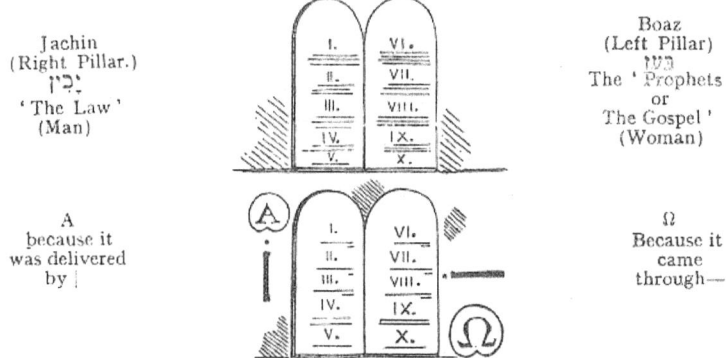

Double Lithoi : The 'Tables' of Stone.

Jachin (Right Pillar.) יָכִין 'The Law' (Man)

Boaz (Left Pillar) בֹּעַז The 'Prophets or The Gospel' (Woman)

A because it was delivered by |

Ω Because it came through —

Fig. 118
The union of | and of — is consequently +, or the 'Cross'

Commandments to the Right); and the 'Gospel' (Five Commandments to the Left). The ten commandments are inscribed in two groups of five' each, in columnar form. The five to the right (looking from the altar) mean the 'Law'; the five to the left mean the 'Prophets'. The right stone is masculine, the left stone is feminine. They correspond to the two disjoined pillars of stone (or towers) in the front of every cathedral, and of every temple in the heathen times.

The pomegranate is a badge of the Plantagenets; in its form it resembles the crescent moon; it is a symbol of the female influence in nature. There is here an unexpected concurrence with the crescent moon. and star of the Orientals; for above the pomegranate--which is figured sometimes as the crescent moon in the heraldic insignia of the Plantagenets--the six-pointed star appears in the hollow of the crescent, with its points in the curvilinear or serpentine form. The crescent moon of Egypt and that of Persia is the thin sickle of the new moon reclining on her back, and seemingly with the star *issuant* from between her horns; which is evidently an Egyptian hint coming from the old hieroglyphic times. This mysterious crescent and star is the badge of the sect of Ali among the Mohammedans, and it plays a most important part in augurial or religious heraldry. The standards of Egypt, Persia, and Arabia are *gules*, or Mars, or the fiery colour. It is the ardent, or masculine, or red colour of Ali. The colours of Turkey, on the other hand, are strictly those of Mohammed, and unconsciously honour the female element in displaying the green, or the *vert*, or the woman's colour, or Friday colour, that of the Mohammedan Sabbath. This green is the *vert*, or 'Venus', of Mecca. The Turkish standard divides *party-per-pale* the masculine red of the sect of Ali with the green of the Hadgi; allotting to the former the place of honour, or the dexter side of the emblazonment.

The Christian altar is divided, as a hieroglyphic, into two halves or sides, before which the representative priest extends his hands, standing before it with his right hand (meaning the 'Law') to the right, and his left hand (meaning the 'Prophets') to the left;

the first of which signifies the masculine (Jewish), and the second the feminine (Christian--because the Saviour was 'born of a woman'), mystic celestial power.

Some monograms or hieroglyphic expressions, meaning the 'Salvator Mundi,' show the Roman letter 'I' (Jesus) in front, in large size; the letter 'H' (which is feminine, and Greek in its origin, meaning here 'Man, *as born of Woman*') much smaller; and behind, interlacing and combining the first two letters, is the single curved or cursive 'S', which stands for 'S.S.', the Holy Spirit, or the Third Person of the Trinity. The whole, in another way, is 'Jesus Hominum Salvator'. Nearly all the sacred monograms, with the intention of making the letter denoting the 'Man' prominent, present the letter 'I' large; in the heraldic language *surtout*, or 'over all'. The monogram of the Saviour is sometimes seen in the 'Ark', or '*vesica piscis*,' which is a pointed oval figure, familiar in Gothic architecture, and shaped like a boat or a shuttle, *counter-changing* the letters and the closing arcs, white and black--the black occupying the left or female side according to the ideas of the Templars. The standards of these soldier-monks were white and black, either oblong or forked.

There are two columns of that heavy, severe order, however grand and impressive, which distinguishes the early Norman period of architecture in England, in regard to which, though abounding in far-off hermetic suggestions, we have seen no notice in antiquarian quarters. These two columns comprise a part of the colonnade in the White Tower, or central tower, of the Tower of London. The capital of the first column is square, but it is rounded at the angles by a cut to the *hypotrachelium*, or base-ring, of the capital. The tops of these cuts are formed by volutes similar to the horns of the Corinthian and Ionic capitals. The male volute is to the right, and is a spiral volve, from which issues a dependent budding flower dropping seed. The volve to the left, which is a series of rings enclosing a point, is female. A twisted perpendicular, like a horn, projects from the base on this left side. The capital of the other column presents a not unusual Norman form of two truncated-tables or faces rounded below and divided in the middle. These we interpret as meaning the 'woman' and the 'man', side by side, and left and right. These glyphs in the two capitals of the columns signify 'Jachin' and 'Boaz', and stand for the 'First Man,' and the 'First Woman'. The mysterious letter 'Tau', which is the same as the Runic Hammer of Thor, and which in truth is a 'Cross,' occupies the centre-point, or, heraldically, the 'honour-point', of the first column to the right. The master-masons were celebrated in their art of concealing myths, or hinting them cautiously in the most difficult and far-off resemblances. The curious reader is referred to our illustration, figs. 119, 120.

The character of the 'Head' which the Templars were charged with having worshipped in their secret 'encampments', or 'mystic lodges', has been the subject of much dispute. Some say it was the head of Proserpine, or of Isis, or of the 'Mother of Nature' presented under certain strange aspects. Others assert that the figure was male, and that of Dis or Charon, according to the classic nomenclature. The object was reputed to be a talisman, and it is called by some the head of Medusa, or the snake-haired visage, dropping blood which turned to snakes, and transforming the beholder to stone. It was this head, or one of a similar description, which was supposed to serve as the talisman or recognitive mark of the secret fraternity or society, headed by Pichegru and others, which was suppressed by Napoleon, and the members of which were tried and condemned as aiming at revolutionary objects. Why Napoleon adopted this mysterious supposed magical head, as he is said to have done, on the suppression and destruction of this revolutionary body--to which we refer elsewhere--and why he chose to place his own head in the centre-place before occupied by this imagined awe-inspiring countenance, and adopted the whole as the star of his newly founded 'Legion of Honour', it is very difficult to say. In the East there is a tradition of this insupportable magic countenance, which the Orientals assign to a 'Veiled Prophet', similar to the mysterious personage in *Lalla Rookh*.

CHAPTER THE SECOND

PRESENCE OF THE ROSICRUCIANS IN HEATHEN AND CHRISTIAN ARCHITECTURE

A QUESTION may here arise whether two corresponding pillars, or columns, in the White Tower, London, do not very ingeniously conceal, masonically, the mythic *formula* of the Mosaic Genesis, 'Male and Female created He them', etc. Refer below to figs. 119, 120.

I. Tor, or 'Hammer of Thor' T(au).

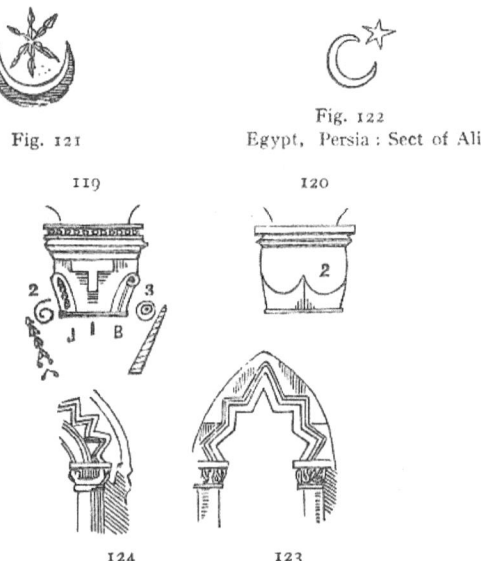

Fig. 121

Fig. 122
Egypt, Persia : Sect of Ali

Figs. 119, 120: Columns to Chapel in the 'White Tower', London. Style, Early Norman, 1081. Fig. 119—(1) Mystic 'Tau'; (2) Male, Right; (3) Female, Left.
Fig. 123: Castle-Rising Church, Norfolk. Fig. 124: Romsey Abbey, Hants.

Fig. 125 : St. Peter's Church, Northampton
Fig. 126 : S—out of the Arms of the +. (Font, Runic and Saxon, Bridekirk Church, Cumberland)

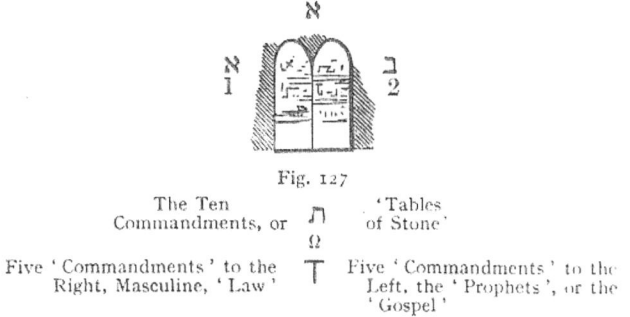

Fig. 127

The Ten Commandments, or ♪ 'Tables of Stone'
Ω
Five 'Commandments' to the T Five 'Commandments' to the
Right, Masculine, 'Law'   Left, the 'Prophets', or the 'Gospel'

2. Corinthian Volutes, or 'Ram's Horns'.

The crescent moon and star is a Plantagenet badge. It is also the Badge of the Sultan of Turkey. Also, with a difference, it displays the insignia of Egypt.

The flag of Egypt is the ensign of the sect of Ali (the second Mohammedan head of religion), which is 'Mars, a Crescent, Luna; within the horns of which is displayed an estoile of the second'--abandoning the vert, or green, of the 'Hadgi', or of Mecca, the site of the apotheosis of Mohammed. The Mohammedan believers of the sect of Ali rely on the 'masculine principle'--more closely, in this respect, assimilating with the Jews; and therefore their distinctive heraldic and theological colour is red, which is male, to the exclusion of the other Mohammedan colour,

Fig. 128 A lamp, Roma Sotteranea ΙΧΘΥΣ   Fig. 129   Fig. 130

Fig. 131: Devices from the Tombs in the Catacombs at Rome

Fig. 132   Fig. 133   Fig. 134   Fig. 135   Fig. 136

green, which is female. The 'Hadgi', or Pilgrims to Mecca, wear green; the Turkish Mussulmans wear red and green, according to their various. titles of honour, and to their various ranks.

The Hospital of St. Cross, near Winchester, abounds in the earliest Norman mouldings. The architecture of St. Cross presents numerous hermetic suggestions.

The identity of Heathen and of Christian Symbols is displayed in all our old churches in degrees more or less conclusive.

The 'Ten fingers' of the two hands (made up of each 'Table' of Five) are called in old parlance, the ten commandments'. 'I will

  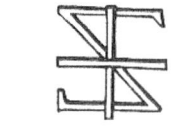

Fig. 137: Monogram of the Three Emblems carried in the Mysteries   Figs. 138, 139: The Heathen Monogram of the Triune

Fig. 140: Monogram of the Saviour

write the ten commandments in thy face' was spoken in fury, in the old-fashioned days, of an intended assault. The hands explain the meaning of this proverbial expression, interpreted astrologically. Palmistry is called Chiromancy, because Apollo, mythologically, was taught 'letters' by Chiron, the 'Centaur'.

The devices on most Roman Bronze Lamps present continual Gnostic ideas.

The Temple Church, London, will be found to abound with Rosicrucian hieroglyphs and anagrammatical hints in all parts, if reference be made to it by an attentive inquirer--one accustomed to these abstruse studies.

These designs supply a variety of Early Christian Symbols or Hieroglyphs, drawn from Roman originals in all parts of the world.

The Æolian Harp, or Magic Harp, gave forth real strains in the wind. .These were supposed to be communications from the invisible spirits that people the, air in greater or lesser number. See figs. 141, 142.

The above music consists of a magical incantation to the air, or musical Charms, supposed magically to

Fig. 141 : Melody (or Melodic Expression) of the Portico of the Parthenon
Fig. 142 : General Melody (or Melodic Expression) of the Pantheon, Rome

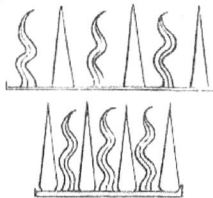

Fig. 143
Alternate Direct and Crooked Radii, or ' Glories ' set round Sacred Objects

Figs. 144, 145 : Collar of Esses

be played from the frontispieces, as musical instruments, of two of the most celebrated ancient religious structures. The Cabalists imagined that the arrangements of the stars in the, sky, and particularly the accidental circumvolvent varying speed of the planets of the solar system, produced music--as men know music. The Sophists maintained that architecture, in another sense, was harmonious communication,

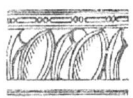  

146    147   148

Fig. 146: Egg-and-Tongue Moulding, Caryatic Prostyle, Pandroseum (Temple of Erechthæus, Athens)
Fig. 147: Moslem: the Crescent and Star: also Plantagenet
Fig 148: Honeysuckle, Greek Stele

Fig. 149: Egg-and-Tongue Moulding, Roman example

 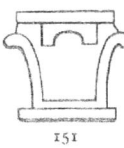 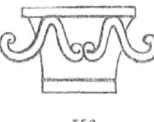

150   151   152

Fig. 150: Rhamasseion, Thebes, Caryatic Portico
Fig. 151: India, origin of the 'Corinthian'
Fig. 152: India, Rudimental Corinthian Capital, as also Rudimental Christian

Fig. 153

addressed to a capable apprehension--when the architecture was true to itself, and therefore of divine origin. Hence the music on fig 141-142. These passages were supposed to be magic charms, or invocations, addressed by day and night, to the intelligent beings who filled the air invisibly. They were played from the fronts of the Parthenon, Athens, and the Pantheon, Rome, according to the ideas of the superstitious Greeks and of the Oriental Christian Church.

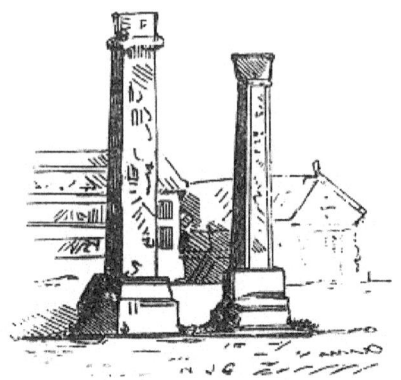

Fig. 154 : Stone Crosses at Sandbach, in Cheshire

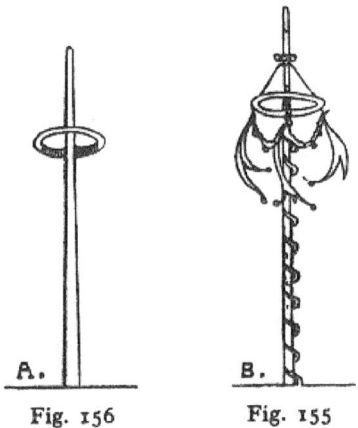

Fig. 156   Fig. 155

In fig. 153 we have a representation of Bersted Church, as seen (magnified) from a rising hill, over a hop-garden, at about the distance of half a mile. Bersted is a little village, about three miles from Maidstone, Kent, on the Ashford road. In the chancel of Bersted Church, Robert Fludd, or Flood ('Robertus de Fluctibus'), the head of the Rosicrucians in England, lies buried. He died in 1637.

157

158

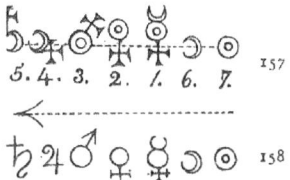

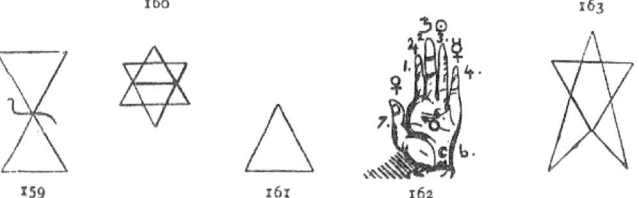

Fig. 157 : Hindoo Monograms of Planets : (1) Mercury, Buddha (Boodh) ; (2) Venus ; (3) Mars ; (4) Jupiter ; (5) Saturn ; (6) Moon ; (7) Sun
Fig. 158 : Astrological Symbols of Planets : (1) Sol ; (2) Luna ; (3) Mercury ; (4) Venus ; (5) Mars ; (6) Jupiter ; (7) Saturn

160

163

159

161

162

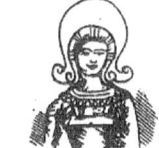

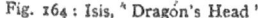

Fig. 159 : Buddhist Emblem
Fig. 160 : 'Shield of David', or, the 'Seal of Solomon'
Fig. 161 : Phallic Triad
Fig. 162 : Astrological Hand : (1) Jupiter ; (2) Saturn ; (3) Sun ; (4) Mercury ; (5) Mars ; (6) Moon ; (7) Venus
Fig. 163 : Indian and Greek

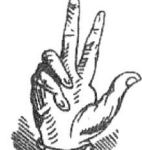

Fig. 164 : Isis, 'Dragon's Head'

Fig. 165 : Hand in Benediction

Apex of the Phallus, the Quatre-feuilles, and the Discus or Round. The lower portion is the Linga, Lingham, or Phallus, Fig. 155 displays the standard Maypole, or authentic Maypole, with all its curious additions; and we add their explanation. In the upper portion we have the 'wreathed'; also the 'Pole' of the ship 'Argo' ('Arco'); otherwise the 'Tree of Knowledge'. The ribbons of the Maypole should be of the seven prismatic colours.

Fig. 156 shows the union of the Phallus and Yoni, and exhibits Unmistakably the destination and purpose of the familiar Maypole.

Fig. 166: Egyptian Alto-Relievo
(British Museum)

Fig. 167: 'Hook of Saturn'
'Crook of Bishops'

Each finger in fig. 162 is devoted to a separate planet. Refer to the engraving of the hand.

Fig. 167, 'Hook of Saturn', 'Crook of Bishops'. 'By hook or crook', meaning, 'By fair means or foul', is a proverbial expression, continually heard.

There are two works which will assist in throwing light upon that mystic system of the ancients, probably originating in the dreaming East, that refers the production of music to architectural forms or geometric diagrams; as columns and entablatures, or upright lines and cross-lines, and mathematical arcs and diagonals, in their modifications and properties, of course are. These books, which will help to explain the passages of music given at figs. 141, 142, are Hay's *Natural Principles and Analogy of the Harmony of Form*, and a very original and learned musical production, entitled *The Analogy of the Laws of Musical Temperament to the Natural Dissonance of Creation*, by M. Vernon, published in London in 1867. Through a strange theory, the music at figs. 141-142 of our book is taken as the expression of the geometrical fronts of the two great temples, the Parthenon at Athens and the Pantheon at Rome, which are supposed to have been built with perfect art. We have 'translated' these phantom Æolian melodies played in the winds (so to express it), and fixed them in modern musical notation.

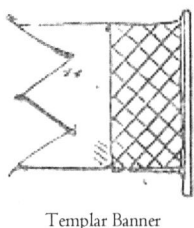

Templar Banner

CHAPTER THE THIRD

THE ROSICRUCIANS AMIDST ANCIENT MYSTERIES. THEIR TRACES DISCOVERABLE IN THE ORDERS OF KNIGHTHOOD

THE. 'Collar of Esses' is supposed always to be a part of the Order of the Garter. The coupled 'S.S.' mean the 'Sanctus Spiritus', or 'Holy Spirit', or the 'Third Person'. The 'Fleurs-de-Lis', or 'Lisses', or the Lilies of the Field', invariably appear in close connexion with St. John, or the 'Sanctus Spiritus', and also with the Blessed Virgin Mary, in all Christian

Fig. 168 : Collar of Esses

symbola or *insignia*. The Prince of Wales's triple plume appears to have the same mythic Egyptian and Babylonian origin, and to be substantially the same symbol as the 'Fleur-de-Lis'. When arranged in threes, the 'Fleurs-de-Lis' represent the triple powers of nature--the 'producer', the 'means of production', and 'that produced': The 'Fleur-de-Lis' is presented in a deep disguise in the 'Three Feathers', which is the crest of the Prince of Wales;

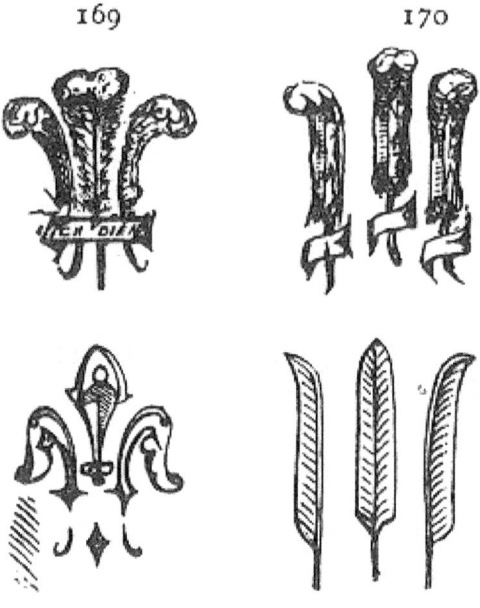

Figs. : 169, 170, 171

in this form the Fleur-de-Lis is intended to elude ordinary recognition. The reader will observe the hint of these significant 'Lisses' in the triple scrolls or 'Esses' coiled around the bar in the reverse of the Gnostic gem, the 'Chnuphis Serpent', elsewhere given. This amulet is a fine opalescent chalcedony, very convex on both sides. It is the figure of the 'Chnuphis Serpent' rearing himself aloft in act to dart, crowned with the seven vowels, the cabalistic gift to Man in his Fall, signifying 'speech'. The re verse presents the triple 'S.S.S.' coiled around the 'Phallus'.

In fig. 170 we have the Prince of Wales's Feathers, from the Tomb of Edward the Black Prince, in Canterbury Cathedral. This badge presents the idea of the 'Fleur-de-Lis', 'Ich Dien!'--'I serve!'

Fig. 171 represents the Egyptian Triple Plumes, which are the same badge as the 'Fleur-de-Lis' and the Prince of Wales's Feathers, meaning the 'Trinity'.

Fig. 172--also (*ante*) referred to as fig. 191--is a Gnostic Gem. It represents the 'Chnuphis Serpent', spoken of above.

A famous inscription (Delphic E) was placed above the portal of the Temple at Delphi. This, inscription

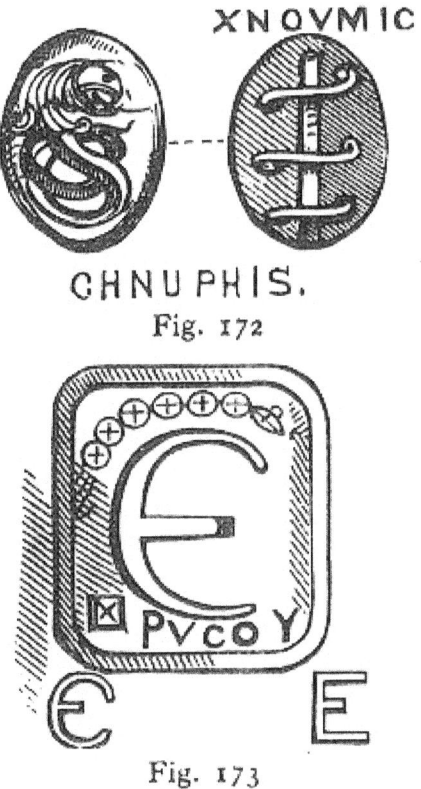

CHNUPHIS.
Fig. 172

Fig. 173

was a single letter, namely, the letter E, the name of which in Greek was E, 'which is the second person of the present of the indicative of the verb ειμι, and signifies 'Thou art'; being as Plutarch has interpreted it, the salutation bf the god by those who entered the Temple. See Plutarch *de E apud Delph*. Lord Monboddo's *Origin and Progress of Language* (1774), vol. ii. p. 85, refers to this letter E.

The Delphic 'E' means the number 'Five', or the half of the Cabalistic Zodiac, or the Five Ascending Signs. This 'Delphic E' is also the Seleucidan Anchor. It was adopted by the Gnostics to indicate the 'Saviour', and it is frequent in the talismans and amulets of the early Christians. It is one of the principal gems of the Gnostics, and is a cameo in flat relief.

One of the charges against the Knights Templars was as follows: 'That they bound, or touched, the head of an idol with cords, wherewith they bound themselves about their. shirts or next their skins'

('Processus contra Templarios', Dugd. *Monast. Ang.* vol. vi. part ii. pp. 844-846, etc.). There is something strange about these cords, cordons, ropes, belts, bands, baldrics (also in the term 'belted earls'). These are always male accessories; except the 'zones', sashes, or girdles, worn as the mark of virgins, which cinctures may yet draw their symbolic meaning from this same '*umbilicus*' in question. The reader will notice also the connexion of these ideas and the practice in the Roman race of the 'Lupercal', at the February Roman religious solemnities (February of the 'Fishes'). At these it was the custom of the runners to flog bystanders, *particularly women*, with thongs or cords; which were probably intended to be the racers' own girdles. Julius Cæsar, Mark Antony, and Calphurnia form a group illustrative of this meaning. Thus Shakespeare:

> Our elders say,
> The barren, touched in this holy chase,
> Shake off the sterile curse.
> --Julius Cæsar, act is sc. 2.

Is this the origin of the custom of the people pelting or .flogging each other at the Italian Carnivals? It seems highly probable. The Carnivals occur at the same time as these Roman *Lupercalia*.

Many early Norman mouldings exhibit various examples of the cable. Thongs, ties, and network are seen to bind all the significant figures in the early English and Irish churches. Is there any connexion between these bonds, or ties, or lacings, with the 'cable-tow' of the initiates among the Masons? Perhaps the 'tow' in this 'cable-tow' means the 'Tau', or stood for it originally. Reference may here be made to the snake which forms the girdle of the Gnostic 'Good Shepherd' in the illustration later in our book (fig. 252). The cable-mouldings in Gothic architecture are intended to carry an important meaning. They are found in the pointed or Christian architecture in continual close connexion with the triplicated zigzag, the vandykes, or '*aquarii*', as we designate them, because all these architectural forms, which are hieroglyphs, mean the feminine or 'Second Principle', and express the sign of Aquarius, with its watery or lunar hints, its twin-fishes, and its Jonah-like anagrams of the 'Redeemer'. Hence the boatlike, elongated, peculiar form called the *vesica piscis*, which is the oblong shuttle-shaped frame continually set over doors and windows and elsewhere in Gothic churches, to contain effigies of the Saviour, or Virgin Mary, or groups from the New Testament in connexion with these Two Sacred Persons. A doorway in Barfreston Church, Kent, supplies an excellent example of the employment of this oblong figure; which is also Babylonian, and means the female member as its starting-point.

In a previous part of our book we give various figures of the prows or cutwater-heads of gondolas, in which we clearly show the origin of their peculiar form, which represents the *securis*, or 'sacrificial axe', that crook originally expressed in the 'hook of Saturn'. The 'Bu-Centaur' indicates the fabulous being, the bicorporate 'ox' or 'horse' and 'Man', as will be found by a separation of the syllables 'Bu-Centaur'. It is the name of the state-galley of the Doge of Venice, used on the occasion of his figurative stately marriage with, the Adriatic, or espousal of the 'Virgin of the Sea', who was Cybele of the 'sacrificial hook'. The hatchet of Dis, the glaive, the halberd, the reaping-hook of Ceres, the crescent moon, the 'Delphic E', are all the same mystic figure. The prow of the gondola exhibits unmistakably the *securis* and *fasces* conjointly, or the axe of the sacrifice and the rods for the scourging of the victim first, if human, and afterwards for his burning--the rods being the firewood. Lictors have their name probably from '*Lled*'. From this peculiar cutwater arose the Dragon-beak, the 'Prow', or 'Frow', the figurehead and fiddle-head. They have all a feminine origin.

Fig. 174

Fig. 174 represents 'S. Johan' (St., John), from an early woodcut of the Twelve Apostles: His right hand is raised in the act of the holy sign, whilst hid left clasps the chalice of the 'S.S.', or Sacrament of Wine; in the cup is a salamander, signifying the 'H. G'. This is St. John the Apostle, the author of the 'Apocalypse'; or the 'Sanctus Spiritus', who baptizes in the mystic Eucharist with the 'Holy Ghost and with Fire'.

The following are the names pf the angels of the planets, according to the Gnostics. At the beginning of all things is Jehovah (Sabaoth), Victory; at the end, the 'Old Serpent' (Ophis). Between these are the Seraphim (Intelligences) and Cherubim (Benevolences), and their representatives. Origen calls the Sun, Adonai; the Moon, Iao; Jupiter, Eloi; Mars, Sabao; Orai, Venus; Astaphai; Mercury; Ildabaoth, Saturn. All this is Gnostic--highest mysticism therefore.

The name Tarasque is given for the Dragon of a Northern Nation. (Qy. the 'Hill of Tara', etc.?) Under the Roman Emperors, and under the Emperors of Byzantium, every cohort or centurion bore a dragon as its ensign (Modestus, *De Vocabul. Rei Milit.*; Flav. Veget. *De Re Militari*, lib. ii. c. xiii.: Georget, *Insig. Europ., loc. cit.*) Matthew of Westminster, speaking of the early battles of this country of England, says: 'The King's place was *between* the Dragon and the Standard'--'Regius locus fuit inter draconem et standardum' (Lower's *Curiosities of Heraldry*, p. 96). This is the undoubted origin of the ensign's 'pair of colours' in a battalion; viz. the first colour, or 'King's Colour', whose place is to the right, is properly the standard; and the second colour, or the 'regimental colour', to which is assigned the left-hand, or female, or sinister place, is the 'Dragon'. The Dragon was supposed to conduct to victory, because its figure was a most potent charm. The standards and guidons of the cavalry follow the same magic rule.

The planets are supposed by the astrologers and alchemists to exercise dominion more particularly in the order following, and to produce effects upon their own appropriate under-mentioned metals, on planetarily corresponding days. These are Sol, for gold, on Sunday; Luna, for silver, on Monday; Mars, for iron, on Tuesday; Mercury, for quicksilver, on Wednesday; Jupiter, for tin, on Thursday; Venus, for copper, on Friday; and Saturn, for lead, on Saturday (Lucas's *Travels*, p. 79; Count Bernard of Treviso). The emblematical sculptures, in which the whole enigma of the art of transmutation is supposed to be contained, are those over the fourth arch of the Cemetery of the Innocents, at Paris, as you go through the great gate of St. Denis, on the right-hand side. They were placed there by Nicholas Flamel.

The old traditions, from time immemorial, aver that it is neither proper for sailors nor for servants of the sea to wear beards. That they have never done so is true, except at those times when profound mythic meanings were not understood or were neglected. This smoothness of a sailor's face arises from the fact that the sea has always been mythologically feminine, and that sailors and men or followers of the sea are under the protection of the 'Queen of the Deep', or the 'Virgin of the Sea'. Hence the figure of Britannia, with her sceptre of the sea or trident, and not that of Neptune.

The Virgin Mary, the 'Star of the Sea', and Patroness of Sailors, rules and governs the ocean, and her colours are the ultramarine of the 'Deep', and sea-green, when viewed in this phase of her divine character. In all representations, ancient or modern, sailors have beardless faces, unless they belong to the reprobate and barbarian classes--such as pirates and outlaws, and men who have supposedly thrown off devotional observance, and fallen into the rough recusancy of mere nature.

Fig. 175 is a very curious design from Sylvanus Morgan, an old herald. Above is the spade, signifying here the *phallus*; and below is the distaff, or instrument of woman's work, meaning the answering member, or *Yoni*; these are united by the snake. We here perceive the meaning of the rhymed chorus sung by Wat Tyler's mob: 'When Adam delved' (with his spade), 'and Eve span' (contributing her [producing] part of the work), 'where was then the Gentleman?'--or what, under these ignoble conditions, makes difference or degree? It is supposed that Shakespeare plays upon this truth when he makes his clown in *Hamlet* observe 'They' (i.e. Adam and Eve) 'were the first who ever bore arms.' By

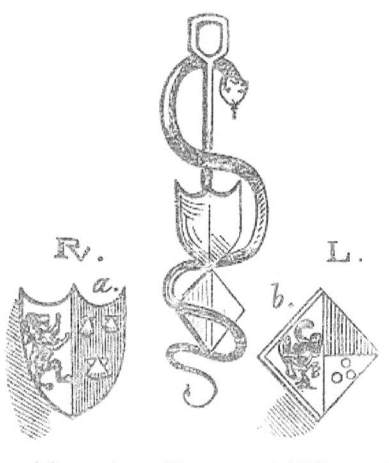

a. ' Baron '   Fig. 175.   *b*. ' Femme '

a reference to the foot of the figure, we shall see what these arms were, and discover male and female resemblances in the shape of the man's 'escutcheon' and the woman's diamond-shaped 'lozenge'. As thus: *a* is the shield of arms, or 'spade', or 'spada', or 'male implement', on man's own side, or dexter side; *b* is the 'lozenge', or distaff, or 'article representative of woman's work', on her proper side, or the left or sinister side.

A chalice is, in general, the sign of the Priestly Order. The chalice on the tombstone of a knight, or over the door of a castle, is a sign of the Knights Templars, of whom St. John the Evangelist was the Patron Saint. The 'cup' was forbidden to the laity, and was only received by the Priests, in consequence of the decree of Pope Innocent III, A.D. 1215. It means the 'S.S.', or Holy Spirit, to which we have frequently adverted.

We have carefully inspected that which has been designated the *crux antiquariorum,* or the Puzzle of Antiquaries, namely, the famous Font, which is of unknown and bewildering antiquity, in the nave of Winchester Cathedral. Milner (a feeble narrator and misty, unreliable historian), in his *History of Winchester,* has the following superficial notice of this relic: 'The most distinguished ornaments on the top are doves "*breathing*"' (they are not 'breathing', they are drinking) 'into phials surmounted with crosses *fichée*. And on the sides' (the north side, he should say, which is faced wrongly, and ought properly to front the east) 'the doves are again depicted with a *salamander,* emblematic of fire; in allusion to that passage of St. Matthew: "He shall baptize you with the *Holy Ghost and with fire*".'

All the secrets of masonry are concealed in the Hebrew or Chaldee language. In the First Chapter of the *Gospel according to St. John* is contained the mythical outline of the Cabala, in its highest part.

'Les anciens astrologues, dit le plus savant les Juifs' (Maimonides), 'ayant consacré à chaque planète, une *couleur,* un *animal,* un *bois,* un *métal,* un *fruit,* une *plante,* ils formaient de toutes ces choses une *figure* ou représentation de l'astre, observant pour cet effet de choisir un *instant approprié, un jour heureux,* tel que la *conjonction,* ou tout autre aspect favorable. Par leurs cérémonies (magiques) ils croyaient pouvoir faire passer dans ces figures ou idoles les influences des êtres supérieurs (leurs modèles). C'étaient ces idoles qu'adoraient les *Kaldéens-sabéens.* Les prêtres égyptiens, indiens, perses--on les croyait lier les dieux à leurs idoles, les faire descendre du ciel à leur gré. Ils menacent le soleil et la lune dé révéler les secrets des mystères.'--Eusebius Iamblicus, *De Mysteriis Egyptiorum*.

The mystic emblems of the religions of India, China, Greece, and Rome are closely similar, and are set forth in the ornaments on the friezes of the temples of all those countries, explaining their general principles. 'Your popular societies are an emanation from the lodges of the Freemasons; in like manner as these proceeded from the funeral pile of the Templars' (*'Castle' of the Tuileries*, year viii). Thus the 'egg-and-tongue moulding ('egg and adder's tongue', for the egg and the serpent were two of the emblems of the Egyptian and Greek mysteries), the griffin, the lion of St. Mark, the honeysuckle-and-lotus ornament, the convolutions and volutes, the horns as floriation springing from the lighted candelabra, the lotus and tori of Egypt, and the Greek ornaments and Roman Templar ornaments, are all related in their religious meanings.

The names of the 'Three Kings', or 'Shepherds'; who descried, the Star of Annunciation in the East, are Caspar, Melchior, and Balthasar. Caspar, or Gaspar, is the 'White One'; Melchior is the 'King of Light'; Balthasar, the 'Lord of Treasures'. Balthasar, or Balthazar, is the Septuagint spelling of Belshazzar.

Linga is the old name of an island near Iona, called the 'Dutchman's Cap'. (Qy. the Phrygian cap?--also the first 'cocked hat', and its recondite meaning?) *Gallus*, or the Cock, is sacred to Mars, whose-colour is *red*. In this connexion, and as bespeaking Hermes or Mercurius, the 'messenger of the dawn', may have arisen the use of the 'cock', as the emblem supposedly of the first descrier of the daily light from the tops of the steeples. It probably signifies the phallic myth. The grasshopper, dragon, arrow, and fox, as weathercocks, have undoubtedly a remote reference to the same idea of symbolizing the 'Prince of the Powers of the Air'.

The form of the Pointed Arch reached the Orientals --as we see in their Temples--in the shape of the Phrygian and Median

Bonnet (Lascelles, 1820). In these strange curves we have mingling the *scarab*, scorpion, Σ, or (--).

Cocks crow at day-dawn. Weathercocks turn to the wind, and invite the meteoric or elementary influences, the 'Powers of the Air'. The question as to the mystic side of all this is very interesting and curious. The fields of the air were supposed by the Rosicrucians to be filled with spirits.

'Tous les Lamas portent la mitre, ou bonnet conique, qui était l'emblème du soleil. Le Dalai-Lama, ou immense prêtre de La, est ce que nos vieilles relations appelaient le prêtre Jean, par l'abus du mot persan *Djehân*, qui veut dire le monde. Ainsi le prêtre Monde, le dieu Monde, se tient parfaitement.'--Volney, *Ruines*, p. 251. (Qy. Prester-John? Qy. also this verbal connexion with '*Saint* John', as if Prêtre John?) In the old Norman-French *Maistre* is frequently met for *Maître*. This Prestre, or Prester (Anglicized), or Prêtre John, is probably no other than the Priest or High-Priest 'John', otherwise Saint John, or the 'Saint-Esprit'. The recognition of the + in the Great Llama, Al-Ama, Ama, Anima (Soul, Spirit), Alma, El-Om, etc., meaning 'white', is very curious. The antiquary Bryant is positively of opinion, from the very names of Columbkil and Iona, that this island Iöna was anciently sacred to the Arkite divinities. The great asylum of the Northern Druids was the Island of Hu or Iona, Vs Colan, or Columba (*Mythology and Rites of the British Druids*, by Edward Davies, 1809, p. 479).

The glories around sacred persons and objects, which have straight-darting and curvilinear or wavy or serpentine rays alternately, are continual in theological or heraldic illustration; which waved and straight rays alternately imply a deep mystery. They are constant symbols in the sacred *nimbi*, and are found upon sacramental cups; they are set as the symbolical *radii* around reliquaries, and they appear as the mystic fiery circle of the Pyx. The *straight* spires and the brandished waved flames, or cherubic (or rather *seraphic*) gladii, or crooked swords guarding Paradise, imply two of the chief Christian mysteries. In the curved spires of flame, alternating with the aureole or ring of glory, there is possibly a remote hint of ♄, or the 'Reconciler of the Worlds Visible and Invisible', or 'S.S.'.

To account for the universal deification of 'horns' in architecture all over the world, as its symbolic keynote, as it were, which sigma has been transmitted into modern emblematic science, and incorporated unconsciously into the ornaments and elevated into the high places, over and over again, even in Christian buildings, an old Talmudist--Simeon Ben-Iochay by name--hazards the startling conjecture that this adoration arose originally in the supernatural light of knowledge of the old day, for the following reasons: the strange explanation which this mysterious writer gives is, that the bovine animals would have themselves become men in their future generations, but for that divine arrest which interfered athwart as it were, and wasted the ruminative magnetic force; which otherwise miraculously would have effected the transformation, by urging the powers of the brain from the radix of the rudimentary templar region into the enormous branching, tree-like, then improvised appendages, where this possibility or extension of the nervous lines became spoiled and attenuate, solidified and degraded. Growth and development are assumed as taken from expansion and radiation off a nervous sensitive centre, by election or affinity governed by an invisible Power operating from without. It is to descend very deep into cabalistic and Talmudical mysteries to gain comprehension of an idea concerning-the origin of this absurd worship of animal horns.

Fig. 176: The Templar Banner, 'Beauséant'

Fig. 177
Arches of the Temple Church, London, Symbol of the B.V.M. Also Delphic E, or Seleucidan Anchor

Fig. 178
Eight-pointed Buddhist Cross, ' Poor Soldiers' of the Temple '

Fig. 179
Teutonic Knights

The cabalist Simeon Ben-Iochay declares that it was in gratitude for this changed intention, and because the creature man became 'Man', and not the bovine creatures--a 'catastrophe which might have happened, except for this diversion of the brain-power into horns' (mere fable or dream as all this sounds!)--that the Egyptians set up the very 'horns,' to worship as the real thing--the depository or 'ark'--into which the supernatural 'rescue' was committed. Thus the horns of the animal--as the idol standing for the means, equally as another representative figure (the phallus), expressive of the mighty means to which man's existence and multiplication was entrusted--were exalted for adoration, and placed as the trophies heroically '*won even out of the reluctance and hostility of nature*', and adored, not for themselves, but for that of which they spoke.

Fig. 180
Knights of Malta

Fig. 181
Cross Potent, Knights Hospitallers

Fig. 182
St. John. (Hospital of St. Cross, Winchester)

Fig. 184
e of Apollinopolis Magna, in Upper Egypt

Fig. 185
Norman Capital, Door-shaft: Honeysuckle-and-Lotus Ornament, early example

Fig. 183
EgyptianTorus, Lotus Enrichment, and various Lunar Symbols

Shakspeare has several covert allusions to the dignity of the myth of the 'Horns'. There is much more, probably, in these spoils of the chase--the branching horns or the antlers--than is usually supposed. They indicate infinitely greater things than when they are only seen placed aloft as sylvan trophies. The crest of his late Royal Highness Prince Albert displays the Runic horns, or the horns of the Northern mythic hero. They were always a mark of princely and of conquering eminence, and they are frequently observable in the crests and blazon of the soldier-chiefs, the Princes of Germany. They come from the original Taut, Tat, Thoth, Teat, whence 'Teuton' and 'Teutonic'. These names derive from the mystic Mercurius Trismegistus, 'Thrice-Master; Thrice Mistress'--for this personage is double-sexed: 'Phoebe above, Diana on earth, Hecate below.'

Fig. 186 : Uræon

Fig. 187 : Winged Disc

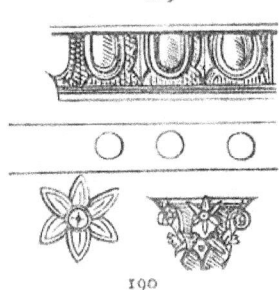

Fig. 188 : Ionic—Greek : ' Egg-and-tongue ' Moulding (two of the Emblems of the mysteries)
Fig. 189 : Grecian Moulding, expressing Religious Mysteries
Fig. 190 : Corinthian—Temple of Vesta. Central Flower, probably the Egyptian Lotus

Fig. 191 : Pantheon at Rome. Fig. 192 : Volute Fig. 193 : Corinthian
Fig. 194 : Ionic Capital, Erecthæum at Athens Fig. 195 : Composite features
Fig. 196 : Temple of Vesta, or the Sybil, at Tivoli ; Ram's Horns for Volutes
Fig. 197 : Temple of Ellora and Bheems-Chlori (Mokundra Pass)
Fig. 198 : India and Greece (similar capitals)
Fig. 199 : Greek—Corinthian : Choragic Monument, Athens

Fig. 177, *ante* (from the arches of the Temple Church, London), is a symbol of the 'Blessed Virgin; it is also the 'Delphic E', or 'Seleucidan Anchor'.

Fig. 200 : Norman Capital : Foliated Ornament, resembling the Honeysuckle and Lotus

Fig. 201 : Canterbury Cathedral : Volutes of the Corinthian form
Fig. 202 : Canterbury Cathedral : Corinthian Scrolls or Horns

The 'horns' of the Talmud account for the mythological *Minotaur*, the Bucen*taur*, Pan and Priapus, the 'Sagittary' or Centaur, the sign 'Sagittarius', and perhaps all bicorporate human and animal forms.

In the group of figures above, showing the various classical forms of the volutes, or flourished horns, in the Corinthian, Ionic, and Composite capitals, a close affinity will be remarked to examples of capitals with horns or volutes from the temple of Ellora, in India, and other Indian and Persian temples: placed under, for comparison, in the illustration.

Various mouldings, both Gothic and Classic, present shapes drawn from the astronomical sign 'Aquarius'. These signs, or ciphers, are significant of the 'Sea' and of the 'Moon'. Glyphs resembling 'fishes' mean Iona, or Jonah. They are also symbols of the 'Saviour', when they occur amidst the relics left by the early Christians, and in forms of the first Christian centuries.

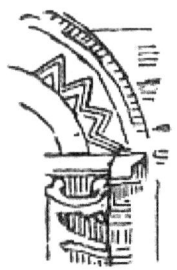

Vertical Arch: Early Norman (Temple Church)

CHAPTER THE FOURTH

ROSICRUCIANISM IN STRANGE SYMBOLS

IN the following part of our book we supply, in a series of figures, the succession of changes to which the most ancient head-covering--in itself a significant hieroglyph--the Phrygian cap, the classic Mithraic cap, the sacrificial cap, or *bonnet conique*, all deducing from a common symbolical ancestor, became subject. The Mithraic or Phrygian cap is the origin of the priestly mitre in all faiths. It was worn by the priest in sacrifice. When worn by a male, it had its crest, comb, or point, set jutting forward; when worn by a female, it bore the same prominent part of the cap in reverse, or on the nape of the neck, as in the instance of the Amazon's helmet, displayed in all old sculptures, or that of Pallas-Athene, as exhibited in the figures of Minerva. The peak, *pic*, or point, of caps or hats (the term 'cocked hat' is a case .in point) all refer to the same idea. This point had a sanctifying meaning afterwards attributed to it, when it was called the *christa*, *crista*, or crest, which signifies a triumphal top, or tuft. The 'Grenadier Cap', and the loose black Hussar Cap, derive remotely from the same sacred, Mithraic, or emblematical bonnet, or high pyramidal-cap. It, in this instance, changes to black, because it is

p. 281

devoted to the illustration of the 'fire-workers' (grenadiers), who, among modern military, succeed the Vulcanists, *Cyclopes*, classic 'smiths', or servants of Vulcan, or Mulciber, the artful worker among the metals in the fire, or amidst the forces of nature. This idea will be found by a reference to the high cap among the Persians, or Fire-Worshippers; and to the black cap among the Bohemians and in the East. All travellers in Eastern lands will remember that the tops of the minarets reminded them of the high-pointed black caps of the Persians.

The Phrygian Cap is a most recondite antiquarian form; the symbol comes from the highest antiquity. It is displayed on the head of the figure sacrificing in the celebrated sculpture, called the 'Mithraic Sacrifice' (or the Mythical Sacrifice), in the British Museum. This loose cap, with the point protruded, gives the original form from which all helmets or defensive headpieces, whether Greek or Barbarian, deduce. As a Phrygian Cap, or Symbolizing Cap, it is always *sanguine* in its colour. It then stands as the 'Cap of Liberty', a revolutionary form; also, in another way, it is even a civic or *incorporated* badge. It is always masculine in its meaning. It marks the 'needle' of the obelisk, the crown or tip of the *phallus*, whether 'human' or representative. It has its origin in the rite of circumcision--unaccountable as are both the symbol and the rite.

The real meaning of the *bonnet rouge*, or 'cap of liberty', has been involved from time immemorial in deep obscurity, notwithstanding that it has always been regarded as a most important hieroglyph or figure. It signifies the supernatural simultaneous 'sacrifice' and 'triumph'. It has descended from the time of Abraham, and it is supposed to emblem the strange mythic rite of the '*circumcisio preputii*'. The loose Phrygian bonnet, *bonnet conique*, or 'cap of liberty' may be accepted as figuring, or standing for, that detached integument or husk, separated from a certain point or knob, which has various names in different languages, and which supplies the central idea of this 'sacrificial rite--the spoil or refuse of which (absurd and unpleasant as it may seem) is borne aloft at once as a 'trophy' and as the 'cap of liberty'. It is now a magic sign, and becomes a talisman of supposedly inexpressible power--from what particular dark reason it would be difficult to say. The whole is a sign of 'initiation', and of baptism of a peculiar kind. The Phrygian cap, ever after this first inauguration, has stood as the sign of the 'Enlightened'. The heroic figures in most Gnostic Gems, which we give in our illustrations, have caps of this kind. The sacrificer in the sculptured group of the 'Mithraic Sacrifice', among the marbles in the British Museum, has a Phrygian cap on his head, whilst in the act of striking the Bull with the poniard--meaning the office of the immolating priest. The *bonnet conique* is the mitre of the Doge of Venice.

Besides the *bonnet rouge*, the Pope's mitre--nay, all mitres or conical head-coverings--have their name from the terms 'Mithradic', or 'Mithraic'. The origin of this whole class of names is Mittra, or Mithra. The cap of the grenadier, the shape of which is alike all over Europe, is related to the Tartar lambskin caps, which are dyed black; and it is black also from its association with Vulcan and the 'Fire-Worshippers' (Smiths). The Scotch Glengarry cap will prove on examination to be only a 'cocked' Phrygian. All the black conical caps, and the meaning of this strange symbol, came from the East. The loose black fur caps derive from the Tartars.

The 'Cap of Liberty' (*Bonnet Rouge*), the Crista or Crest (Male), and the Female (Amazon) helmet, all mean the same idea; in the 'instance of the female crest, the *knob* is, however, depressed--as shown in the figures next.

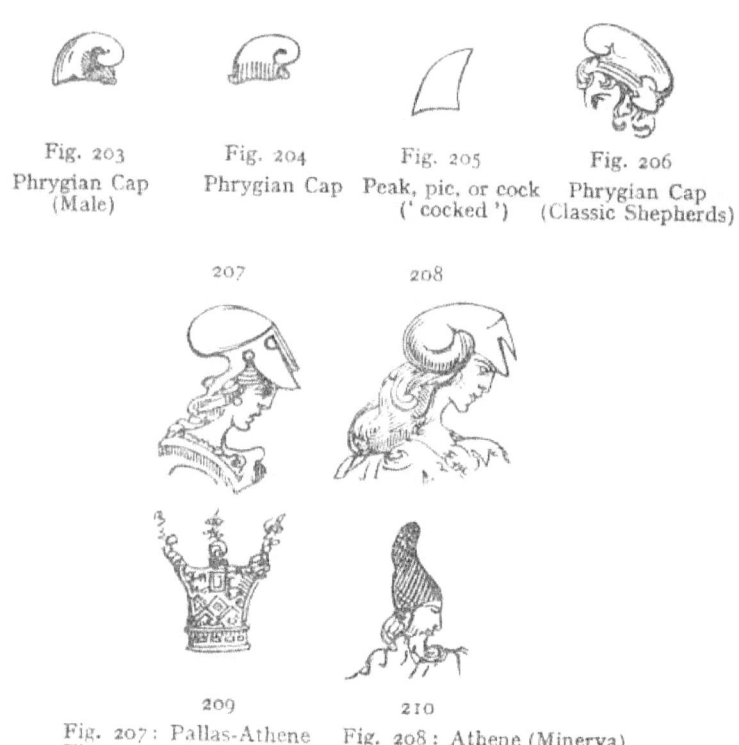

Fig. 203 Phrygian Cap (Male) Fig. 204 Phrygian Cap Fig. 205 Peak, pic, or cock ('cocked') Fig. 206 Phrygian Cap (Classic Shepherds)

Fig. 207: Pallas-Athene Fig. 208: Athene (Minerva)
Fig. 209: Jitra, Persia Fig. 210: Persia

The forms of Grenadier caps, and of those worn by Pioneers also, are those of the head-covers of the Fire-workers or Fire-raisers (Vulcanists) of an army. All the black fur caps--militarily called busbies are Bohemian, Ishmaelitish, heathen, irregular; their origin lies in the magic East.

Few would suspect the uniform of the Hussars to have had a religious origin; both the flaps which depend from their bushy fur caps, and the loose jacket or *dolman* which hangs from their left shoulder, are mythic. 'The long triangular flaps, which hang down like a jelly-bag, consist in a *double* slip of cloth, which, when necessary, folds round the soldier's face on each side, and forms a comfortable night-cap. In our service, *one single slip* is left to fly.'--Sir Walter Scott. to T. Crofton Croker, 7th July 1827. (Qy. whether the above-named *double* fly of the Hussar Cap be not the dependent ears or horns of the original Motley?) The Hussars wear the original fur cap of Tubal-Cain, or the Smiths, or 'Artful Workers in Nature'. The name Hussar is borrowed from the Oriental exclamation to (or invocation of) 'Al *huza*', 'Al-husa', or Venus, or Aphrodite--the original patroness of these Ishmaelitish irregular light troops. The *dolman* or pelisse, properly worn on the left shoulder of the Hussar, has its signification and origin in the following act related in Scripture, which refers to a certain Rosicrucian myth: 'Shem and Japheth took a garment'(a cover or extra piece of clothing), 'and laid it upon both their shoulders' (on the left shoulder of each), 'and went backward, and covered their father Noah.' It is astonishing how successfully this mythic act, with its original strange Rosicrucian meaning, should have been hidden away in this apparently little corresponding, trivial fact, of the wearing of the Hussar loose cloak or pelisse (*pallium* or pall) on the left or sinister shoulder; which is the shoulder nearest to the *woman:* because the *Talmudists say that Man was Made from the left hand.*

Regarding the Templar *insignia*, we may make the following remarks. The famous flag, or 'Beauséant', was their distinguishing symbol. Beauséant--that is to say, in the Gallic tongue, *Bien-séant*; because they are fair and honourable to the friends of Christ, but black and terrible to His enemies: 'Vexillum bipartitum, ex Albo et Nigro, quod nominant "Beau-séant", id est; Gallica lingua, "*Bien-séant*", eo quod Christi amices candidi sunt et benigni, inimices vero terribiles atque nigri' (Jac. de Vitr. *Hist. Hierosol.* apud *Gesta Dei*, cap. lxv).

Fig. 211
Motley or Scaramouch: 'Bonnet Conique,' cloven and set about with bells

Fig. 212
Knight's head-gear, with 'torse'

Fig. 213
Cap of Maintenance

Fig. 214
Tartar or Cossack Fur Cap, with double pendants

Fig. 215
Mediæval Cap of Estate

Fig. 216
Double Mitre—Horns of the Jester or Buffoon, set about with bells or jingles

Fig. 217
Fool's Cap. This shape has Egyptian indications

Fig. 218
Bulgarian; also worn by the Pandours

Fig. 219
Hussar and Cossack

Fig. 220
Hussar Conical Cap

Fig. 221
Artillery

Fig. 222
Sapeur, Pioneer

Fig. 223
Fur Cap of the Sword-bearer (mythic *gladius*) of the City of London

Fig. 224
Turkish

Fig. 225
Judge, in imitation of the Egyptian Klaft: the black Coif, placed on the sensorium, is the mark or 'brand' of Isis (Saturn)

The Cardinal de Vitry is totally uninformed as to the meaning and purpose indicated in this mysterious banner. Its black and white was originally derived from the Egyptian sacred 'black and white', and it conveys the same significant meanings.

Now, in the heraldic sense--as we shall soon see--there is no colour *white*. *Argent* is the silver of the moon's light, the light of the 'woman'; or it is light generally, in opposition to darkness, which is the absence of all colour. White is the synthesis and identity of *all* the colours--in other words, it is light. Thus white is blazoned, in the correct heraldic sense, as also in reference to its humid, feminine origin (for, as the old heralds say, 'light was begotten of darkness', and its 'type, product, and representative, woman, also'), as the melancholy or silver light of the moon, 'Argent'; also, in the higher heraldic grade, 'Pearl', as signifying tears; lastly, 'Luna', whose figure or mark is the crescent ☽, or ☾; which is either the new moon (or the moon of hope), or the moon of the Moslem (or 'horned moon resting on her back'). Black (or *sable, sab., sabbat, Sat.*, Saturn) is the absence of light, and is blazoned 'sable', diamond (carbon, or the densest of matter), 'without form and void', but cradle of possibilities, 'end' being taken as synonymous with 'beginning'. It is *sab.*, or Saturn, whose mark is ♄, and who is both masculine and feminine--sex being indifferent to this 'Divine Abstraction, whose face is masked in Darkness.'

Lykos--'wolf', *lykê*--'light'; whence comes *Lux* (Volney, 1st English edition, 1792, p. 378). 'Je' and 'V' are of Tartar origin. It is probable that St. John's College at Cambridge is the *Domus Templi* of the Round Church of the Templars there. The present St. John's is only of modern foundation. There is annexed to, or connected with, this church an almshouse called 'Bede's House', the name of which has puzzled all the antiquaries. There is little doubt that this was the original *Domus Templi*, the house of Buddha, corrupted into Bede, and meaning 'wisdom'.

A Discourse concerning the Tartars, proving (in all probability) that they are the Israelites, or Ten Tribes which, being taken captive by Salmaneser, were transplanted into Media. By Giles Fletcher, Doctor of Both Laws, and sometime Ambassador from Elizabeth, Queen of England, to the Emperor of Russia. This was found in Sir Francis Nethersole's study after his death (*Memoirs of the Life of William Whiston*, 1749)

Mr. Cavendish, an eminent chemist, 'had reason to be persuaded that the *very water itself* consisted solely of inflammable air united to dephlogisticated air.' This last conclusion has since been strengthened very much by some subsequent experiments of Dr. Priestley's (see p. 299 of *Morsels of Criticism, tending to illustrate some few passages in the Holy Scriptures upon Philosophical Principles.* 2d. edition, 2 vols. 8vo. London: J Davis, Chancery Lane, 1800).

The jewel of the Rossi-crucians (Rosicrucians) is formed of a transparent red stone, with a red *cross* on one side, and a red *rose* on the other--thus, it is a *crucified rose*. The Rossi--or Rosy--crucians' ideas concerning this emblematical red cross and red rose probably came from the fable of Adonis--who was the sun whom we have seen so often crucified--being changed into a red rose by Venus (see Drummond's *Origines*, vol. iii. p. 121). *Rus* (which is *Ras* in Chaldee) in Irish signifies 'tree', 'knowledge', 'science', 'magic', 'power'. This is the Hebrew *R--as*. Hence the Persian *Rustan* (*Val. Col. Hib.* vol. iv: pt. i. p. 84). 'The ancient Sardica, in lat. 40° 50′, is now called "Sophia"'; the ancient Aquineum, Buda, or Buddha. These were, I believe, old names restored' (*vide* D'Anville's *Atlas*). The society bearing the name of the Rosicrucians (or Rosicruxians) is closely allied with the Templars. Their emblem is a monogram or jewel; or, as malicious And bigoted adversaries would say, their 'object of adoration' is a 'red rose on a cross'. Thus:

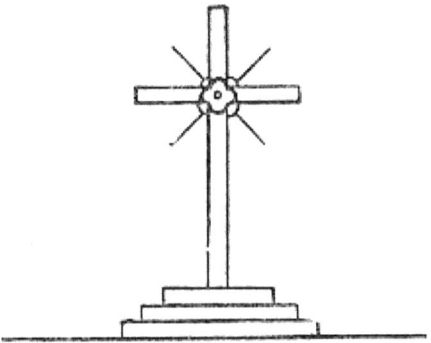

Fig. 226

When it can be done, it is surrounded with a glory, and placed on a Calvary. This is the Naurutz, Natsir, or Rose of Isuren, of Tamul, or Sharon, or the Water-Rose, the Lily Padma, Pema, Lotus 'crucified' for the salvation of man--crucified in the heavens at the Vernal Equinox. It is celebrated at that time by the Persians in what they call their Nou-Rose, i.e. Neros, or Naurutz (Malcolm's *History of Persia*, vol. ii. p. 406). The Tudor Rose, or *Rose-en-Soleil* (the Rose of the Order of the Garter), is the Rosicrucian 'Red Rose', crucified, with its rays of glory, or golden sunbeams, or mythical thorns, *issuant* from its white, immaculate 'centre-point', or 'lily-point'--all which have further occult meanings lying hidden in theurgic mysticism. All these are spoken in the famous 'Round Table' of the Prince (and Origin) of Christian knighthood, King Arthur. His table is now hanging on the wall, dusty and neglected, over the. 'King's Seat or Bench' in the Court-House on the Castle Hill of our ancient Winchester. But upon this abstruse subject of the Round Table we have spoken more fully in another place. See Elias Ashmole.

Pope John XIV, about the year 970, issued a Bull for the baptizing of bells 'To cleanse the air of devils'; with which it was imagined to be full in the time of storms or of public commotion. To this end, the kettledrums of the Lacedæmonians were also supposed to be used on all extraordinarily harmful occasions. Pagodas are uprights and obelisks, with the same meaning as other steeples, and their angles are set about with bells, which are agitated in the wind, and are supposed to exercise the same power of driving off evil spirits. Vesper bells secure spiritual serenity. The bells of the churches are tolled in thunderstorms still, in some parishes in England, supposedly to disperse the clouds, and to open their rifts for the returning sunshine.

Edward the First of England was in every way an extraordinary man. There are certain reasons for supposing that he was really initiated in Eastern occult ideas. It is to be remembered that he made the Crusade to Palestine. He invited to England, Guido dalla Colonna, the author of the Troy-book *Tale of Troy*; and he also invited Raymond Lully into his kingdom. Raymond Lully is affirmed to have supplied to Edward six millions of money, to enable him to carry on war against the Turks. The origin of the rose-nobles is from the Rosicrucians.

No. I. Catherine-wheel window--12 columns. Query, the 12 signs, with the Rose, Disc, or Lotus, in the centre? From a Saracenic fountain near the Council-House, Jerusalem. This fountain seems to be built of fragments; the proof of which is that this inscribed stone (No. 2) is placed over half the *discus*. The whole structure, though Oriental or Saracenic, abounds with Gothic or pointed features. Such are the frets, the spandrel-work, the hood-moulding, etc.

No. 3. Query, 'Aquarii'? The *Aquarii* always indicate the Lunar element, or the female. The Baptisteries dedicated to St. John, or to the S.S., are eight-sided. The *Baptisteria* in Italy follow the same emblematical rule. The sections into which the Order of the Knights of Malta were divided were eight, answering to the eight points of the cross, which was their emblem. The Order was composed of eight nations, whereof the English, which was one, disappeared at the Reformation.

The colours of the monastic knightly orders were the following: The Teutonic Knights wore white, with the eight-pointed black cross; the Knights of Malta wore black, with the eight-pointed white cross. The

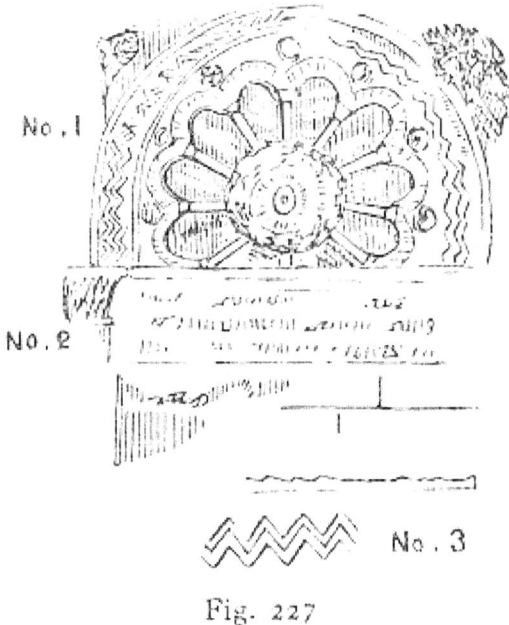

Fig. 227

foregoing obtained their Black and White from the Egyptians. The Knights Templars, or Red-Cross Knights, wore white, with the eight-pointed Bhuddist red cross displayed on their mantles. The Guardian of the Temple Chapel was called '*Custos Capellæ*, (*Capella*, a 'kid', 'star', 'she-goat', also 'chapel').

Attila, surnamed the Scourge of God', is represented as having worn a 'Teraphim', or head, on his breast-- a snaky-haired head, which purported to be that of Nimrod, whom he claimed as his great progenitor. This same Medusa-like head was an object of adoration to the heretical followers of Marcion, and was the Palladium set up by Antiochus Epiphanes, at Antioch, though it has been called the visage of Charon. This Charon may be 'Dis'-- or the 'Severe', or 'Dark', Deity.

The human head is a magnet, with a natural electric circle moving in the path of the sun. The sign of this

Fig. 228: Hindoo Pagoda at Tanjore

ring is serpentine, and is Σ; each man being considered--as far as his head is concerned--as magnetic. The positive pole of the magnet is the *os frontis, sinciput, os sublime*. The negative pole is the *occiput*.

Tonsure of the head is considered as a sacred observance. Hair (*in se*) is barbarous, and is the mark and investiture of the beasts. The Cabalists abstained from wine and marriage. Tonsure means 'the sun's disc' in the East. 'Les Arabes, dit Hérodote, lib. iii. se rasent la tête en rond et autour des tempes, ainsi que se rasait, disent-ils, Bacchus' (Volney, *Ruines*, p. 265). 'La touffe qui conservent les musulmans est encore prise du soleil, qui, chez les Égyptiens, était peint, au solstice d'hiver, n'ayant plus *qu'un cheveu sur la tête*.' 'Les étoiles de la déesse de Syrie et de la Diane, d'Ephèse, d'où dérivent celles des prêtres, portent les douze animaux du zodiaque.'

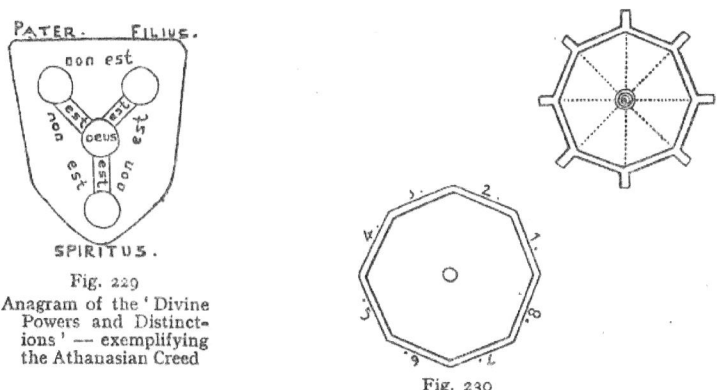

Fig. 229
Anagram of the 'Divine Powers and Distinctions'—exemplifying the Athanasian Creed

Fig. 230

Fig. 230, Chapter-Houses of York Cathedral and of Salisbury Cathedral. Most of the Chapter-Houses of the Cathedrals are eight-sided. In this they imitate the eight-sided or 'Bhuddist' cross of the Templars. This is the crown, cap, capital, chapiter, tabernacle, mythic *domus templi*, or *domus Dei*. They are miniature, mystical Round Churches, or 'Tors'. The Chapter-Houses oblong in shape are imitative of the 'Ark' of the Mosaical Covenant. All the Basilicas are of this figure. The symbol is a parallelogram, or an oblong, when the shape adopted is that of the temples. It then is the *navis*, 'nave', or ship--which is the 'Argo'.

'Les Chinois l'adorent dans Fôt. La langue chinoise n'ayant ni le B ni le D, ce peuple a prononcé Fôt ce que les Indiens et les Perses prononcent Bôt, Bot, Bod, Bodd, ou Boùdd--par où bref Fôt, au Pegou, est devenu Fota et Fta." Query, Pthah (Vulcan) of the Egyptians, and the Teutonic *F*'s in 'Friga' (the Runic Venus), 'Ffriga'--'Friday'? *B--F*, *P--F*, are interchangeable letters (see Arabic and Sanscrit vocabularies).

The Æolic Digamma is the *crux* of philologists. The ancients pronounced every word which began with a vowel with an aspirate, which had the sound of our *w*, and was often expressed by β or υ, and also γ.

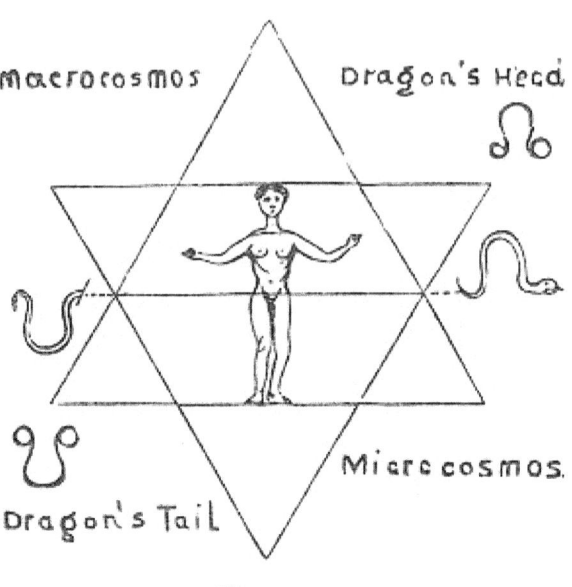

Fig. 231

For this the figure of a double Γ, or ꟻ, was invented, whence the name Digamma; which was called Æolic, because the Æolians, of all the tribes, retained the greatest traces of the original language. Thus, the Æolians wrote or pronounced Foίνος, Fελέα, *velia*. The Latin language was derived from the Æolic dialect, and naturally adopted the Digamma, which it generally

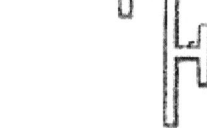

Fylfot: Digamma (Dr. Valpy's crest)
A notable Rosicrucian, Cabalistic, and Masonic emblem

expressed by *V*. These significant, mysterious sounds and characters-- *V, W, B*, and *F*--are reputed to be the key of the Lunar, or Feminine, Apotheosis. The symbol (or that meant in the symbol) is the keynote, as it were, of all Grecian architecture and art; which is all beauty, refinement, and elegance, with power at the highest.

This is the foundation mark of the famous symbols--

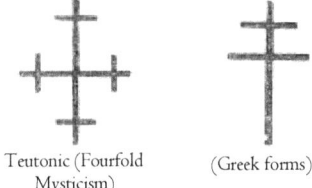

Teutonic (Fourfold Mysticism)   (Greek forms)

This latter double Cross (in ascension) is indicative of the Left-Hand Greek forms, or of the Eastern Church.

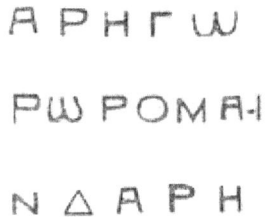

CHAPTER THE FIFTH

CONNEXION BETWEEN THE TEMPLARS AND GNOSTICISM

THE branch sect of the Gnostics, called Basilideans, who were properly Ophites, arose in the second century, deriving their name from Basilides, the chief of the Egyptian Gnostics. They taught that in the beginning there were Seven Being's, or Æons, of a most excellent nature; in whom we recognize the cabalistic Seven Spirits before the Throne. Two of these first Æons, called Dyamis and Sophia--that is 'Power' and 'Wisdom'--engendered the, angels of the highest order. The name of Abraxas; the Deity of the Gnostics, is made up of 'the numerical letters representing the total 365--the aggregate of days of the solar year. The 'manifestation' of Abraxas rests in his Son, Nūs (knowledge), or Christ, the chief of the Æons, who descended to earth and assumed the form of 'Man'; was baptized, and crucified in appearance (Mosheim's *Eccles. Hist.* vol. i. pp. 181-4). The Manichæans, who deny the reality of the Crucifixion of the Son of God, and whose tenets concerning the Saviour Jesus are peculiar, derive their name from Manes, or Mani; and their doctrine was first disseminated in Persia about the year 270. They speak mysteriously of the *Anima Mundi*, or 'Hyle'; they call this principle a deity, and agree with the Rosicrucians in asserting that it is a power presenting itself at once in reverse to the world and to the heavens, in as far as that, while it is dark to the one, it is light to the other; and contrariwise. The Gnostic hierarchy consisted of an arch-priest or patriarch, twelve. masters, and seventy-two leaders or bishops. The Gnostics called Matter, or Body, 'evil', and 'darkness', and seemed uncertain whether, in its operations, it were active or passive. It was believed by these sectaries that there were successive emanations of intelligent beings--these were the Æons (αἰῶνες), producing the various phases in creation. In this way, there arose in time a mighty being, the Demiurge, who set to work on the inert matter then existing, and out of it formed the world. The reconcilement, or restoration, is to the Bhuddistic *pleroma*, or fullness of light. It is absorption into 'annihilation', or into victory, oblivious of the vexations of 'life'. Here, in this fullness of light--or independence of all worlds, or of life, according to Man's ideas--the Supreme God has His habitation: but it is not 'nothingness', according to our ideas of nothing; it is so only because it has not anything in it comprehensible. The Alexandrian Gnostics inclined to the opinion that Matter was inert, or passive; the Syrian, Gnostics, on the contrary, held that it was active. Valentinus came from Alexandria to Rome about A.D. 140. St. Augustine fell under the Gnostic influence, and retained their beliefs from his twentieth to his twenty-ninth year--viz., from 374 to 383 A.D. Their books have for titles: the *Mysteries*, the *Chapters* or *Heads*, the *Gospel*, and the *Treasure*. Refer to Beausobre, Walch, Fuësslin, and Hahn.

The Gnostics held that Christ's teaching was not fully understood even by His disciples; and therefore He promised to send, in due time, a still greater Apostle, the Paraclete, who should effectually separate truth from falsehood. This Paraclete appeared in Mani.

The West Front of Lichfield Cathedral displays accurately the mythic idea of the union of the Male and Female Principles in the parallel double towers, which are uniform.

The claims for the real reading of the Egyptian hieroglyphics are distinct and unhesitating, as put forward by the Egyptologists; who, if industry could have succeeded, certainly would have realized their desire. But it is extremely doubtful whether, after all, they are not very widely astray. The late Sir George Cornewall Lewis, in his *History of Ancient Astronomy*, has disposed conclusively of the assumed correctness of most of these interpretations. The Egyptologists, the principal of whom are Champollion, Rawlinson, Dean, Milman, Sir George Lewis (perhaps the best critic), Professor Wilson, Sir Gardner Wilkinson, Dr. Cureton, Dr. Hincks, M. Oppert, Mr. Fox Talbot, with a large amount of ingenious and very plausible research and conjecture, have not truly touched or appreciated these enigmas. They yet remain, baffling the curiosity of the moderns; and they are likely to preserve their real mysteries unread as long as the stones of the Pyramids and the remembrance of the Sphinx--if not her visible figure--themselves endure. We believe that there is no adequate mystical comprehension among modern decipherers to read the hopeless secrets--purposely evading discovery--which lie locked in the hieroglyphics: the most successful readings are probably guesses only, founded on readily accepted likeness and likeliness.

The Temple Church, London, presents many mythic figures which have a Rosicrucian expression. In the spandrels of the arches of the long church, besides the 'Beauséant', which is repeated in many places, there are the armorial figures following: 'Argent, on a cross gules, the Agnus Dei, or Paschal Lamb, or'; 'Gules, the Agnus Dei, displaying over the right shoulder the standard of the Temple; or, a banner, triple cloven, bearing a cross gules'; 'Azure, a cross prolonged, potent, issuant out of the crescent moon argent, horns upwards; on either side of the cross, a star or'. This latter figure signifies the Virgin Mary, and displays the cross as rising like the pole, or mast of a ship (*argha*), out of the midst of the crescent moon, or *navis biprora*, curved at both ends; 'azure, semée of estoiles, or'. The staff of the Grand Master of the Templars displayed a curved cross of four splays, or blades, red upon white. The eight-pointed red Bhuddist cross was also one of the Templar ensigns. The temple arches abound with brandished *estoiles*, or stars, with wavy or crooked flames. The altar at the east end of the Temple Church has a cross *flourie*, with lower limb prolonged or, on a field of *estoiles*, wavy; to the right is the Decalogue, surmounted by the initials, A. Ω. (Alpha and Omega); on the left are the monograms of the Saviour, I C·X C; beneath, is the Lord's Prayer. The whole altar displays feminine colours and emblems, the Temple Church being dedicated to the Virgin Maria. The winged horse, or Pegasus, argent, in a field gules, is a badge of the Templars. The tombs of the Templars, disposed around the circular church in London, are of that early Norman shape called *dos d'âne*; their tops are triangular; the ridge-moulding passes through the temples and out of the mouth of a mask at the upper end, and issues out of the horned skull, apparently, of some purposely *trodden* creature. The head at the top is shown in the 'honour-point' of the cover of the tomb. There is an amount of unsuspected meaning in every curve of these Templar tombs; but it would at present too much occupy us to more fully explain.

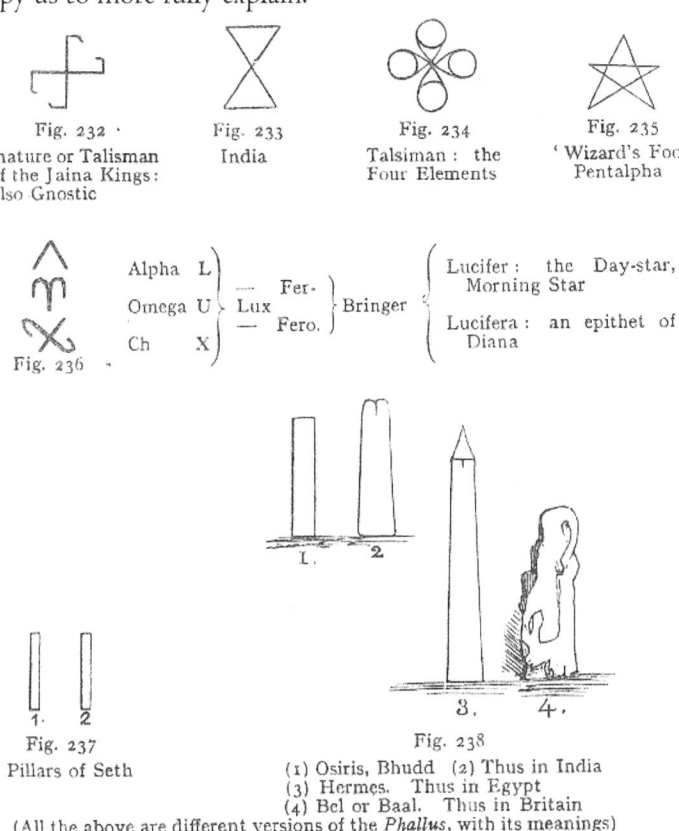

Fig. 232
Signature or Talisman of the Jaina Kings: also Gnostic

Fig. 233
India

Fig. 234
Talsiman: the Four Elements

Fig. 235
'Wizard's Foot Pentalpha

Fig. 236

Alpha   L
Omega U   — Fer-
              Lux   Bringer
Ch   X   — Fero.

Lucifer: the Day-star, Morning Star
Lucifera: an epithet of Diana

Fig. 237
Pillars of Seth

Fig. 238
(1) Osiris, Bhudd (2) Thus in India
(3) Hermes. Thus in Egypt
(4) Bel or Baal. Thus in Britain
(All the above are different versions of the *Phallus*, with its meanings)

The crook part of a Bishop's staff shows the undulating curve of S.S. issuing out of the foliations: meaning the Blessed Virgin Mary. This is particularly observable in the statue of William of Wykeham, the founder, at St. Mary's College,

Winchester; who, holding the spiritual crook in the left hand, gives the usual benediction of the two extended fingers with his right. The crook is the Shepherd Crook of the 'Second Person', and of the 'Holy Spirit'.

We now give a series of Gnostic Talismans, from originals. The reader is requested to refer to our numerous figures and symbols from the Temple Church,

Fig. 239

Fig. 240

Fig. 241
Jacinth : Gnostic Gem

Fig. 242
'Mithraic Sacrifice' Gnostic

Figs. 239-242

London, and to the insignia of the Templars, as displayed in all countries, for hints as to their connexion with the mysterious beliefs constituting that which is called Gnosticism.

Concerning the Pillars of Seth (see fig. 237), Josephus asserts that No. 1 was existent in his time. It is a Cabalistic tradition that No. 2 was destroyed in the Deluge. Notice also their resemblance to the Phallus or Phallos, Lingam or Lingham. Lithoi = Ll-th-oi.

Figs. 239-240, represent, under different aspects, the armed Abraxas, the chief deity of the Gnostics. In fig. 239 he is displayed with characteristics of Apollo, or the Sun rising in the East, in the *quadriga* or four-horsed chariot. Fig. 240: 'Abraxas brandishing his whip, as if chasing away the evil genii.

Fig. 243
Egyptian Apis, or Golden Calf

Fig. 244
Cancer grasping with One Claw at the Lunar Crescent : Gnostic Gem

On his shield; the titles IΨ. IAΩ. Neat work. Green jasper' (*The Gnostics*, p. 201).

The '*Uræon*', or winged solar disc, or egg, from which issue, on reversed sides, the two emblematical asps, has certain characteristics which ally it with the '*Scarabæus*'. Both Uræon and Scarabæus are symbols continual on the fronts of the Egyptian temples, and they are principally placed over the portals; they are talismans or charms.

Fig. 248: 'Osiris', or the 'Old Man'; a terminal figure. At the foot, the celestial globe and masonic pentagon, or 'Solomon's

Seal'. The field is occupied by symbols and letters, seemingly Hebrew. The whole design is mediæval, hardly a production of even the lowest times of the Empire. This is one of the pieces most evidently bespeaking a 'Rosicrucian' origin. Deeply cut in a coarse-grained green jasper (*Gnostics*, p. 213).

Fig. 249: Anubis walking; in each hand, a long

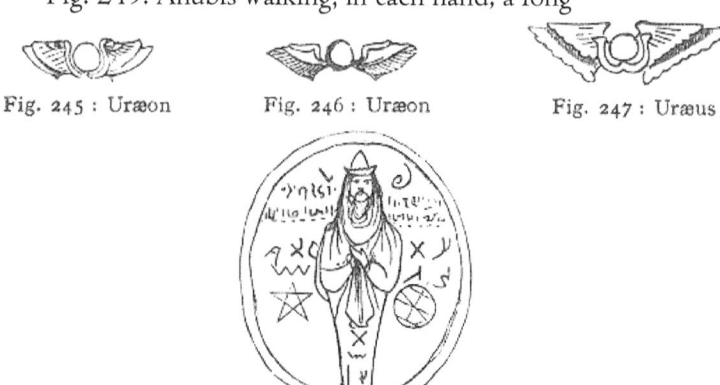

Fig. 245 : Uræon   Fig. 246 : Uræon   Fig. 247 : Uræus

Fig. 248

Egyptian sceptre terminating in a ball; in the field, the sun and moon (adjuncts marking the astrological character of this talisman, which therefore must be ascribed to the class of Abraxoids). The whole enclosed in a sunken circle. Rev. MIXAHA, between four stars. The Cabalists make Michael the Angel of the Sun. Plasma of bad quality (*The Gnostics*, p. 200).

Fig. 250: This object is the 'Chnuphis Serpent', to which frequent reference has been made in our book. The 'Serpent' is raising itself in act to give the mythic dart. On its, head is the crown of seven points or vowels. The second amulet presents the name of the Gnostic 'Unknown Angel', with the four stars in the angles. This is Michael or the 'Saviour', the 'Chief of the Æons', seventy-two in number, and composed of six times twelve; there being three 'double decades', for the night and for the day, in each lunar period or sign of the zodiac; each of which consists of thirty degrees. In another aspect, this symbol stands for the Gnostic

Chief Deity Abraxas, the letters of whose name make up the number of days of the solar circle. The following group of figures gives some of the significant hieroglyphs from the Egyptian sculptures. (*a*) Plume, 'Spiritual Power' (*b*) Jackal, 'Priesthood'. (*c*) Tau, Fleur-de-Lis, Crux-Ansata. (*d*) Placenta, 'Religious Solemnities'. (*e*) Horns, 'Power'. (*f*) Anser, 'Prudence'. (*g*) 'Nonage'. (*h*) Asp, 'Sovereignty'. (*i*) Hawk, 'Sagacity'. The Lotus-headed Sceptre means 'Religious Authority'. A Snake-headed Rod or Staff signifies 'Military Dominion'. A Snaky Rod or Sceptre is the 'Lituus' or 'Augur's Divining-rod', when it is curved at the lower as well as the upper end. It is said that this was the sceptre of Romulus.

We give in another place the Procession of the 'Logos', or 'Word', according to the Gnostics,

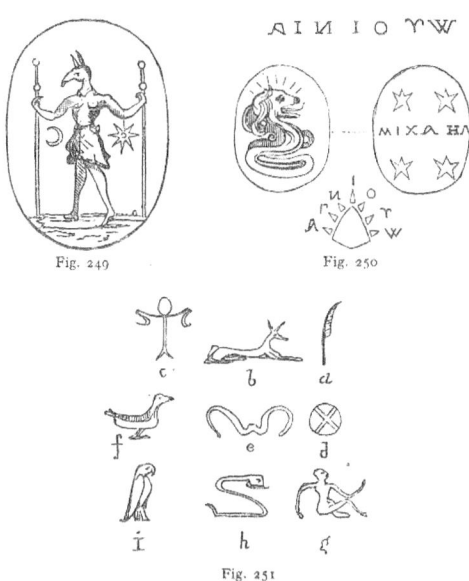

Fig. 249   Fig. 250

Fig. 251

Fig. 252: 'The Good Shepherd bearing upon his shoulders the Lost Lamb, as he seems to the uninitiated eye: but on close inspection he becomes the double-headed Anubis; having one head human, the other a jackal's, whilst his girdle assumes the form of a serpent, rearing aloft its crested head. In his hand is a long hooked staff. It was perhaps the signet of some chief teacher or, apostle among the Gnostics, and its impression one of the tokens serving

Fig. 252

for mutual recognition mentioned by Epiphanius. Neatly engraved in a beautiful red sard, fashioned to an octagon form; a shape never met in the class of antique gems, though so much affected in Mediæval art, on account of its supposed mystic virtues' (*The Gnostics*, p. 201).

One of the Gnostic Gems, reputed the most efficacious of amulets, is of red jasper, and presents the Gorgon's Head ('Gorgoneion'), with the legend below, 'ΑΡΗΓΩ ΡΩΠΟΜΑΝΔΑΡΗ', 'I protect Rhoromandares'.

In India, the 'Great Abad' is Bhudda; Bauddha, Buddha, or Baddha. There is a connexion. suggested here with the 'Abaddon' of the Greeks. In the same way, a relation may be traced with 'Budha's Spiritual Teacher'; who was the mythic Pythagoras, the originator, of the system of transmigration, afterwards transplanted to Egypt, and thence to Greece. Thus in Sanscrit it is 'Bud'ha-Gooros'; in Greek it is 'Pythagoras', in English it is 'Pythagoras'; the whole, 'Budha's Spiritual Teacher'.

The *crista*, or crest, or symbolic knob of the Phrygian cap or Median bonnet, is found also, in a feminine form, in the same mythic head-cover or helmet, for it unites both sexes in its generative idea, being an 'idol'. In the feminine case--as obviously in all the statues of Minerva or Pallas-Athene, and in the representations of the Amazons, or woman-champions, or warriors--everywhere the cap or helmet has the elongated, rhomboidal, or globed, or salient part in reverse, or dependent on the nape of the neck. This is seen in the illustration of the figure of the armed 'Pallas-Athene', among our array of these Phallic caps. The whole is deeply mythic in its origin. The ideas became Greek; and when treated femininely in Greece, the round or display--which in the masculine helmet was naturally pointed forward, saliently or exaltedly (the real '*christa*', or 'crest')-- became reversed or collapsed, when worn as the trophy on a woman's head. On a narrow review of evidence which evades, there is no doubt that, these classic helmets with their 'crests', this *pileus*, Phrygian cap, Cap of Liberty, or the Grenadiers' or Hussars' fur caps, or cocked hats, have all a phallic origin.

The Cardinal's 'Red Hat' follows the same idea in a different way; it is a chapel, chapter, chapiter, or chapeau, a discus or table crimson, as the mystic feminine 'rose', the 'Queen' of Flowers, is crimson. The word 'Cardinal' comes both from *Cardo* (Hinge, Hinge-Point, 'Virgo' of the Zodiac), and also from *Caro*, It. *Carne*, flesh--the Word made flesh.' It is probable that these mythological hints and secret expressions, as to the magic working of nature, were insinuated by the imaginative and ingenious Greeks into dress and personal appointments. In the temples, and in templar furniture, mythological theosophic hints abound; every curve and every figure, every colour and every boss and point, being significant among the Grecian contrivers, and among those from whom they borrowed--the Egyptians. We may

ΘΕΟΥ - ΘΕΟΥ
Fig. 253
'Bai', a Prize

Fig. 254
Gnostic Invocation

assume that this classic Grecian form of the head-cover or helmet of the Athenian goddess Pallas-Athene, or Minerva, not only originated the well-known Grecian mode of arranging women's hair at the back, but that this style is also the far-off, classic progenitor of its clumsy, inelegant imitation, the modern chignon, which is only an abused copy of the antique. In our deduction (as shown in a previous group of illustrations) of the modern military fur caps--particularly the Grenadier caps of all modern armies, as well as those of other branches of the military service--from that common great original, into which they can be securely traced, the mythic Phrygian cap when red, the Vulcan's *pileus* when black, we prove the transmission of an inextinguishable important hint in religion.

The following are some of the most significant talismans of the Gnostics:

Fig. 255

Fig. 256   Fig. 257

In fig. 255 we have the representation of the Gnostic Female Power in Nature--Venus, or Aphrodite, disclosing in the beauty, grace, and splendour of the material creation. On the other, or terrible, side of her character, the endowments of Venus, or of the impersonated idea of beauty, change into the alarming; these are the attributes of the malific feminine elementary genius born of 'darkness' or 'matter', whose tremendous countenance, veiled as in the instance of Isis, or masked as in that of the universal mythological Queen of Beauty, inspires or destroys according to the angle of contemplation at which she is mythically revealed.

Fig. 256 (A) is the crested 'Snake', curved as the symbol of the 'Dragon's Tail', traversing from left to right the fields of creation, in which the stars are scattered as 'estoiles', or waved serpentining flames--the mystic 'brood' of the 'Great Dragon'. The reverse of this amulet (B) presents the 'crescent' and 'decrescent' moons, placed back to back, with a trace or line, implying that the 'Microcosmos', or 'Man', is made as between the 'Moons'. This figure suggests a likeness to the sign of the 'Twins', and to that of the February 'Fishes'.

Fig. 258

Fig. 257 is the mythological 'Medusa's Head', terrible in her beauty, which transforms the beholder to stone. This direful head is twined around with snakes for hair, and the radii which dart from it are lightning. It is, nevertheless, esteemed one of the most powerful talismans in the Gnostic, preservative group, though it expresses nothing (in a strange, contradictory way) but dismay and destruction.

Fig. 258 is referred to in a previous part of our book as fig. 313.

CHAPTER THE SIXTH

STRANGE SPECULATIONS OF THE TRANSCENDENTALISTS

'HAD Man preserved his original innocence and refused to taste of the means of that bitter and condemned knowledge (or power of recognition) of good and evil, as then there would have been none, of that physical deficiency asserted to be debited to Women, would there likewise have been no females engendered; no propagation of the human species? By some the preference of the robust to the delicate sex is accounted beyond all question as self-evident. A certain class of philosophers have made no scruple to call a woman an imperfect and even monstrous animal. These have affirmed that nature, in generation, always intends a male, and that it is only from mistake or deficiency, either of the matter or the faculty, that a woman is produced.' The oriental ethics have degraded woman to the level of a chattel. It is Christianity alone, in the discovery of the Divine Mary 'Virgin-Mother', 'Mother-Virgin'--that has elevated 'Woman', and found for 'Her' a possible place (of course as a Sexed-Sexless, Sexless-Sexed 'Idea') in Heaven--or in that state other than this state; irradiated with the 'light', breathing with the 'breath' of Divinity.

Almaricus, a doctor at Paris in the twelfth century, advances an opinion that, had the state of innocence continued, every individual of our species would have come into existence a complete 'MAN', and that God would have created them by Himself, as He created Adam. He theorizes that woman is. a defective animal, and that the generation of her is purely fortuitous and foreign from nature's intent. He therefore infers that there would have been no women 'in a state of innocence'. On the other hand, there exists a counterbalancing singular idea, combated by St. Austin in his *City of God,* Book xxii. chap. xvii.; and of which its partisans take upon themselves to say that at the universal resurrection this imperfect work (woman) will be rendered perfect by a change of sex; all the women becoming men--grace and finish being then to complete the work of the human form, which nature (in Man) only, as it were, had left coarse, unfinished, rough-hewn. These ideas resemble closely the conclusions of the alchemists (or of the Rosicrucians when applying to practical art), who declare that nature, in the production of metals, always *intends* the generation of gold, and that it is only from accidental diversion or interposing difficulty, or from the deficiency of the virtue or faculty, that the working out of the aim falls short, and issues (bluntly and disappointed) in another metal--the blanker, blacker, and coarser metals being, in fact, only as the 'DISEASES' of matter, which aims at clear perfect *health*--or *as gold.* Here the alchemists contend that their superhuman (in apparent-sense) science, felicitously applied, 'completes the operation', and transmutes or compels-on, 'into gold' what weaker-handed nature was compelled to 'forego' as 'iron'. Thus nature always intends the production of male (sun--gold--fire being the workman, or 'agent'); but that, in the production of female (silver as against gold--the moon--sublimated matter, or 'patient'), nature's operation miscarries; the effort degenerates into struggle, and struggle submits in failure. Therefore; 'Female'. But this shortcoming, when the Divine perfecting-means (in another state, and through another nature or 'mode') is applied, will be rectified. And in the universal resurrection, Women will transcend into the nobler creature, and, changing sex or ceasing sex, will become--'Woman'd-Men': Both sexes interchanging 'sex' to form the 'Angel', or rather blending sex and uniting sex--bicorporate no longer, but becoming 'Ideal'--fit spirit-populace, winnowed of materiality and of humanity. 'Unintelligible to the *intellect* as Music, but beautiful to the *heart* as Music.'

Yet it must be understood that no man's *dreams* (dreams, we have elsewhere contended, quite contrary to the usual ideas, are *real things*) are wholly and altogether evil and vain; for that cannot be except men were utter (or outer) devils; which also cannot be so long as we live in the human nature, for Man's Fall was not like the Fall of the Evil Angels; for these latter fell into the Dark Abyss, or Original. Wrathful Principle (the Rosicrucian 'Refuse' or 'Lees' of Creation, without, or beyond; nature and creature, and therefore there was for them no help or recovery). But, on the contrary, Men fell and were saved thereby (the Knowledge of Good and Evil), that is, *into* Nature and Creature, which is Man's inexpressible happiness, as not being left destitute of Hope or the Regenerating Seed of the Woman. For there does centrally dwell in the human nature that which the wise man galls the Voice of Wisdom, or conscience-recall; which in the suggestion of the Immortal Sorrow, planted deep in the soul of man for his 'Lost Paradise' (of which the very air and hint and proof to him, is Music--Man's Music--with its *shadow* of discords). And this Immortal Sorrow languishes to Redemption in repentance. Thus the pathetic languishment of the Saviour (and Sufferer), Jesus Christ: 'My soul is sad, even unto death!' Hence the 'Garden' of 'Agony'.

This is the *Genius Optimus*, the 'Soul of the Soul' and the 'Eye of the Mind'--that part *incapable* of damnation even in the greatest sinner (this was Cromwell's firm reliance and belief, and his last question to his attendant chaplain bore reference to the assurance of it). This is the last supernatural power which can and will defend man from all the assaults of evil angels, and unto this holy principle and benevolent upspring the dictates and the efforts of all Good Angels and Spirits do tend, it being a great part of their work and business to assist man, and to defend and preserve him from the inward incursions of the multitude of the malignant Spirits in their various degrees.

Trithemius, a noted Rosicrucian, asserts that 'never any good Angel appeared in the shape of a woman.' Van Helmont, in the ninety-third chapter of one of his books, has these words: 'If an Angel appear bearded, let him be accounted an evil one; for a Good Angel hath never appeared with a beard. The truth is, a woman is the weaker vessel, and was first in the Transgression. Therefore, that sex is an emblem of weakness and a means of seduction. And therefore there is no reason why the Good Angels, amongst whom there is no difference of sex, should elect to appear as a female; but rather, being a species of creature above humankind, they assume the shape of the most excellent of that kind (only feminine in regard of grace and beauty); and for the same reason they may appear without beards, both because "hair is an excrement", and verges greatly, in the more conspicuous instances, to the brutish nature, as also more especially in their beardless, beautiful, glorified aspects, and graceful delicacy and yet *power* of form, to express their perpetual virgin-youth, unspoiled heavenly beauty, and immortal star-born vigour. Hair being an abhorred, tentacled, reaching-out or brute-like animal superflux--the stigma or disgrace of the glorious spark of light or nearly suffocated human entity, condemned to its earth-birthed investiture or body--it can have nothing about the parts of the "Deified Idea of Man"--or the various classes of the Blessed Angels.' The contrary of all this is to be assumed of the evil Genii or the Recusant Genii (Luciferent and yet Lucifugent), except in regard to their power or knowledge. For the 'Soul of the World' and 'Matter', and to an important one-half, the 'Means of the World'--are 'Feminine'. For Night (which is the other side of the curtain of Day) is Feminine. Thus Bœhmen and Plato; as representing all the closest-of-thought of the centuries.

All the above is the reproduction of the singular ideas of the 'Idealists' of the Middle Ages.

CHAPTER THE SEVENTH

ROSICRUCIAN ORIGIN OF THE ORDER OF THE GARTER. DEDUCTIONS, AND PROOFS, FROM HISTORICAL AUTHORITIES

THE natural horns of the Bull or the Cow--both which animals were deified by the Egyptians, and also by the Indians, who particularly elected the Cow as the object of religious honour--were the models from which originally all the volves and volutes, presenting the figure of curved horns, or the significant suggestion of the thin horns of the crescent or growing moon, were obtained. The representative horns figured largely afterwards in all architecture, and were copied as an important symbol expressive of the second operative power of nature. The 'Lunar' or 'Feminine Symbol' is the universal parent of the Hindoo and Mahometan returned arches; find therefore, also, of the Horse-shoe curves of the Arabian arches, and the hooked curves of all Gothic architectural reproduction, whether in arches or otherwise. The Egyptian volutes to the pillars, the Egyptian horns everywhere apparent, the innumerable spiral radii distinct in all directions, or modified, or interpenetrating the ornamentation of buildings in the East; the Ionic volutes, the Corinthian volutes, which became pre-eminently pictorial and floral in their treatment in this beautiful order, particularly in the Greek examples (which are, however, very few); the more masculine volves and volutes, or horns, of the Roman solid, majestic columns; the capitals to the ruder and more grotesque of the Indian temples; the fantastic scrolls and crooks and oval curves, abounding on the tops of the spiring columns in the Gothic or, more properly to call it, the Romantic architecture called 'pointed'--all have a common ancestor in the horns of the bull, calf, or cow. All these horns are everywhere devoted in their signification to the Moon. It is in connexion with this secondary god or goddess, who is always recognizable through the peculiar appendage of horns,--it is in proximity to this god or goddess, who takes the second place in the general Pantheon, the Sun taking the first--it is here, in all the illustrations which the mythic theology borrows from architecture, or the science of expressing religious ideas through hieroglyphical forms--that the incoherent horns reiterate, always presenting themselves to recognition, in some form or other, at terminal or at salient points. Thus they become a most important figure, if not the most important figure, in the templar architecture everywhere--of India, of Egypt, of Greece, of Rome, even of the Christian periods--all the Christian ages, earlier and later.

The figure called Nehustan--the mysterious upright set up by Moses in the Wilderness--was a talisman in the form of a serpent coiled around the mystic 'Tau'. This is a *palladium* offered for worship, as we have explained in several places.

In a previous part of our book, we have brought forward certain reasons for supposing that the origin of the Most Noble Order of the Garter was very different from that usually and popularly assigned. The occurrence which gave rise to the formation of the Order, and which explains the adoption of the motto, does not admit of being told, except in far-off, roundabout terms; propriety otherwise would be infringed.

We may say no more than that it was a feminine *accident*, of not quite the character commonly accepted and not quite so simple and ordinary as letting fall a garter. But this accident, which brought about the foundation of the exalted Order, pre-eminently 'Rosicrucian' in its hidden meanings--however clear it becomes when understood, and however sublime, as the Rosicrucians asserted it was, when it is apprehended in its physiological and also in its deeply mythic sense--could not, of necessity, be placed before the world, because ordinary persons could not have appreciated it, nor would they have felt any other idea than repulsion and disbelief at the statement. The commonplace, coarse, unprepared mind instantly associates indecency with any explanation, however conclusive, which cannot for obvious reasons be spoken 'on the house-tops'. We are now ourselves, against our desire, compelled to speak circuitously about the real, successfully concealed, very strange origin, in our modern ideas, of this famous 'Order of the Garter'. The subject is, however, of very great consequence, because there is either meaning of the highest force in this, which may be called the 'brotherhood of princes', as the Order undoubtedly is in a high sense; or there is no particular meaning, and certainly nothing challenging startled attention. There is either truth in the abstract, occult matters which the Order supposedly is formed to whisper and to maintain, or there is only empty, meaningless pretence and affectation. There is grandeur and reality in its formalities, or the whole institution is no more than a parade of things that have no solidity, and an assumption of oaths and obligations that regard nothing of consequence--nothing of real, vital seriousness. We seek thus to *ennoble* the 'Order' in idea, by giving it conclusively the sanction of religion, and rendering to it the respect due to the mighty mystery which may be suspected to lie in it; which it *was* supposed to emphasize, *whatever it be held now*. We are inclined to view with surprise--although in no grudging, prejudiced, spirit--the obtrusion of the 'Crescent and Star,' the symbol of the Grand Signior, Soldan, or Sultan of Turkey, the Representative of Mohammed, the 'Denier of Christ', according to his supposed religious obligations. It is certainly an anomaly to admit the denier of Christ in an Order intended to exalt into vital distinct recognition the Divinity of Christ as 'the Saviour of Mankind'. How can the Sultan of Turkey, or any Mahometan, or any disbeliever, discharge the oaths which he is solemnly assumed to take in this respect? We are disposed to contemplate the addition of the Moslem banner--the direct contradiction and neutraliser of the ensigns of the Christian knights--suspended in the Chapel of the Order, the Chapel of St. George at Windsor, as a perplexing, uncomfortable intrusion, according to assumed correct Christian ideas. We fear that the admission of this heathen knight may possibly imply heraldically the infraction of the original constitutions of the Order, which created it as exclusively Christian. The 'Garter' is specially devoted to the Virgin Mary and to the honour (in the glorification of 'Woman') of the

Saviour of Mankind. The knights-companions are accepted; supposedly, as the special initiated holy guard bf the Christian mysteries, and they. are viewed as a sworn body of 'brothers', by day and night, from their first association, bound to maintain and uphold, in life and in death, the faith that had Bethlehem for its beginning and Calvary for its end. The bond and mark of this brotherhood is the Red Cross of Crucifixion. The 'Red Cross' which is the 'Cross' of the 'Rosicrucians'--thence their name.

Even the badge and star and symbol of this most Christian Order, if ever there were a Christian Order--which presents this red or sanguine cross of the Redeemer, imaged in the cognisance of His champion, or captain, or chief soldier, St. George or St. Michael, the Trampler of the Dragon, and Custos of the Keys of the Bottomless Pit, where the devils are confined--protests against the mingling of this Mussulman banner with the Red Cross, which opposed it in the hands of the Crusaders, and in those of all Christian knights. Now all the Christian 'Garter' badges only seem to appeal and to protest quietly and under allowance, with 'bated breath' as it were (as if afraid), deficient in firmness and life, leaving results to chance, and abandoning expostulation to be regarded or disregarded (or taken up faintly) *according to circumstances.*

These are matters, however, which properly appertain to the office, and lie in the hands of the dignitaries of the Order of the Garter. These officials are its Prelate and 'Garter' himself (the personified 'Order'), who are supposed, because of the sublime duties with which they are charged, to be the guardians of the meanings and the myths of an Order of Knighthood whose heraldic display in one form or other covers the land (or covers the world), and must be interpreted *either as talisman or toy.* The Bishop of Winchester is always the chief ecclesiastical authority of the Order. Remark here; as the sanctions of this 'Most Noble Order', that in Winchester we directly alight upon 'King Arthur and his Knights of the "Round Table"'--what the 'Round Table' is, we have explained elsewhere. In these days without faith, wherein science (as it is called in the too arbitrary and overriding sense) has extinguished the lights of enthusiasm, leaving even our altars dark, desecrated, and cold, and has eliminated all possible wonder from the earth, as miracle from religion, and magic from the sensible or insensible fields of creation--in these questioning, doubting, dense, incredulous days, it is no inconsistency that the gorgeous emblazonments of the Garter should provoke no more curiosity or religious respect than peculiar ornaments do, signifying anything or nothing.

But to return to the import of the title of the Order of the Garter. This is a point very engrossing to heralds, antiquaries, and all persons who are interested in the history, traditions, and archæology of our country. The origin of the Order would be trivial, ridiculous, and unbelievable, if it be only thought due to the picking up of a lady's garter. It is impossible that the great name and fame of this 'Garter' could have arisen alone from this circumstance. The Garter, on the contrary, is traceable from the times of King Arthur, to whose fame throughout Europe as the mythic hero there was no limit in his own period. This we shall soon show conclusively from the accounts of the Garter by Elias Ashmole, who was 'Garter King of Arms', and who was one of its most painstaking and enlightened historians; besides himself being a faithful and conscientious expositor and adherent of the hermetic Rosicrucian science. The 'Round Table' of King Arthur--the 'mirror of chivalry'--supplies the model of all the miniature tables, or tablets, which bear the contrasted roses--red and white, as they were originally (and implying the female *discus* and its accidents)--with the noble 'vaunt', or motto, round them--'Evil to him', or the same to him, 'who thinks ill' of these natural (and yet these magical) feminine circumstances, the character of which our readers will by this time not fail to recognize. The glory of woman and the punishment of woman after the Fall, as indicated in Genesis, go hand in hand. It was in honour of Woman, and to raise into dignity the expression of the condemned 'means' (until sanctified and reconciled by the intervention of the 'S.S.', or of the Holy Spirit, or of the Third Person of the Trinity), which is her mark and betrayal, but which produced the world in producing Man, and which saved the world in the person of the Redeemer, 'born of Woman'. It is to glorify typically and mystically this 'fleshly vehicle', that the Order of the 'Garter'--Or 'Garder'--that keeps it sacred was instituted. The Knights of the Garter stand sentinel, in fact, over 'Woman's Shame', at the same time that they proclaim her 'Glory', in the pardoned sense. These strange ideas are strictly those of the old Rosicrucians, or Brethren of the 'Red Cross', and we only reproduce them. The early writers saw no indecency in speaking openly of these things, which are usually hidden away, as improper to be spoken about.

The blackness or darkness of 'Matter', or of the 'Mother of Nature', is figured in another respect in the belongings of this famous feminine Order, instituted for the glory of woman. Curious armorists, skilled in the knowledge of the deep sacred symbolism with which the old heralds suffused their illustrations or emblazonments, will remember that *black* is a feature in the Order of the Garter; and that, among figures and glyphs and hints the most profound, the 'Black Book', containing the original constitutions of the Order--from which 'Black Book' comes the important 'Black Rod'--was *lost*, or taken away for some secret reason before the time of Henry the Fifth. See various pages, *ante*, for previous remarks about the 'Garter'.

Elias Ashmole mentions the Order in the following terms: 'We may ascend a step higher and if we may give credit to Harding, it is recorded that King Arthur paid St. George, whose red cross is the badge of the Garter, the most particular honours; for he advanced his effigy in one of his banners, which was about two hundred years after his martyrdom, and very early for a country so remote from Cappadocia to have him in reverence and esteem.'

In regard to the story of the Countess of Salisbury, and her garter, we shall insert the judgment of Dr. Heylin, who took great pains to ascertain its foundation. 'This I take to be a vain and idle romance', he says, 'derogatory both to the founder and the Order, first published by Polydore Virgil, a stranger to the affairs of England, and by him taken upon no better ground than *fama vulgi*, the tradition of the common people--too trifling a foundation upon which to raise so great a building.'

The material whereof the Garter was composed at first is an *arcanum*, nor is it described by any writer before Polydore Virgil, and he only speaks of it in general terms. The Garter was originally without a motto [14]. As to the appointments of the Order, we may gain the most authentic idea of them from the effigies of some of the first knights. Sir William Fitz-warin was buried on the north side of the chancel of the church of Wantage, in Berkshire, in the thirty-fifth year of the reign of King Edward the Third. Sir Richard Pembridge, who was a Knight of the Garter, of the time of Edward the Third, lies on the south side of the cathedral of Hereford. The monument of Sir Simon Burley, beheaded A.D. 1388, was raised in the north wall, near the choir of St. Paul's, London. It is remarkable that, Du Chesne, a noted French historian, is the source from which we derive the acknowledgment that it was by the special invocation of St. George that King Edward the Third gained the Battle of Cressy; which 'lying deeply in his remembrance, he founded', continues Du Chesne, 'a chapel within the Castle of Windsor, and dedicated it in gratitude to the Saint, who is the Patron of England.' The first example of a Garter that occurs is on the before-mentioned monument of Sir Francis Burley; where, on the front, towards the head, are his own arms, impaling his first wife's, set within a garter. This wants the impress, or motto. Another shield of arms, having the same impalement placed below the feet, is surrounded with a collar of 'S.S.', of the same form with that about his neck. It was appointed by King Henry the Eighth, and embodied in the Statutes of the Order, that the collar should be composed of pieces of gold, in fashion of Garters; the ground enamelled blue, and the letters of the motto gold. In the midst of each garter *two roses* were to be placed, the innermost enamelled red, and the outermost white; contrarily, in the next garter, the innermost Rose enamelled white, and the outermost red, and so alternately; but of later times, these roses are wholly red. The number of these

---

[14] A proof that it did not originate with Edward the Third.

Garters is so many as to be the ordained number of the sovereign and knights-companions. At the institution they were twenty-six, being fastened together with as many knots of gold. And this mode hitherto has continued invariable; nor ought the collar to be adorned or enriched with precious stones (as the 'George' may be), such being prohibited by the laws of the Order. At what time the collar of 'S.S.' came into England is not fully determined; but it would seem that it came at least three hundred years since. The collar of 'S.S.' means the Magian, or First Order, or brotherhood. In the Christian arrangements, it stands for the 'Holy Spirit', or 'Third Person of the Trinity.' In the Gnostic talismans, it is displayed as the bar, curved with the triple 'S.'. Refer to the 'Cnuphis Abraxoids' occurring in our book, for we connect the collar of 'S.S.' with the theology of the Gnostics.

That the Order of the Garter is feminine, and that its origin is an apotheosis of the 'Rose', and of a certain singular physiological fact connected with woman's life, is proven in many ways--such as the double garters, red and white; the twenty-six knights, representing the double thirteen lunations in the year, or their twenty-six mythic 'dark and light' changes of 'night and day'.

There are 13 Lunations in the Year, or the Solar Circle:-- twice 13 are Twenty-Six, the dark and the light renewals or changes of the Moon (which is feminine). The dark infer the red rose, the light imply the white rose; both equally noble and coequal in rank with parallel, but different, Rosicrucian meanings. These mythic discs, or red and white roses, correspond with the Twenty-Six Seats, or 'Stalls', around the 'Round Table' (which is an Apotheosis), allowing two chief seats (or one 'Throne') as preeminent for the King-Priest, Priest-King, in the 'Siege-Perilous.' The whole refers to King Arthur and his Knights of the Round Table; set round as sentinels ('in lodge') of the *Sangreal,* or *Holy Graal*--the 'Sacrifice Mysterious', or 'Eucharist'.

'But how is all this magic and sacred in the estimate of the Rosicrucians?' an inquirer will very naturally ask. The answer to all this is very, ample and satisfactory; but particulars must be left to the sagacity of the querist himself, because propriety does not admit of explanation. Suffice it to say, that it is one of the most curious and wonderful subjects which has occupied the attention of antiquaries. That archaeological puzzle, the 'Round Table of King Arthur', is a perfect display of this whole subject of the origin of the 'Garter'; it springs directly from it, being the same object as that enclosed by the mythic garter, 'garder', or 'girther.'

King Edward the Third chose the Octave of the 'Purification of the Blessed Virgin' for the inauguration of his Order. Andrew du Chesne declares that this new Order was announced on 'New Year's Day, A.D. 1344'. There were jousts holden in honour of it on the 'Monday after the Feast of St. Hilary following--January 19th'. There are variations in the histories as to the real period of the institution of the Garter; most historians specifying the year 1349 Ashmole states that a great supper was ordered to inaugurate the solemnity of the institution, and that a Festival was to be annually held at *Whitsuntide* (which means the 'S.S.'); that King Edward erected a particular building in the Castle, and therein placed a table ('Round Table') of 200 feet diameter, giving to the *building itself* the name of the 'Round Table'. He appropriated £100 per week--an enormous sum in those days--for the maintenance of this table. In imitation of this, the French King, Philip de Valois, instituted a 'Round Table' for himself at his court. Some say that he had an intention of instituting an order of knighthood upon the same 'feminine subject', but that he was anticipated by King Edward; which shows that it was something more than an accident and a mere garter which inspired the idea of this Rose forming the mystery. The knights were denominated 'Equites Aureæ Periscelidis'. King Edward the Third had such veneration for the Blessed Virgin Mary, that he ordained that the habit of his Knights of the Garter should be worn on the days of her Five Solemnities. Elias Ashmole states that the original of the Statutes of Institution had wholly perished long before his time. There was a transcript existing in the reign of Henry the Fifth, in an old book called *Registrum Ordinis Chartaceum*. Though the Order was instituted so long ago as in the year 1344, it was not till the reign of Charles the Second that the Knights were empowered to wear the star they use at present embroidered on their coats. The rays are the 'glory' round the 'Red Cross'.

Sir John Froissart, the only writer of the age that treats of this institution, assigns no such origin as the picking up of the Countess of Salisbury's garter; nor does he adduce the words of the motto of the Garter as having been spoken by King Edward the Third when encountering the laughter of his court, and assuring them that he would make the proudest eventually wear it as the most illustrious badge. There can be only one conclusion as to the character of the investment which was picked up; and which article of dress makes it clear that the Countess of Salisbury--or the lady, whoever she may be, who has succeeded in becoming so wonderfully celebrated in the after-ages of chivalry-- should have rather been at home, *and at rest*, than inattentive to saltatory risks in engaging in a dance or in forgetful gambols at a crowded court. There was no mention of this supposed picking up of a garter for 200 years, nor was there anything referring to such an origin occurring in any of our historians other than Sir John Froissart, until Polydore Virgil took occasion to say something of it in his notices of the origin of the Order. In the original Statutes of the Order (which is a most important point in the inquiry) there is not the least conjecture expressed, nor does the compiler of that tract entitled *Institutio clarissimi Ordinis Militaris a prænobili Subligaculo nuncupata*, prefaced to the *Black Book of the Garter*, let fall any passage on which to ground the adroit conclusions about the Garter. Polydore does not mention whose garter it was; this he cautiously declines to do. He says that it was either the Queen's, or that of the King's mistress-- meaning Joan, Countess of Salisbury, with whom it was supposed the King was in love, and whom he believed when she was bravely holding out for him against the Scots, in her Castle of Wark- upon-Tweed; but she was certainly no mistress of the King's, in the injurious and unworthy sense. It is to be particularly noticed that the Latin words *subliGAR subligaculum*, mean *not* a 'garter' but 'breeches, drawers, or trousers'. It was therefore not a garter for the leg, but a cincture for the body, which was thus picked up publicly, and elevated for honour, as such an unexpected illustrious object; one around which the most noble knights were to take enthusiastic oaths of the most devoted religious homage. Now, unless there had been some most extraordinary meaning under all this (lying under the apparent but only apparent, indecency), such an idolizing of a garter could never have occurred, and the whole occurrence ages ago would have been laughed into oblivion, carrying the sublime honours of the 'Garter' with it. Instead of this, the Garter is the highest token of greatness the Sovereign of England can bestow, and it is contended for and accepted with eager pride by Princes. 'Subligaculum, *breeches, drawers, trousers*'. 'Subligatus, *cinctured, bound, etc., wearing drawers*'. The origin of the 'Garter' is proven in this word not to be a garter at all.

It is most generally supposed that it was on January 19th, 1344, that King Edward instituted his famous Order of the Garter. This period, it will be perceived, was almost within an octave of the purification of the Blessed Virgin Mary; under whose patronage, and under the guardianship of St. George on, earth (St. Michael in heaven; both these Saints being the same, with earthly and spiritual attributes refluent respectively) King Edward placed his profoundly religious Order. The whole was a revival of the 'Round Table' of King Arthur, or the apotheosized female *discus* in certain mythical aspects. To confirm us in our assertion of the feminine origin of the Order of the Garter--which many in their ignorance have questioned--we may state that one of the old chroniclers, though somewhat guardedly, as befitted those great persons of whom he spoke, declares that the lady who let fall her garter, or 'garder', was the *Queen*, who had suddenly left the courtly assembly in some confusion, and was hastening to her own apartments, followed by the King, who, at first, did not perceive the reason when the spectators avoided lifting the article, being aware to whom it belonged; but who raised it himself, and called aloud, not the words of the motto of the Garter, which the historian says that the Queen herself spoke, but giving an intimation that he would, spite of their laughter, 'make the proudest of the refusers wear the rejected cincture as the grandest badge that knighthood ever bore'. Rightly viewed, this little evaded incident--which we desire to restore to its proper place of due respect in the knowledge of Englishmen--is the most conclusive proof of King Edward's nobleness and greatness of heart, and of his chivalrous, inexpressibly gallant delicacy; an instance admirable to all future generations, and worthy of the most enduring applause. The reader finally is referred to our observations in a previous part of our book for evidence in our justification. In the foregoing we, give the Rosicrucian view of the origin of the 'Garter'. It is the centre-point round which have converged the noblest ideas and the most illustrious individuals in the world. It is still the proudest and most solemn badge, and the chiefest English knightly dignity. Strangely enough, too, this whole history of the 'Garter' teaches, as its moral, the greatness of the proper independence of shame, and the holiness of its unconsciousness.

Also the gallantry and the knighthood of the holding sacred these strange natural things.

CHAPTER THE EIGHTH

ROSICRUCIAN SUPPOSED MEANS OF MAGIC THROUGH SIGNS, SIGILS, AND FIGURES

THE Dragon's Head and Dragon's Tail are the points called Nodes, in which the ecliptic is intersected by the orbits of the planets, particularly by that of the moon. These points are of course shifting. The Dragon's Head is the point where the moon or other planet commences its northward latitude; it is considered masculine and benevolent in its influence. The Dragon's Tail is the point where the planet's southward progress begins; it is feminine and malevolent. The Dragon mystically is the 'self-willed spirit', which is .externally derived into nature by the 'fall into generation' (*Hermes Trismegistus*).

The same fine, catholic nature--which in its preternatural exaltation appears so very precious in the eyes of the philosopher--is in the common world defiled; abiding everywhere in putrefactions and the vilest forms of seemingly sleeping, but in reality most active, forms of life.

According to Ennemoser, 'Magiusiah, Madschusie' signified the office and knowledge of the priest, who was called 'Mag, Magius, Magiusi', and afterwards 'Magi' and 'Magician'. Brucker maintains (*Historia Philosophiæ Criticæ*, i. 160) that the positive meaning of the word is 'Fire-Worshipper', 'Worship of the Light'; to which opinion he had been led by, the Mohammedan dictionaries. In the modern Persian the word is 'Mag', and 'Magbed' signifies high-priest. The high-priest of the Parsees at Surat, even at the present day, is called 'Mobed'.

The mythic figure placed in the front of the Irish Harp--the meaning of which we have explained in a previous part of our book, and which is now represented as a woman with the lower parts twined as foliage, or as scrolls, into the body of the harp--is properly a Siren. This 'Siren' is the same as Venus Aphrodite, Astarte, the Sea-Deity, or Woman-Deity, the Dag, Dagan, Dagon, or idol of the Syrians, Tyrians, or Phœnicians; hence her colour is green in the Iona, Ierne, or Irish acceptation. The woman or virgin of the Irish Harp, who is impaled on the stock or 'Tree of Life'--the Siren whose fatal singing means her mythic Bhuddistic or Buddhistic 'penance of existence'--the Medusa whose insupportable beauty congeals in its terror the beholder to stone, according to the mythologists--this magic being is translated from the sign of Virgo in the heavens, and sent mythically to travel condemned the verdant line of beauty, or the cabalistic *benedicta line a viriditatis*. The whole of the meaning, notwithstanding its glory, is, none the less, 'sacrifice'. The Woman of the Harp of the Seven Strings, or the seven vocables, vowels, or aspirations, or intelligent breathings, or musical notes, or music-producing planets (in their progress); is purely an astrological sigma--although a grand one--adopted into heraldry. In the old books of heraldry, the curious inquirer will find (as will all those who doubt) this 'Woman' or 'Virgin' of the 'Irish harp'--to whom, in the modern heraldic exemplification, celestial wings are given, and who is made beautiful as an angel (which in reality she is, the other form being only her disguise) represented as a dragon with extended forky pinions, and piscine or semi-fish-like or basilisk extremity. There is a wonderful refluent, or interfluent, unaccountable connexion, in the old mythology, between the 'Woman', the 'Dragon', or the 'Snake' and the 'Sea': so that sometimes, in the obscure hints supplied in the picturesque suggestive ancient fables, it is really difficult to distinguish one from the other. The associations of an interchangeable character between dark and light, and 'Dragon' and 'Hero', ascribing to each some mystic characteristic of the other, cannot be all fabling accident. There are hints of deep mysteries, transcendent in their greatness: and beauty, lying under these things in some concealed, real way. To bring these to the surface, to discover their origin, and, to the justifiable and guarded extent, to assign them properly, has been our aim. There must have been some governing, excellent armorial reason, special and authorized, for the changing of this first figure of a dragon into a woman, or a siren, or virgin, on the Irish Harp; and this fact assists the supposition of an identity, at some time, of these two figures, all drawn from the double sign 'Virgo-Scorpio' in the Zodiac. There is a strange confirmation of the account of Creation in the *Book of Genesis*, in the discovery of the 'Woman and Snake' in the most ancient Babylonian or Chaldæan Zodiac. The Indian zodiacs and the Egyptian zodiacs repeat the same myth, slightly varied in certain particulars. The different versions of the story of the Temptation and Fall, in the main respects, are the same legend, only altered to suit ideas in every varying country. Traversing all the long-descended paths of the mythologies, this singular, but in reality sublime, myth preserves its place, and recurs up to the last in its identity. The first chapter of Genesis seems to us to be clearly found here in the signs of the Zodiac; which we know are derived from the earliest astronomical studies, and which extraordinary hieroglyphical zodiacal figures descended originally from the summit of the famous Tower of Bel, or Belus--the first observatory where the movements and the story of the stars were at the outset noted, and handed as from the earliest expositors of the secrets of the heavens. This 'Procession of Twelve' (in the origin it was the 'Procession of Ten'), under the name of the Zodiac, tells, in its 'signs' the history of the making of the world, according to the Chaldæans and Egyptians, and also, in the hidden way, according to the account in the Bible.

As the little and the large have sometimes a closer connexion than is ordinarily supposed, we will pass on now to some more familiar and commonplace examples.

It may be worth while to dwell with greater minuteness on the little-understood origin of those light auxiliary troops, as they were organized originally, the modern Hussars. This irregular, lightly-equipped European cavalry plays an important part as a skirmishing or foraging force. We are all accustomed to see the elegantly appointed light cavalry called Hussars, and doubtless many persons have frequently wondered as to the origin of that *dolman*, pelisse, or loose jacket, which is worn, contrary to all apparent use, dangling--an encumbrance rather than a cover or defence--on the trooper's left shoulder. This pelisse, richly embroidered in the Eastern fashion, is always the genuine distinctive mark or badge, with the Wallachian or Hungarian, or Oriental, busby of the Hussar. The precise time when this originally loosely disciplined and heathen soldiery came into Europe is not fixed. They now form a dazzling and formidable branch of light-cavalry service everywhere. All armies of modern times possess regiments of Hussars. They came originally from Tartary and the East, and they brought with them their invariable mark, the rough fur cap, or Ishmaelitish or 'Esau-like' black head-cover. They adventured into the West with the now thickly ornamented and embroidered 'trophy', called the pelisse or 'skin-coat ('*pel*' from *pellis*, 'skin'; thence 'pall').

In these modern tasteless, ignorant days all these distinctive learned marks are obliterated in the equipment of troops. We may also instance, as proofs of disregard and of bad taste, the blundering dishonour offered to the majestic Obelisk brought to England in 1878, in the choice of its inappropriate site, and in the ignoring, for state reward, those who brought it to this country.

This pelisse is an imitation or reminder, and is the very remote symbol, or garment, or 'cover of shame,' as it is called, with which, for very singular cabalistic reasons (which, however, do not admit of explanation), the two dutiful sons of Noah covered and 'atoned' for that disgrace of their father, when, after he had 'planted a vineyard, and had drunken of the wine, he lay disgracefully extended in his tent', and was seen by his son Ham; whom Noah denounced. The Hussars (under other names) were originally Eastern, Saracenic, or Moslem cavalry. The horse-tails and jingles, or numberless little bells, which ought to distinguish the caparisons of Hussars to the modern day, and which are part of the special insignia of their origin, are all Oriental in their character, like the bells of the wandering Zingari, 'Morris', or Moresque, or Gypsy, or Bohemian fantastical dancers. Deep-lying in the magical ideas of the Eastern peoples was the sacredness, and the efficacy against evil spirits, of their small bells, like the bells of the Chinese pagodas. All bells, in every instance, even from the giant bell of the Dom-Kirche or Duomo, or the cathedrals of Kasan or Casan, Moscow or Muscovia generally, down to the 'knell', or the 'sacring' or warning bell of the Romish Mass (which latter 'signal' has a signification overpowering in its profundity), are held to disturb and to scare and drive off evil spirits. These were supposed, according to the old superstitious ideas, to congregate thickly, with opportunities accidentally offered either in the din of battle to impair invisibly the exertions of the combatants, or in the church to spoil the Eucharist, by tempting the celebrating priest, or hampering or hindering the ceremonial and its triumphant sacred climax.

The Eastern name of Venus is *Al-Huza* or *Husa*, which stands for the Egyptian 'Divine Woman', or Isis.

'Hussey', with its inflections of opprobrium, in the vernacular--strangely to say in regard of the champions mentioned above, who are the followers and the children of Venus. Venus 'Hussey', as in a certain sense she may be considered.

Al-Huza means the hyacinth, acacia, or lily, sacred to the 'Woman', or to the complying and therefore productive powers of nature. The word 'Hussar' comes, through circuitous paths of translation, from its original *Al-Husa*. These Hussars are the alert, agile, armed children, or soldiers, of Cybele. It is well known that the knights of old--particularly the Crusaders when they returned to the West--adopted the Oriental fashion of covering their appointments and horse-furniture with bells, the jingle raised by which, and at the same time the spreading or flying-out, in onset, of the *lambrequin* or slit scarf attached to the helmet, with the shouted war-cry, or *cri de guerre*, struck terror into the opposed horse and rider. Naturalists suppose that even the spangled tail of the peacock, with its emerald eyes, answers a similar, purpose, when spread out, of frightening animals who intend an attack. The knights, therefore, may have borrowed the hint of thus, startling their foes, and of confusing them with the sudden display of colours and disturbing points--as if sprung from a spontaneous, instant, alarming centre--from the peacock when startled by an enemy. The bird has also his terrifying outcry, similar to the knight's *mot de guerre*, or individual 'motto'.

The Hebrew priests were directed to fringe their garments round about with 'bells and pomegranates', in the words of the text. The use and intention of these 'bells and pomegranates' have been subjected to much discussion, particularly a passage which we now cite:

'A golden bell and a pomegranate, a golden bell and a pomegranate, upon the hem of the robe round about.' And it shall be upon Aaron to minister: and *his sound shall be heard* when he goeth in unto the holy place before the Lord, and when he cometh out, *that he die not* (*Exodus*. xxviii. 34-35).

The reason supposed in the Targum for the directions given to the priest in these two verses of the chapter containing the law is, that the priest's approach should be *cautious* to the innermost 'Holy of Holies', or sanctuary of the Tabernacle. The sound of the small bells upon his robe was intended to announce his approach before his, actual appearance, in order to recall the attention of the 'Angel of the Lord' to the fact of the coming of a mortal, so that He who was supposed to be then personally descended, and possibly 'brooding' (to make use of the words of *Genesis*), in the secret shrine or penetralia, might be allowed *time* (according to the ideas of men) to gather up and concentrate His presence--which 'no man can be permitted to behold [15] and live'--and to withdraw. For the Divinity to be seen by the profane eye is guilt and annihilation to the latter; therefore the gods and all spirits have, in every account of their appearance, been seen in some worldly form, which might be acceptable to, and supportable by, a human face. There is, theoretically, such contrariety, and such fatal difference to the constitution of man, in the actual disclosure of a spirit, that it is wholly impossible except by his death; therefore spirits and divine appearances have always been invested in some natural escape or guise, by the medium of which the personal communication, whatever it might be, might be made without alarm, and without that bodily

---

[15] Unless self-disclosed.

disturbance of nervous assent which should destroy. This alarm would, by the utter upsetting of the mind, and the possible fatal effect, otherwise have rendered the disclosure impossible. The denial of the interior parts of a sanctuary, or adytum, to the priests of the temple, or even to the chief hierarch sometimes, is supposed to have arisen on this account. Mythological story is full of the danger of breaking in unpreparedly upon spiritual presences, or of venturing into their haunts rashly or foolhardily. The real object and purpose of the veil to the Hebrew Temple, and of the curtains and enclosures ordered in the Jewish ceremonial complicated arrangements, are certainly of this class. Thus, in the idea that God did really pass down at chosen times from Heaven, even in a possible visible shape, to His Altar (though not, perhaps, in the form expected by man in his ignorant notions), the sacred place was carefully shut in, and all access to it set round with rigid, awful caution. There is fine and subtle meaning in that old expression in *Genesis*, 'to brood', as if to be fixed or rapt, and thus to be self-contained and oblivious, even inattentive. The ancients--the Greeks especially--constructed their temples originally without roofs, in order that there might be no obstacle interposed by them to the descent of the God to the temple which was especially raised in His honour. He was imagined, at favourable opportunities, to descend--either visibly or invisibly--into His appropriate temple; and it was not to seem to exclude, but rather in every way to invite straight from the supernal regions, that the ancients left open the direct downward way to the penetralia. From this sacred point, when the God was supposed to be expected or present, every eye, even that of the High-Priest, was shut out. The covered temple, or the ceiled temple--of which the chapter-house, or particular temple, with a 'crown', or 'cap', or 'cover', presents the small example--is the *domus templi* or *domus Dei*, where the 'Manifested God' is supposed to be enclosed, or wherein the 'Man is made Flesh'--the microcosmos or spirit within his cincture, or walls, or castle of comprehension, or of senses.

CHAPTER THE NINTH

ASTRO-THEOSOPHICAL (EXTRA-NATURAL) SYSTEM OF THE ROSICRUCIANS-THE ALCHEMIC MAGISTERIUM OR 'STONE'

THE letters of all languages are significant marks or symbols, which have the 'Twelve', or rather the original 'Ten Signs' of the 'Zodiac' for their beginning. Of these letters there is a certain group which has, in the characters of all languages, a secret hieroglyphical, hagiographical reference to the originally single, and afterwards double, sign 'Virgo-Scorpio', which is supposed to give the key to the secret or cabalistic 'Story of Creation'. These letters are S and Z, L and M; or rather a group, which is marked by Λ, Π, M, Σ, S, Z--L, M, V, W. The significant aspirates, or 'vowel-sounds', follow the same rule. The 'Snake-like Glyph', or 'mystery of the Serpent', or disguise, in which the 'Recusant Principle' is supposed to have invested himself, has coiled (so to say), and projects significant curves and inflections, through all this group of letters and sounds; which is perceivable, by a close examination and quick ear, in all languages, living and dead. The sigma presents itself to the eye (that recognizes) in the Hebrew, the Sanscrit, the Persian, the Arabic, the Coptic, the old Gothic, the Georgian or Iberian, the Ancient Armenian, the Ethiopic or Gheez, the Sclavonic, the Greek, the Latin, the Samaritan, the Irish, the Etruscan--of all which alphabets, and the symbols serving for their 'numerals', we had prepared a comparative table, to prove the identity of the sign 'Virgo-Scorpio' and its ciphers; but we forbore in deference to our limits (and from other circumstances), which did not advisedly admit of the addition.

A comparative display of all marks or symbols which give occult expression to the 'female side of nature', and its astronomical and astrological signs, affords the same result of identity. The marks of the 'signs' ♍ and ♏, and their ciphers, are interchangeable, and reflect intimately from one to the other. It must be remembered that the sign Libra--our modern September--the 'hinge-point' or 'balance-centre' of the two wings of the celestial Zodiac--was an addition by the Greeks. Here, according to the Sabæan astrological tradition, the origin of 'Good and Evil', of the malific and the benevolent 'cabalistic investments of nature', the beginning of this 'two-sexed', intelligent sublunary world, were to be found--all contained in the profoundest mysteries of this double sign.

The cabalistic theory, and the Chaldæan reading is, that the problems of the production of the sensible world are not to be read naturally, but *supernaturally*. It was held that man's interior natural law is contained in God's exterior magical law. It followed from this that present nature is secondary nature: that man is living in the 'ruins' of the angelic world, and that man himself is a 'ruin'. Man fell into the degradation of 'nature' as the result of the seduction by the woman (to sexual sin), which produced the 'generations' according to Man's ideas. The strange theories as to the history of the first world prevalent among the Cabalists imply that the appearance of 'woman' upon the scene was an 'obtrusion' in the sense of a thing unintended; even accidental and unexpected in a certain (non natural) sense. Thus her advent upon the scheme of creation--to use one of their mysterious expressions--was at a late spoiled and evil period of the world, which had sunk from the 'supernatural' into the 'natural'. As woman had no part in the earliest world, and as her origin was altogether of another nature and from other sources than that of man, the traces of her introduction, and the hints as to her true character, are to be found mystically in the original sign 'Virgo-Scorpio', double-sided (yet identical) at first but afterwards divided. These divided 'personalities' were set thereafter in mythologic opposition. The reader is referred to the previous Zodiac, fig. 12, where will be found the diagram illustrative of this idea, which was originated amidst the magic of the Syro-Chaldæans; it yet remains the key to all the mythologies and to all the religions.

The sign 'Virgo-Scorpio' stands, in the present order of things, or in this non-angelic or mortal world, as a divided sign, because in the 'World of Man' as 'born of Woman'--enmity has been, placed between the 'Snake' and the 'Woman'. Thenceforth, from the 'Fall', and as a consequence of it, they are, in opposition. The sign of the 'Balances' is placed between, as the rescuing heavenly shield, miraculously interposed, separating, as the tremendous 'Ægis', the two originally conjoint signs, and simultaneously presented 'both ways' (to speak in figure), defending 'each from destruction by either'--'until the time shall be complete!'--which means the Apocalyptic 'New Heaven and New Earth'.

Marks, movements, or influence from the side of 'Scorpio', or from the sinister side, are malign, and mean danger; because they represent the 'Old Serpent', or, in other terms, the 'Great Deep', or 'Matter'. Of such magic character are the letters 'S' and 'Z', and all their compounds; because this originally 'single' sound, or letter 'S-Z, Z-S', came into the world representing its sinful side. Man is pardoned through the 'Promise to the Woman', and 'Woman' is saved because through her the 'Saviour of the World', or the 'Rescuer of the World', or the 'Deified Man', or the 'Sacrifice', came into the world. Woman has the intermediate office of reconciling and consoling. In the abstract sense, as '*virgo intacta*' (or holy unknowing means), woman is free and unconscious of that deadly 'Original Sin', which in the disobedience to the Divine Command (to refrain from that 'Fruit' with 'Eve', or with the 'Natural Woman'), lost 'Man' his place in the scheme of the 'Immortal World'. All this is part of the cabalistic view of the Mysteries of Creation. The Cabalists say that the 'Lost Man' Adam should not have yielded to those which he found the irresistible fascinations of Eve, but should have contented himself--to speak in parable--with 'his enjoined, other impersonated delights', *whom* he outraged in this preference, winning 'Death' as its punishment: We conceal, under this term, a great Rosicrucian mystery, which we determine to be excused explaining more particularly, and which must ever remain at its safest in the impossibility of belief of it. This is of course obscure, because it is a part of the secret, unwritten Cabala, never spoken of in direct words--never referred to except in parable.

In the views of the refining Gnostics, woman is the accidental unknowing 'obtrusion' upon the universal design. The ideal woman (as 'ideal virgin') is spiritually free (because of her nothingness except 'possessed') from the curse and corruption of things material. From these ideas came the powers superstitiously imagined to be possible in the virgin state, and capable of being exercised by virgin woman.

All the marks and forms connected with these proscribed letters 'S' and 'Z' have, on their material and worldly side, the character of charms, sigils and talismans, in the evil sense, or dark sense. They were supposed to be means of magic by the old soothsayers. The celebrated Lord Monboddo produced a very elaborate treatise--quite contrary to recognized ideas--to show that speech was *not natural to Man*, but that language was a result of the Primeval Fall, and that the punishment of Babel signified the *acquisition* of the tongues, and not the 'confusion of language'. This idea is sufficiently startling.

A general display of the 'Esses' (S.S.) and the 'Zeds' (Z.Z), and their involutions, combinations, and sounds in all languages, would result in a persuasion of their serpentine origin. The forms of these snake-like glyphs and their cursive lines in all the alphabets will, on examination, present the same suspicious undulation. These letters have an intimate refluent connexion with all the signs which mean the 'Sea', the 'Great Deep', 'Matter in the abstract', or the 'Personified Receptive Feminine Principle', which eventually is to be the Conqueror of the 'Dragon' or 'Enemy'. We thus desire to show the unity of the myths and the forms made use of, for the expression of religious ideas in the glory of 'Woman'. Woman, in fact, is the maker of Nature; as we know Nature.

ASTRO-THEOSOPHIC CHART (No. 1)
WESTERN OR ROMAN RITE

A, Alpha
(North Celestial Pole)

'MYSTERIUM'

Dominion of the Moon in Man's Body, as she passes through the Twelve Zodiacal Signs

1. Aries, Head and Face . . . ♈
2. Taurus, Neck and Throat . . . ♉
3. Gemini, Arms and Shoulders . . . ♊
4. Cancer, Breast and Stomach . . . ♋
5. Leo, Heart and Back . . . ♌
6. Virgo, Venter . . . ♍
7. Libra, Reins and Loins . . . ♎
8. Scorpio, Genitalia . . . ♏
9. Sagittarius, Hips and Thighs . . . ♐
10. Capricorn, Knees and Hams . . . ♑
11. Aquarius, Legs and Ankles . . . ♒
12. Pisces, Feet and Toes . . . ♓

'MYSTERIUM'
Sun Rises
East
Holy of Holies
Crown of Glory
Crown of Thorns
Apse or Apsis
'The Blessed Lady'—'St John'

Man's Side   Woman's Side
(Sun)   (Moon)
Dexter   Sinister

North Transept   South Transept
(Chief Nail)   (Second Nail)
Right Hand   Left Hand

Body

'Place of' Fons'   'Nave, from 'Navel',
Two Nails, in the   'Ship', or 'Ark'

                      'Fountain', or 'Font'
Male : Sacred   Latin Rite, in the Feet;
Pillar—Jachin   Female : Sacred
                      Pillar—Boaz

Wine   Bread
'Twin Western Towers, or Spires
Galilee', 'West Porch for the People
West
Sun Sets
Night

Axis inclined
(Ecliptic)
(Regulating the Seasons, and the hours of the Day and Night):

(Chapter-House)
(As deliberative Judgment Seat)

Cor or 'Choir' (Equatorial)

South Meridian
(South Celestial Pole)
Ω, Omega

One Nail in the Greek Rite

319

ASTRO-THEOSOPHIC CHART (No. 2)

EASTERN OR GREEK RITE

PROCESSION OF THE 'LOGOS', OR 'WORD', ACCORDING TO THE GNOSTICS

' MYSTERIUM³.

' Concludimus itaque, cum Trismegisto, mundum esse Dei imaginem homino vero mundo, et quod per consequens propter suam cum mundo similitudinem, homo haud improprie mundus minor seu microcosmus dicendus, et in omnibus more mundi majoris seu macrocosmi sit considerandus.'
' Tertius Parvus μικρόκοσμος. Ipse in tres distinguitur cælos (questio hic præsertim de interno esi).'

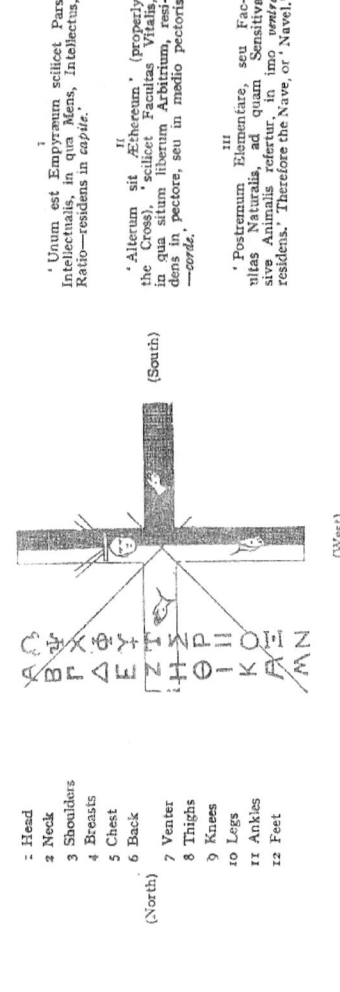

(East)

(North)

1 Head
2 Neck
3 Shoulders
4 Breasts
5 Chest
6 Back
7 Venter
8 Thighs
9 Knees
10 Legs
11 Ankles
12 Feet

(South)

(West)

Robertus de Fluctibus (Robert Flood, or Fludd), Rosicrucian

' Unum est Empyræum scilicet Pars Intellectualis, in qua Mens, Intellectus, Ratio—residens in *capite*.'

II
' Alterum sit Æthereum,' (properly the Cross), scilicet Facultas Vitalis, in qua situm liberum Arbitrium, residens in pectore, seu in medio pectoris —*corde*.

III
' Postremum Elementare, seu Facultas Naturalis, ad quam Sensitiva sive Animalis refertur, in imo *ventre* residens.' Therefore the Nave, or ' Navel.'

We wish the reader particularly to take notice that the above singular notions are in no way shared by us, further than as occurring in our account of some of the strange reveries of the 'Illuminati.' or 'Gnostics'; due, therefore, in our comments.

'I will put enmity between thee and the woman, and between thy seed and her seed; it shall bruise thy head, and thou shalt bruise his heel' (*Genesis* iii. 15).

A careful and critical inspection of all the alphabets or letter-forms, whether cursive or fluent, or rigid and rectangular--as in the Greek, and still more obviously in the Latin--will show that certain ideas are expressed pictorially in them. Two principal ideas seem to be furtively suggested. These are the upright or *phallus*, and the cross-line or 'snake', whether the horizontal be undulated or direct. In the Greek letters these ideas make the form. The first letters, according to the Cabalists, were the original 'Ten Signs of the Zodiac', which contained mythologically the history of the 'making of the world'. These 'Ten Signs' afterwards multiplied and produced other broods of letters (when the original magical knowledge was veiled); some of which were the cuneiform and early tree-like alphabets. There seems to be an 'event' symbolized or pictured, in the alphabets. This mystic idea, which is hidden in the hieroglyphics called letters, is supposed by the more profound of the Talmudists to be the introduction of 'Man' into the world, through the very fact and in the force of his 'Fall', or as arising through the 'Temptation', the chief agent or efficient in which is the 'Snake'. Thus every letter is an anagram of 'Man, Woman, and Snake', in various phases of the story. Each letter has embodied in it the 'Legend of the Temptation', and conceals it safely in a 'sign'.

'Ut omnia uno tenore currunt, redeamus ad mysticam serpentis significationem. Si igitur sub serpentis imagine Phallicum Signum intelligimus, quam *plana sunt et concinna cuncta pictura lineamenta*. Neque enim pro Phallo poneretur Serpens nisi res significata cum typo accurate congrueret' (*Jasher*, editio secunda, p. 48).

The late Dr. Donaldson has a dissertation upon the word עקב, which is translated 'heel' in *Genesis* iii. 15. He adduces *Jeremiah* xiii. 22, and *Nahum* iii. 5, and, comparing the words made use of in the original, shows that the 'heel' is a euphemism, as are the 'feet' in *Isaiah* vii. 20. His exhaustive argument demonstrates that the part intended to be signified by the word is *pudenda muliebria*. The whole proves the extreme importance--in the mythical and magical sense--of this unexpected figure, and throws quite a new philosophical light on it. These views fortify completely our Rosicrucian explanation of the origin of the Order of the Garter, and other kindred subjects, fully heretofore discussed in our book. This significant connexion of the two figures--the *phallus* and the *discus*--explains the text in *Genesis* i. 27: 'Male and Female created He them', i.e., זָכָר *gladius*, sword'; נְקֵבָה, 'sheath'. In this latter word, the part which characterizes the female is used for the woman herself. Qy., in this connexion *Kebah* ('case', or 'container', or 'deep'), the Caaba at Mecca, and Keb or Cab, standing for Cabala, Kabbala, Gebala, Kebla, or 'Ark', or 'Mystery'--the grand central point of all religions?

A modern learned writer, Thomas Inman, M.D., gives the following as an interpretation of the passage: 'Thou shalt bruise his *head*, and he shall bruise thy *heel*': 'Gloriam fascini congressio tollit et caput ejus humile facit, sed infligit injuriam moritura mentula, quum impregnationem effict et uteri per novas menses tumorem profert.' This may explain the reason why the cube of the Phrygian Cap, in the ancient sculptures of the 'armed female', is worn in reverse, or at the back of the head, as shown in figs. 207 and 208.

The celebrated philosopher, Petrus Gassendus, assailed the system of Robertus de Fluctibus, or Robert Flood, and criticized it at great length, in his work entitled *Examen in qua Principia Philosophiæ Roberti Fluddi, Medici, reteguntur*, published at Paris in 1630. But he never really seized the spirit of Flood's system, and he wasted his force. He did not comprehend, .nor could he ever realize, the Rosicrucian views with. the largeness of insight of a man of great critical powers, which Gassendus otherwise undoubtedly possessed. Gassendes, however, was a prejudiced theologian, and was ill calculated. for a disquisition upon a secret philosophy so remote and subtle. Before an insight of greater depth, of more readiness, and less obstinacy, the difficulties presented by Flood melt away, even converting into brilliancy in new proofs. His exhaustive logical positions indeed, the necessity of his theorems--are soon recognized by an investigator, when he shakes off trammels and clears himself of prepossessions. But a rapid and complete philosophical grasp, extraordinary in its decision, is indispensable. Flood's system is profound, shadowy, difficult, and deep-lying. Short of consummate judgment, and clear, fine mind, in those to whom they are submitted, Flood's ideas, in their very strangeness and apparent contradiction, startle and bewilder, because they contradict all the accepted philosophies, or at least all their conclusions, and stand alone. The ordinary recognized knowledge, hired from the current accumulation, opposes him. Flood's deeper teaching, by its very nature, and through the character of those from whom it sprung, is secret, or at all events evading, where the knowledge is not wholly suppressed.

As an instance of the impossibility of accepting Flood's ideas, if these were such, Gassendus charges him with a stupendous puzzle, that of passing the entire interpretation of Scripture over, not to the Mystics only, but to Alchemy. This is fully commented upon in the latter part of this work. Gassendus asserts, as the opinion of Flood, that the key of the Bible mysteries is really to be found in the processes of alchemy and of the hermetic science; that the mystical sense of Scripture is not otherwise explainable than by the 'Philosopher's Stone'; and that the attainment of the 'Great Art', or of the secrets which lie locked, is 'Heaven', in the Rosicrucian profundities. Old and New Testament, and their historical accounts, are alike hermetic in this respect. The 'Grand Magisterium', the 'Great Work' as the Alchemists call it, is mythed by Moses in *Genesis*, in the Deliverance from Egypt, in the Passage of the Red Sea, in the Jewish Ceremonial Law, in the Lives of the Patriarchs and

Prophets, such as Abraham, David, Solomon, Jacob, Job. In this manner the true Cabalists are supposed to be Alchemists in common with the Magi, the Sages, Philosophers, and Priests, when these possessed the 'true and only knowledge'. The 'Just Man made Perfect' is the Alchemist who, having found the 'Philosopher's Stone', becomes glorified and immortal by the use of it. To be said to 'die' is when the material elements can no longer maintain or cohere. To 'rise' is when the immaterial life or spark is liberated out of its perishable temporary investment. To be 'glorified' is when the powers, or independence, are attained which properly appertain to the supernaturally perfect 'Light', into which, like Enoch or Elijah, the Rosicrucian is transfigured, and in which he knows 'all', can be 'all', and do 'all'. It is this 'draught of immortality' which enables him to assume what form he will, by passing through Nature as its master, and renewing his body by means of his art projected by Nature through, to the other side of Nature.

The adept stands in the place of Nature, and does that with the obstruction of matter--separating by dissolution the pure from the impure--which it takes unassisted Nature ages, perhaps, to effect. The Alchemist is supposed to be superior to Nature to that extent, that he can pass through it (that is, through its appearances), and work on it, and in it, on the other side. It is here--in this true *Anima Mundi*, or 'Soul of the World'--that the Alchemist, or Rosicrucian, regathers the light dispersed or shaken out of its old broken forms. Gold is the flux of the sunbeams, or of light, suffused invisibly and magically into the body of the world. Light is sublimated gold rescued magically, by invisible stellar attraction, out of the material depths. Gold is thus the deposit of light, which of itself generates. Light in the celestial world is subtle, vaporous, magically exalted gold, or 'spirit of flame'. Gold draws and compels inferior natures in the metals, and, intensifying and multiplying, converts into itself. It is a part of the first-formed 'Glory' or 'Splendour', of which all objects and all souls are points or parts.

Gassendus asserts that when the Rosicrucians teach that the 'Divinity' is the 'Light' or the 'Realization of Creation', displayed from the beginning (A) to the end (Ω) of the whole visible or comprehensible frame, they mean that the Divine Being is not possible or existent, according to human idea, unless 'He', or the 'Original Light', is manifested or expressed in some special 'comprehensible' other light or form. The 'Second' reflects the glory of the 'First Light', and is that in which the 'First' displays. This second light, or *Anima Mundi*, is 'Manifestation', or the 'Son as proceeding from the Father'. This synthesis is the light, breath, life, *aura*, or Sacred Spirit. It is the solar or golden alchemical soul, which is the sustainment and perfection of everything.

The pendulum of the world beats between inspiration and expiration. This is the breath of the angels who 'burn and glow' (scriptural expression), in the pulsative access and re-inforcement of the 'soul of the world'. This 'breath of the angels' is made human in the mechanism of the heart, and is eternal; but becomes personal and limited in the 'world of man'--down, in inhalation, *to* a point, and *up*, in exhalation, *from* that point. So Jacob Bœhm. All lies between hermetic rarefaction and condensation--mortal and spiritual both.

'Is not the Devil the "Deep Darkness", or "Matter"? the "*terra damnata et maledicta*", which is left at the bottom of the process of the Supreme Distiller, who condenses and evokes the "Light" from out of it? Is not "Lucifer" the "Lord of the False Light", and the "Splendours of the Visible World"? Can the Prince and Ruler of this Relegate or Lower World soar with his imitations? Can the "Adversary" pass into the "Region of God's Light"? Can he rise anew to combat in that Heaven where he has already encountered the "Mighty Ones" who have driven him down; and can he there spread again, like a cloud, his concentrate darkness?' The Cabalists and Talmudists aver that Scripture, history, fable, and Nature, are alike obscure and unintelligible without their interpretation. They aver that the Bible is the story of heavenly things put forward in a way that can be alone comprehensible by man, and that without their Cabala, and the parables in which they have chosen to invest its revelation, not religion only, but even familiar Nature--the Nature of Things and of Men--is unintelligible. It has been a common opinion, and it so remains, that there is no such thing as the Philosopher's Stone, and that the whole history and accounts of it are a dream and a fable. A multitude of ancient and modern philosophers have thought otherwise. As to the possibility of metals transmuting from one into the other, and of the conversion of the whole material into gold, Libavius brings forward many, instances in his treatise *De Natura Metallorum*. He produces accounts to this effect out of Geberus, Hermes, Arnoldus, Guaccius, Thomas Aquinas (*Ad Fratrem*, c. i.), Bernardus Comes, Joannes Rungius, Baptista Porta, Rubeus, Dornesius, Vogelius, Penotus, Quercetanus, and others. Franciscus Picus, in his book *De Auro*, sec. 3, c. 2, gives eighteen instances in which he saw gold produced by alchemical transmutation. To those who allege the seeming impossibility, he rejoins, that difficult things always seem at first impossible, and that even easy things appear impracticable to the unskilled and unknowing.

The principles and grounds for concluding that there may be such an art possible as alchemy we shall sum up as follows. Firstly, it is assumed that every metal consists of mercury as a common versatile and flexible base, from which all metals spring, and into which they may be ultimately reduced by art. Secondly, the *species* of metals, and their specific and essential forms, are not subject to transmutation, but only the individuals; in other words, what is general is abstract and invisible, what is particular is *concrete* and visible, and therefore can be acted upon. Thirdly, all metals differ, not in their common nature and matter, but in their degree of perfection or purity towards that invisible 'light' within everything, or celestial 'glory' or base for objects, which has 'matter' as its *mask*. Fourthly, Art surmounteth and transcendeth Nature; for Art, directed upon Nature, may in a short while perfect that which Nature by itself is a thousand Years in accomplishing. Fifthly, God hath created every metal of its own kind, and hath fixed in them a principle of growth, especially in the perfect metal gold, which is the master of the material, and which in itself has magnetic seed, or magic light, an unseen and heavenly power, unknown in this world, but which can by Art be evoked, be made to inspire and multiply and take in all matter.

It is said of the alchemical philosophers, that no sooner did they attain this precious 'Stone' or 'Power', than the very knowledge of it, in the magic surprise, at its existence, delighted them more than aught that the world could give. They made greater use of it in its supernatural effects upon the human body than in turning it upon the base matter, to make 'gold' of this latter, which they treated with contempt. And in answer to those who would ask what was the reason that those supposed greatest of all philosophers did not render themselves and their friends rich by a process so speedy and thorough, it was rejoined, that they wanted not, that they were satisfied in the possession of the ability, that they lived in the mind, that they rested satisfied in theory and declined practice, that they were so overcome and astonished at the immensity of the power accorded by God's grace to man, that they disdained to become gold-makers to the greedy, or suppliers to the possible idle and mischievous needy, and that they were afraid to be made the prey and sacrifice of avaricious, cruel tyrants; which would be but too surely their fate if they were, through vainglory, or temptation, or avoidable effects of force, to make known their wondrous gifts, or to disclose or betray the fact of the supernatural method of their existence--clearly at the safest in being disbelieved, and being looked upon as lie or delusion.

Therefore these conclusive reasons, and others similar, impelled the Society to hide from the world, not only their stupendous art, but also themselves. They thus remained (and remain) the unknown, 'invisible', 'illuminated' Rosicrucians, or Brethren of the Rosy Cross; regarding whose presence and intentions no one knows anything, or ever did know anything, truly and in reality, although their power has been felt in the ages, and still remains unsuspectedly conspicuous: all which we think we have in some measure proved.

And shall still farther establish (we hope), before we arrive at the end of our book.

CHAPTER THE TENTH

ROSICRUCIAN 'CELESTIAL' AND 'TERRESTRIAL' (MEANS OF INTERCOMMUNICATION)

'CONSCIENTIOUS readers will thank the man who states accurately that which they agree with, but will be almost equally grateful to the man who states clearly what they most dissent from. What they want is either truth or error; not a *muddle between them*.'

The reason of the real superlative importance of the ideas entertained by people respecting the Rosicrucians, is that they were REALLY magical men, appearing like real men; carrying, in very deed, through the world *eternally forbidden secrets*--safe, however, in the fact that they were sure never to be believed. De Quincey, who has written the most lucid and intelligible (until this present work) speculation concerning these profoundest of mystics; and which account, though (most naturally) *humanly* lucid and intelligible--*groping* as it were at the claims of these men--is yet as far from the truth and as different to the real beliefs of the Rosicrucians as darkness is from light; De Quincey says; in exemplification of the grandeur of their mystery: 'To be hidden amidst crowds is sublime. To come down hidden amongst crowds from distant generations is *doubly sublime.*' This appears in *The London Magazine* of 1821; reprinted, corrected, enlarged, and greatly improved in the last edition of his collected works in volumes, published by Groombridge, Paternoster Row. De Quincey, Works, Vol. 6: Secret Societies, p. 235.

It is very little reflected upon, but it is no less a truth, which (because profound) is therefore contradictory--that if you take away Man from out the universe, that no universe remains. There cannot be any proof of there being anything outside of us when you take away Man, TO WHOM ALONE THE WORLD IS. For to any other intelligence than Man's, the world real CANNOT BE. And hence arises a curious question. It is, whether space as occurring AS AN IDEA in sleep (which implies time) would be real space? The truth of time, and of space, depend alone upon this question. Consider the depth of void ('something') into which thought has the power to extend. Consider the preposterous (in our senses) wall of separation (utterly IMPOSSIBLE to our POSSIBLE) which divides living human life (or 'living possibility') from the life (and the 'possibility') of the world *even next-off* this world. Not to speak of possibly multitudinous other worlds (or other possibilities), which stretch--for all we know to the contrary--we know not whither. And these 'possibilities' or metaphysical intelligible worlds--of what kind, of what nature, or of what (whether pleasant or unpleasant) character we can conceive not. We understand not *what* they are; or *how* they are; or *why* they are. Indeed--penetrating down to this truth--we know not why WE ourselves exist, or what we ARE. For we, that is, the human race, are not intelligible. Creation is not intelligible. That single word SOMEHOW alone covers the whole of our knowledge. The entire ground next-off this ground of senses (or of nature) is wholly conjecture. Nature itself--*away from us*, and *not us*--may be 'UNNATURAL', for all we know to the contrary. For Man himself is only a 'PHENOMENON', and HE alone MAKES nature, which exists not without Him. All the foregoing is the groundwork of the arguments of the deep Buddhists in regard to the *real* nature of things.

  The result of all these sound and only possible philosophical conclusions is, that there is nothing left for man but *entire submission*--entire subjection to the UNKNOWN POWER--the humbleness of the UNKNOWING CHILD. And herein we see the force of that *dictum* of the Saviour: 'Unless ye become as one of THESE' (little children), 'ye shall in nowise see the 'Kingdom of God.' Certainly, we are unable to know absolutely (that is, philosophically) that WE OURSELVES EXIST. (Berkeley, in showing that our senses are only *medium*, but not *means*, implied that we did not exist.) By a side-glance, as it were, we can suspect whether 'Life' itself be only a 'grand DREAM' which may be, or be not; be anything, or be nothing. There is no such thing as pain or pleasure, radically; without a medium which makes it pain or pleasure. And both are only 'disturbance', *made pain or pleasure from without*. Our pain may be pleasure in another differently-constituted nervous method (or medium of) existence. Our pleasures may be pains (or PENALTIES) elsewhere. This possibility, which is the foundation of supernaturalism--or of the doctrine of the 'intelligent population of the elements'--proves that pain, and pleasure, and the countless shades between them, necessitate the idea of *body*, or of *capacity*, of some kind or other: because capacity is 'state', and state is 'material'. So says Paracelsus; so says Van Helmont; so says Jacob Boehm. Nothing can be anything,' unless it is fixed in something material.

Hume, in demonstrating that in reality there is 'no connexion between cause and effect', proved that there is some *delusion* between cause and effect; and therefore that life *may be* a dream. Benedictus Spinoza, in his merciless logic, although he was a man so interpenetrated with the idea of Deity, as to be called 'The God-intoxicated man', proved that GOD MUST BE 'MATTER'; in evaporating, or exhausting, or '*calculating Him the closest* OUT of His own works'. So much for the AUDACITY of mind--mind which is 'knowledge', knowledge which is the 'devil'; the devil which is the 'DENIER'. Our highest knowledge--the most refined 'sum-up' of the thinnest-sifted (until disappearing, *evanishing*) metaphysics, is peremptorily passed back upon us when we essay beyond the frontier of 'second causes'. All is guess over that brink. All is cloud where this pathway--turn Which way we will--ends. Man's human arms are insufficient to lift as 'weights' aught than second causes--'CAUSED CAUSES'. He falls asleep, helpless, when the Great Veil is dropped over him to insulate his understanding. All is possible in 'SLEEP', because 'DREAMS' are in sleep. God is in sleep. And God, who is in sleep, although He is a reality AWAY from us, is a delusion, when sought to be demonstrated TO us. And sleep, which is men's thoughts, or rather *the dreams are* that are in his (man's sleep), is the stumbling-block over which the whole comprehensible theory of man parts into nothing and falls into absurdity; as in which dream he is himself ALONE, perhaps, made. These general ideas of the profound constitute the 'BYTHOS' of the GNOSTICS, and the 'MAYA', or annihilation, of the BUDDHISTS--however defectively interpreted heretofore, where these sublime subjects have not been wholly misunderstood or thought absurd--

Firstly.--In the affairs of God Almighty and the world there is some mighty reason--*ab extrâ*--which contradicts itself; inasmuch as it contradicts reason--*having no reason.* But *because* it contradicts reason, it proves itself to HAVE a REASON-- divine and ABOVE REASON--which is human; that is, INTELLIGIBLE ONLY. It follows from this, logically, (even)-- that in being 'UNINTELLIGIBLE' it is master of the 'INTELLIGIBLE'. Therefore 'MIRACLE' is superior to 'REALITY'. Because miracle is true (being impossibility and wonder), and reality is untrue, being possible, and *therefore limited* (in the face of the *illimitable*). Reality (reason) is satisfied, and complete, and 'full'--so to speak. While the 'impossible', and therefore the 'supernatural', must be true, because it *encloses* nature: which is only intelligible up to its certain point of nature. (But not beyond.) Nature *itself being yet to be accounted for--* inasmuch as NATURE is NOT REASONABLE. What is truth? There is no truth--inasmuch as nature itself, which must necessarily be the basis of everything, is not *true truth*, but only apparent truth.

Secondly.--So long as Nature must have a 'farther'--or a 'whereto'--beyond the present apparent 'whole' (and forward to which, in the necessity of things it must pass)--it may be reasonable--that is, all of TRUTH APPARENT. (The Cabalists (Rosicrucians, the Brothers of the 'CRUCIFIED ROSE') say that 'Man' is unintelligible, that 'Nature' is unintelligible, that the Old Testament, with its Genesis, its Pentateuch; that the New Testament, with Christianity and the 'Scheme of Redemption', that all is unintelligible without their *secret*--to the world wholly forbidden '*interpretation*'). But it cannot be TRUE TRUTH; or abstract, positive truth. Man is made. Man is not a maker. In other words, man gets nothing that is outside of him. He only obtains that which is already in him. He is in his world. He is of his world. But he is not of another world. His helplessness--unsupported--is perfectly ridiculous. He only lives--forgetting himself. He '*falls asleep*', blindly '*into his morrow*'. If he had independent power he would not do this. He would *know* his 'morrow'. (This is the contention of the Buddhists.)

Now, in regard of real truth, it has been settled for very many ages that there is no possibility of there ever being such. '*Cogito; ergo sum.*' I am; because I am. Existent only to the periphery of consciousness--no more.

Thirdly.--For there is something in the ring outside which (converging) makes the centre--or, in other words, that creates consciousness. That which insulates is greater than that which it insulates. 'Power' is only escaped 'Rest'. The 'Living' out of the 'Dead'.

Fourthly.--Thus IMPOSSIBILITY, alone, makes POSSIBILITY POSSIBLE.

Fifthly.--The 'made' cannot know its 'maker'; otherwise it would be 'its maker itself'. For the MAKER knows that which It (HE) makes, up to the farthest possible limit of its making or prolongation. Every man's morrow (*not yet arrived at him*) is already PAST to the SUPERIOR INTELLIGENCE that is altogether independent of 'morrows'--that is, ordinary morrows. 'The ANGELS have their manacles on the wrists of the MEN-MOVERS.' Men think they act their own intentions; but in reality they act *other agents'* intentions. In this 'delusion' perhaps lies the reconcilement of that unresolvable puzzle by MAN--at least, in his waking, or real, state--'Free-Will' and 'Necessity'. Free-will is 'necessity' UPWARDS, while necessity is 'free-will' DOWNWARDS; or mutual reversal of the *ends of the same lever*--GOD'S INTENT-TONS. This is as far as MAN is concerned; for Fate is Fate as regards the universal frame of things; the human reason being capable of grasping *no possibility* otherwise.

CHAPTER THE ELEVENTH

THE PRE-ADAMITES. PROFOUND CABALISTIC OR ROSICRUCIAN SPECULATIONS

THE monastic or separate (sexual) state, where nature is ignored and its suggestions and the indulgence of the seductive individual *appetite* is held to be ruinous (to the spiritual aims of the human creature), is a dangerous--nay, almost an impossible abnegation. From the spirit-side, in this respect, nature is held abominable. Its practice is the shutting of the heavenly door. Thus fleshly incitements are AWFUL; and yet--such are the contradictions of nature--they are necessitated. We must 'whip' the body, as it were, 'into wood' before we can drive the devil therefrom.[16] We must fast and watch, and watch and fast. We must reduce our robustness into leanness. Our physical graceful, worthy or handsome 'selves', we must punish down into everything that is incapable and pitiable. We must become *pitiless* in our body's own maceration and mortification. Meanwhile (in faith, and in reliance on the efficacy of our penances) we grow into holiness-intensifying into SAINT-HOOD. The lights of the soul are to shine through the rents and fractures of the flagellated and punished body, until the fleshly sense or enchantment and enticement is trampled-up, through the destruction of its *medium*, into *life other than this life*.

But truly, in this view, the necessities--or rather the requirements--of nature cannot be set at naught --cannot be contended with. Religion evades this question. *Men* suffer to a very grievous extent. To descend to realities in this living world of flesh of ours. Farther, however, in natural arrangements. The most cruel nervous disorders, such as the *furor uterinus*, hysteric spasms, and a whole train of vengeful mischiefs, chiefly attack such women as have throughout life *refused* the pleasures of love. Many fatal affections, such as mania, epilepsy, and so on, prey

---

[16] And thereout.

upon those of *both sexes* who have imposed upon themselves too severe refraining or bridling. This incidence is ingrain in nature. But the dangers resulting from the abuse of these amiable pleasures are much more formidable. Pp. 38, 39, of *Curiositates Eroticæ Physiologiæ* (1875). Woman's physical constitution adapts her for love. 'Excitements *more numerous*, and of more *exquisite sense*, are *bestowed on Woman*'--Casanova, *Physiology*, 1865, p. 78, quoting from Swedenborg. 'Polarity of the Two Sexes--*Vito-electro galvanic*. Attractive power is effected from within'--Casanova (1865), p. 25. 'The slumber of the body seems to be but the waking of the soul'--Grindon, on 'Life'--Casanova, *Physiology*, p. 39. But (until proven) she is rigid, and to a certain extent (like virgins usually) insensate, and even rebelliously irresponsive.

All the '*pittoresques*', to the number of twelve, invented by the Greek courtesan Cyrene, as being the best in which to signalize that particular loving mystery which has everything (enjoined) under it; all those enchanting modes of sympathy which Phyleiris and Ashyanase published, which Elephaseus composed in Leonine verse, and which afterwards the Roman Emperor Nero caused to be painted on the Walls of the Imperial Banquetting Hall, in his famous Golden Palace, by the first artists of Rome, all these prove that women are much better adepts in the *ars amandi* and its mysteries than men--that they have a much keener relish for its intricacies, to which they deliver themselves up--*with the chosen object*--with a delight and *abandon unknown to man*. In short, in all the solicitation of love, women are the most inventive, assiduous, intense and persevering. Catherine the Second of Russia possessed boundless power. She set no limits to her gratification in the sensual respect. She was imperial and magnificent in her luxurious enormities. Her will was law--she was the 'modern Messalina'; she richly earned the title which was accorded to her of literally being (no small distinction in its way) '*la più futatrice nel mondo*'. But, on the other hand, there were wonderful contradictions to this state of irregular eagerness. Maria (Mariana) Coanel, wife of Juan de la Cerda, not being able to bear the absence of her husband, preferred committing suicide to yielding to the otherwise irresistible temptations of the flesh--as she found them in their occasional assaults. The extraordinary unconsciousness and ignorance of some women is remarkable--however rare; especially in these, in some respects, scarcely modest, all-knowing times. Isabella Gonzaga, the wife of the Duke of Urbino, passed two years with her husband still remaining a virgin; and so great was her ignorance of the matrimonial usage that, until enlightened, she had imagined all married women lived as she lived; and she received the new knowledge in all simplicity.

Greek pictorial and statuary art was suffused with ideas of matchless and--of immortal beauty. The curves and undulation of form, the enchanting and enchanted art which peopled Grecian landscapes with shapes of ravishment and Greek temples with wonders: the eye that saw, the hand that traced, the taste that toned, the delicacy that softened--all was exquisite, all was successful. The most intensely poetical and subduing (nay, the most religious, moving one to tears), and the most gloriously beautiful object in the whole universe, is the naked form of a symmetrical woman. This is difficult to understand--but it is true. The reason may be--sorrow that such a glorious object--Divinity's handiwork, as a 'present' to Man--should perish. Reflect upon matter immediately following.

No wonder that the ancients made a woman (thus) in object of idolatry. In the excess--in the super-excelling--of their refinement, other ideals were reached. Beauty became *bifurcated* (so to express), and irregular; heated as it were into a sinister--a devilish (*forbidden*) temptation, for passion of taste. Excess, or a deviating superflux or *overdoing*, of desire supervened. Longing became delirious: because 'Lucifer', or the 'Lost One'--'Unchastened Presumption'--had passed his lightning-like availing spear of *apotheosizing*, enchanted, tempting DEATH through the transmuted 'human female body'; advanced and addressed in its snaring graces to Hell's perfectness.

The 'Sexes' were 'Two'. But 'Beauty' was 'One'. Beards have naught of beauty, apart from strength. Beards are barbarous--hence their name. Hair is of the beasts, '*excrementa*'; '*tentacula*'. The Greek artists exercised their talents in the production of a kind of beauty mixed of that of the 'Two Sexes', merging and blending the softness and enchanting shapeliness of the one with the aggressive picturesque roundness and boldness of the other. Each (separate) was the acmé of picturelike propriety and grace. But the third 'Thing' was a 'New Thing'--otherwise a miracle--a new sensation. Hence Paris, hence Adonis, hence Ganymede, hence the loves of Salmacis and Hermaphroditus, hence the 'feminine' Bacchus, hence Hylas--hence these deities, in tresses, of neither sex, and yet of both. Greek art in this respect presents a phenomenon. As a phenomenon we must recognize and regard it. The flower is *supra-natural*, treasonous, and abhorrent. It is 'a flower of Hell'. Nevertheless, it is a 'flower'. And thus the idea dominates the *alternate 'shaded' and 'shining' halves* of the whole world; of all art; of all philosophy; of all RELIGION. Philosophy must not ignore, or affect not to see, or decline hypocritically, or too nicely (not wisely), to consider these powerful--these ALL POWERFUL--factors. This whole round of subjects intimately refers to the Rosicrucians, and to their supposed 'unintelligible' beliefs. They are intelligible enough to the 'knowing ones'; but they are not to be divulged.

The most difficult problem of the Greek artists was to exercise their talent in the production of a kind of beauty mixed with that of the Two Sexes, and time has spared some of the masterpieces. Such is the figure known under the name of the *Hermaphrodite* (*Hermes-Aprodite; Venus-Mercury*). In the classic times, both amongst the Greeks and Romans, as also in Oriental countries, a cruel and flagitious *violation* of nature (not supposed-so; even accepted as sacred) produced this beauty by enforcing sacrifice of a peculiar kind on young male victims. In the case of true Hermaphroditism, that which art could only effect by dispossession, nature brings about by super-addition, or rather by concurrent transformation or mutual 'coincidence'. The idea even lies '*perdue*' (like a silver snake) in the supposed origin of 'Mankind. The most extraordinary ideas as to the origin of the human race have been entertained by speculative thinkers, and by theologians. The celebrated William Law believed that the First Human Being was a creature combining the characteristics of both sexes in his own individual person. 'God created man in His own Image. In the Image of God created He him.' Some controversionists consider that there is. a LONG space due (but not allowed) between the foregoing and the succeeding: 'Male and Female created He THEM'.

'Increase and Multiply, and replenish the earth.' This command was given on the Sixth Day. Eve was not created until the Seventh Day. Hence Eve must have been born of Adam--or separated from him 'Ejus autem imago ea est quæ exhibetur, *ore* videlicet *excellentissimo*, ut sunt Arnobii verba, et specie inter virginem et puerum eximia. Catullus hoc idem voluit. Carm. 64.

> Quod enim genus figuræ est, ego quod non habuerim?
> Ego mulier, ego adolescens, ego ephebus, ego puer,
> Ego gymnasii fui flos, ego eram decus olei.

Marcianus Capella, Lib. i.:

> Atys pulcher item curvi et puer almus aratri.

Caput autem tectum *mithra Phrygem* indicat.'

Laurentii Pignorii Patavini Magnæ Deum Matris Idææ et Attidis initia. Amstelodami Andreæ Frisii. MDCLXIX.

Admitting, moreover, that the term 'Day'--as used in *Genesis*--is employed to express an indefinite period of time, in order to form Woman, God deprived Adam of his *androgyne* character, and reduced him to a Being having one sex only. And here steps in a fanciful idea of some speculative thinkers; which (however extravagant) is very poetical and beautiful. They ask in specifying the question--in serious truth a not-altogether improbable conjecture--whether the irresistible inclination and the otherwise mysterious, unaccountable drawing-together and sympathy of two persons who meet for the first time and find themselves mutually charmed (they cannot tell how or why); or who even 'hear' or 'read' of each other; whether even the continual natural inclination which impels 'man to woman' and 'woman to man' be not the spirit-reflex and the atoning 'Penance' (there is a great amount of *sadness* which mingles in the delight of these feelings) of the 'Original Grand Human Division'. And that this extra-natural (and yet natural) inclination which draws One Sex towards the Other be not the movements of Fate (lying down deep-buried in the necessities of things); and that the whole is the active tendency and forced (however latent, sometimes) searching through the world for the 'Missed' and 'Lost Half' (whether feminine, whether masculine), to once more embrace and supernaturally in rapture in the recognition to become ONE again? Hence, perhaps (also), that inconstancy and feebleness of decision and 'puzzled distress' ('seeing through the glass darkly') so aboundingly manifest in human nature, becoming dramatic in a thousand ways in the confusions of history--a stupendous scheme of contradictions itself.

May such affinities--and such unsuspected enchantment in this hard, practical, disbelieving world--lie mysteriously deep as the eternal secret of original human fellowship and society? And may even the amusement and the wonder of uninterested spectators and standers-by arise only from their having the unimagined fact (to them) of dream and magic being presented, while this unaccountable show is the secret foundation (as dream started at the beginning of time) of all the sentimental phenomena of the world? In all the infinite gradations of love, and passion, and sympathy (and in the experience of their opposites), we may be witnessing the baffled attempts of the whole round of human-nature--of the succession of the generations in the centuries--life being hopelessly too short, and circumstances controlling everything; we may be seeing the efforts of the 'Halves' to recover 'Each Other'. The masculine half of mankind wandering unconsciously to find its fellow-feminine, and the female half of the human family urging (from its nature) with the still more lively and more sensitive, and more acutely disappointed at repeated failure--quest. Each sex in its half-individuality, and prosecuting through time its melancholy 'penance', straining blindly towards that 'Shadow', the complement and double of 'Itself'. Vain indeed in the nature of things must be that human search to find, in this world, the supernaturally divorced 'Half'. For that other 'Half-Self' originated in 'another world', and thence started on a 'Dream-Pilgrimage' as a Shadow, or Spirit, recognizable only through the *imagination* (a mischievous, deluding faculty) of a real person, to recover its other original Half in 'This World'. We doubt, indeed, whether *in this world* (and were the original duality of persons true) that in this state of flesh the discovery would be welcome, even were discovery and recovery possible. Such is the preordainment of fate (which has made circumstances), that the halves of this first-junction may wander all the world over and exhaust the generations, and all time, in the search, and yet never meet; save at that 'Grand Assize' or General Resurrection where impend the New Heaven and the New Earth; and at which Final Consummation the two parts of the same Unit might be united never to be sundered more--complete and summed as. the 'One Being'--sexless in the bosom of DIVINITY; where there is 'neither marriage, nor giving in marriage'.

But the reader will find, in the latter part of the book, plausible theories--nay, cogent arguments, scarcely to be refuted-- not only as to the possible (and likely) incorporation of spirits; but as to the difference of sexes among them, with natural incidents, and apparently contradictory results from their semi-spiritual, semi-bodily Rosicrucian conditions.

The idea that Adam and Eve were both originally Hermaphrodites was revived in the thirteenth century by Amaury de Chartres. He held--among other fanciful notions--that at the end of the world--both sexes *should be re-united in the same person.*

Some learned Rabbis asserted that Adam was created *double*; that is, with two bodies, one *male* and the other *female*, joined together by the shoulders; their heads (like those of Janus) looking in opposite directions. And that, when God created Eve, He only *divided* such body in Two. Others maintained that Adam and Eve were each of them, separately, an Hermaphrodite.

Other Jewish authorities, among whom are Samuel Manasseh and Ben-Israel, are of opinion that our Great Progenitor was created with Two Bodies, and that 'HE' separated them afterwards during Adam's sleep; an opinion founded by these writers upon the second chapter of *Genesis*, verse 21: 'the literal translation of the Hebrew being: 'He (God) separated the Woman from his side, and substituted Flesh in her place.' This idea resembles that of Plato. Origen, St. Chrysostom, and St. Thomas believed that the Woman was not created till the Seventh Day. But the most generally received opinion is, that Adam and Eve were created on the *Sixth*. These particular notions--extravagant as they must be admitted to be--as to the original 'single-dual, dual-single' characteristics of Adam and Eve are eminently Platonic--nay, cabalistic.

Plato proceeds to account for the love which some men have for some women, and *vice versa*. 'The males', he says, 'which are halves of an Androgyne, are much given to women; and the women, which are the halves of an Androgyne, are passionately fond of men. As for the women' (a not uncommon Case) 'who indulge an inclination for their own sex, they are the halves of the Androgyne females who were doubled, and the men who exhibit a liking for other men are the halves of the males who were also doubled. In the beginning there were three kinds of Human Beings, not only the Two which still exist (namely, the Male and the Female)--but a Third, which was composed of the Two First.' Of this last sex--or *kind*--nothing remains but the tradition, and the name. 'The Androgynes, for so they were called, had not only both the male and female faces, but also possessed the sexual distinctions of both. Of these creatures, likewise, nothing now exists but the *name*, which survives as a stigma, and which is considered *infamous*.' Nature had made this, the fact; as 'out of' nature. The reason assigned for the different shape of these three kinds was that 'the males were formed by the *Sun*; the females by the *Earth*; and the mixed race of Androgynes by the *Moon*:--which partakes both of the *Sun* and the *Earth*.'

Ecclesiastical writers declare that such an Eunuch was the Holy Evangelist, St. John, whom Jesus loved beyond all His other disciples, who lay upon Jesus' bosom; who, while Peter tardily advanced, flew, borne on the wings of virginity, to the LORD; and penetrating into the secrets of the Divine Nativity, was emboldened to declare what preceding ages had been ignorant of. 'In the Beginning was the Word. And the Word was with God, and the Word was God.' Reynardi *Opera*, vol. viii. p. 252.

If the disciples of the doctrine of 'evolution' or 'selection of the fittest' are right--if your Darwins, your Huxleys, your Herbert Spencers, your Leweses, your dense unimaginative men (only specious philosophers), are correct in their deductions of correlation--'bowing-out God' [17] as it were (in sublimity of *fools'* not '*mad*' presumption), 'exterior of His own Creation'--then reverence, and devotion, and martyrdom, and the sacredness, and the magic of *virginity*, must be the merest ludicrous superstition and figment. Is MAN alone in his world? Are there OTHERS in it with him? The ancients universally held virginity as a real magic, transcendental, mysterious something, which exercised power *supernaturally* both through Heaven and through Earth. It was an unnatural-natural outspring set apart and sacred 'of the Gods'. None but the barbarous touch, the brutal touch, could profane it. It worked miracles.

'Tis said that the Lion will turn and flee
From a Maid in the pride of her purity.

For maidhood and virginity is a phenomenon *independent of Creation*, and bears through the worlds visible and invisible--the worlds immortal--the impress and seal upon its forehead of *GOD'S REST*, and 'Refusal', not of His ACTIVITY and 'Consent'. Hence its sacredness in all religions and under all beliefs. '*Voilà pourquoi, pendant les persécutions, il y eut tant de vierges chrétiennes outragées par leurs bourreaux, qui ne faisaient qu'appliquer l'antique loi romaine, en vertu de la quelle une vierge ne pouvait pas être mise à mort.*'--*L'Antiquité la plus*

---

[17] 'Bowing-out', or 'complimenting-out'; to express in a strong figure--but not inapt.

reculée jusqu'à nos jours, par Pierre Dufour, vol. 3, chap. i. p. 29. Bruxelles, J. Rosez, 1861. The reason for this lies very deep, and is very refined and very true. It will be seen, on adequate reflection, that the heathen executioners, in exercising their supposed *human* right of death-giving in law, did not dare touch the 'property of the Gods' in death, owing to their superstition; and they therefore made their victims 'things' in 'getting godhood' (so to speak) 'out of them' before the death-penalty. This was the reason why, in the old English executioners' practice, women were always burnt or strangled at the stake, but not hanged vulgarly like men or dogs. It was a tribute to the supposed sacredness of women's characteristics, and from the fact of her (phenomenal) character. 'Les Juges Païens qui prenaient un odieux plaisir à les frapper dans ce qu'elles avaient de plus cher. Mais leur virginité était un sacrifice qu'elles offraient chastement à Dieu en échange de la couronne du martyre. "Une vierge", disait Saint-Ambroise, "peut être prostituée et non souillée." "Les vierges", dit Saint-Cyprien, "sont comme les fleurs du Jardin de Ciel".' Pierre Dufour. '*Le viol des vierges chrétiennes n'était donc dans l'origine qu'un préliminaire de la peine capitale, conformément à l'usage de la pénalité romaine.* Vitiatæ prius a carnifice dein strangulatæ.' Suetonius, *dans la vie de Tibère:* Pierre Dufour. '*L'Histoire de Prostitution*'.

'Because Virgins by a received custom were not to be strangled, he caused the Hangman first to deflower a Virgin, and then to strangle her'. Tacitus. Suetonius. Edward Leigh's *Analecta de Primis Cæsaribus*. And when *forced*, the author might have added, became still more glorious flowers (or lights) of Paradise, We live, in nature, in contradiction--in 'impossibilities' that make 'possibilities'. Our 'forms' ignore 'ourselves'. Maidhood is the possibility of bearing joy beyond compare (the human-natural joys locked therein)--the first, last, and best of this world's pleasures--through the world; and yet withstanding the use of it. Refraining in the carrying the precious casket from 'one world' (*through the world for which it is intended 'as the temptation'*) into 'another world'. It is the successful resistance and baffling of the Devil, who lures in this mysterious respect, with his most exquisite inducement. Hence the reason of our King Edward the Confessor being marked as the 'Saint; for he 'forbore his wife Edith'. This is the *raison d'être* of all triumph of the kind: Virginity in itself (strangely as it may sound for mankind), though without its infraction heaven could not be--for it is our senses that make heaven--is a Key of Heaven. Hence the inherent sacredness of the--human--'Act' all the world over; and highest so in the religions of the most civilized peoples, those which have risen to the highest refinement. Mary Magdalen was the *first* at the tomb of the Redeemer, and was the *first* to whom our Lord showed Himself. It was through a WOMAN that our race was rendered possible. This must never be forgotten.

It is not difficult to discover how inveterate the belief of their system, which seems naturally to account for everything, has become to the Materialists; who (to use a wild figure) have identified the *time* that has got into the watch with the *reason that the watch goes*. Their whole work is the falling-in-love-with and believing their own work. It would be cruel to make these men believe. It would be the dispossession of themselves, out of themselves. Their scope, and range, and judgment are an impenetrable world's presumption; working only from the centre outwards--as from 'particulars' to 'generals'--the false way. These accepted *reasonable reasoners* do not see that if God's reasons had been man's reasons man would never have been; because MAN has no place *in reason*--he is not reasonable. It is the self-assertion and the self-presumption that is at fault--mere miserable self-conceit produces these men:--volubility--and reading--provide them with a cloud of words wherewith they may (and do) confuse. They have dared in their lofty (toppling) philosophical climbing--like the men of Babel--or 'Babble', as the tongues afterwards became--forcing into their Heights of Metaphysics (as it were) to *look down* upon God--spying Him at His work! Impious--mad stupidity;--trusting *brains*, in which the Devil (or Denier) forges lies--forgetting that *Darkness is only the reversed side of Light*, as light is only the presented side of Darkness--and that Both are the Same. We should know no light without darkness, which shows us the light; just in the same way as we see the wrong side of the light in seeing the darkness when the welcome light appears--so to speak.

These men want contradiction. They are ruined in their own self-esteem. They are floated upward in the pride of knowledge-- with wings of wax. They grape in, the *débris* of nature. Their knowledge is scientific knowledge. Knowledge as an acquisition to enlighten (its only use) is as ashes with the fire all out of it-- fire which is faith. These philosophers are converted into the vehicle of the comprehension of their own theories: and there they rest, absorbed and occupied in these alone. Self-centred, complete, satisfied, distrustless, they fortify themselves in their triumph, and become incompetent to see aught that shall challenge their own fixed ideas. In regard to these merely scientific people, an apt and a forcible remark has been made: 'Natural selection can only preserve such slight variations as are immediately useful. It cannot provide a savage with brain *suited to the remote needs of his civilized descendants some thousands of years later.*' All is progressive, and all is development, with these philosophers. They have no idea of cataclysm. When the whole world is the offspring--when the mountains, with the mutilated and the riven faces which they present to us, are the children--thunderstricken--of the INTELLIGENT (*sudden* to the world sometimes, snapping 'gradations' and 'evolutions' with *miracle*), MASTER, GUIDE and GOD of ALL! Thinkest thou that those skies have forgotten to be in earnest, because thou goest mouthing through the world like an ape?' Be what you wish to be then, and go down into the dust! Very probably your fate it may prove to be; though it may be the lot of some others to escape. By humbleness--by FAITH!

Revelation and supernatural disclosure, quite different to progress and circumstantial natural advance--as the 'nature of nature'--are to be inferred from the apparition of certain deplorable maladies--diseases which puzzle and bewilder as to their true character; which lead us astray, sometimes, as to their likeliest best treatment. The ideas of the ROSICRUCIANS as to the real (hidden and unsuspected) origin of these diseases, which seem--large as is the catalogue of maladies--so *contrary* to all the physiological, natural groundwork upon which (so to say) man's health and healthy exercise of his nature expand and expound, are speculative and *recherché* in the extreme. Such querists ask in vain where such diseases--so momentous, so super-horrid--could have first sprung. Philosophers of this class affirm that there is nothing of these in the *true character of man*. That these diseases stand aloof, and are of themselves. That they bear in themselves *proofs* of the indignation (intelligent) exterior to man; to some violent invasion and inversion--to some inappeasable outrage of God's law. Flesh and blood has become an accursed--a super-accursed *weed*, from the devils having gained access to it. Man's unholy passions have hurried him into an abyss of physical perdition, wherein he has obliterated his 'image' and gifts, and done things (worse than the beasts) *beyond the laws* of his impress; wide already as the area of the exercise of those laws was, *even for evil*. The penalty has pursued the original guilt through the generations and still survives; because Man has dared to intrude into the 'DISORDERS OF DARKNESS', and brought back out of ORCUS and made physical guilt and horror which were the property of the devils and within the compass of their range, alone, of accursed activity, but which *were not for him--were not naturally for him*. Hence the marks and tokens of this supernatural 'cancer', some of the imported effects--otherwise lying out of his reach as being far above what his limited nature could endure without utter consumption of itself--of the 'FIRST FALL'. Conquest is wide-spread just according to the weakness and incidence of the subjected. Fire finds its easy prey in dry leaves and in light combustible. These 'immortal-mortal' diseases spread and ramified, and spread and ramify (though with diminution now), with an extension, and with a vigour, just in the proportion of the necessitated surrender arising from the incompetency and inability to resist; these hitherto supersensual and supernatural terrors had found an access into this real world of BODY, and there the disaster revelled in its appropriate forms in its newly-found dominion. 'The imagination of man is evil continually.' There are blots and imperfections which have fastened upon Man's very mortal composition or body. His nature is struggling to free itself of the contagion. But the poison is not poison of this world. The generations suffer in all the crowd forward--in all their procession and replication for the sin--for the unbelievable sin--for the wanton, out-of-the-way wickedness of predecessors. This is the theory as to the origin of certain diseases, which are considered 'NOT HUMAN'; but which have been conveyed-to, and are inherited by, those who have no affinity with these inflictions by their nature or by the intentions of the 'EXTERIOR PROVIDENCE'. Man has brought all this upon himself, as farther fruits and newer penalties arising from the First Great Lapse, and in farther proof, in still more degrading and still more disfiguring decadence, of the imbibing of the first sweet poison--so deliciously and yet so treacherously (lecherously) brewed by the First Great Tempter:--Nameless--Anonymous--with 'Its' Janus Mask, and offering to that 'Phenomenon', man, under 'Its' many 'Names'. Man is another ruin, perhaps, in a series of *several previous ruins*, of which mortality has lost all trace.

The terms superstition and science are counter-changed. In reality science may be the superstition, and superstition the truth (otherwise the 'science', assumed as truth). Scientific men are the most superstitious of any class, for they have raised an idol which they call science, and therefore truth (why, *therefore*, forsooth?); and they have fallen down and worshipped Science (their own ignorance) as God. They have taken themselves out of themselves, and worshipped 'themselves'--otherwise their heads, instead of their hearts; their reason (their head), which is no reason (no head) really, instead of their hearts, or their emotions and instincts; which are true, and which are infallible--because they contradict the apparent and the reasonable, *which is never true.* Hence we cannot know God through God, or rather through the Intellect; but we must know God through the 'Saviour', or through the heart or affections; which entity, or sum of heart and affections, is Second God, or Man 'in the image', etc. The Third 'Person' of the Trinity is the Holy Ghost, or 'Recognition' in which 'Both' are--'Seen in the Spirit', wherein, and absorbing the 'Two Others', is interfluent, miraculous, instant union and 'ASSUMPTION' of God and Means, in 'Belief'. This is the groundwork of all religious systems. God's anger (the 'denunciation' or the 'shaking-off' by the All-Pure and the All-Powerful) is shown in those immortal (become fleshly), or 'Spirit-Cancers' (so to speak), imported, as adaptations to the nature of physical man, into *body-corporate* (that is, intelligible): the supernatural become natural.

'Enfin, un des plus grands hommes qui aient porté le flambeau dans les ténèbres de l'art médical: *Grand Chirurgie* (liv. i. ch. 7) "La vérole", dit-il avec cette conviction que la génie peut seul donner, "a pris son origine dans le commerce impur d'un Français lépreux avec une courtisane qui avait des bubons vénériens, laquelle infecta ensuite tous ceux qui eurent affaire à elle. C'est ainsi", continue cet habile et audacieux observateur, "c'est ainsi que la vérole, provenue de la lépre et des bubons vénériens, à peu près comme la race des mulets est sortie de l'accouplement d'un cheval et d'une ànesse, se répandit par contagion dans tout l'univers." Paracelse considérait, donc, le vérole de 1494 comme "un genre nouveau dans l'antique famille des maladies vénériennes."' Pierre Dufour, tome quatrième, p. 292.

'Un saint laïque', dit Jean Baptiste van Helmont dans son *Tumulus Pestis*, 'tâchant de diviner pourquoi la vérole avait paru au siècle passé et non auparavant, fut ravi en esprit et eut une vision d'une jument rongée. du farcin, d'où il soupçonna qu'au siége de Naples, où cette maladie parut pour la première fois, quelque homme avait eu un commerce abominable avec une bête de cette espèce attaquée du même mal, et qu'ensuite, *par un effet de la justice divine*, il avait malheureusement infecté le genre humain.' Pierre Dufour, tome quatriéme, chap. xx. p. 292.

'Manardi, Mathiole, Brassavola, et Paracelse disent que l'infection vénérienne est née de la lèpre et de la prostitution.' Pierre Dufour, tome quatrième, p. 297 (8vo edition).

Nothing can exceed the importance of the foregoing observations in regard to the welfare (bodily and spiritually) of Man; especially in these questioning, inquisitive modern times, when everything is brought to the front, and remorselessly (although often foolishly, because conceitedly) canvassed. Such names as the great (much-libelled) Paracelsus, the prince of chemists and physiologists, and that of Van Helmont, the most subtle and profound of magnetists and psychologists, secure attention among the best-informed, and carry their own consummate guarantee--the most convincingly to the adepts. MEN of REFLECTION are needed to comprehend these theories and speculations, and to weigh this evidence.

CHAPTER THE TWELFTH

THE ADAPTED ROSICRUCIAN CONTEMPLATION. INTRUSION OF SIN. RUINS OF THE OLD WORLDS.

THE extraordinary philosophy of the Rosicrucians (and of the Rosicrucian system) is best explained (though it is all erroneous as to the true meanings of the Brothers of the 'R. C.') through the following, charges which were brought forward to the disparagement of these famous men. Petri Gassendi Theologi Epistolica Exercitatio. In qua Principia Philosophiæ Roberti. Fluddi Medici reteguntur. Parisiis, apud Sebastianum Cramoisy, via Jacobæa sub Ciconiis, M.DC.XXX.

'*Primo.* Totam scripturam sacram referri ad alchymiam, et principia alchymistica. Sensum scripturæ mysticum non esse alium, quàm explicatum per alchymiam, et philosophicum lapidem. Non interesse ad ilium habendum cujus religionis sis, Romanæ, Lutheranæ, aut alterius. Catholicum ilium solum esse, qui credit in Lapidem Catholicum, hoc est Philosophicum, cujus ope homines Dæmonia ejiciant, linguis loquantur novis, etc.

'*Second.* Cum Deus sit quædam Lux per totum mundum diffusa, illum tamen non ingredi in ullam rem, nisi privs assumpserit quasi vestem spiritum quendam æthereum, qualis opera alchymiæ extrahitur, et quinta essentia vocatur. Facere proinde Deum compositionem cum hoc spiritu æthereo. Residere cum illo præsertim in sole, unde evibretur ad generationem, et vivificationem omnium rerum. Deum hoc modo esse formam omnium rerum, et ita agere omnia, ut causæ secundæ per se nihil agant.

'*Tertio.* Compositum ex Deo, et Spiritu isto Æthereo esse animam mundi. Purissimam partem hujus animæ esse naturam angelicam, et cœlum empyreum, quod intelligatur permistum esse omnibus rebus. Dæmones etiam particulas esse ejusdem essentiæ, sed malignæ materiæ alligatas. Omnes animas tam hominum, quam brutorum, nihil esse aliud, quam particulas ejusdem animæ. Eandem animam esse Angelum Michaelem, seu Mitattron.

'*Quarto.* Quod est amplios, eandem mundi animam esse verum Messiam, Salvatorem, Christum, Lapidem Angularem, et Petram universalem, supra quam Ecclesia, et tota salus fundata sit. Hanc nempe esse præcipuam partem Philosophici Lapidis, quæcum addensata rubescat, exinde dicatur esse sanguis Christi, quo emundati, et redempti sumus. Neque enim nos emundari sanguine Christi humano, sed hoc divino, et mystico.

'*Quinto.* Hominem justum esse alchymistam, qui Philosophico Lapide invento, illius usu immortalis fiat. Mori tamen dici, cum partes corruptibiles abijicit; Resurgere, cum fit incorruptibilis; Glorificari, cum proinde easdem dotes assequitur, quæ tribuuntur corporibus gloriosis. Hommes quihuc evaserint "FRATRES CRUCIS ROSEÆ" dictos, scire omnia, posse omnia, non arbitrari rapinam esse se equales Deo, cum eadem in illis sit mens, quæ in Christo Jesu.

'*Sexto*. Creationem none esse productionem rei ex nihilo, ut nos vulgo intelligimus nihil. Materiam (quam sæpissime tenebras vocant) esse id, quod proprie appelletur nihil; ac proinde cum Deus dicitur creare, aut facere aliquid ex nihilo, intelligi creare, aut facere ex materia. Moysen, cum Creationem Mundi descripsit, fuisse alchymistam, itemque Davidem, Salomonem, Jacob, Job, et omnes alios; adeo ut etiam yeti Cabbalistæ nihil aliud quam alchymistæ sint; itemque Magi, sapientes, philosophi, sacerdotes, et alii.' Marinus Mersennus significantly adds: 'Quæso autem, nisi ista sunt impia, quid potest esse impium?'

In the first place, the whole of the Sacred Scriptures are a grand mystical puzzle referring to ALCHEMY, and to the universal alchemic process. The mystical sense of the Old and the New Testaments is none other than the HISTORY OF ALCHEMY--originated in the *Cabala* (with the secrets contained therein), and the *rationale* of that called 'The Philosophers' Stone'. It matters not to the question of these secrets fixed what religions be professed; whether Christian, whether those of the 'Sects', whether infidel and heathen. That only is 'Catholic' which lies in the 'Stone'--otherwise *practical magic*; whereby Demons are commanded, good spirits evoked, and the innermost hidden resources of nature, and the Spirits of Nature, laid bare and availed-of.

Secondly.--When Deity is said to be 'Light', pervading and vivifying all nature, He enters not in anything unless a *mask* of the object is adopted as the medium in which He fixes. This *aura* (or the deliquescence of the uproused light) is the infinite Ethereal Spirit. The spring or the moving spirits, or the means, of alchemy evolve out of it. They are fivefold in their exercise or delimitation. God is indeed *identical* with this supreme spirit. And the radiant or intense material-nucleus is the lucid conflux-spot or the SUN stored (by its spirits) with vigour, sensitiveness, and intelligence. From this Intense Centre or Fiery Blaze of Power (the Sun), agitations and life vibrate in masterdom from the middle-point to circumference. God, thus, in producing, is said to be identified with Matter, and He so fills (and IS) that there are not (nor can there be) secondary causes, except to Man; who can *only know second causes*. This, be it noted, is 'Berkeleyism' on the one side, and its opposite, or 'Spinozism', on the other--both being the same thing in reality; looked at *from either side*; or from before and from behind.

Thirdly.--Composed of this 'mask', and of this infinite medium or Divine Movement, is the general investment (or spirit) called the 'Soul of the World'. The purer part of this sensitive, responsive soul is, in its own nature, of the breath of the angels (*for 'the Angels were made'*). The *anima mundi* is the Flaming Spiritual Region, in which all things live. Even the devils are portions of this efflux, which is the general life. But the Rebellious Spirits (the *vis inertiæ*, or the *laziness*, so to speak), of matter--dense, contradictory, inaccessible--are buried or lost--and were afterwards *chained*--in inapprehensive matter. All particular 'sentiences'--whether of the brutes or man--are nothing other than parts of the whole lucid spirit. Of the same soul (in essence) is the Archangel Michael, or Mitattron. Also all the Angels in their Sevenfold Regions; both of the Bad, and of the Good; of the Dexter and of the Sinister Sides of Creation.

Fourthly.--Which is still more dreadful (in appearance), the same *anima mundi*, or Soul of the World, is the real Messiah, Saviour, Christ, the 'Corner-Stone of the Temple', the 'Temple' itself (the universe) the 'STONE' (*Petram Universalem*), or 'ROCK' (Peter--St. Peter), upon which the Church, and Salvation, is founded. This is the mystical end and scope of that longed-for Beatitude--or Magical Transfiguration--the 'Philosophers' Stone', or 'Foundation'. Which (being to be obtained 'out of the material' by 'supernatural' means) when contracted into itself, and concentrated and intensified, glows (or martyrises) into *flaming red*, or possession, or Glorified Agony (made Heaven). From thence it is said to be the 'Blood' of Christ (and the 'Gross' of Christ), which 'blood' was shed for the redemption of the world from the penalties of the (First?) FALL (by Which We Are). By means of the 'Great Sacrifice' mortality is purged into purity back into the celestial fire, and redeemed from Hell or Matter. However, we are not redeemed by the blood of a 'Human' Christ, but by the atoning blood *in a divine and mystical sense*. (See corresponding plates.)

Fire is contention--whether holy or unholy. Heat, intensified in the struggle, agitates furiously to FIRE. Fire, triumphing and mastering the matter which lends it its material and strength, when passing into victory brandishes *into the calm and the glory of victory*, and becomes yellow in its flaming precious. gold, and quiet LIGHT intense as the grandest phenomenon-- sprung up skywards; or against gravity; therefore *reversing* nature's principal law. The intenser the darkness, or the mass of matter (the Rosicrucians' 'other side' of Spirit, and of Light), the greater the Light, and the greater the spirit and vivacity and force in the Liberation *into Light* (and into Spirit) of the Darkness and the Matter; when *its* farthest-winnowed atoms are forced asunder in the darts of the fire, and turned '*inside-outwards*'. See preceding pages. This is the 'Holy Grail', or 'Sangreal', or 'Sang-Reale' or Fire', or 'Mighty Redeeming Magic', sought by the Champions, or the Knights, of King Arthur's Round Table. See Supplementary Explanations.

Fifthly.--The 'Just Man made Perfect' is the Alchemist (or rather, Rosicrucian) who, having found the Philosophers' Stone (San Graal, or Holy Grail, or '*Sang Reale*' or 'Holy Rapture' or Magic Birth into the Celestial Fire, or flame of Self-Extinguishment, or of 'Ecstasy'), becomes immortal (and disappears, or 'dies' to the world). His 'chariot of fire' being that of Enoch, or 'Translation'. To die is simply the falling asunder and disintegration of the mechanism of the senses, which have contracted inwards and formed (in life) the prison of the soul--a prison of pains and penalties; from between the bars of the windows of which (or out of the eyes) the suffering, languishing SPIRIT looks for the often long-coming releasing GREAT SPIRIT-DEATH. The flitting is of the flickering flame (consciousness) out of the urn. To 'Rise'--is to cast off the chains of mortality. To become 'Glorified' is to discover *in one's own identity* the glorious, godlike gifts or MAGIC--which are the wings upon which to rise. Those men who have passed (as through a door) in their lifetime from the 'hither' side (or world) to the 'thither' side (or the world invisible)--following into the LIGHT the divine beckon to Paradise of the ANGELS of LIGHT, are the BROTHERS of the ROSY CROSS, or the ROSICRUCIANS, as they have been called; who 'know everything', can 'do anything', and have even arrogated to themselves, when in them should be set up the same angelical-magical spirit which was in the Christ-Jesus, to be of the 'COUNCIL of GOD'. Though, in the world, they were the humblest of the servants of the Almighty.

In the Sixth Place,--Creation is not the making of things out of nothing, which we understand commonly (or vulgarly) of God's work in the beginning of the universe or of Creation. Matter, which the Rosicrucians frequently refer to as Darkness, is that only which is properly, to be called 'Nothing'. Thus when God is said to create, or make something out of nothing (to do which is impossible), it is to be understood that He worked with material, or with DARKNESS, which is the 'Blank side' or the 'Other Side of Light; turned away'. These profound metaphysical distinctions are the key of all the Theologies. Moses, when he describes the Creation of the World, is the Alchemist, relating in parable the generation of the solids, and the flowing-over into the border-country (out of the flesh) of the Invisible--WHERE EVERYTHING ULTIMATELY IS. The history of David, Solomon (of the 'Temple'), Jacob (of the 'Ladder; or Staircase from Earth to Heaven, and from Heaven to Earth', etc.), Job; the accounts of the Heroes of the stories of the *Apocrypha* (the most concealed or recondite of the 'things hidden'--*thence its name*), etc., are cabalistic and alchemical, similarly to all the mythologies, which are, in their fanciful and mystic range of supposed facts, cabalistic and alchemical. The true *Cabalistæ* are none other than Alchemists and Rosicrucians. Likewise the Magi, Wise Men, Philosophers, Priests, and Heroes; from Jason and the 'Three Kings' to King Arthur, and from Adam, Noah, Abraham, and

Moses, to Numa, Paracelsus, Borrichius, Robertus de Fluctibus (nearer our own time), AND OTHERS.

The Rosicrucian system took the following forms:--These Philosophers believed that there were Two Principles in the Beginning--Light and Darkness, or Form and the Material *out of which the Form was*. That before the Creation (distinctively so called), the Light Itself was as 'Divinity Latent' or 'At Rest'. In the Creation, or in the production of things, Divinity became active, aroused, and inventive. By whatever name distinguished, or by whatever style identified, Moses' description of Creation is to be taken as the process of alchemy, as worked by Nature itself, being her Form; to which head are referred the kingdoms of darkness, or chaos, and the Light emerging out of its own bosom or DARKNESS.

After the active movement from the centre, or evolvement, or Creation, the radiation and counter-working or interchange of Light and Darkness in crossing and encountering irritated mutually, naturally; became expansive and contractive angularly--thence pyramidal and starry. And in the relative counterbalancing contemperation, the diversity of things arose at the points of the masterdom into form or Light. The medium in which the elements were (and the elements themselves) now grew 'in their natures'. From these various rudiments of being--(in the vehicle Light) the archetypical scheme arranged itself; which, 'One' in essence, was 'Triple' in procession or 'parade'. Hence the TRINITY.

But it is Incomprehensible, obviously, *without the means to comprehend it*--which is CHRIST. Christ the 'PENALTY'--Christ the 'SACRIFICE'. Christ the 'Glass' of the 'Universe', in which 'God' saw 'Himself'. But 'Christ' is not 'God' any more than the 'Glass' is the 'Seer'. From the TRINITY and the vivifying *substratum* in the mathematical four corners of the world, comes the ineffable name--'*Tetragrammaton*'. The archetypical 'Idea' is also called Reflective--Intelligible--Informed--Superessential--Endless in resource.

Object--Subject--Result: or the Three 'Persons' of the Trinity. The reflection of God is in the Archetype which is the Second Principle, or 'Macrocosmos' (created worlds), exhibiting 'Either Side', or 'Will' in 'Action'. This is displayed in Three Divisions, or Spheres--called (1st) the 'Empyræum' (God). (2nd) The 'Ethereæum' (the 'Saviour'). (3rd) The 'Elements' (the Virgin Mary). Light emanates in the Sephiroth ('CABALA') or 'Sevenfold' rotation--hence the 'production of phenomena'. In uniting with the Ethereal Spirit, it becomes the Soul, or 'Responsive Sentience of the World'. The further elucidation of the Rosicrucian theological system, in its general features--*so far as in hint or parable submitted to unenlightened comprehension*--will be found prestated in previous pages, and elsewhere.

The Rosicrucians contend that music, or melody--*which is enchantment*--pervades all nature in its prosperous or intended progress, although it is only the wail, or plaint, of the instinctive soul on its 'wounded', or 'sacrificed', or '*Ruined Side*'. It mourns for its 'Original Lost Paradise'. The music of the spheres is no unreal thing, but real as is the atmosphere of the spirits; for 'music is the atmosphere of the spirits', and discords (though the necessity, support, and balance of Creation) are a medium for the coarse and low spirits, who inundate, as it were, the lees and the settlings of nature. In discords, or in the inharmonious strife amidst the sounds, the rabble of the spirits (so to term them) are stimulated to their envious and spiteful, or malific or freakish and blundering, bad life. Beauty is not, however, necessarily beauty--it may be *seduction*. For the higher grades of the recusant or rebellious spirits who find their power in the original permission that there '*might be phenomena*' are beautiful in their assumption--or usurpation--of the lovely forms of spirit-life and of nature. And they will prevail, sometimes, even against the best efforts of the Angels of Light. The Cabalists whisper that God 'made the world' by the 'means of music'--that music, as man knows music, is essentially a power; that it is the faint, much-changed, much-enfeebled, sole relic, and tradition, and reminder of Man's Lost Paradise; that (through it originally) everything was possible, as the gift of God; which explains the classic fables of Orpheus, Amphion, and the mythological wonder-workers in music; that music is modulated in the movements of the planets according to the rearrangement of the post-diluvian world, and in conformity with the readjustment of the solar-system after mysterious aberration or cataclysm; that mortality cannot hear, and that the human soul is so debased that it only catches intermittently the faint echo of the continuous universal music which in other--now material--senses is the life and growth and splendour of everything.

> There's not the smallest orb, that thou behold'st,
> But in his motion like an angel sings,
> Still quiring to the young-eyed cherubims:
> Such harmony is in immortal souls;
> But, whilst this muddy vesture of decay
> Doth grossly close it in, we cannot hear it.

Music is magic, is sacred, and a power--as all harmony must be;--the nerves of the world--the aspiration of living things--the spell which breaks up and extols--into super-added, super-natural life--the 'Real' into the 'Ideal'. Harmony--or the mysterious solace and satisfaction and happiness at heroism which we feel--is found in the beauty of the human figure, the glories and graces of all growing objects and moving or unmoving natures. Success in nature, and in life, with their changes--as man knows 'nature' and 'life'--arise from the interstarry, mechanical modifications, and the incidents (and, the apparent interference and intertangle) through the restless movement of the planets. All the glorious seeming mechanism of the starry sky shows so as mechanism only to the *measuring senses* of man; but in reality it may be the play of Infinite Spirit. (See accompanying Charts, A, B, C.) The planets of our own system may be directed in their 'continual-speaking' changes by their several crowds of governing spirits. Spirits being everywhere the directors of matter, its solids are only to be separated by soul or energy--as the wedge (directed by the will) cleaves inert or resistant solids. Music is always in the air. Man has no ears for it, unless it is *enlivened* to, or finds access to, his senses. But *his heart is its home*--if he has a heart, and not an 'animal's mechanic throbbing-machine' only. Air is the breathing of nature. Music is always in the air--more particularly at night, for Nature (being born of it) is necessarily more nervously sensitive at night, whether for the 'beautiful' or the 'dreadful'; because both are equally exciting and fascinating--basilisks both-- as they are mysterious. We obtain by pulsation, or scientific commotion of the air, by musical instruments, the music out of it; and our fine nerves are the fine sensitives (born of God), as the harp played upon to receive it. *Otherwise there is no sense in music.* Otherwise our passions could not be stirred by it. These are storms and convulsions (rendered beautiful) certainly not born of God's original 'REST'. Rather they come of the stirring ambitions of Lucifer--uprising--'Son of the Morning', 'Son of the Awakening'--'Son' of the 'Sun'. Music and its success depend upon the prosperous progress of the Planets which make it, as (in Astrology) they prearrange, order and fix the fates of men. It is no inconsistent thing to say that, in the Rosicrucian sense, every stone, flower, and tree has its horoscope (we know that there are no two leaves alike), and that they are produced and flourish in the mechanical resources of the mysterious necessities of *astrology*--every object bearing its history in its lines and marks (sigillated magnetism), as inspired by the Great Soul of the World; which is all continual changing *purpose*, urging restlessly towards 'REST'.

'Nullam esse herbam, aut plantain inferius, cujus non sit stella in firmamento, quæ eam percutiat, et dicat ei, cresce.' *Exercitatio in Fluddanam Philosophiam*, p. 228. Parisiis, 1630.

Or back again to that from which it came. Moving in the *arc* of the pendulum between the two points--Life and Death (as we know Life and Death)--beyond which the 'swing' of this world's 'Creation' points, cannot pass--OR BE.

CHAPTER THE THIRTEENTH

INDIAN MYSTERIOUS ADORATION OF FORMS. THE UNITY OF THE MYTHOLOGIES FOUND IN THE BHUDDISTIC AND MOHAMMEDAN TEMPLES

GENERAL note on the *Sacti Puja*. POWER means the good goddess, *Maya Maia* (i.e. Delusion). She is also called Bhagala, Vagula, Bagala-mukhi. She has neither images nor pictures. The Girl in the Indian sacred, secret Temple rites, who figures as the representative of Sacti, is the supposed embodiment of the goddess offered for worship. The word Sacti corresponds to genius, or 'sylph', of the Rosicrucian creed. The doctrine of guardian angels and of patron saints is conveyed in these Hindoo meanings in the machinery of the 'sylphs'.

During *Puja*, the Yogini is supposed to be in an exalted visionary state (*guyána nidra*), wherein, like the sibyls among the ancients, and the modern *clairvoyantes*, she answers questions in a delirious manner, and is supposed to be for the time inspired. *The Foreign Quarterly Review*, No X. for February 1830; art. viii.: '*Histoire Critique de Gnosticisme, et de son influence sur les Sects religieuses et philosophiques des six premiers siècles de l'ère chrétienne. Ouvrage couronné par l'Académie Royale des Inscriptions et Belles Lettres*. Par M. J. Matter, Professeur. 2 tomes, avec planches, 8vo, Paris, 1828.' The third volume is of small size, and contains eleven plates of gems and symbols. This book proves Gnosticism to be identical with the Sacti creed of the Hindus. Edward Sellon advances this. See *Annotations on the Sacred Writings of the Hindus, being an epitome of some of the most remarkable and leading tenets in the faith of that people*. Printed for Private Circulation, 1865. London.

Brühm Atma, the Breathing Soul, is, according to the Hindoos, a spiritual Supreme Being, coeval with the formation of the world. In process of time the Hindoos appear to have adopted a material type or emblem of Brühm. A rude block of stone began to be set up. This was the '*Phallus*', or, as they termed it, the

'*Linga*'. This emblem had reference to the Procreative Power seen throughout nature, and in that primæval age was regarded with the greatest awe and veneration. This simple and primitive Idolatry came by degrees to diverge into the adoration of the elements, particularly Fire, and at length developed itself by the institution of an emanation from *Brühm Atma* in his Triune capacity, as Creator, Preserver (or 'Saviour'), and Destroyer. These attributes were deified under the names of *Brahma, Vishnu,* and *Siva,* on whom were conferred three *gunas,* or qualities, viz. *Rajas* (passion), *Sat* (purity), and *Tumas* (darkness). This is the *Trimurti.* 'Trimurti' (three-formed *Murti*), signifying also an image. Our vital souls are, according to the *Vedanta,* no more than images, or εἴδωλα of the 'Supreme Spirit'--*As. Res.* vol. iii. It may be concluded that the most exalted notion of worship among the Hindus is a service of *fear.* The Brahmins say that the other Gods are good and benevolent, and will not hurt their creatures; but that Siva is powerful and cruel, and that it is necessary to appease him. As fear is, and must be everywhere, the most potent feeling. Thence vital and active physical religion. Distrust and fear of the external phenomena of the world, as meaning mischief to us (it means the greatest --apparently--in Death), created religion. Fear creates respect--respect is attention to an object, and therefore dread of it. Because we are not acquainted with its possible operation upon ourselves in regard of our being interfered with or injured. Hence all religion is selfishness apart from 'inspiration', which the world (in its folly) calls 'superstition'.

The most popular representation of the Divine Being in India is unquestionably the *Linga;* a smooth stone rising out of another stone of finer texture, *simulacrum membri virilis et pudendum muliebre.*

This emblem is identical with *Siva* in his capacity of 'Lord of all'. It is necessary, however, to observe that Professor Wilson, while admitting that 'the *Linga* is perhaps the most ancient object of homage adopted in India', adds, 'subsequently to the ritual of the *Vedhas,* which was chiefly, if not wholly, addressed to the

Elements, *and particularly to Fire*. How far the worship of the *Linga* is authorized by the *Vedhas* is doubtful, but that it is the main purport of several of the *Puranas*[18] there can be no doubt.'[19]

The universality of *Linga puja* (or worship) at the period of the Mohammedan invasion of India is well attested. The idol destroyed by Mahmoud of Ghizni was nothing more than one of those mystical blocks of stone called Lingas. The worship of Siva under the type of the *Linga* is almost the only form in which that Deity is reverenced. The Linga of black or white marble, and sometimes of alabaster slightly tinted and gilt, is placed in the middle of the Hindu temples. This is a Chinese hint. The Chinese Pagodas are Phalli, storied 'Tors', or Obelisks; abounding in bells to be agitated in the winds to drive off the crowds of roving malignant spirits. The whole of China may be mystically said to be populated by '*Bells* and the Dragon'. Speaking of Siva and Pawáti, M. de Langlet says 'Les deux divinités dont-il s'agit, sont très souvent et très pieusement adorées sous le figure du Linga (le Phallus des anciens), et de l'Yoni dans leur mystérieuse conjonction. L'Yoni so nomme aussi Bhaga (pudendum muliebre). *Madheri,* douce; et *Argha,* vase en forme de bateau.' Benares is the peculiar seat of the Linga or Phallic worship. No less than forty-seven Lingas are visited, all of pre-eminent sanctity; but there are hundreds of inferior note still worshipped, and thousands whose fame and fashion have passed away. It is a singular fact, that upon this adoration of the procreative and sexual Sacti (or power) seen throughout nature, hinges the whole strength of the Hindu faith. Notwithstanding all that has been said by half-informed and prejudiced persons to the contrary, this *puja* does not appear to be prejudicial to the morals of the people. Nearly all the *Pujas* are conducted with the frequent ringing of bells, and the object of this is twofold--first, to wake up the

---

[18] *Puranas* (New Testament), the Modern Scriptures of the Hindus, as distinguished from the *Vedhas* (as Bible), or more Ancient Scriptures. Wilson on Hindu Sects--*As. Res.* vol. xvii.

[19] *As. Res.* vol. xvii. pp. 208-10.

attention at particular parts of the service; and secondly, to scare away malignant *Dewtas* and evil spirits; precisely, in fact, for the same reasons as they are used at the celebration of Mass in Roman Catholic countries.

Prakriti, the mother of gods and men, one with matter, the source of error, is identified with Maya or delusion, and coexistent with the Omnipotent, as his *Sacti,* his personified energy, his bride. *Prakriti* is inherent *Maya,* 'because she beguiles all things'.--*As. Res.* xvii. It is stated in one of the *Purans* that *Brahma,* having determined to create the universe, became androgynous, male and female (or 'reflector' and 'reflected'); the right half having the sex and form of a man, the left that of a woman. In his images he is sometimes thus represented, and is then termed Ardnari. 'This is *Prakriti* of one nature with *Brühm--*illusion, eternal, as the soul so is its active energy, as the faculty of burning is in fire.' The Sacti system bears a striking affinity with Epicureanism. It teaches Materialism, and the Atomic System of the 'Confluence of Chance'. Compare the *Ananda Tantram,* c. xvii. with Lucretius, lib. iii. On the base of Minerva's statue at Sais, whom the Egyptians regarded to be the same as Isis, a goddess who bears so striking an analogy to the Hindu *Prakriti* or nature, there was this inscription: 'I am everything that was, that is, that is to be. Nor has mortal ever been able to discover *what I am.*'--Plutarch, *De Iside et Osiride,* S. ix. According to the immediate object of worship is the particular ceremony, but all the forms (lighter or heavier) require the use of some or all of the five *Makaras: Mánsa, Matsya, Madya, Maithuna,* and *Mudra,* that is, fish, flesh, wine, women, and certain charms or mystical gesticulations with the fingers. Suitable *muntrus,* or incantations, are also indispensable, according to the end proposed, consisting of various seemingly unmeaning monosyllabic combinations of letters, of great imaginary efficacy. 'The combination of H and S is principal, and is called *Prásáda-Mantra,* and described in the *Kulárnava.*'--Wilson, *As. Res.* In many of the religious observances solitude is enjoined, but all the principal ceremonies culminate in the worship of Sacti, or POWER, and require, for that purpose, the presence of a young and beautiful girl, as the living representative of the goddess. This worship is mostly celebrated, in all due serious religious formality, in a mixed society; the men of which represent *Bhairavas*, or *Viras*, and the women *Bhanravis* and *Nayikas*.

The female thus worshipped is ever after denominated Yogini, i.e. 'attached' (set apart, sacred). This Sanscrit word is in the dialects pronounced *Jogi* and *Zogee*, and is equivalent to a secular nun, as these women are subsequently supported by alms. The leading rites of the *Sakti-Sodhana* are described in the *Devi-Radhasya*, a section of the *Rudra-Yámala*. It is therein enjoined that the object of worship should be either 'A dancing-girl, a female devotee (or nun), a courtesan, a *Dhobee* woman, a barber's wife, a female of the Brahminical or Sudra tribe, a flower-girl, or a milkmaid'. Appropriate *muntrus* are to be used. She is to be solemnly placed *naked* (as a sacred, unapproachable 'Thing', or object), but richly ornamented with jewels and flowers--the triumphant spoils of glorious nature--*on the left* of a circle (inscribed for the purpose), with *muntrus* and gesticulations. The circle, or vacant enchanted space, must be rendered pure by repeated incantations and rites; being finally baptized *with wine* by the peculiar *mantra*. The *Sacti* is now sublimized or 'apotheosized'; but if not previously initiated, she is to be farther made an adept by the communication of the radical *Mantra* or last charm whispered thrice in her ear, when the object of the ceremony is complete. The finale to this solemnity is what might be concluded as likely, but--strange to say--accompanied throughout by *muntrus* and forms of meditation and of devotion incomprehensibly foreign to the scene. In other aspects this presentation of the 'Yogini' is a '*Sacrifice*', and the whole meaning of the rites is sacrificial--rites performed *before an altar*, and implying--superstition undoubtedly--but deep mystery and some profoundest suggestions. (Wilson, *As. Res.* vol. xii. 225: on Hind. Sects. Vide *Rig Veda*, Book ii. c. viii. ss. 13, 14, 2nd attham, 8th pannam, Rigs B. 14, which contain the *Sucla Homa Mantram*, etc.)

The caste-mark of the *Saivas* and *Sactas* consist of three horizontal lines on the forehead, with ashes obtained if possible *from the hearth*, on which a *consecrated fire* is perpetually maintained.

The *Sacti* (or 'Sacred Presence') is personified by a naked girl, to whom offerings are made of meat and wine, which are then distributed amongst the assistants. Here follows the chanting of the *Muntrus*, and sacred texts, and the performance of the *mudra*, or gesticulations with the fingers. The whole service terminates with orgies amongst the votaries of a very licentious description. This ceremony is entitled the *Sri Chakra*, or *Purnabisheka*, THE RING or 'Full Initiation'. This method of adoring the *Sacti* is unquestionably acknowledged by the texts regarded by the *Vanis* as authorities for the excesses practised. Wilson, on Hind. Sects, vol. xvii. *As. Res.* Ward, on the Vaisnavas, p. 309.

In Gregory's Works (*Notes and Observations upon several difficult passages in Scripture*, vol. i. 4to. London 1684) is to be found a significant comment. '*Noah prayed daily in the Ark before the body of Adam*', i.e. before the PHALLUS, or Regenerator (Adam being the primitive 'Phallus', or great Procreator of the Human Race)--(under its present circumstances, and in the existing dispensation). 'It may possibly seem strange', Gregory says, 'that this orison should be daily said before the body of *Adam;* but it is a most confessed Tradition among the Eastern men that Adam was commanded by God that his dead body should be kept above ground till a fullness of time should come to commit it פיוססאלאוע to the *middle of the earth* by a priest of the Most High God.' See previous pages. This 'middle of the earth' is Mount Moriah--the Meru of India.

The 'Brazen Serpent' continued to be worshipped by the Jews, and to have incense offered to that Idol, till the reign of Hezekiah: 'For, it being written in the Law of Moses "Whosoever looks upon it shall live", they fancied they might obtain blessings by its mediation, and therefore thought it worthy to be worshipped. Our learned Dr. Jackson observes that "the pious

Hezekiah was moved with the greater indignation against the worship of this image, because in truth it never was--nor was intended to be--a type of our Saviour, but a figure of His Grand Enemy"', etc.

The Jews relapsed into idolatry by the adoration of the Golden Calf; set up, too, not by a few schismatics, but by the entire people, with Aaron at their head. The calf-superstition was doubtless a relic of what they had seen in Egypt in the worship of Apis and Mnevis. Next we have the 'Golden Calves' set up by Jeroboam at Dan and Bethel. Then follows (*Judges* viii. 22, etc.) the worship of Gideon's Ephod. 'The Ephod made by Gideon with the spoil of the Midianites became after his death an object of idolatry' (ibid., p. 41). We have also Micah's images and the 'Teraphim'. We learn from St. Jerome (who received it by tradition from the ancient Jews, and indeed it is so stated in *Numbers* xxv. 1, 2, etc.; xxiii. 28, and numerous other passages of the Old Testament) that the Jews adored Baal Phegor (Baal-Pheor), the Priapus of the Greeks and Romans. 'It was'; he says, 'principally worshipped by women; *colentibus maxime feminis* (Baal-Phegor).' Maimonides observes that the adoration offered to this Idol, called Pehor, consisted in discovering ------. Chemosh, probably the same as Baal-Pheor, also received the homage of the Jews, as also did Milcom, Molech, Baal-berith (or Cybele), and numerous others--all of the same sexual cast.

From all this in regard to their irregular worship--or rather (mysteriously) to their *regular* or assigned worship, it will be seen that the Jews fell into Idolatry (and Phallic Idolatry, too) to an extent interpenetrating, again most mysteriously, the whole scope of their religion. There will consequently not appear anything so very startling in the supposition that the Ark of the Covenant contained symbolic objects referring to Phallic ideas. We have seen that the 'Stone', or 'Pillar', of Jacob was held in particular veneration--that it was worshipped and anointed. We know from the Jewish records that the Ark was supposed to contain the tables of stone. And if it can be demonstrated that these stones implied a Phallic reference, and that these 'tables' were identical with the symbolism accompanying the sacred name Jehovah, Iehovah, or Yehovah, which, written in unpointed Hebrew, with four letters is--IEVE or IHVH (the HE being merely an aspirate and the same as E)--this process leaves us the two letters I and V (or, in another of its forms, U). Then if we add the I *in* the U we have the 'Holy of Holies'; we also have the Linga and Yoni and Argha (Ark or Arc) of the Hindus, the 'Iswarra' or 'Supreme Lord'. In all this may be found--mystically--the 'Arc-Celestial' replicating-in upon itself--symbolically and anagrammatically-- and presenting itself as identical with the 'Lingayoni' of the 'Ark of the Covenant'. Gregory observes that the '*middle* of the Ark was the place of prayer--made holy (consecrated) by the presence of Adam's Body.' (Refer to the glyptic symbolism, the mystical engraving of the 'Ark', placed among the full-page plates. Thence 'Man' was the Cabalistic (Rosicrucian) *Microcosmos* or 'Little World', in contradistinction to the causer, or pattern, or original-- *Macrocosmos,* or 'Great', or 'Producing' ('Outside'), or 'Originating World'.

'The body of Adam was embalmed and transmitted from father to son, till at last it was delivered up by Lamech into the hands of Noah.' Again, the '*middle of the Ark*' was the place of prayer (and worship) made holy by the presence of 'Adam's "Body".'--Gregory, p. 118. 'And "*so soon as ever the day began to break*" Noah stood up towards the "body of Adam",' etc., etc., 'and "prayed" (or "worshipped").' Here was the origin of the 'Eucharist', as the reader will clearly see farther on (see accompanying plate).

The most ancient monuments of Idolatry among the Gentiles were consecrated pillars (Lingas), or columns, which the Jews were forbidden to erect as objects of divine homage and adoration. And yet--a most extraordinary contradiction--this practice is conceived to arise from an imitation of Jacob, who 'took a stone' and 'set it up', etc. Further, 'this stone was held in great veneration in subsequent times by the Jews, and removed to Jerusalem.' They were accustomed to 'anoint this stone'; and from the word *Bethel,* the place where the pillar was erected, came the word Bœtylia among the Heathen, which signified rude stones, or uprights, which they worshipped either as 'symbols of Divinity', or as 'true gods', animated (at certain times) by the heavenly power. Thence the name 'Bowing Stones' amongst the Welsh-- not as stones to be 'bowed to', but 'bowing of themselves', like the modern 'tipping-discs' or other supposed enchanted idols or consultative tables or objects. Indeed it would seem not improbable that the erection of the Pillar of Jacob actually gave rise to the worship of Phallus among some of the Pagan peoples. 'For', says Lewis, 'the learned Bochart asserts that the Phœnicians (at least as the Jews think) first worshipped this *very stone* which Jacob set up, and afterwards consecrated others in imitation and in reminder of it.'

It is to little purpose that we are reminded that the Jews were forbidden by their law to 'make unto themselves any graven image'; for, as Lewis shows in the following passage, there may be exceptions to this, as to every other general rule. 'Notwithstanding', he says, 'the severity of the Law against the making of Images, yet, as Justin Martyr observes in his Book against Trypho, it must be somewhat mysterious, that God in the case of the "Brazen Serpent" should command an image to be made, for which one of the Jews confessed he never could hear a reason from any of their Doctors.' According to Theodoret, Arnobius, and Clemens of Alexandria, the *Yoni* (then become *Ioni;* thence *Ionia* and *Ionic*) of the Hindus was the sole object of veneration in the Mysteries of Eleusis (Demosthenes, *On the Crown*).

CHAPTER THE FOURTEENTH

DOCTRINE AND RATIONALE. THE EMBODIED 'CHILDREN OF THE ELEMENTS', BOTH OF HEATHEN AND OF CHRISTIAN PERIODS

IL est avéré pour les Théologiens et les Philosophes, que de la copulation de l'homme, mâle ou femelle, avec le Démon, naissent quelquefois des hommes. Et c'est de la sorte que doit naître l'Antichrist, suivant bon nombre de Docteurs: Bellarmin, Suarez, Maluenda, etc. Ils observent en outre que, par une cause toute naturelle, les enfans ainsi procréés par les Incubes (Exterior Spirits, with more or less power, enabled to embody themselves with male human characteristics, and drawn to earth with the desire to form alliances with women--as hinted in the Bible), sont grands, très-robustes, très-audacieux, très-superbes, et très-méchants. Voyez là-dessus Maluenda; quant à la cause en question, il nous le donne d'après Vallesius, Archiatre de Reggio.

'Ce que les Incubes introduisent *in uteros* n'est pas *qualecumque, neque quantumcumque*--mais abondant, très-chargé d'esprits et sans aucune sérosité. Ceci est d'ailleurs pour eux chose facile: ils n'ont qu'à choisir des hommes chauds, robustes, et *quibus succumbant;* puis des femmes de même tempérament, *quibus incombant.* Tels sont les termes de Vallesius. Maluenda confirme ce qui a été dit plus haut, prouvant, par le témoignage de divers Auteurs, classiques la plupart, que c'est à pareilles unions que doivent leur naissance: Romulus et Rémus, d'après Tite-Live et Plutarque; Servius-Tullius, sixième roi des Romains, d'après Denys d'Halicarnasse et Pline l'Ancien; Plato le Philosophe, d'après Diogène Laërce et Saint Jérôme, Alexandre le Grand, d'après Plutarque et Quinte-Curce; Séleucus, roi de Syrie, d'après Justin et Appien; Scipion l'Africain, premier du nom, d'après Tite-Live; l'empereur César-Auguste, d'après Suétone; Aristomène de Messénie, illustre général grec, d'après Strabon et Pausanias. Ajoutons encore l'Anglais Merlin or Melchin, né d'un Incube et d'une Religieuse, fille de Charlemagne. Et, enfin, comme l'écrit Cocleus, cité par Maluenda, ce Hérésiarque qui a nom Martin Luther.'

On lit aussi dans la Sainte Écriture, *Genèse, chap.* 6, *verset* 4, que des géants sont nés du commerce des Fils de Dieu (the 'Angels of God') avec les Filles des Hommes (the 'Daughters of Men'). Ceci est la lettre même du texte sacré. Or, ces géants étaient des hommes de *grande stature*, comme qu'il est dit dans

Baruch, chap. 3, *verset* 26, et de beaucoup supérieurs aux autres hommes. Outre cette taille monstreuse, ils se signalaient encore par leur force, leurs rapines, leur tyrannie; aussi est-ce aux crimes des Géants qu'il convient d'attribuer la cause première et principale du Déluge, suivant Cornélius â Lapide, dans son *Commentaire sur la Genèse.*

Ces animaux Incubi (spirits capable of incorporating themselves and of borrowing forms to effect their purpose without 'alarming'--asserted to be an 'essential Rosicrucian tenet') ces animaux naitraient-ils dans le péché originel, et auraient-ils rachetés par le Seigneur Christ? La grâce leur serait-elle conferèe, et par quels sacrements, sous quelle loi vivraient-ils, et seraient-ils capables de Béatitude et de Damnation?

Dans un monastère de saintes Religieuses vivait comme pensionnaire une jeune vierge de noble famille, laquelle était tentée par un Incube qui lui apparaissait jour et nuit, et, avec les plus instantes prières, avec les allures de l'amant le plus passionné, la sollicitait sans cesse au péché. Elle cependant, soutenue par la grâce de Dieu et la fréquentation des sacrements, demeurait ferme dans sa résistance. Mais malgré toutes ses dévotions, ses jeûnes, ses vœux; malgré les exorcismes, les bénédictions, les injonctions faites par les exorcistes à l'Incube de renoncer à ses persécutions; en dépit de la multitude de reliques et autres objets sacrés accumulés dans la chambre de la jeune fille, des flambeaux ardents qu'on y entretenait toute la nuit, l'Incube n'en persistait pas moins à lui apparaître comme de coutume *sous la forme d'un très-beau jeune homme.* Enfin, parmi les doctes personnages consultés, à ce propos, se trouva un Théologien d'une grande érudition: lequel, observant que la jeune fille tentée était d'un temperament tout à fait flegmatique, conjectura que cet Incube devait être un démon aqueux (il y a en effet, comme en témoigne Guaccius, des démons ignés, aériens, flagmatiques, terrestres, souterrains, ennemis du jour).'

We may here remark that the above expresses some of the notions of the Rosicrucians in regard to those that they denominate: '*Les Enfans Aériens et Les Enfantes Aériennes*', their *Ondins* and *Ondines*, their *Sylphs* and *Sylphides*, their *Gnomes* and *Gnomides*, their *Kebels*, *Kebelles* or *Kobolds* (*Krolls* or *Krolles*), and their *Salamanders* and *Salamandrines.*

'Le Théologien érudit ordonna qu'on fît immédiatement dans la chambre de la jeune fille une fumigation de vapeur. On apporte en conséquence une marmite neuve en terre transparente; on y met une once de canne aromatique, de poivre cubèbe, de racines d'aristoloche des deux espèces, de cardomome grand et petit, de gingembre, de poivre long, de caryophyllée, de cinnamome, de canelle caryophyllée, de macis, de noix muscades, de storax calamite, de benjoin, de bois d'aloès, et de trisanthes, le tout dans trois livres d'eau-de-vie demipure; on place la marmite sur des cendres chaudes, afin de faire monter la vapeur fumigante, et l'on tient la chambre close. La fumigation fait arriver l'Incube, mais qui, cette fois, n'osa jamais pénétrer dans la chambre. Seulement, si la jeune fille en sortait pour se promener dans le jardin ou dans le cloître, il lui apparaissait aussitôt tout en restant invisible aux autres, et lui jetant ses bras autour du cou, lui dérobait ou plutôt lui arrachait des baisers, ce qui faisait cruellement souffrir cette honnête pucelle, Enfin, après nouvelle consultation, notre Théologien ordonna à la jeune fille de porter sur elle de petites boulettes composées de parfums exquis, tels que musc, ambre, civette, baume de Pérou et autres. Ainsi munie, elle s'en alla se promener dans le jardin où sur-le-champ lui apparut l'Incube, furieux et menaçant; toutefois, il n'osa point l'approcher, et après s'être mordille le doigt, comme s'il méditait une vengeance, il disparut pour ne plus revenir.--*Confesseur de Nonnes*, homme grave et très-digne de foi.'

Je sais que beaucoup de mes lecteurs, la plupart peut-être, diront de moi ce que les Epicuriens et bon nombre de Philosophes Stoïciens disaient de S. Paul (*Actes des Apôtres*, c. 17, v. r8): 'Il semble qu'il annonce des divinités nouvelles', et tourneront ma doctrine en ridicule. Mais ils n'en seront pas moins tenus de détruire les arguments qui précèdent, de nous dire ce que c'est que ces Démons Incubes, vulgairement appelés *Follets*, qui n'ont peur ni des exorcismes, ni des objets sacrés, ni de la Croix du Christ; et enfin de nous expliquer les divers effets et phénomènes relatés par nous dans l'exposition de cette doctrine.

The above passage is very curious, since it gives the key (a matter which has puzzled every speculator) as to the meaning of the masquerade and 'Folly' and antic system which prevails in the Catholic application of the Christian Doctrine at the 'Pre-Lent' period, and the recurring Festivals, or the Jovial, Mercurial, Venus-patronized periods. *Folle: Follets* (m), *Follettes* (f), Folletins (m.), Folletinnes (f). These are the names of the male and female masquerading, gambolling 'Follies', or Fays or Elves or Sprightly Spirits--under their various fanciful names, and in their picturesque, sportive, masquerading disguises--the 'pied-populace' of that 'world-turned-upside-down', in the general male and female interchange and frolicsome 'Glorying'--the Carnival, or Grotesque (in reality, religious) Celebration of all countries.

Dancing is also sacred in certain senses. The 'Precentor' of the Cathedrals was originally the Leader of the *Choirephists*, or Chorephists, or Corephests. Thence Coriphes, or Coryphées, for female dancers.

Luxure et humidité sont deux termes correspondants: ce n'est pas sans raison que les Poëtes ont fait naître Vénus de la mer, voulant indiquer, comme l'expliquent les Mythologues, que la luxure a sa source dans l'humidité. Lorsque les Incubes s'unissent aux femmes dans leur corps propre et naturel, sans métamorphose ou artifice, les femmes ne les voient pas, ou, si elles les voient, c'est comme une ombre presque incertaine et à peine sensible. *Quando vero volunt se visibiles amasiis reddere, atque ipsis delectationem in congressu carnale afferre, sibi indumentum visibile assumunt, et corpus crassum reddunt.* Par quel art (magic), ceci est leur secret. Notre philosophie à courte vue est impuissante à le découvrir.

Hector Boethius, Hist. Scot., raconte aussi le cas d'un jeune Ecossais qui, pendant plusieurs mois, reçut dans sa chambre, quoique les portes et fenêtres en fussent hermétiquement (note: this word comes from the 'Hermetic Brothers', or the Rosicrucians) fermées, les visites d'une Diablesse Succube (as it was supposed or assumed, perhaps wrongfully) de la plus ravissante beauté; caresses, baisers, embrassements, sollicitations, cette Diablesse (or Temptress) mit tout en œuvre, *ut secum*--ce qu'elle ne put toutefois obtenir de ce virtueux jeune homme. A worthy example to youth: 'especially in this generation' will be an exclamation vividly rising to the mind of the reader.

D'autres fois aussi le Démon, soit incube, soit succube, s'accouple avec des hommes ou des femmes dont-il ne reçoit rien des hommages, sacrifices ou offrandes qu'il a coutume d'imposer aux Sorciers et aux Sorcierès, comme on l'a vu plus haut. C'est alors simplement un amoureux passionné, n'ayant qu'un but, un désir: posséder--la personne qu'il aime. Il y a de ceci une foule d'exemples, qu'on peut trouver dans les Auteurs, entre autres celui de Menippus Lycius, lequel, après avoir maintes et maintes fois--avec une femme, en fut prié de l'épouser; mais un certain

Philosophe, qui assistait au repas de noces, ayant deviné ce qu'était cette femme, dit à Menippus qu'il avait affaire à une *Compuse*, c'est-à-dire à une Diablesse Succube; aussitôt notre mariée s'évanouit en gémissant.--Lisez là-dessus Cœlius Rodiginus, *Antiq.*, livre 29, chap. 5. These extraordinary narrations form the basis, and supply the material, for Keats's poem *Lamia* and Coleridge's poetic sketch '*Christabel*'.

Nous avons de plus, à l'appui de notre thèse, *l'Evangile de S. Jean*, ch. 10, v. 16, où il est dit: 'J'ai encore d'autres brebis qui ne sont pas de cette bergerie: il faut aussi que je les amène, et elles entendront ma voix, et il n'y aura qu'une seule bergerie et qu'un seul berger.' Si nous demandons quelles peuvent être ces brebis qui ne sont pas de cette bergerie, et quelle est cette bergerie dont parle le Seigneur Christ, tous les Commentateurs nous réspondent que la seule bergerie du Christ c'est l'Eglise, à laquelle la prédication de l'Evangile devait amener les Gentils, qui étaient d'une autre bergerie que celle des Hebreux. Pour eux, en effet, la bergerie du Christ, c'était la Synagogue, d'abord parce que David avait dit (*Psaume* 95, v. 7): 'Nous sommes son peuple et ses brebis qu'il nourrit dans ses pâturages'; puis, parce que la promesse avait été faite à Abraham et à David que la Messie sortirait de leur race, parce qu'il etait attendu par le peuple Hébreu, annoncé par les Prophètes, que étaient Hébreux, et que son avénement, ses actes, sa passion, sa mort et sa résurrection étaient comme figurés d'avance dans les sacrifices, le culte et les cérémonies de la loi des Hébreux.

Les Anges ne sont pas tours de purs esprits: décision conforme du deuxième Concile de Nicée. Existence de créatures ou animaux raisonnables autres que l'homme, et ayant comme lui un corps et une âme. Et quoi ces animaux diffèrent-ils de l'homme? Quelle est leur origine? Descendent-ils, comme tous les hommes d'Adam, d'un seul individu? Y a-t-il entre eux distinction de sexes? Quelles sont leurs mœurs, leurs lois, leurs habitudes sociales? Quelle sont la forme et l'organization de leur corps? Comparaison tirée de la formation du vin. Ces animaux sont-ils sujets aux maladies, aux infirmités physiques et morales, à la mort?

Naissent-ils dans le péché originel? Ont-ils été rachetés par Jésus-Christ, et sont-ils capables de béatitude et de damnation? Preuves de leur existence.

De la Démonialité et des '*Animaux Incubes et Succubes*' ('Children of the Elements'); *où l'on prouve qu'il existe sur terre des créatures raisonnables outres que l'homme, ayant comme lui un corps et une âme, naissant et mourant comme lui, rachetées par N. S. Jésus-Christ et capables de salut ou de damnation.* Par le R. P. Louis Marie Sinistrari d'Ameno, de l'Ordre des Mineurs Réformés de l'étroite Observance de Saint-François (xviie siècle). Publié d'après le Manuscrit original découvert à Londres en 1872, et traduit du Latin par Isidore Liseux. (Seconde Edition.) Paris, Isidore Liseux, 5 Rue Scribe, 1876.

A translation of this exceedingly curious book into English was afterwards simultaneously published in London and Paris.

CHAPTER THE FIFTEENTH

ROBERT FLOOD (ROBERTUS DE FLUCTIBUS), THE ENGLISH ROSICRUCIAN

IT is a reflection on the knowledge of the compilers of all books treating of the history and topography of Kent, that perhaps the most remarkable man born in it--because his pursuits lay out of the beaten track of recognition or of praise--should not be mentioned in any of the descriptive or biographical works that we have met with concerning that county--undoubtedly one of the most interesting in England. In some general biographies and dictionaries the name of Robert Fludd, Doctor of Medicine, etc., does occur. But the notices concerning his life are very scanty, possibly because there was little material for them existent in his own age. We have, in our studies of the Rosicrucian doctrines, purposely made the life of Dr. Robert Flood an object of close examination. We have searched for every possible personal memorial of him. We have been rewarded with, however, but fragmentary matter. Our information concerning his life is quite the reverse of extensive, notwithstanding our intimacy with his writings.

Our ideas and conviction in regard of this truly great man being what they are, the extreme curiosity, and the vivid interest, may be divined with which we set out on our first expedition to discover, and to make ourselves fully acquainted with his place of birth, and his own place and the seat of his family. It was in the afternoon of a summer day that we sought out the village of Bersted, situate a few miles distant from Maidstone in Kent, on the Ashford Road. Flood is buried in the ancient church (a small one) of Bersted--a village, or rather hamlet, boasting an assemblage of larger or smaller houses around a green, none of any considerable pretension; cottages--neat specimens of English rural cottages they may be called, with small gardens, varying gables, and crossed lattices. There are woody grounds and picturesque hop-plantations enclosing this quiet, homely-looking place; with its solemn church up an elevation in the corner of this extensive triangular green--with excellent smooth cricket-space in the centre. The church in which he lies!--what words for such a man. To us--or to any Rosicrucian student who knew who he was and what he had done--he was the whole country. His influence extended from, and vivified everything--this, the whole way from 'The Star'--the old inn, or rather hotel, from which we had started in the morning in order to pilot our way thither; through the quiet country, passing few people and only small groups of cattle straggling along the sunshiny road.

It was with feelings just as reverential, just as melancholy, and greatly as enthusiastic, as those with which we contemplated the tomb of Shakespeare in Stratford-on-Avon, that we stood (knowing the man, as it were, so well) silent and absorbed--revolving many--many thoughts--before the oblong slab of dark slate-coloured marble--(greatly like Shakespeare's again)--which covered the place of last deposition of Robertus de Fluctibus--as into which parallel he had latinized, according to the usage mostly of the Elizabethan period, his name--Robert Fludd or Flood. Flood's monument occupies a large space of the wall of the chancel on the left hand, as you stand before the altar looking up the body of the small church towards the door. The monument is singularly like Shakespeare's, even allowing for the prevailing architectural fashion of the time. There is a seated half-length figure of Flood with his hand on a book, as if just raising his head, from reading, to look at you. The figure is nearly of life-size. There is, moreover, a very striking similarity in Dr. Flood's grand thinking countenance to that of Shakespeare himself, and his brow has all the same breadth, and is as equally suggestive of knowledge and of power.

The church of Bersted is very small and old. The square tower of the church is covered with masses of dark ivy. The grassy ground slopes, with its burial mounds, from about the foundation of the old building towards the somewhat distant village of Bersted. The churchyard descends in picturesque inclination, and is divided by a low brick-wall; over which, here and there, flowers and overgrowth have broadly scaled from the garden of the old-fashioned, though neat-looking rustic, picturesque parsonage. There is a winding green lane, with high hedges, which leads down to the village. All is open, and quietly rural. It is true English scenery, homely and still. The large trees, and the abundance of turfy cover over the whole ground-view, pleases. The rustic impression and the deep country silence befit that spot where one of the most extraordinary thinkers in the English roll of original men lies at rest. When we were in this neighbourhood, and on the first occasion that we sought out Bersted, it was a calm grey summer's afternoon. The still clouds, which seemed to prolong the grey general haze dwelling on the more distant landscape, were impressive of a happy--quietly happy--repose. And as we stood on our return towards Maidstone--having spent, we believe, upwards of three hours in meditative notice either in the church or musing and strolling round it--the slopes of the hopgrounds presented a field of view of light, lovely green. Out of this low-lying landscape to which we reverted, Bersted Church tower rose small. It has four sculptured bears ('Bersted, Bearstead') at the four angles, for pinnacles, to the square tower. These miniature bears, perched upon the summit, looked to me at about half-a-mile's distance like four crows. The distant wooded hills showed faint to the eye. There was no wind. The air was warm and silent. The country was green and luxuriant.

Robert Flood was a Brother of the Rosy-Cross. He is called the English Rosicrucian. To those who never heard his name, the titles of his books will suffice to prove the wonderful extent of his erudition, and the strange, mystical character of the man. We would warn every inquirer to place not the least reliance upon any account which they may meet of Robert Flood in any of the ordinary biographies, or in any Encyclopædia or other book professing to give an account of the Rosicrucians. We beg the curious not to believe one word--except dates, and scarcely these--that are to be found in accepted scientific treatises, or otherwise, purporting to speak of Flood, or of his compeers. These are all at fault--*and ignorant*--particularly and generally.

Robert Flood was the second son of Sir Thomas Flood, Treasurer of War to Queen Elizabeth. The name was originally Lloyd, and the family came from Wales. Robert Flood was born at Milgate House, of which edifice one corner still remains built in the manor-house which was erected on its site when the old house fell to ruin. Milgate House is situated near Bersted. Flood was born in the year 1574. He was entered at St. John's College, Oxford, in 1591. He travelled for six years in France, Spain, Italy, and Germany. He was a member of the College of Physicians, London. He was M.B., M.D., B. A., and M.A. The latter degree he took in 1605. He began to publish in 1616. He died at his house in Coleman Street, London, in the year 1637. Flood is also stated by Fuller to have lived in 'Fanchurch' Street.

The list of Flood's works comprise the following:--

1. *Utriusque Cosmi, Majoris et Minoris, Technica Historia.* Oppenheim, 1617. In Two Volumes, Folio.

2. *Tractatus Apologeticus Integritatem Societatis de Rosea-Cruce defendens.* Leyden, 1617.

3. *Monochordon Mundi Syunphoniarum, seu Replicatio ad Apologiam Johannis Kepleri.* Francfort, 1620.

4. *Anatomia Theatrum Triplici Effigie Designatum.* At the same place, 1623.

5. *Philosophia Sacra et vere Christiana, seu Meteorologia Cosmica.* At the same place, 1626.

6. *Medicina Catholica, seu Mysterium Artis Medicandi Sacrarium.* The same, 1626.

7. *Integrum Morborum Mysterium.* The same, 1631.

8. *Clavis Philosophiæ et Alchymiæ.* The same, 1633.

9. *Philosophia Mosaïca.* Gondæ, 1638.

10. *Pathologia Dæmoniaca.* The same, 1640.

The above account of Flood's Rosicrucian works is from Fuller's *Worthies*.

There are notices of Dr. Flood in the *Athenæ et Fasti Oxoniensis*; in Chalmers' *Biographical Dictionary* under the names of Flood, Mersenne, and Gassendi; in Granger's *Celebrated Characters*; and in Renaudot, *Conferences Publiques*, tom. iv. page 87. Also in Brucker.

Upon Flood's monument there are two marble-books bearing the following titles:--*Misterium Cabalisticum*, and *Philosophia Sacra*. There were originally eight books represented in all; 'studding' the front of the tablet (as the look of it may be described). The inscription to his memory is as follows: viii. Die Mensis vii. A°.D^m., M.D.C.XXXVII. (8th September 1627). Odoribus vrna vaporat crypta tegit cineres nec speciosa tvos ovod mortale minvs tibi. Te commitimus vnum ingenii vivent hic monumenta tui nam tibi qui similis scribit moritur-que sepulchrum pro tota eternum posteritate facit. Hoc monumentum Thomas Flood Gore Covrte in-oram apud Cantianos armiger infœlissimam in charissimi patrui sui memoriam erexit, die Mensis Augusti, MDCXXXVIII.

In the life of the astronomer Gassendi will be found some mention of the career, and of the distinctions, of Robert Flood. A work of Gassendi's bearing the title '*Epistolica Exercitatio, in qua precipua principia philosophiæ Roberti Fluddi deteguntur, et ad recentes illius libris adversus patrem Marinum Mersennum scriptos respondetur*' was printed at Paris in 1628. This piece was reprinted in the third volume of Gassendi's works published at Paris in 1658, under the title of *Examen Philosophiæ Fluddanæ*, etc. Flood wrote two books against Mersennus, who had assailed his philosophy. The title of the first book was *Sophia cum Moria Certamen, in quo Lapis Lydius a falso structore Patre Marino Mersenno, monacho reprobatus, voluminis sui Babylonici in Genesi figurata accurate-examinat*. This work was published in Folio at Francfort in 1629. The name of the second book was *Summum bonorum, quod est verum magiæ, Cabalæ, Alchymiæ, Fratrum Rosæ-Crucis Virorum. subjectum indictarum scientiarum laudem, in insignis calumniatoris Fr. Mar. Mersenni dedecus publicatum, per Joachim Frizium*, 1629.

In this Book, which we now bring to a close in its Fourth Edition, we have traced and expounded the philosophy of the authentic Rosicrucians, as developed in the folios of the celebrated Dr. Flood, 'Robertus de Fluctibus'. We are the first Author who has brought forward Flood's name to the reading world, justified his claims, and made him known through the most laboured and long-studied translation with continual reference to hundreds of books in all languages, dead and living, which bore reference to Flood's sublimest philosophical speculations. All the world has heard of the Rosicrucians--few or none have ever taken the trouble to ascertain whether the stupendous and apparently audacious claims of these philosophers were rightly or wrongly estimated--that is, whether to be adjudged as founded on the rock of truth, or seeking steadiness and root only in the sands of delusion. The Author began his inquiries, in the year 1850, in a spirit of the utmost disbelief; thus taught by the world's assumptions and opinions. Much of this indoctrinated preoccupation the wise man has to unlearn in his progress through life. Fogs, and prejudices, and prepossessions cleared from the Author's mind as he advanced.

After the very considerable space of thirty-six years of study of the Rosicrucians, the Author of this work ends (*as* he ends). Let the candid reader, himself, judge in what frame of mind the Author of the 'Rosicrucians' concludes. How should any one complete an inquiry in regard to the Majestic Brothers of the Rosy Cross, otherwise the Rosicrucians? The story of the Rosicrucians is of the widest interest. The proof of this fact lies in the accumulation of letters from persons in every condition of life addressed to the Authors of the present work since the publication of the First Edition from all parts of the world; anonymously, or with particulars of names, etc.

The celebrated author of the *Confessions of an English Opium Eater* (Thomas de Quincey), in his *Rosicrucians and the Free-Masons*, originally published in The London Magazine of January 1824, also continued in the succeeding number, has this remarkable passage: 'Rosicrucianism is not Freemasonry. The *exoterici*, at whose head Bacon stood, and who afterwards composed the Royal Society of London, were the antagonist party of the Theosophists, Cabbalists, and Alchemists. *At the head of whom stood Fludd*; and from whom Freemasonry took its rise.'

Thus we leave the Rosicrucians--as men--(just as we ought to leave them)--in the same mystery as that state of really impenetrable mystery in which we find them. Let the mask and the 'mystery' still remain before them, concealing them and their purposes in the world.--As it is enjoined!

CHAPTER THE SIXTEENTH

NOTICES OF ANCIENT AUTHORITIES

THE following extraordinary work--which is so rare and so valuable (see below) *in its original edition,* that we have reason to believe the Authors of the 'Rosicrucians' can congratulate themselves in being the possessors, in all probability, of the *only* copy in existence--was suppressed, wherever found, on its appearance. The author, in reality, was never known. It is considered probable that this book had a paramount effect in bringing about, and in compassing the success of, the Reformation.

Disputatio Nova contra Mulieres; qua Probatur eas Homines non esse. Anno MDXCV. *Theses de Mulieribus quod Homines non sint.* Cum in Samaria, ut in campo omnis licentiæ, liberum sit credere et do cere, *Jesum Christum,* Filium Dei Salvatorem et Redeptorem animarum nostrarum, una cum Spiritu Sancto non esse Deum, licebit opinor etiam mihi credere, quod multo minus est, mulieres scilicet non esse Homines--et quod rode sequitur--Christum ergo pro its non esse passum, nec eas salvari. Si enim non solum in hoc regno tolerantur, sed etiam a magnatibus præmiis afficiuntur, qui blasphemant Creatorem, cur ego exilium aut supplicium timere debeo, qui simpliciter convicior creaturam? præsertim cum eo modo ex Sacris literis probare possim, mulierem non esse hominem, quo illi probant Christum non esse Deum.

Admonitio Theologicæ Facultatis in Academia Witebergensi, ad scholasticam juventutem, de libello famoso et blasphemo recens sparso, cujus titulus est: *Disputatio Nova contra Mulieres, qua ostenditur, cas hommes non esse.* Witenbergæ. Excudebat Vidua Matthæi Welaci, Anno MDXCV (1595).

Defensio Sexus Muliebris, Opposita futilissimæ Disputationi recens editæ, qua suppresso Authores et Typographi nomine blaspheme contenditur. Mulieres Hommes non Esse. Simon

Gediccus S.S. Theol. Doct., etc. Lipsiæ, Apud Henricum Samuelem Scipionem, Anno MDCCVIII (1708).

Auctor hujus *Dissert. rarissima* credit: valeat Acidalius. Vide, inter alios, Freytagii Analecta--de *libris rarioribus*, p. 5. (Very ancient handwriting in the copy itself) 'Acidalius died, aged 28 years only, 1595.' Hallam's *Lit. Hist.* p. 14. This is only surmise. The authorship of the book is unknown. It was rigorously suppressed.

CHAPTER THE SEVENTEENTH

MYSTERIES OF THE ANCIENTS
THE ARK OF NOAH

NOTE *to Plate* '*Mysterium*': The explanation of this engraving will be found at a previous page. The ancient volume from which it is taken is very rare, and bears the following title:

Antiquitatum Iudaicarum LIBRI IX:

In qüis, præter Ivdæe, Hierosolymorum, et Templi Salomonis accuratam delineationem, præcipui Sacri ac profani gentis Titus describuntur (auctore Benedicto Aria Montano Hispalensi). Adiectis formis æneis. Lvgdani Batavorum. Ex officina Planteniana apud Franciscum Raphelengium--1595.

The Ark of Noah--the medium of escape from the Deluge, and the mythic means of the perpetuation of the Human Family (afterwards Race). The Post-Diluvian 'Signs of the Zodiac' are here correctly designated as in number 'Twelve'. Let the judicious Reader remark that twelve times thirty are Three-Hundred-and-Sixty, which is *not* the number of the degrees of this symbolical plan. There are twelve divisions in this ark. The centre space is that through which the 'Dove', or 'Raven', escaped out into the 'open' in search of its new home, or into the restored world when the waters 'went down' or 'disappeared'. Each of the twelve spaces in the accompanying plan contains twenty-five degrees, which make an aggregate of three hundred degrees. The mythical figure contained in the Ark is presumably that of Noah. It is also evidently the symbolical figure of the 'Saviour', and typically only that of Noah; for the hands are 'crossed', and the feet and hands bear the marks of the 'Incision'--the 'Nails of the Crucifixion (or Passion)'. Twenty-five, the number of the degrees in each space or sign of this 'Noachic Ark', Arca, or Chest (Gigantic), are the number of the Knights of the Garter; with the reserved 'twenty-sixth', or Kingly or Sovereign Seat. In this respect the ark may be regarded as the grand mythic 'Idea' of the 'Round Table'; as that was the production of the central mythic 'Idea' of the 'Sangreal', or 'Sangreil'--*Refer to the Engravings, and to the Rosicrucian comment throughout both parts.* See pages generally, and the whole of the Chapters referring to the 'origin' of the Order of the 'Garter'.

CHAPTER THE EIGHTEENTH

CABALISTIC ILLUSTRATIONS. THE SAN-GRËALE, GREAL, OR HOLY GRËALE

THE engraving No. 4 at the end gives the mystical idea, or suggestion, of the Round Table of the Knights of King Arthur, which is again typical of the San Grëal. The romance of Guyot, or at least the traditional fable of the *San Grëal*, spread over France, Germany, and England. In the twelfth century the dogma of transubstantiation not being yet defined by the Church, the *chalice*, the mark of the Knights Templars, had not the deep mystic meaning which it received in the following century. The *graal* signifies a *vase*. The San Grëal is identified with the vessel in which Jesus celebrated the Holy Supper, and which also was used to receive His blood flowing from the wound inflicted upon Him by the centurion Longinus.

Walter Mapes, the historian of the San Grëal, ascribes to it a supernatural origin. He gave out that God was its real author, and had revealed it, in a celestial vision, to a holy hermit of Britain towards the year A.D. 720. This writer makes Joseph one of the *coryphœi* of his history of the San Grëal. After forty-two years of captivity Joseph of Arimathæa, the guardian of the Grail or Grëal, is at last set at liberty by the Emperor Vespasian. In possession of the sacred vessel, and a few more relics, and accompanied by his relations and disciples Hebron and Alain the Fishermen, he travels over a part of Asia, where he converts Enelach, King of Sarras. He then goes to Rome, and thence to Britain, where he preaches the gospel and performs thirty-four miracles. He settles in the Island *Yniswitrin*, Isle of Glass (the Grëal is of emerald, and consequently green), or *Glas*tonbury, where he founds an Abbey (Glastonbury Abbey), and institutes the Round Table (Arthur did this), in imitation of the Holy Supper, which was partaken of at a 'Round Table' with the Twelve Disciples, in their mythical *double-places*, twenty-four in all, and with the double chief-seat, or 'cathedra', for the President or the 'Saviour'. Lastly, the apostle of the Britons builds a palace, in which he preserves his precious relics, the Sacred Cup (refused to the Laity as a communion), which takes the name of San Grëal, the bloody spear (the 'upright' of the St. George's Cross, to whom the 'Garter' is dedicated), with which the centurion Longinus pierced the side of the Lord, from whence issued 'blood and water'--the Rosicrucian heraldic colours (royal), *Mars*--Red; *Luna*--Argent (or 'Fire' and 'Water'). There are Eight Angels, one to each half-heaven, or dark or light sides, guarding the Four Corners of the World.

The Sacred Cup is identified with the vessel of the Holy Supper. The Templars are the successors of the Knights of the Round Table. Their successors again were the Knights of Malta, with their Eight 'Langues', or Nations--each represented in a blade of, or ray, of the Eight-pointed RED Templar Cross.

The Temple Church, London, was dedicated to St. Mary. The Grëal is a sort of oracle. It is, so to speak, at the orders of the 'Mother of God', to execute all 'Her' commands. Parsival--the German champion-hero--thinks of transporting the Grëal to the East, from whence it originally came. He takes the San Grëal, embarks at Marseilles with the Templars, and arrives at the court of his brother Feirifix in India. The Sacred Cup manifests a desire that Parsival should remain possessor of the 'Grëal', and only change his name into that of Prester John (Prestre, or Prêtre, Jehan, or John). Parsival and the Templars settle in India. After the disappearance of the Grëal in the West, King Arthur and the Knights of the Round Table, losing the 'central object', or the 'Rose' (Rosicrucianism) of the Table, go on a scattered (Knight-Errant or romantic) championship in search of it. They travel over the world--but in vain. They cannot find the 'Grëal'. For it is for ever *hidden* in the far 'East', or in the land of the 'Sun'. Wolfram von Eschenbach tells us that Meister Guyot-le-Provençal found at Toledo an Arabian book, written by an astrologer named Flegetanis, containing the story of the marvellous vase called 'Grëal'.

The sacred vase, or the San Grëal, was placed, according to the myth of Guyot, in a Temple (or Chapel), guarded by Knights *Templeis* or *Temiplois* (Knights Templars). The Temple of the Grëal was placed upon a mountain in the midst of a thick wood. The name of this mysterious mountain (like the Mount Meru of the Hindoos and Olympus of the Greeks) hints sublimity and secrecy. Guyot calls it *Mont Salvagge*, wild or inaccessible mountain (or 'Holy Way'). The Grëal was made of a wonderful 'Stone' called *Exillis*, which had once been the most brilliant jewel in the 'Crown of the Archangel Lucifer'--the gem was emerald (green; Friday; the unlucky in one sense, the 'sacred' woman's day in another sense). This famous legendary stone was struck out of the crown or helmeted double-rayed or double-springing 'winged' crown--mythically--of the Prince of the Archangels ('Lucifer'), in his conflict with the opposing 'general of the skies'--Saint Michael, the 'Champion of Heaven'; and the combative guardian of innocence and of 'virginity' (mark). This immortal 'Stone'--the Grëal--fell into the 'Abyss'. It was mythologically recovered.

The 'Stone' was brought from heaven (rescue) by Angels, and left to the care of Titurel, the First King of the Grëal, who transmitted it to Amfortas, the Second King, whose sister '*Herze*'-loïde was the mother of Parsival, the Third King of the San Grëal. (These are the Three Kings of Cologne, or the Three Magi or Astrologers.) A great many towns pretended to possess this holy relic. In 1247 the Patriarch of Jerusalem sent the San Grëal to King Henry the Third of England, as having belonged to Nicodemus (see the *Gospel of Nicodemus*) and Joseph of Arimathæa. The inhabitants of Constantinople, about the same time, also fancied that a vessel which they had long esteemed as a sacred relic was the San Grëal. The Genoese also felt certain that their *canto catino* (Catillo, v. a. (L.) 'to lick dishes'; *Catinus*, i. m. (L.) 'a dish') was nothing else than the San Grëal. The same (or similar) modifications of the myth are to be noticed in a romance, in prose, entitled *Percival-le-Gallois*. Not only is the Round Table considered in this book as an imitation of the 'Holy Supper', but the author goes so far as to give it the name of San

Grëal itself. In the *Romance of Merlin*, written towards the end of the thirteenth century, it is said that the *Round Table* instituted by Joseph in imitation of the Holy Supper was called 'Graal' that Joseph induced Arthur's father to create a third *Round Table* in honour of the Holy Trinity.

The San Grëal: an Inquiry into the Origin and Signification of the Romances of the San Grëal. By Dr. F. G. Bergmann, Dean of the Faculty of Letters at Strasburg, and Member of the Royal Society of Antiquaries, Copenhagen. Edinburgh: Edmonston and Douglas, 1870. We quote the above in parts.

Round Table
(Mythical)

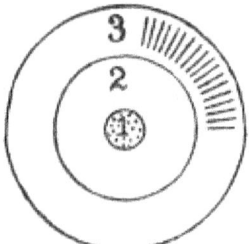

1. ROSE 'Crucified'
2. ROSE 'restored to Life'
3. 'CONSUMMATION'

CHAPTER THE NINETEENTH

THE ROUND TABLE IS THE RATIONALE OR APOTHEOSIS OF THE MOST NOBLE THE ORDER OF THE GARTER

HONI-SOIT QUI MAL-Y-PENSE

THE Round Table of King Arthur is a Grand Mythological Synthesis. It is a whole Mythology in itself. It is perennial. It is Christian. By tradition, the Round Table of King Arthur devolves from the very earliest period. The illustration opposite a previous page was copied from the original with great care and attention. King Arthur, in the principal seat, is idealized in the person of King Henry the Eighth, in whose time the Round Table is supposed to have been repaired and refaced. In the Revolution, Cromwell's soldiery, after the capture of Winchester, and in the fury at the imputed idea of *idolatry* (the Round Table is the English 'Palladium'), made a target of it. The marks of many balls are still conspicuous.

The five-leaved Roses (Red and White Roses; *Rhodion*, Rhodes--Knights of Rhodes or of Malta, the successors of the Templars) typify the Ten Original Signs of the Zodiac. Red-Rose, Five Signs (Aspiration or Ascension); White Rose, Five Signs (or Leaves), Descension (or 'Con'-descension, or S.S., or Holy Ghost (the key of the whole *apotheosis*; according to the mystical Jacob Bœhmen).

The whole is radiant (notwithstanding that the rays are *green*; otherwise expressive of the '*Linea Viridis*', seu '*Benedicta*

Viriditas'--Rosicrucian). (See former pages) out from the 'seed-spot', or 'Golden Sun' (Grand Astronomical Central Flame), in the centre. This double-rose, 'barbed' or 'thorned', Sol, is (in this form) the Tudor Rose (the *Rose-en-Soleil*, be it remembered, was another of the Tudor badges); denoting the union of the Houses of York and Lancaster in the person of Harry the Eighth.

It will be observed that each Knight of the Round Table is seated as at the base of an *obelisk*. The architectural 'obeliscar' form (rayed, or spread, or bladed) is universal, all the world over, both in old times and modern times. The Egyptian Obelisks are sacred to the Sun. The Paladins of Charlemagne were Twelve in number. The Marshals of France should be twelve in number. The Judges of England, according to old constitutional *rationale*, should be twelve; as the number of a Jury are twelve. All these are mythical of the Twelve Signs, or Divisions, of the Zodiac, the Twelve Jewish Tribes, the twelve oracular stones in the breastplate of the High Priest of the Jews, and, in the Christian aspect of the mysticism, the Twelve Apostles; with the 'Reprobate Condemned Central Sign' as Judas, the Traitor. The whole is Cabalistic in the highest degree; *and therefore ordinarily unintelligible*. It signifies the Second Dispensation, or the astrological reproduction and rearrangement of the Zodiac, when the original Ten Signs of the Ecliptic (mythically the *gladius* of the Archangel Michael) became Twelve; and when the mystic system underwent the GREATEST CHANGE--presenting a new traditionary and reproductive face. (Refer to Chapter on the origin of the Order of the Garter, previous, and thenceforward.)

 510. *Perceval Le Galloys; Tresplaisante et Recreative Hystoire du Trespreulx et vaillant Chevallier Perceval le galloys jadis chevallier de la Table ronde. Lequel acheva les adventures du sainct Graal. Avec aulchuns Picts belliqueulx du noble chevallier Gauvaīn. Et aultres Chevalliers estans au temps du noble Roy Arthus, non auparavant Imprime.* On les vend au Pallais a Paris. En la boutique de Jehan logis. Jehan sainct denis, et Galliot du pre. [A la fin] Et fut acheve de Imprimer le premier jour de Septembre. Lan mil cinq cents trente [1530]. Folio. 𝕭𝖑𝖆𝖈𝖐 𝕷𝖊𝖙𝖙𝖊𝖗, fine woodcut border to title, woodcuts, old french olive morocco extra, gilt edges, 1351. Aug. 1879. 29 New Bond Street.

CHAPTER THE TWENTIETH

REMARKS UPON TWO CURIOUS BOOKS

THE following old book is a very extraordinary one; as the design and tendency of it will puzzle most persons who are acquainted with the nature of the antagonistic relations which were supposed to exist between the Church of Rome and the Rosicrucians. The book is exceedingly scarce and valuable:

Rosa Jesuitica, oder Jesuitische Rottgesellen, das ist, Eine Frag ob die Zween Orden, der ganandten Ritter von der Neerscharen Jesu, und der Rosen-Creuzer ein einiger Ordensen. per J. P. D. a S. Jesuitarum Protectorum. Prague, 1620. (4to.) This is a truly curious tract upon the 'relations of the Jesuits and the Rosicrucians'.

A very curious book upon the subject of the peculiar and fanciful *attributed* notions of the Rosicrucians, and which drew a large amount of surprised and 'left-handed' attention when it first appeared, was that which bore the title (in its improved edition-- published without a date): *Comte de Gabalis, ou Entretiens sur Les Sciences Secrètes. Renouvellé et augmenté d'une Lettre sur ce sujet.* This book was brought out at Cologne. The printer's name was Pierre Marteau. Bound up with the copy in the possession of the present Authors of the Rosicrucians is another volume bearing the following title: *La Suite du Comte de Gabalis; ou Nouveaux Entretiens sur les Sciences Secrètes, touchant La Nouvelle Philosophie.* This latter work was published at Amsterdam, with no year mentioned of its publication, by Pierre Mortier. Upon the title-page of the first-named of these books appears the 'rescript' 'Quod tanto impendio absconditur, etiam solum-modò demonstrare, destruere est.--'Tertullian.

These works were considered--although written from the questioning and cautiously satirical point--as unwelcome and even obnoxious; even among those who freely commented on religion. Nevertheless they provoked (and still provoke) extraordinary curiosity.

CHAPTER THE TWENTY-FIRST

REMARKS RELATING TO THE GREAT MYSTIC, ROBERT 'DE FLUCTIBUS'

THE noted mystic, Jacob Bœhm, was born in the year 1575, and is said to have died in the year 1619. He was undoubtedly acquainted with the volumes of Robertus de Fluctibus, known as the 'English Rosicrucian'.

There is considerable doubt whether there were not two Robert Fludds, and whether, in reality, the theories and the mystic ideas of the one were not accepted as arising from the other. The following attestation will sufficiently establish these important facts:

'Quelques bibliographes ont confondu Robert Flood' (the Rosicrucian Philosopher), 'avec un autre Robert, dominicain Anglais, nè a York, et qui florissait dans le 14° siècle.

'Ce religieux avait fait aussi des recherches et laissé des écrits sur les Mysterès de la Nature, et ce qui l'avait fait surnommer "Perscrutator" (le "Chercheur"). Jean Pits et Jacques Echard, d'après Jean Leland, lui attribuent: *De impressionibus aëris; de Mirabilibus Elementorum de Magia Cæremoniali; de Mysteriis Secretorum; et Correctorium Alchymiæ*.'--Biographie Universelle:--Tome Quinzieme, p. 109, *et supra*.

The character of the above books by Robert Flood, the Dominican, and the close similarity of his studies with those of the famous Robert Flood, or 'Robertus de Fluctibus', of Milgate House, in Kent, would seem to come very near to proof that there was some family descent from the one to the other. The circumstances will at all events go a long way towards establishing a possible connexion or relationship between the first Robert and the second Robert; though divided through such a long space of time as intervenes between the fourteenth century and the period of James the First and Charles the First.

In all the matters treated of in this book, in the meaning and purpose of art--such as music particularly--the grand philosophical contention is, whether the world may be said to have 'sprung'--to apply the word thus--from FEELING, or was constructed--so to describe the mythic: making of nature--from SCIENCE. In this distinction lies everything of philosophic abstraction in regard to the subjects 'POWER' and 'LOVE', as originators of the scheme of things.

We may put the question in other words as a theosophic speculation, whether 'Man'--and therefore 'art'--is from the HEAD, or the HEART. We think entirely the latter, in as far as 'LOVE' is greater than 'WISDOM', and is its ruler. In this great fact lies all the hope of the world. By wisdom and justice the world is naught. Mercy and love (the 'IMMORTAL PITY') alone saves the world. Therefore contrition. Therefore sacrifice. Therefore submission--submission and innocence 'like as little children'.

It follows from the above that to this possible relaxing of the sternness of punishment ('JUSTICE') the saints penetrated. This means the theosophic, all-sufficient (because accepted) 'Propitiation,' or the sacrifice of the 'SAVIOUR', or of the 'sensitive side of human nature'. In this emotion from the heart lies all religion, and all that we can know of ourselves of hope. All that by any possibility we can know of ourselves--'OF HOPE'.

The following are certain Masonic observations:

(I. N. R. I.) These significant letters (or symbols) may be interpreted:
'Igne Nova Renovatur Integra'.
INRI: Jes. Naz. Rex. Judæ.

The office of the Rosary contains fifteen repetitions of the 'Lord's Prayer'. It comprises One Hundred and Fifty Salutations of the Blessed Virgin Mary. In the astronomical and astrological reference this implies: Firstly, the fifteen lunations (half of thirty days), or the feminine half-dark, mystic, naturally unconscious--magic--insensible corporeal changes incident of each month. The second instance carries reference to the magic semi-diameter of the ever-revolving solar circle, or the mythical 'Ezekiel's wheel', to which we have referred (cabalistically) in various places.

CHAPTER THE TWENTY-SECOND

ALCHEMY. THE POWER OF PRODUCING GOLD AND SILVER, THROUGH ARTIFICIAL MEANS. DOCTRINE OF THE ROSICRUCIANS

THE persuasion as to the possibility of the convertibility of the metals, and as to the existence of a master-means of improving and intensifying generally through all nature, until the confine was approached; and then by supernatural method (that is, supernatural to the world of man), that this border-line or limit (apparently so invincible) was passed over (indeed *evaded*) with power of return into the world with the fruits of the daring exploration openly in the hands:--this idea, which nothing could drive out of the mind, was fixed--spite of all the sense of those who supposed such contradictions. The proper cool-headed realization of the impossibilities, so far as Nature made them impossibilities, was not entertained.

There was much that urged--as a prime motive--such destruction as that effected by the Caliph Omar, on his conquest of Alexandria, in his committal to the flames of the famous Alexandrian Library. This destruction is usually taken as a reason for this elimination or extinguishment of previous accumulations of such imagined priceless value. It was not jealousy, but *fear*, that actuated the Caliph Omar.

The object of the Sultan, in regard to this immense collection of writings, is well known, and is usually attributed to the dogmatism and narrowness of his views in regard to his Mohammedan beliefs:--namely, that if the books contained any philosophy which justified or explained, or enforced, the religion of Mahomet, or any wisdom which could be interpreted as explanatory of it, it was needless, because all such was already contained in the *Koran*; and that if it taught other things, or advanced any contrary religious beliefs, it was correspondingly mischievous, and as such should be relentlessly destroyed. Thus the Caliph took up such a position that he was right both ways.

All the secrets of alchemy were supposed to be contained in the Alexandrian Library.

The sun is alchemic gold. The moon is alchemic silver. In the operation of these two potent spirits, or mystic rulers of this world, it is supposed, astrologically, that all phenomena are produced. It is a common opinion, and it is a generally assumed idea, even among the most learned, that that which is called *The Philosophers' Stone* is a mere fable. It prevails as an assurance in all books of instruction, or of learning, that it is purely *romantic*--a delusion--a wild idea--poetical, and therefore necessarily untrue. But all poetry--even *poetry*--is true enough in a certain way, and whilst it is conceived in the mind, just the same as the *colour* of the flower, which has nothing to do with the flower. It is very difficult to get over the assertions of competent persons as to the possibility of making gold. The chemical records abound with accounts of its artificial production, and of its having been exhibited under extraordinary--and certainly (necessarily) under secret circumstances. A multitude of ancient and modern philosophers have contended that in the secret spirits of nature, urging towards the light, and towards the sun, which is gold (*Chrysos*, or the 'Saviour'), there was a movement in all matter towards extrication, and therefore out of the *curse* of nothingness, or of 'matter'. Thence the precious gold, prepared and purged by the scorching fire. As to the possibility of metals being transmuted from one into the other, 'doctored', as we may say, in the skill of the alchemists, and 'purged' by the fierce conflagration, clear of their defacements, defilements, and *diseases*, into the divine *angelic* gold--responsive to the sun's brightness;--as to this stupendous art--believed in by the ancients, wholly discredited by the moderns--Libavius brings forward many instances in his treatise *De Natura Metallorum*. He produces accounts to this effect out of Geberus, Hermes, Arnoldus, Guaccius, Thomas Aquinas (*Ad Fratrem*, c. I), Bernardus Comes, Joannes Rungius, Baptista Porta, Rubeus, Dornesius, Vogelius, Penotus, Quercetanus, and others. Franciscus Picus (in his book

De Auro, sec. 3, c. 2) gives *eighteen* instances in which he saw gold produced by alchemical transmutation.

The principles and grounds for concluding that there may be such an art *possible* as alchemy, we shall sum up as follows. Firstly, it is assumed that every metal consists of mercury as a common versatile and flexible base, from which all metals spring, and into which they may be ultimately reduced by art. Secondly, the *species* of metals and their specific and essential forms are not subject to transmutation, but only the individuals; in other words, what is general is abstract and invisible, what is particular is *concrete* and visible, and therefore can be acted upon. Thirdly, all metals differ, not in their common nature and matter, but in their degree of perfection or purity towards that *invisible light* to which all matter tends for its relief or *rescue*--that celestial, imperishable glory, which necessarily in the world of sentience or possibility of recognition to itself (or oneness), must have 'matter' (in this world made up of senses, and of the avenues to those senses) as its '*mask*', or the vehicle in which it is to be, and out of and exterior to which all is magic or miracle. Fourthly, art or design or contrivance in its own respects, and directed by the immortal resource or intelligence which is a matter of spiritual tradition, a pitying gift to man in his lost or fallen state, surmounteth and transcendeth Nature--as we see every day in the mastery of the soul of man over his fleshly lusts, which otherwise would urge him into daily ruin. For Art directed upon Nature, may in a short while--seeing the *end* of things, and not being 'put-off' by their *appearances* only--perfect that which Nature, by itself, is a thousand years in accomplishing. Fifthly, God has created every metal of its own kind, and hath implanted in them a really vital, *restless* principle of growth, struggling against diseases and interruptions; as we see in the efforts of the metals--especially in the perfect metal, gold, born of the sun--which is the king of the material, and which in its healthy state overflows with magnetic seed or sparks of *magic light*, welcomed by the aerial world, and usurped only by the devil for his bad purposes in this world of dazzling shows. The true spiritual side of this golden well-spring of lucidity--free of all debasement of matter--is never seen in *this* world. But it is the medium of connexion, and is the golden bridge--one-half gold, as it refers backwards to man from the fountain of all life and light, the Sun, and the other half forward, into the celestial and heavenly eternal GOD'S LIGHT! Thus gold, and light, as its consequence, can by art (assisted by the angels, and farthered by prayer) be evoked, be made to fructify and grow, and can inspire and multiply, and take in ALL matter.

We will now compress (into certain well-considered passages) some of the ideas of that very remarkable chemist and speculative philosopher, B. V. Van Helmont, advanced in his *Paradoxal Discourses concerning the Macrocosm and Microcosm, or the Greater and Lesser World, and Their Union.* [20]

Metals consist universally of a hot and a cold sulphur. They are as of male and female; in respect to both of which, the more intimately they be united or naturally interwoven, the nearer those metals approach to the nature of gold. And from the difference and disparity of this union (according to the proportion and quantity of every one), arises the distinction of all metals and minerals--that is, in the due proportions, as the said sulphurs are more or less united in them.

If metals be produced, and consist by the union of these two, where then is there room for a third principle in metals--which is vulgarly called salt--and which is spoken of by the chemists; who make salt, sulphur, and mercury the principles of all metals?

But this is indeed only an enigmatical speech of the chemists. For when we see that the superfluous combustible sulphur, which is found in great quantity in the ore of the perfectly united metals, is by mortification, transmutation, or calcination, changed into an acid salt, it ceaseth to be sulphur. Now, forasmuch as all of the said sulphur can be changed into a salt, so as that it cannot be rechanged into brimstone back again (because the salt serveth only as a means to dissolve the two perfect sulphurs in order to

---

[20] London: Printed by J. C. and Freeman Collins, for Robert Kettlewel, at The Hand and Scepter, near S. Dunstan's Church in Fleet Street. 1685.

unite them); and whereas the white incombustible sulphur can never be changed into salt, how can we then make out three parts or principles which concur to the composition of metals? For two fathers to one mother would be monstrous and superfluous; forasmuch as both of them are but one and the same. Likewise, also, there cannot be two mothers to one father, in order to the bringing-forth of one birth, for so there would be two births, out of each mother one. For it cannot be denied that to generate a child, whether boy or girl (of which the one hath more of the father's nature and property, the other more of the mother's), there needs only a union of man and wife, and it is impossible that a third thing should be superadded essentially.

This visible, glorious, spiritual body may lead us to endless glorious thoughts and meditations; namely, if we consider that in all the sands created by God, there is a little gold and silver from whence all other beings do exist and have their being, as proceeding from their father, the Sun, and their mother, the Moon. From the sun, as from a living and spiritual gold, which is a mere fire, and beyond all thoroughly refined gold, and, consequently, is the common and universal first created mover (even as is the heart of man), from whence all moveable things derive all their distinct and particular motions; and also from the moon, as from the wife of the sun, and the common mother of all sublunary things.

And forasmuch as man is, and must be, the comprehensive end of all creatures, and the Little World (in whom all seeds exist and are perfected, which thenceforth can never be annihilated), we shall not find it strange that he is counselled (*Rev.* iii. 18) to buy gold 'tried in the fire' (the Greek words imply gold all or thoroughly fired, or all a mere *fire*), that he may become rich and like unto the sun, as on the contrary he becomes poor when he doth abuse the arsenical poison, so that his silver by the fire must be burnt to dross, which comes to pass when he will keep and hold the 'menstrual blood' (out of which he in part exists), for his own property in his own thoughts and outworkings, and doth not daily offer up the same in the fire of the sun, to the end the

'Woman' may be 'clothed with the Sun', and become a 'Sun', and thereby rule over the Moon; that is to say, that he may get the Moon 'under his feet', as we may see, *Rev.* xii.

Forasmuch as we are here treating concerning gold, it will not be inconvenient to query yet further, Whether is anything more to he considered and taken notice of about gold--namely, How many sorts of gold there be? And how gold is properly formed?

There are three sorts of gold.

Firstly. There is a white gold, which hath the weight and all the qualities of gold except the colour; for it is white as silver, and hath either lost its colour or hath not yet attained it.

Secondly. The second sort of gold is of a pale yellow colour.

Thirdly. The third sort is a high, yellow-coloured gold. But how little the tincture or colour doth, that is in gold, we may perceive from what follows:

1. In that the first sort, namely, the white gold, in its substance is as ponderous as any other gold, from which hint or instance we may see how little the colour conduceth to the being of gold; seeing it is not at all, or very hardly to be perceived in its weight and substance.

2. The whole body of common gold is nothing else, and cannot consist of anything else, but silver, which is a perfect body, and wants nothing of being gold but the fiery male tincture. If now it should happen that a certain quantity of silver should be tinged into gold with one grain of tincture, and that the said grain should be only sufficient to turn it into gold, without giving it the true colour to supply this, we have already showed that the gold-beaters and gilders know how to give it a fixed yellow gold-colour.

It may be further queried, how it comes to pass that antimony and copper can give to pale gold its perfect colour, and so can help others, whereas they cannot help themselves. As also, whence it is that they can communicate this colour to gold, and not to silver or any other metal, and not to themselves.

Forasmuch as gold doth want this colour, and must have it as its due and property, which it hath either had before, and now lost it, or hath not yet attained to it, but must attain it for the future; wherefore the gold, to satiate itself, takes in this gold-colour in order to its perfection, and can naturally take no more than it ought to have.

There remains yet one considerable question to be asked, namely, forasmuch as it has been said that gold naturally takes in no more of a golden-colour than it stands in need of for itself, and that a tincture which must first turn the Imperfect metals into silver (as being the body of gold), and afterwards tinge them into gold, must consist and proceed from gold and silver (for no third or strange thing can be here admitted), and yet the said tincture must not be gold or silver, but the very principle and beginning of gold and silver, and so be partaker of the end and perfection of gold and silver, and have the sulphur of gold and silver in it: for that bodies of one nature (as before mentioned), cannot mechanically enter into each other, as being both of them equally hard to be melted. The tincture, therefore, must needs be and consist of just such a sulphurous nature--(namely, which is easily fusible)--as the sulphur of gold and silver is of, which hath given them their form, and as it was before it entered into the composition of gold and silver, at the beginning of their being made such. And forasmuch as the said tincture is to tinge the other metals through and through not mechanically but vitally and naturally, it must of necessity abound with the said perfect metallic yellow and white tincture. Now silver and gold (according to what has been said) cannot mechanically take in more than they stand in need of themselves. The question therefore is, From whence such a tincture as this must be taken. And this question, in itself, may be said to include the whole challenge to the powers of alchemy.

We are likewise to weigh and consider how it can be, that such a little body of one grain should naturally be able so to subtiliate itself, as to be able to pierce a body of a pound weight in all its parts; which commonly is held to be impossible, because they suppose the metals to be mere gross bodies, and that one body cannot penetrate another.

Ask Nature of what she makes gold and silver in the gold and silver mines, and she will answer thee, out of red and white arsenic; but she will tell thee withal, that indeed gold and silver are made of the same. For the gold which is there in its vital place where it is wrought and made, is killed by the abundance of arsenic, and afterwards made alive again and volatilized, to bring forth other creatures, as vegetables and animals, and to give unto them their being and life. From whence we may conclude, that gold is not only in the earth, to be dug thence and made into coin and plate: for should we suppose this, it would follow, that an incomprehensible great quantity of gold must have been created in vain, and be of no use at all, there being vast quantities of gold which never are, nor ever can be, dug-up. And now to draw a parallel between the divine part or soul of man, and the purged and perfected gold.

Seeing that man, as a perfect and express Image of God, had all created beings, and consequently all living creatures in himself, and that therefore it would have been unnecessary to bring the outward living creatures outwardly to him; must it not then be supposed, that this was done inwardly in the centre, wherein Adam then stood. And that in this centre he gave to all creatures their proper and essential names, forasmuch as this could not have been done by him, in case the essential living ideas of the said creatures had not been in him, from which he gave forth those essential names, as water gusheth out from a living fountain. And may we not therefore with evidence conclude from hence that the 'Garden of Eden' was not only an outward place without man. Doth it not also clearly appear from this that the 'Garden of Eden' was not only a place 'without man?' For that when Adam by his 'FALL' had lost the inward life out of the centre (which proceeds from the centre to the circumference), *and was come into the circumference*, his eyes were 'opened' so that now he was fain to take in his light from without from the outward world, because his own 'inward world' was hid and shut up from him;

and now he saw his earthliness and bodily nakedness (which is the present state of all men in the world), for before he was 'full of light' from the continual irradiation 'from the centre'.

Pure gold is the sediment or settlement of 'light'. It is the child of the 'Sun', and is implanted and perfected by him.

CHAPTER THE TWENTY-THIRD

THE OUTLINE OF THE CABALA, OR KABBALAH. ITS MYSTIC INDICATIONS. THE PURPOSE OF THE GREAT ARCHITECT OF THE UNIVERSE IN THE SENSIBLE AND SPIRITUAL WORLDS (NATURAL AND SUPERNATURAL), AND THE CHARACTER OF THEIR RECIPROCITY, AND DOUBLE-WORKING

WHAT is more dream-like than the transactions in the Apocalypse? To ordinary comprehension, the mysteries of the Cabala, and the outline (spiritual) of the beginning of things, suggested in the Revelation of Saint John, are equally unintelligible.

It seems natural to believe, that the All-Powerful, All-Wise Deity hath, before all time (as far back as we can imagine), formed and governed a world of spiritual beings, active, conscious, having understanding and reason to conduct them, and '*passions*' to stimulate them. We may also conceive, that in so enormous a rebellion as that of Lucifer, where so many orders of operative spirits were drawn in, that several (or many, or a multitude) of these did more eminently *transgress* than others. Some, from the heights of arrogance and pride, against the Almighty Dispenser of Rewards; and others through malice and envy, and some by other specious pretences, according to the powers and capacities they enjoyed in their several states of subordination, in which they were placed; and therefore, at that period, when they shall be solemnly tried, different degrees of punishment will be awarded against them; and for a larger or shorter time, in proportion to their crimes. As confinement is also a reasonable intermediate punishment, until their general trial and sentence; so also, according to their offences, it may be reasonable to believe, that the degrees of confinement may be greater or less, and they may have more or less enjoyment of life and sensations, in proportion to their crimes. That, accordingly, some may be deprived of life and sensation, and be entirely unconscious, until the General Judgment. Some may be deprived in part, and for part of the time, and be conscious sometimes; and yet, when conscious, may be deprived of the memory of past actions, or any knowledge for the time to come; whilst others may know both, and fear and tremble at the approach of their trial and judgment.

Since the Divine Being has an infinite variety of purposes and occupations in which to employ, and infinite extensions and limitations of rewards and punishments to dispense to conscious free spirits, who may deserve rewards and punishments, and may have passed on and 'thrilled', and grown into power; so these entities rose into higher, and nobler, and more fully-informed life in the ever-springing and ever-fluent Creation. The innumerable items in this physical world, ever resigning, ever renewed, ever balanced, (subsiding to evil; recovering to good): these were in active motion. All this state of restless, universal conflict or competition; of affirmation, and of negation, in different degrees, both as to duration and intenseness; at the time of the formation of the scheme of the 'Cosmos', in the developing of the (speculative) Mosaic creation, was perhaps the area of the operations of the lapsed spirits. These had been doomed to a state of silence, by being deprived of their sensations, and had been chained down to the abysses of the several suns, or chaos of planets, by the impulse of gravitation, or mutual attraction (gravity being, magically, the magnetic, sensitive, '*angelical effluvium*' spoken of by Robertus de Fluctibus and the Rosicrucians). Such may have had an opportunity of gaining degrees and impetus back again into angelic life, in recovery out of the soulless densities of matter (that meant by the 'darkness' allegorized by Moses); and reappearing, in the new order of things, in the beautiful form of new efforts at life--star-raised--astrologically raised--vegetables, growing plants, and flowers (sexed, even, in their own mysterious differences and forms and fashions), or [21] animals, in their higher or lower, or pure or impure kinds. These animal or 'plantal souls' come from the metamorphosed 'spirits'-world' (all this is perfectly possible,

---

[21] This agrees with the Pythagorean ideas, and with those of Lucretius.

however strange and mysterious), being, in their seeds, dispersed not only over the surfaces of the several suns and planets ('if particles of light are spiritual forms'), but also throughout all the matter in the several stars, through infinite space. Those who are doomed to a long inactivity until a future judgment are within the surfaces of the several globes, and are not to 'take life' during this present period, or reign of things. That to such as the Deity thinks proper, only a fossil, vegetable, or animal, brutal life was to be given, until the conflagration of this globe. It has been a doctrine advanced in the mysticism of the Gnostics, that only for such as our Saviour Jesus Christ had interposed for mercy, a state of probation was allowed. These are the condemned (the conquered 'Hosts of the "First Fall"'--that fall of the 'Angels'). This class of spirits by their entering human bodies (having been allowed sufficient machine, and adequate physical means), combined the *synthesis* of reason, memory, and judgment, which combination makes them accountable for their behaviour and actions here. At the same time others, who have not these powers, at the last Judgment are to be doomed according to their *former* crimes; crimes *of the nature and character of which* poor human nature--incapable and childish as it is--can form no idea;-- humanity having been never intended for a comprehension of the *supernatural, mighty secrets*--resting alone in the hidden MYSTERIES OF GOD! These crimes of the lapsed spirits (committed in their former state), before they were imprisoned in these globes, are as totally unimaginable by men, as crimes, and the 'wherefore', and the 'nature' of crimes, in the human mature state, are not known by children.

Let us consider a little the nature of that mysterious thing-- in reality, the Master of the World--called 'Fire'. The 'body' and the 'spirit' are alike traceable into it. The human scale or register of fire is nothing; because our instruments--thermometers, pyrometers, and so forth--fail at a given point. They cannot inform us of the intensities of heat or of cold (instant destruction) which shoot upward, or downward, from either end, baffling mortal computation or idea, flying through hundreds of degrees by leaps, impossible of recognition by man. Thus man knows nothing of Fire, except the ordinary comfortable little *minimum* of fire--which, answering his purposes in certain indispensable respects, when risen into magnitude, destroys him as his master in a moment, and all his belongings--nay, the whole world, and *its* belongings, and everything conceivable. FIRE, in fact, devours every cosmic possibility.

Many particles of light lose their motion when they enter into the pores of the several bodies around us, and many remain and adhere to the bodies they enter; so that, we apprehend, vegetables consist, in great part, of these particles, which makes them so inflammable; and that the *pabulum* of our material fire is nothing more than the imprisoned rays or particles of light, when united to salts, and other particles of body; and that the strong heat and motion of fire, when kindled, is nothing more than the struggle of the imprisoned or fettered rays to break from the salts and aqueous particles they are united with; and, when that motion becomes exceeding quick, Fire then glows, and is thrown off in lucid rays. Where the struggle is strongest, as in metals, sulphurs, and consolidated impenetrability, the fire and flame is intense, as requiring a stronger motion to break up the atoms into brightness, and to liberate that 'flower', glory, or crown of heat, which we call flame--flame and light, nature's last achievement and brandishing victory. Out of the solidest matters for burning, comes the fiercest and the most abundant Fire; until the masses of fiery molecules burst (being turned inside-out) into the blaze of the brightest of Light! The whole late mass is then passed into the 'unknown', leaving the ruin only as ashes, *with the whole power out.*

An opinion was put forward in the middle ages that our souls were all originally in the first Adam; and that both our spirits and bodies are all come from him; and, by throwing off one tegument or skin after another, at each conception, we at last appear in the world in the condition we are now in. But this seems to be too much of a piece with the materialists, who may believe our souls, like matter in their conception, divisible infinitely; for this would confirm their hypothesis, that our souls are material, and infinitely divisible; and that there are souls *within souls*, looking backwards as far as thought can reach; for myriads of millions are included in the vehicle of one, since so many souls or animalcules are thrown off at each act of copulation, as we now observe by microscopes, when in the least drop of the *semen* there are such surprising numbers seen. This would also confirm their opinion, who imagine that souls take up no room or place in space, by being infinitely small; and may thus, in a manner, be conceived not to be anywhere. Whereas, from the powers we observe in ourselves, and other spiritual beings, we must take up room, and be extended in space, since we act in a limited part of it. It is impossible that souls, in the spiritual sense, can be born into this world out of so much waste.

In the cabalistic, which is; therefore, the astrological view, the sun in every vortex is the centre and lowest part; the ascent is from the sun, the descent to it. A vortex may be divided into four concentric orbs or worlds (unequal), and termed the utmost, or highest, *Aziluth;* the next, *Briah;* the third, *Jetzirah;* the lowest, or inmost, *Asiah* (or *Asia*). The first, *Aziluth* ('absorbed in divine contemplations'), extends from the margin of the vortex to Saturn; the second, *Briah* (social or political), from Saturn to Mars; the third, *Jetzirah* (leonine and belluine), from Mars to Mercury; the fourth, *Asia* (mechanical), from Mercury to the frigescent Sun. *Asia*, superior, from Mercury to the atmosphere of the now frigid star. *Asia*, inferior, the atmosphere and body of the frigid star itself. Hence, perhaps, Saturn and Jupiter were worshipped by the sons of darkness, corrupting old traditions at the will of their Prince, the Old Serpent (as the causer of all visible things), and as presiding over counsel and benignity, as apparent, and as to work in a world which is half-shadow. Mars and Venus over the irascible and concupiscible. Mercury over ingenuity and human production, or 'making', technical and mechanical. These are all astrological meanings and interpretations. All souls, even *Aziluthic* were clothed with corporeal vehicles, they being the means of sensation and commerce, the highest gratifications of animal, or perhaps of all created natures. The deeper immersed these entities are in the vortex, that is in matter (or 'darkness'), the more gross the vehicle; and yet supplying the most abundant means--contributing the most of power--to the Fire, or the Light, because all *comprehensible* FIRE and LIGHT is material. There is a revolution of human souls through all the four worlds (the Four Elements, or the four corners of the universe of the Rosicrucians, *Aziluth*, etc.), either by divine fate, or their own fault. The periods are unequal, especially the *Aziluthic* and *Briathic*. The legitimate revolution of angelic souls is no lower than *Asia*, superior. Their vehicles are richer in the exquisite sensual gratifications than the human; but their souls are less gifted with the possibility of the divine aspiration than the human. This mystery lies at the very base of the cabalistic profundities, which form the first step upon which, in mounting upwards out of man's ordinary nature, the true Rosicrucians (humblest, and yet haughtiest, of the children of men) place their feet. Hence the above-referred-to 'darkened' angels--a certain number, at least, of them, fell first by breaking-forth into '*Jetzirah*', without Divine Leave, out of that region cabalistically denominated '*Briah*', in which, and in '*Aziluth*', innocence reigned universally. And there the augmented delights and vigour of their vehicles, through the greater heat and increased magnificent fulgency of the sun, allured them, and strengthened them, to those inordinate deeds (impossible to be comprehended by man), by the *divine magic* of those regions, and to the traitorous embassy of that proud princely genius, the 'Rebel Leader' amongst the principal Archangels, known afterwards by many names, but herein by that of *Ophioneus*, or *Lucifer*, 'Bringer of Light', or 'Morning Star' (*Lux-fero*)--which brought to them the name of Rephaim, or giants; and to human souls the lapse out of '*Briah*', by joining the rebel angels. This is the cabalistic, theosophical or mystical story of the 'First Fall'--or that of the 'Angels'. Souls which degenerate into the vivified region, cabalistically called '*Asia*', not through their own fault, but by divine fate, return safe into '*Aziluth*', neither broken by adversity, nor softened by pleasures, aided in all states, by Grace Divine. This is the meaning of the 'Elect', or the chosen of God.

In '*Aziluth*' the souls of men and angels, wholly intent on the adoration of the Supreme Master, and occupied in sublime wonderings, neglect and scarcely perceive the life of the natural vehicle--'that of wants'. From the celestially igneous and vivacious, and illuminated character of this life, and of the magic *aura*, or matter of this supernatural region, it is named *cœlum empyræum*. This was Adam's state before Eve was created, and before the 'sexes' became possible, or the distinctions of 'sex' sprang into existence. For, whereas Adam owed his birth to God, who made him out of matter, Eve owed her birth to Adam, who produced her out of 'ruined' matter. Thus we see the necessity of the Saviour, 'born of Woman', through the pardon, under penalties, which in the continual generations absolve the sin--the seed of the WOMAN 'bruising' (crushing) the SERPENT'S Head. Eve was the 'Feminized Adam', and was the 'First in the Fall', misinterpreting the Devil as a God: but out of this temptation, and as a result of its success, arises the 'possibility of Man'--the great stumbling-block to all the disbelievers, who are unable to rise into any supernatural idea. In '*Briah*'--or the region in which descent was furthered, the *Aziluthic* ardour being abated, the view became turned to the outward world, or the world of physical construction, and to the life, and sensations, and sustainment of the vehicle. This became the state *after* the formation of Eve. Then arose the transaction between God and the Soul of the Messiah concerning his 'Passion', and the 'Redemption of the World'. The soul of the Messiah profited so much in the cabalistic '*Aziluth*', and adhered to the eternal *Logos* with so strict a love, that, at length, they were united into one 'Person' (*Partzuph*)--(this is the mystic doctrine of the Gnostics)--with the highest *aziluthic*, or rather *hyperaziluthic* union, as Soul and Body, into one Individuality, thence rightly called the Son of God, name or nature ineffable. This Divine Messiah is constituted by God the Father, Ruler of all Souls, human and angelical, King of Kings, and Lord of Lords. Upon his undertaking to become the Saviour of the Lost World--thence arose his union with the divine *Logos,* which was completed and declared. (*John* xvii. 5; *Heb.* i. 6; *Philippians* ii. 6-8; *Ps.* lxxii. 5, according to the Septuagint.) Its mystical primæval duration until the sun of this vortex (the solar system) cooled into a planet (rather comet), through the rebel Rephaim overturning all order and beauty; and therefore deprived of the solar light and heat, the principle of their magic power and operations, and before the moon became frigid, and was struck off from the bulk of the earth, and set rolling, circumvolving, in its new magic, *feminine* light--maker of the sensitives--as a satellite to our world. The chaotic comet being formed into a habitable earth through the force of gravitation, and, physically, in the exertion of the powers centripetal and centrifugal, solidifying it into a globe, the lapsed human souls—having drank of the 'river of Lethe' to make this new state of trial and purification (here we encounter the Buddhistic system) more attainable and effectual, sank into terrestrial bodies. All this, and the new operations arising in place of that divine magic so greatly abused by them in their former state, and in their cabalistical state, called '*Jetzirah*'--*Gen.* iii.

The *Jetzirathic* Rephaim of the *Cabala* esteemed themselves *Elohim* (Gods) in their supernaturally drunken and mad frolics, as being experimentally skilled in all sorts of contrivances, good and evil, through the use and abuse of magic. And so the Serpent persuaded Eve it would be with her. Whence the name of *Jetzirah,* the Cabalistic term for this development, from the Chaldaic, or foundation--Hebrew '*jatzar*', to form 'good and evil' magically, not mechanically.

Catachismus, Cabalisticus, Mercavæus Sephirothicus. Refer to a very valuable old Book, published in London, in the possession of the authors of this present work and entitled '*A Miscellaneous Metaphysical Essay, or, An Hypothesis concerning the Formation and Generation of Spiritual and Material Beings, with Their Several Characteristics and Properties, and how far the several surrounding Beings partake of either property. To which is* added *Some Thoughts upon Creation in General, upon Pre-existence, the Cabalistic Account of the Mosaic Creation, the Formation of Adam, and Fall of Mankind; and upon the Nature of Noah's Deluge. As also upon the Dormant State of the Soul, from the Creation to our Birth, and from our Death to the Resurrection. The whole considered upon the Principles of Reason, and from the Tenor of the Revelations in the Holy Scriptures.* By an Impartial Inquirer after Truth.--London.' (No name or date.)

It is impossible to tell now who was the author of this remarkable work. It was, in fact, an explanatory treatise on the *Cabala.*

We have, as far as allowable, given the Rosicrucian interpretation thereof. The whole range of these subjects is pre-eminently mysterious and Phallic. For Phallicism seems to rest as the basis of everything, as it proffers undoubtedly as the foundation and the meaning of all the mythologies. It follows from this, that this human state must be a supernatural (natural) place, of inquietude, and of penitential suffering; and that this place of trial--the world--is only a state of purgation and of trouble, introductory to some other--and it is to be hoped--better state. 'The whole Creation groaneth and travaileth in pain together, until now.'--St. Paul.

The following suggestions are from Scripture:

'And those "*members of the body*" which we think to be "*less honourable*", upon them we bestow "*more abundant honour*".'--I *Cor.* xii. 23.

'But God hath chosen the foolish things of the world to confound the wise, and God hath chosen the weak things of the world to confound the things which are mighty; and base things of the world, and things which are despised hath God chosen, yea, and things which are *not*, to bring to nought things that *are*.'--I *Cor.* i. 27 and 28.

'For it is written, I will destroy the wisdom of the wise, and will bring to nothing the understanding of the prudent.'--I *Cor.* i. 19.

'He that overcometh shall not be hurt of the second death.'--*Rev.* ii. II.

'To him that overcometh will I give to eat of the hidden manna, and will give him a white stone' (the *'Philosophers' Stone?'*) 'and in the stone a *new name* written, which no man knoweth saving he that receiveth it.'--*Rev.* ii. 17.

'And he that overcometh, and keepeth my works unto the end, to him will I give power over the nations.'--*Rev.* ii. 26.

'And I will give him the Morning Star.'--*Rev.* ii. 28.

'And I will write upon him my New Name.'--*Rev.* iii. 12.

'He that overcometh shall inherit all things; and I will be his God, and he shall be my son.'--*Rev.* xxi. 7.

'We discover that, not only is the "Garden of Eden" an allegory in itself, but the whole structure of the Bible is an allegory, beginning with Creation, (as described by Moses), and ending with Christ's spiritual, or clairvoyant, appearance to St. John in the *Revelation.*'

The whole is, however, indicative of pure spiritual life.

CHAPTER THE TWENTY-FOURTH, AND LAST

CABALISTIC PROFUNDITIES

IT is an assertion of the occult philosophers that the meaning and purpose of life is altogether mistaken:--necessarily--that is, in the 'Necessity of Things'--mistaken. That, inasmuch as *he lives*, man is incapacitated for pronouncing upon the *nature of his life;* being it--*itself.* He being as a 'Liver'--'It'--(i.e. 'Life', 'Itself'). Philosophy and common sense take it for granted that life needs consciousness, or some form in which the consciousness may be, in order that the liver may 'live'. Abstract philosophy asserts that the liver (living), UNLIVES (in the true sense), *for the very purpose of living*. In other words, it is concluded that, as man is the 'thing seen', the individual cannot ever go out of himself, 'to see himself'; that the 'judged at the bar' cannot cease his character to become another character, and thus 'change places' with his judge, and thus become the judge on the bench, going out of 'himself', to become 'something other' than himself, and to judge of what he is, himself. Now this, obviously, cannot be in common-sense, or in any sense. Thus, this philosophy is applied in the hermetic sense. The alchemists contended that it is possible (by art) to obtain out of the boundless, holy, unappropriated eternal Youth of Nature, a wherewithal, by means of which to 'wreak'--to use a strange word. Thus there could be miraculous renewal, even out of the powers of nature. No one knows the purposes of God, nor can any one limit the powers of God.

'*Angelicarum* animarum *revolutionem,* quanquam ad terrestrem regionem proprie, dictam haud pertingit, ad superiorem tamen partem mundi *Asiathici* et atmosphœram extendi. Nec tamen nisi parcius et compendiosius hisce de rebus egimus in *Cabbala Philosophica;* in *Geneseos,* Cap. 2 & 3.

Animas, quæ non *sua* quidem culpa, laborant, sed *Divino* quodam *Fato,* in mundum *Asiathicum* delabuntur. Divina quadam vi munitas ac agitatas tuto certoque in mundum Aziluthicum reverti.

Animam *Messiæ* in mundo Aziluthico tan tum profecisse et tam arcto amore ac unione cum Divino Intellectu, sive æterno *Logo* coaluisse ut tandem summo plane gradu *Aziluthico* vel potius *Hyperaziluthico*, et si scholastici loqui liceat Hypostatico, cum eo unitus esset, adeo ut Anima *Messiæ* et Divinus *Logos* unafieret פרעוף, i.e. unapersona (ut anima et corpus unus Homo) quæ recte appellanda esset Filius DEI.

Electrum vero in *medio Ignis* est Elementum Divinum cælestis vortices materiæ inclusum et interspersum.'

✻   ✻   ✻   ✻   ✻

'Upward of the "server" or of the heavenly-assisted influences.' Sphara Litera (M) signata, representat Mundum Briathicum, ubi observanda.

	(Sephiroth)	(Nomina)	(Angeli)	(Chori Angelorum)
1.	Kether	אהיה	Jehuel	Seraphim.
2.	Chochmah	אהֹהי	Raphaël	Ophanim.
3.	Binah	אהֹה	Cherubiel	Cherubim.
4.	Daath	היֹהא	Schemuel.	
5.	Chesed	הֹהיא	Zadkiel	Schinanim.
6.	Gebhurah	הֹהאי	Tarschisch	Tarschischim.
7.	Tiphereth	האֹהי	Chasmel: alii	Chaschmalin.
8.	Nezach	האֹיה	Metatron Usiel	Malachim.
9.	Hod	היאֹה	Chasmel	Bene Elohim.
10.	Jesod	יאֹהה	Zephaniah: alii Jehuel	Ischim.
11.	Malchuth	יהֹהא יהאה טדי לא	Michaël	Arelim.

FINIS

'Soli deo gloria per Christum.'

'*Kabbala Denudata seu doctrina Hebræroum Transcendentalis et Metaphysica atque Theologia scriptum Omnibus Philologis, Philosophis, Theologis omnium religionum, atqu: Philo-Chymicis*. Sulzbaci, Typis Abrahami Lichtenthalbri--1677.'

Extracts from the Cabala

THE 'SECOND RUIN'

In which Second Ruin the origin of the strangely great, strangely mysterious religion of the first Buddhism, or first Buddhistic (or more properly Bhuddhistic) system is to be found.

'When the old primæval world was ruined.'

הוה׳ chavvah. R. Moscheh inquit, sic appellari Malchuth, quia est vere est Mater omnis viventis, et uxor Adami primi sub mysterio מה to quod refert numerum ארם. *Pardes. Tr.*, 23, c. 8.

חופה׳ *Thalamus, vel cælum nuptiale*, sub quo sponsus et sponsa consecrantur. Kabbalistæ totum systema Aziluthicum in Chuppah præfigurant. Kether enim est Tectum. Chocmah Parietes; Binah ostium; Chesed, Gebburah, Nezach et Hod quasi brachia in introitu Thalami constituta; Tiphereth et Malchuth sponsus et sponsa intra Thalamum per Jesod, qui est Paranymphus. *Pardes. Tr.*, 23, c. 8. Kabbala Denudata, p. 338.'

Morum trium est terra, de qua ibidem; sicut trium nominum receptaculum est Adonai, a quo omnium judiciorum fit executio. Hinc intelligitur mysticum illud *Genes*, 42, vers. 33. Vir אדֹנִי הָאָרֶץ Dominus terræ. *Conf. Jehosch.*, 3, vers. 11.

'*Arca*, est Malchuth: unde in eam ingressus dicitur Noach, i.e. *Jesod. Gen.*, 6, 9, *Pard.*

'Duodecim ergo signacula Tetragrammati et 4 vexilla eorum sunt hæc: Vexillum primum; vexillum secundum; vexillum tertium; vexillum quartum.

'Duodecim autem Tribus in hæc vexilla distribuuntur. Vexillum 1. Juhudah, Jissaschar, Sebulon. Vexillum 2. Reuben, Schimeon, Gad. Vexillum 3. Ephraim, Menanche, Binjamin. Vexillum 4. Dan, Asser, Napthali.

'Duodecim vero menses cum 12. Signis et limitibus Zodiaci in 4 Quadrantibus anni ita locantur.

דר׳ Incola inhabitans. Omnium interpretum consensu vocatur Malchuth. Et in Schaare Zedek additur ratio, quod sit דירה hospitium Tetragrammati Tiphereth, vel quod habitet in tonos sicut scriptum est: *Lev.*, 16, 16, qui commoratur cum eis in medio immunditiarum eorum. R. Moscheh autem dicit, דר esse nomen Lapidis pretiosi; item spinarum et tribulorum. Atqui sit et hæc mensura se habet, quippe a qua provenit bonum et malum Dicetque quod a דר venit vox דרום meridies. Ipse autem R. Moscheh hanc vocent applicat ad Binah, in Malchuth ergo illius respectu erit. *Pard. Tr.*, 23, c. 4.' *Kabbala Denudata.* Ed. 1677. Salzbuch.

'Cerva amorum. *Prov.*, 5, 19. Ita vocatur Malchuth potissimum ob mysterium *novilunii* quando sc. ista in altu porrigit Cornua, quæ sint Cornua. Hod gloriosa in ipsa apparentia quando nova sit h. m. ☽: aliquando tamen cornu unum altius est altero h. m. ☽: sit tradit R. Schimeon ben Jochai in Raja Mehimna, hac adjecta ratione: Hæc variare secundum diversitatem renovationis. Vel enim æqualis sit ab utroque loco: et tunc cornua equalem habent altitudinem. Si vero a parte plus accipit, ita ut hæc sinistræ prævaleat, tunc cornu unum elevatius est altero: atque tunc vocatur *cerva amorum*, ob mysterium amoris et Chesed seu benignitatis in ipsa prævalentis. Si autem sinistrum prævalet latus, vocatur אלת השחר: *cerva nigricans* seu diluculi caliginosi. *Ps.*, 22, 1, nim. ob nigredinem et anxietatem cui subjecta est in exilio.'

'Lurking principles in the physiology of the human construction.' Extracted from *Cabala*: חבעלת Rosa. Est Schechinah, juxta *Cant.*, 2, 1. Ratio datur in *Sohar Sect. Æmor*, quod sicut Rosa crescit ad aquas, et emittit odorem bonum, sic Malchuth hoc gaudeat nomine, cum influxum affugit a Binah, quæ bonum elevat odorem. Item: quod tunc sic vocetur, cum copulari desiderat cum Rege: cum vero Eidem jam adhæret per oscula, nominantur טוטנה Crinorrhodon; juxta *Cant.* 5, 13. *Pardes Tractat.*, 2, 3, c. 8. *Kabbala Denudata.* Ed. 1677. Salzburg. P. 333.

'Sed a muris versus exteriora sunt turmæ malignæ ad latus sinistrum, non quidem supra, sed infra tantum. Et caput omnium catervarum malarum est Samaël: et illæ omnes sunt autores jurgiorum et odii, et non pertinent ad habitatores atrii Regii; sed extra degunt extra tertium aggerem et extra muros, qui circum castra. Et huc pertinet illud *Num.*, 5, 2, de exclusione

Leprosorum, fluentium; et aliorum immundorum; quæ sunt tres catervæ. Isti dicuntur inquinare l. c. attendunt enim, quam accuratissime sicubi peccatis se polluant homines, atque turn in supernis eos accusant. Atque sic dicitur *Psal.*, 104, 4. Faciens angelos suos spiritus, ministros suos ignem flagrantem. Hinc Aqua ad El, Ignis ad Elohim, Aër ad Tetragrammaton, et Terra ad Adonai refertur. Ordinem reperies *Gene.*, I, 2, ubi inter tenebras (quibus Ignis æquipollet) et aquas, ferri dicitur spiritus, ut inter Elohim et El est Tetragrammaton. Receptaculum autem quod a דר veniat vox דרום meridies. Ipse autem R. Moscheh hanc vocent applicat ad Binah, in Malchuth ergo illius respectu erit. *Pard. Tr.*, 23, c. 4. *Kabbala Denudata*. Ed. 1677. Salzbuch.

'Cerva amorum, *Prov.*, 5, 19. Ita vocatur Malchuth potissimum ob mysterium *novilunii* quando sc. ista in altu porrigit Cornua, quæ sint Cornua Hod gloriosa in ipsa apparentia quando nova sit h. m. ︶: aliquando tamen cornu unum altius est altero h. m. ︶: Sit tradit R. Schimeon ben Jochai in Raja Mehimna, hac adjecta ratione: Hæc variare secundum diversitatem renovationis. Vel enim æqualem accipit influxum a dextra et a sinistra, et renovatio æqualis sit ab utroque loco: et tunc cornua equalem habent altitudinem. Si vero a parte dextra plus accipit, ita ut hæc sinistræ prævaleat, tunc cornu unum elevatius est altero; atque tunc vocatur *cerva amorum*, ob mysterium amoris et Chesed seu benignitatis in ipsa prævalentis. Si autem sinistrum prævalet latus, vocatur: השחר :אלט *cerva nigricans* seu diluculi caliginosi.-- *Ps.*, 22, I, nim. ob nigredinem et anxietatem cui subjecta est in exilio.'

Pairing (human) is synthesis--it is the union of 'Half-Sex', Man (so assumed in this abstract sense), and 'Half-Sex', Woman (so assumed, also, in this abstract sense). The union of these 'Two' half-sexes is the establishment of a 'Whole' Sex-- Hermaphrodite: (Hermes-Aphrodite. Venus-Mercury). The mechanical definition of the exercise of Sex is power of blissful *protrusion;* human organic-advance; willed, conscious magnetism (for an end):--with climax of dissolution and destruction (in the end).--Perishing as in the 'flower' of this 'stalk'. Thus Cornelius Agrippa and Paracelsus--thus the mystic anatomists, like Fludd and Van Helmont. Thus, the Mythologists say that the orders are to be taken as identical, although, in fact, they are directly contradictory. It is these things, which are set against each other, which constitute the stupendous and irresistible natural temptation (obtained out of shame or out of denial, and disgrace), of all this enchanted side of life.

טבור' Umbilicus. Est schechinah, quatenus adhuc occulta; Corpus enim est Tiphereth, et venter Malchuth de parte Binah; sub mysterio אה. Sed Tibbur est notio Jod, quatenus est in ventre et in Tiphereth. Et hoc est punctum illud, quo fundamentum habet mundus, quod vocant Tibbur seu medium terræ; nempe punctum Zijon. Et forte Tibbur est *Jesod. Pard. Tr.*, 23, c. 9. חטוקיהם Ligaturæ illarum.' (*Kabbala.*)

There is nothing in the lower and sensible world, that is not produced, and hath its image, in the superior world. Since the form of the body, as well as the soul, is made after the image of the Heavenly Man, a figure of the forthcoming body which is to clothe the newly descending soul is sent down from the celestial regions to hover over the couch of the husband and wife when they copulate, in order that the conception may be formed according to this model. We have before declared in our chapter on the mystic anatomy, enlarged upon by Cornelius Agrippa, that the human 'act' by which the power of perpetuation has been placed in the exercise by man, and has been elevated into the irresistible natural temptation, is rightly a solemnity or magic endowment, or celebration to which all nature not assents simply, but concurs, as the master-key, however blindly or ignorantly, or brutally often practised. *The Sohar*, iii. 104, a, b, declares that 'At connubial intercourse on earth, the Holy One (blessed be he) sends a human form which bears the impress of the divine stamp. This form is present at intercourse, and, if we were permitted to see it, we should perceive over our heads an image resembling a human face. And it is in this image that we are formed. As long as this image is not sent by God, and does not descend and hover

over our heads, there can be no conception; for it is written 'And God created man in his own image' (*Gen.* i. 27). This image receives us when we enter the world; it develops itself with us when we grow; and accompanies us when we depart this life, as it is written: 'Surely man walked in an image'.

The followers of this secret doctrine of the *Kabbalah* claim for it a pre-Adamite existence. It is also called the secret Wisdom, because it was only handed down by tradition through the initiated, and its whole story indicated in the Hebrew Scriptures by signs which are hidden and unintelligible to those who have not been instructed in its mysteries. 'All human countenances are divisible into the four primordial types of faces which appeared at the mysterious chariot-throne in the vision of the prophet Ezekiel; viz. the face of man, of the lion, the ox, and the eagle. Our faces resemble these more or less according to the rank which our souls occupy in the intellectual or moral dominion. Physiognomy does not consist in the external lineaments, but in the features which are mysteriously drawn in us.'

The following are fragments from the *Cabala*:

'Ad Kether, Mundus Intelligentiæ, Sphæra prima, que dat facultatem omnibus stellis et circulis.

'Ad Chochmah, sphæra motus diurni.

'Ad Binah, sphæra otava stellarum fixarum, et duodecim signorum cælestium, cum quibus combinantur duodecim menses.

'Ad Gedulah--Saturnus.

'Ad Gebhurah--Jupiter.

'Ad Tiphereth--Mars.

'Ad Nezach--Sol.

'Ad Hod--Venus.

'Ad Jesod--Mercurius.

'Ad Malchuth--et in medio locatur Terra.

'Figura T. representat Hortum-Eden, ejusque septem mansiones: ubi in circuitu est murus Paradisiacus et sequuntur septem palatia; in medio autem arbor Vitæ.

Ut legitur *Deuter.* 30, 15. "Vide, exhibui coram te vitam et onum, mortem et malum", etc., added locum *Proverb*, 31, 11, 2. Beatus, qui intelligit insigne hoc mysterium, quia ex eo potest intelligere mysterium albedinis et Lunæ a principio ad finem' (pre-eminently indicative of the mysteries of the Rosicrucians). 'Hinc etiam Lepra continetur sub mysterio Labani Aramæi. Qui hoc intelligit, etiam capiet mysterium Lepræ, quæ signum est, quod clausus sit mundus dilectionem unde Targumice *Lepra* dicitur.'

* * * * *

'These are sexual notions--in fact as such must be everywhere'--'Et Malchuth, quando locata et alligata est inter Jesod et Binah etiam vocatur Fœdus. Et hoc est mysterium הפריעה Denudiationis: quia circumcisio refertur ad Jesod et denudatio ad Malchuth. Et propteria dicitur: Qui circumcisus est, et non denudatus, idem est, ac si circumcisus non esset; quia fodicat portam ingressus, quæ est Malchuth, et Ista est denudatio.

'Appetitus bonus et prava concupiscentia. Vid. *Sohar, Sect. Lechlecha*, 57, 227; *Vajera*, 68, c. 269; *Vajischlach*, 95, c. 379; *Toledoth*, 82, c. 325; *Vajischlach*, 101, c. 406; *Vajescheb*, 106, c. 424; *Mikkez*, III, c. 445 *sqq.*, etc., etc. Also *Kabbala Denudata*. Ed. 1677. Salzburg.

'Ignis אש Fire. Cum in viri appellatione, id est in איש reperiatur, ו, quasi dicatur ו אש Ignis Joddatus, id est masculinus. Si autem componantur ambo, inde fit אשיה Ignis Dominio.' Et unus quidem Ignis, remoto omni dubio, est ad dextram; estque *Ignis albus*; Alter autem est ad sinistram; *Ignis* nemper *ruber.* quæ apparent ex יהֹ, ubi Jod dextrum, He, sinistrum designat. *Pardes Rimmonim Tract.*, 23, c. I, h, t, Videantur plura de Uxore in Sohar, Part Sect. Breschith, fol. 39. Col. 154, 155.

'Cum purum non dicatur, nisi respectu prioris impuritatis. Fundamentum ergo sanctitatis est in Chesed, supra qua Chochmah; cui nomen *sancti* tribuitur; et hinc per dextram sanctitas venit super omnia. Sed fundamentum puritatis est in Gebhura; quia igne Gebhuræ omnia dealbatur.' *Ligaturæ illarum, Trabeationes, Exod.,* 27, 10, 11, etc.

'In Tikkunim hoc nomen applicatur ad Hezach et Hod; quod se invicem colligant, ut fiant unum in copula: vel fulciendo, quod sint Trabeationes Domus, et Domus firmetu super eas, quatenus. Sunt Jachin et Boas. Vel quatenus sunt in classe Tiphereth et Malchuth, qui inter ambas istas uniuntur. Pardes I, c.'

* * * * *

'The exercise of the mysteries.'--

יין Vinum. Hæc vox absolute posita refertur ad Gebhurah. Sed si album intelligitur inclinare censeatur ad Chesed, cum rubrum sit vis Gebhuræ: Dicitur autem *bonum*, quando miscetur aquis; subintelligendo aquas Chesed, unde bonum provenit, ut dictum sub בוט. *Eccl.*, 7, 12; *Jeches.*, 10, 20; *Pard. Tr.*, 23, c. 10. Vid. *Soh.*, Sect. Noach, 54, c. 216; *Lechlecha*, 61, c. 244; et *Toledoth*, 81, c. 321; *Vajikra*, 5, c. 19; *Schemini*, 17, c. 67; *Æmor*, 46, c. 182; *Fol.*, 48, 192; *Pinchas*, 114, c. 454; *Debharim*, 123, c. 491.' *Cabala Denudata*. SALZBACH edn., 1677.

סגידן, *quasi clausura*, (et Leprosus מוסגר quasi clausus, sive quis Leprosus sit simpliciter (primo aspectu, ut nulla inclusione opus est) sive mundari queat; quod est mysterium magnum. Lepra enim venit ob linguam malum; quæ omnia clara sunt; omni enim proveniunt e scaturigine serpentis antiqui, qui causa est, ut claudantur portæ Rachamim. Ille autem qui intelligit mysteria hæc magna, de comestione Adami ab arbore cognitionis tempore præputii, etiam intelliget, quare vocetur *Arbor cognitionis;* et quare vocetur *Boni et Mali. Kabbala Denudata*, p. 495. (Edn. 1677.)

THE END

www.ingramcontent.com/pod-product-compliance
Lightning Source LLC
Chambersburg PA
CBHW050119170426
43197CB00011B/1643